LATIN AMERICAN SOCIETIES IN TRANSITION

Robert C. Williamson

Westport, Connecticut
London

Library of Congress Cataloging-in-Publication Data

Williamson, Robert Clifford, 1916–
    Latin American societies in transition / Robert C. Williamson.
      p.   cm.
    Includes bibliographical references and index.
    ISBN 0–275–95750–0 (alk. paper). — ISBN 0–275–95751–9 (pbk. :
alk. paper)
    1. Latin America—Social conditions—1982– 2. Social change—
Latin America. 3. Social conflict—Latin America. I. Title.
HN110.5.A8W486   1997
306' .098—dc20   96–26879

British Library Cataloguing in Publication Data is available.

Library of Congress Catalog Card Number: 96–26879
ISBN: 0–275–95750–0
    0–275–95751–9 (pbk.)

First published in 1997

Praeger Publishers, 88 Post Road West, Westport, CT 06881
An imprint of Greenwood Publishing Group, Inc.

Printed in the United States of America

The paper used in this book complies with the
Permanent Paper Standard issued by the National
Information Standards Organization (Z39.48–1984).

10 9 8 7 6 5 4 3 2 1

Contents

Figures and Tables

FIGURES

TABLES

Preface

The vast amount of literature on Latin America appearing during the last few decades testifies to the growing interest North Americans have found in their neighbors to the south. Most of these works focus on historical-political and economic problems, often with little examination of the social structures that shape Latin American societies. Knowledge of demography, rural and urban life, and ethnic and status relationships is critical for understanding the political and economic fabric. In other words, although the author draws on materials from all the social sciences, the frame of reference is sociological. The book presents in an organized form the findings from an ever-growing number of studies about Latin American society. On the basis of this accumulated research it is possible to make some valid generalizations about the societies that now constitute more than half of the population of the Western Hemisphere.

Considering the diversity and constant change in Latin America, it may seem presumptuous to generalize about a score of nations with varying cultural traditions and differing rates of developing. Indeed, an observer must avoid arriving at stereotypical notions about these societies. National, regional, and other subcultural variations are stressed in this book. Yet despite their diversity, Latin American cultures have some features in common.

This book begins with a brief introduction of the political and economic patterns and an examination of Latin America as a social system. The text focuses on social processes and structures as well as the major social institutions. The findings of Latin American, European, and North

American social scientists are incorporated into the analysis. Throughout the book a prevailing theme is the extent to which Latin America is a
society in conflict and change, with no illusion that these properties are
unique to Latin America. Inevitably, because of their size or importance,
some areas of Latin America receive more emphasis than others.

Change often connotes a succession of prolonged crises. For one thing,
with a high birthrate and a rapidly declining death rate, Latin America's
population has outgrown its food supply. From an overpopulated countryside, migrants have fled to urban centers, doubling the population of
many cities in little more than a decade. Moreover, the economy has failed
to produce an adequate standard of living for well over half the population. Besides an overhauling of the agricultural system, one option is industrialization, even though its implementation and results are often
problematic. Indebtedness and capital and skill formation, among other
problems, remain nearly insurmountable barriers to industrialization.
Other observers may focus on the arbitrariness of the political process.
The alternation of authoritarian regimes with quasi-democratic interludes
is not altogether surprising in an area in which basic economic dilemmas
are fundamental. Nevertheless, no serious analysis would suggest that
Latin America is autonomous in these economic and political decisions.
All too often the area has been subordinate to the needs of other power
structures, usually the United States.

As with many societies undergoing a succession of crises, there is a
lack of articulation of subsystems within the total social system of Latin
America. As in every society, systems compete for power with varying
degrees of success or failure. In contrast to most pluralistic societies in
the West, feudalistic structures have persisted well beyond their effectiveness in Latin America. Among the questions raised in this book are
those concerning the interrelationships between different systems: How
does the ethnic structure relate to stratification based on criteria other
than race? What avenues of mobility are to be found in the class system?
What are the linkages between rapid urbanization and the economy? How
is the power distributed between the older oligarchy and the new commercial and industrial elites? What is the role of an emerging middle class?
To what degree can urban migrants move beyond their marginal position
in a competitive urban society? How effectively can Latin America function in the international scene?

The author's approach is both descriptive and analytic. It is committed to
the position that both planned and unplanned events impinge on all parts of
the social system. Consequently, the pattern of orientation of the various
subsystems to stability and change is a recurring focus of this book.

In writing this book I am aware of the contribution of a number of
organizations and persons. Among these are the Fulbright Commission
that awarded me professorships and lectureships in Chile, Colombia, and

El Salvador. I am especially grateful for the stimulation and insights of my students and colleagues at the National University of Colombia, University of the Andes, Catholic University of Chile, National University of El Salvador, and Lehigh University. No less I want to express my appreciation for the support I received from the Social Science Research Council and the Office of Research of Lehigh University. For reading portions of the manuscript I wish to thank Alvin Cohen, Joan Z. Spade, Hannah W. Stewart-Gambino, and especially John M. Hart. However, they bear no responsibility for any deficiencies in the text. Finally, there has been the constant encouragement of my wife, Virginia Lorenzini Williamson.

LATIN AMERICAN
SOCIETIES
IN TRANSITION

Chapter 1

What Is Latin America?

Until the past few years, Latin America was a universe apart to most North Americans. Even now, only a sensational incident such as a Chilean earthquake, a riot by university students against an emissary from Washington, or a mass murder by a drug lord can command our attention. We are interested in areas where we fear economic competition, notably East Asia—but also, recently and marginally, Latin America. If most North Americans have any genuine concern abroad, it is about their traditional homeland, in Europe. The major exception to this seeming indifference to Latin America is found among the twenty-six million Mexican Americans, Puerto Ricans, Cubans, and other Latinos living in the United States who feel a deep affinity to Latin America.

More than half a century ago, President Franklin Roosevelt initiated the "good neighbor" policy, and hemispheric questions, colored mainly by commercial and military interests, have preoccupied the federal government ever since. The real awakening to the existence of Latin America came with the establishment of Communist rule in Cuba in 1960. Although most North Americans viewed the change with alarm, especially at the time of the missile crisis in 1962, the problem forced us to recognize a wide spectrum of Latin America's economic, political, and social dislocations. It is ironic that much of the impetus to progressive action on the part of the United States was an almost paranoid reaction to the threat of Communism. With the end of the Cold War in 1991, North Americans felt less concern with the problems of other nations.

The acknowledgment of deep-seated crises in the lands south of the Rio Grande occasionally surfaces in aid programs, notably the Alliance for Progress outlined by President John Kennedy in 1961. However inadequate the scope of this and related programs such as the Peace Corps, they dramatically underline the change from an almost arrogant posture of the U.S. government in the past to an intermittently enlightened attitude since 1960. Lip service to aid programs continues, and occasionally they are implemented. President George Bush pledged an "Enterprise for the Americas," but few specifics emerged other than NAFTA (North American Free Trade Association), which was approved in 1993 by Congress at the urging of President Bill Clinton.

The United States moved toward a human rights theme under President Jimmy Carter, followed by an anti-Communist crusade (or in the judgment of many observers, an antidemocratic interference) in Central America during the Reagan administration. If the United States intermittently intervenes economically with significant aid programs, it also intervenes militarily. Early in this century Theodore Roosevelt had his "big stick" policy. Subsequent administrations chose to occupy certain countries (notably the Dominican Republic, Haiti, and Nicaragua) with military troops. Under Hoover and Roosevelt, military occupation was gradually withdrawn. Later, in the Cold War, intervention again became an option. The White House turned to a military situation in Guatemala in 1954, Cuba in 1961, and the Dominican Republic in 1965. Our largest military commitment focused on El Salvador and Nicaragua in the 1980s. The only direct use of U.S. military troops was the invasion of Panama in 1989. These excursions of the 1980s under the Reagan and Bush administrations were criticized at home and abroad, both in Europe and Latin America. For nearly all social scientists, the search for a solution of social, political, and economic problems by the use of force is regarded as counterproductive.

In other words, one may argue as to what degree the United States is a benefactor or an inhibitor in Latin America's social and economic growth. On the one side are the decisions of the U.S. government to permit autonomy, as when the Carter administration attempted to find an equitable settlement of the Panama Canal grievance. On the other side is the support of the Contras during the Reagan period. There is little question as to the effort of the United States to dominate events in the hemisphere.[1]

DEFINING THE AREA

Latin America is conventionally designated as including twenty nations (if we exclude the Guianas and a few other peripheral areas) with a combined population of some 480 million people. Next to Africa it is the most rapidly growing area of the world, with an average population increase of 1.9 percent per year. If the present birthrate continues, the population will grow more than 30 percent by the year 2025.[2] The term "Latin America" itself is misleading since it ignores many people who are in no way Latin. For instance, millions of African Americans in Brazil and the Caribbean area and an almost equal number of Indians or Native Americans in a dozen countries are marginal to Latin culture. In addition, several million Northern Europeans, Anglo-Americans, and Asians have made Latin America their home.

No less than for other areas of the world, generalizations in regard to Latin America are problematic. The extreme diversity is illustrated by the scope and contrasts of the physical character of area. Sheer size is impressive, even in the air age. Nearly six thousand miles separate northern Mexico from Patagonia; Buenos Aires is farther from Mexico City in air hours than Seattle is from London. The size of the area is nearly three times that of the continental United States, and Brazil itself equals the area of Europe.

The location of Latin America is also significant. Although physically in the Western Hemisphere, South America, or at least Brazil, is nearer to Africa than to North America. Natal is only 1,900 miles from Dakar. In reality, the entire continent lies east of Jacksonville, Florida, and a large area is as close to Europe as to the United States.

The Problem of Classification

In keeping with other areas of the world, developed or underdeveloped, it is difficult to consider Latin America as a completely meaningful unit, for it is composed of highly different cultural regions. Even at the most superficial level, five areas can be designated: (1) predominantly *mestizo*, or racially mixed, countries: Mexico, El Salvador, Honduras, Panama, Colombia, and Venezuela, which represent different economies and political orders; (2) nations with a large Indian or Native-American minority (or a majority): Guatemala, Ecuador, Peru, Bolivia, and possibly Paraguay; (3) nations of predominantly European ethnicity: Argentina, Chile, Uruguay, and Costa Rica, different as they are from each other; (4) Brazil with its Portuguese heritage, supplemented by African Americans along the northern coast and Indian tribes in the interior; and (5) the Caribbean populations, varying from European and African in Cuba and the Dominican Republic to a French- and Cajun-speaking population in Haiti. Although not properly regarded as Latin American, Trinidad is largely African and East Indian; Jamaica and other islands are inhabited by African Americans oriented to a British tradition; and finally there are the French outposts of Martinique and Guadeloupe. To most observers, Latin America rivals or surpasses Africa and Asia in racial and national diversity.

At the same time, ethnic patterns are only one of several possible criteria. One could choose geographic bases for categorizing the area. As one sees in Figure 1.1, no less than thirteen different natural areas are found in Latin America. In a broader sense, the mid-latitude countries such as Argentina, Uruguay, and Chile differ sharply from the tropical ones. This kaleidoscope presents certain difficulties as radically different topography, climate, soil, and vegetation play a critical role in determining how people live. In most of Latin America, at least the countries facing the Pacific, there are three very distinct zones—the coast, the sierra, and the *oriente*, in which altitudes vary from sea level to over ten thousand feet. These climatic zones mean a different agriculture and lifestyle. Another striking feature is the varying assortment of natural resources (for example, Brazil so richly blessed in contrast with poorly endowed Argentina).

Another possible breakdown—and not necessarily a very useful one— is based on the particular nation's role in the trade world. For instance, some countries specialize in tropical and subtropical crops, which include sugar (Cuba and the Dominican Republic), coffee (Brazil, Colombia, El Salvador, and Guatemala), bananas (Costa Rica, Ecuador, and Honduras), and cocoa (Ecuador). Second, extractive industries have traditionally dominated the economy of Mexico, Peru, Bolivia, and Chile, and oil has dominated in both Mexico and Venezuela. Third, the production of cereals and live stock is critical in Argentina and Uruguay. The difficulty with this kind of grouping is that several different kinds of economic activities are found in the same country; both industry and agriculture count heavily in Argentina. In several countries the majority of workers are employed in agriculture, whether in a subsistence peasant economy or in a large plantation type designed primarily for export. Furthermore, industrialization began in a few countries before World War I and after World War II became a central preoccupation. With the possible exception of Cuba in its commitment to sugar, the priority of one or two products in the economy is gradually passing from the scene. Assessing nations on the basis of their contribution to the world market no longer has the significance it had in the past.

A slightly more meaningful classification might be level of economic and social development. Although the gross national product (GNP) of North America is several times higher than for all Latin America—a somewhat misleading comparison—marked differences appear between various nations, as seen in Table 1.1. Traditionally, the per capita high-income group includes Argentina, Uruguay, Chile, Cuba (prior to the U.S. embargo), and Venezuela (until the fuel crisis). In the middle range are Mexico, Brazil, Colombia, Panama, Costa Rica, and at one time Peru, a group accounting for more than half of Latin America's total population. The third group is the less developed economies, often with large Indian or peasant societies existing apart from the national economy: the Do-

FIGURE 1.1
Latin America: Natural Regions

**LATIN AMERICA:
NATURAL REGIONS**

1. Gulf-Caribbean Coastal Lowlands
2. Antilles (West Indies)
3. Pacific Littoral:
      Coastal Plains & Valleys
4. Cordilleran Ranges,
      Intermontane Basins &Plateaus
5. Llanos
6. Guiana Highlands (& associated
      coastal lowlands)
7. Amazonia
8. Brazilian Highlands (& asspciated
      coastal lowlands)
9. Peruvian-Atacama Desert
10. Middle Chile
11. South Chile
12. Patagonia & Northwest Argentina
13. La Plata -Paraná Basin

Kilometres
0 200 400 600 800

Source: Alfonso González, "Physical Geography and Settlement Patterns," in *Latin America: Its Problems and Its Promise*, ed. Jan Knippers Black (Boulder, Colo.: Westview Press, 1984), 21.

TABLE 1.1
Population and Economic Development as Reflected by Income

	Estimated Population in Millions	Per Capita Gross National Product in U.S. Dollars*
	1996	1995
Middle America		
Costa Rica	3.6	2,380
El Salvador	5.9	1,480
Guatemala	9.9	1,190
Honduras	5.6	580
Mexico	94.8	4,010
Nicaragua	4.6	330
Panama	2.7	2,670
Caribbean		
Cuba	11.0	----
Dominican Republic	8.1	1,320
Haiti	7.3	---
Puerto Rico	3.8	7,060
Tropical South America		
Bolivia	7.6	770
Brazil	160.1	3,370
Colombia	38.0	1,220
Ecuador	11.4	1,310
Paraguay	5.0	1,570
Peru	24.0	1,690
Venezuela	21.8	2,760
Temperate South America		
Argentina	34.7	8,060
Chile	14.5	3,560
Uruguay	3.2	4,650
United States	265.2	25,860

Source: World Population Data Sheet (Washington, D.C.: Population Reference Bureau, 1996).
   *Some of the figures may be misleading because of currency fluctuations.

minican Republic, Nicaragua, El Salvador, Guatemala, Honduras, Ecuador, Paraguay, Bolivia, and Haiti. It is relevant that Haiti has approximately one-eighth the per capita income of Brazil or Mexico. That is, countries can be in very different phases of their economic development. The concept of "development" is not especially significant for Haiti. In view of its role in the international petroleum world, it is risky to compare Venezuela with, say, Uruguay, even though one can assess nations according to the level of their industrialization.

Still another axis along which Latin American republics might be scaled is the stage of political or democratic progress. Democracy is a relative term in Latin America, and probably in all parts of the world. Alternative terms include protodemocratic, semidemocratic, miltary, authoritarian, and bureaucratic-authoritarian regimes.[3] In a broad classification of government models, several nations show a relatively weak potential for representative government; *caudillo* or "strong man" rule characterized the political scene for most of the history of the less developed nations. A second rubric points to the intermittent democratic regimes appearing in a wide variety of countries: Ecuador, Peru, and Bolivia and to a larger extent in more advanced nations, for instance, Brazil and Argentina. A third cluster of nations is committed to democratic processes, however different their expression of democratic rights. Historically, Venezuela and Costa Rica have been the most consistently democratic; with the exception of the 1970s, Chile and Uruguay are solidly democratic, with Mexico not far behind and Colombia sporadically democratic. Still, this classification is hazardous, as most nations offer exceptions to almost any generalization about their political style.

Another approach prefers a complex model based on social cohesiveness as determined by the number of known acts of violence and repression.[4] But the location on this scale and other scales for a given country shifts in time. A striking question is the degree to which the democratic process is open or closed. Most Latin American governments operate according to a corporatist model, in which various power centers—the agrarian elite, industrialists, the military, professionals, and labor unions—have access to power but a large portion of the citizenry, especially peasants and the lower proletariat, are virtually ignored. This corporatist tradition has its roots in medieval Spain and affects even relatively modern nations such as Argentina.[5] On a hopeful note, Latin America exhibits at present the most democratic profile in its history.

Diversity and Unity

In a number of respects, one cannot overemphasize the heterogeneity of Latin America, either physically or culturally. It would be as meaningless to place any given country or given individual in a rigid classification scheme as to equate a Texas cowhand, a Mississippi poor white or black sharecropper, or a Manhattan artist or secretary as typical North Americans. Similarly, a gaucho of the pampas, a Neapolitan fisherman or Ukrainian storekeeper in Buenos Aires, or a fifth-generation sheep herder in Patagonia may have little more in common than their present status as Argentine citizens and socialization in the Spanish language.

The geographic diversity of Latin America is shown in Figure 1.1, in which Alfonso González finds no less than thirteen natural regions stretching from the tropics to Patagonia. With full realization of the risks of oversimplification, Charles Wagley sees six distinct regions in Brazil (the Amazon basin, the Northeast Coast, the arid Northeast or *sertão*, the far South, the industrial Middle States, and the Western frontier).[6] Each could be a separate country with differing economies, ethnic strains, and ways of life. Throughout Brazil exist national and regional dichotomies: the modern and archaic, city and country, and the *litoral* (coast) and the *sertão* (dry interior of the Northeast). As a much smaller country, Ecuador has the *costa*, the *sierra* or highlands, and the *oriente* or interior Amazon basin. Quito and Guayaquil enact the "tale of two cities," one a melange of colonial Spain and Indian cultures held together by a quasi-modern governmental bureaucracy, the other a bustling commercial and transportation center. Even within the U.S. Commonwealth of Puerto Rico there exist several distinct socioeconomic subcultures.[7] As another variant, Cuba is a Communist state and has its own pattern of development, with incomplete homogenization of its national culture.[8]

All in all, Latin America presents a panorama of contrasting landscapes, climates, races, nationalities, and belief systems, in addition to its highly stratified social systems. For instance, Uruguay and Bolivia could scarcely be further apart in their historical development, economic growth, and ethnic composition. The historical background is relevant. Unlike North America which was colonized (notwithstanding the savage treatment of its indigenous population), Latin America was conquered, with *conquistadores* and *bandeirantes'* psychosocial heritage enduring into the early twentieth century. The southern countries, especially Argentina and Uruguay, were less affected by this exploitive attitude.[9]

Despite the appearance of almost complete diversity, one finds suggestions of cultural unity. For one thing, all countries except Haiti trace their heritage to the Iberian peninsula. As implied above, most cultures emerged as a blend of Spanish feudalism (itself influenced by Arabic as well as Roman vestiges) superimposed on indigenous sources, notably in Middle America and upper South America. This unity reflects a Hispanic tradition and is identifiable in courtship practices, style of architecture, and culinary habits, whether one is in Monterrey, Mexico or Córdoba, Argentina. The Hispanic heritage appears in several traditions; for instance, the style of the home built around a patio, deference toward the male (hardly unique to Latin America), and love of poetry and music. If Latin America renounced Spanish political rule, it did not reject its lifestyle or intellectual leadership.

The Spanish language is a common link for eighteen of the twenty republics. Even though several million Ecuadorians, Peruvians, and Bolivians speak Quechua or Aymara and most Paraguayans are as much at home in Guaraní as in Spanish, national consciousness for the majority of these people is based on communication in Spanish. Likewise, the use of Portuguese is a major factor in holding together so composite a nation as Brazil. It may be added that New World Spanish and especially Portuguese are different colloquial languages from their European counterparts, just as American English differs from English spoken in Britain or Texans and New Englanders do not sound the same.

Not least, Roman Catholicism contributes a sense of cultural integrity to Latin America, since 85 percent of the population is at least nominally attached to this institution. The Church has a pervasive if declining influence on a number of other institutions. Even gender role expectations are indirectly influenced by the Church. However, at present, religious and social ideologies are in ferment, especially among the younger clergy.

Nationalism is another source of unity. Although it appeared as a somewhat parochial movement early in the century, the concept of nationhood has tended to consolidate political sentiment throughout Latin America. Presumably, all Latin America rejects colonialism and the economic penetration of foreign powers, which formerly were European but during this century has been the United States. Generally this suspiciousness is milder and more ambivalent than the xenophobia found in former colonial areas of the world, such as Africa and the Near East.

Nationalistic sentiment is gradually being integrated into a broader regionalism: the establishment of the Central American Economic Union in 1960 and the Latin American Free Trade Association (LAFTA) in 1961 was a refreshing departure from the older chauvinistic policy. Adverse economic developments did little to strengthen these organizations but new linkages with new names were formed in the 1980s. As nearly half the trade for much of Latin America (except the Southern Cone nations) is with the United States, attention in the 1990s is focused on a free trade area for all the Americas. Despite diversity in their policies and goals, many Latin Americans are aware of the advantages of a regional grouping in defense against the major economic powers. Latin Americans now look beyond their region and see the necessity of a more global approach. As mentioned previously, NAFTA and other proposed cooperative ventures are now a reality. Also, new technologies, market processes, and power relationships make the boundary between developed and developing areas a fuzzy one. Still, pressures both within and outside each nation prevent a firm policy on specific issues.

THE ECONOMIC FABRIC

As more than a score of volumes analyze the Latin American economy, the present discussion introduces only a few basic economic problems and their relationship to the society. Among these are the area's dependence on natural resources and Latin America's traditional role as a supplier of these products to Western Europe and the United States. However, the economies of the twenty republics are fairly diverse and not reducible to simple explanations. Differing ideologies continue to surface during this century. We may outline a few of the dominant theories and examine how they have worked over the last several decades.

Economic Theories and Models

Dependency. Dependency is the subjection of local or regional economies to the leading Western powers, particularly the United States. This theory considered the economic situation of Latin American as one of colonialism, that is, a mercantalist relationship or economic subordination of Latin America to Spain and later to the United States and Europe. Many Latin American economists held this theory during the middle of this century. In this context, underdevelopment and overdevelopment represent two sides of the same coin. The revelation of the activities of multinational corporations, for example ITT (International Telephone and Telegraph), has underlined the dependency thesis. The European and North American domination of mining, transportation, and other interests in these countries may have been of advantage, for example, in the early years as a prelude to Peru's own industrial takeoff in the 1960s. Nevertheless, this kind of economic dominance was of questionable value to the society or to the needs of the later welfare-oriented regimes. Reactions against dependency or colonialism appeared as early as 1938 in Mexico with its oil resources. By the 1960s nationalization of mineral and fuel resources was the rallying cry from Venezuela to Chile. In the 1980s, the insistence of the International Monetary Fund (IMF) about fiscal responsibility introduced another version of dependency.

One problem with the dependency theory is the fallacy that interrelatedness means underdevelopment. Buenos Aires and São Paulo actually profit from their attachments to the outside economic world. Another weakness of the theory is its failure to examine the specific connections between different segments of the economic and social structure. Notably, the inadequacies may stem more from the sharp disparities of economic rewards within the nation than from subordination to outside forces.

Import Substitution. This theory focuses on the revamping of the economy by the manufacture of capital and consumer products in order to reduce dependency. The effect of two world wars and the Great Depression made Latin America conscious of the need to move out of its dependency relationship.[10] As inspired by the Economic Commission of Latin America and the Argentinian economist Raúl Preibisch, the theory was known as *structuralism* with stress on industrialization. Actually, industrialization began in advanced countries like Argentina in the nineteenth century. For most nations, the drive to industrialization came during and after World War II. Increasingly, the state played a role in this process, with inflation resulting as money had to be printed to underwrite this expansion. The need to industralize remains with Latin America, even though more sophisticated economic theories have reshaped the idea of import substitution. Stagnation, growing unemployment, lower consumption levels, and rural decline are all to the point. These problems were difficult enough for larger nations, impossible for smaller ones such as Ecuador or Bolivia. In other words, import substitution, a centerpiece of the modernization, failed.

Modernization. Modernization is a loose combination of various processes and overlaps, including import substitution and structuralism, as it emphasizes the need to industrialize but with more demand to innovate and diversify the economy. Stress is on urbanization, along with educational and technological advances, foreign investment, removal of trade barriers, and reducing the relative contribution of the agricultural sector in the national economy. One version would make the nation economically autonomous; another more current model looks at the nature of our global economy. The global model is more than occasionally criticized by economic nationalists as a form of neocolonialism—especially when the national economy lies under the dictates of the World Bank, IMF, and other international agencies, as in the 1980s when enormous debts were incurred.

Even Marxists believe that developing countries have to incorporate capitalist features in order to prepare for a proletarian transformation. According to nearly all economists, a serious aspect of modernization and structuralism is the cost of rapid industrialization and urbanization because they result in government underwriting of the socioeconomic infrastructure. Inflation occurs when the government prints money with no genuine revenue. The wealthy resist paying taxes and the taxability of the middle and lower classes is limited.[11]

Neoliberalism. This theory focuses on freeing the economy from state controls, as inspired by the "Chicago Boys" (or the influence of economists from the University of Chicago) in the Pinochet regime in Chile. This relatively new doctrine must be viewed in the context of competing and sometimes overlapping economic models. For one, it is a reaction to Marxism and state welfare. Indeed, neoliberalism asserts a laissez-faire approach in its encouragement of entrepreneurship. It is also an attack against state intervention, which has been associated with inflation because of pump priming by the government. Neoliberalism emphazises privatization, deregulation, export expansion, and foreign economic penetration. At the same time, it adheres to "structual adjustment"; that is, the need to achieve solvency as defined by the IMF. Interestingly, experiments with neoliberalism have appeared in both authoritarian and democratic societies with not altogether consistent results.[12]

As implied, these theories are hardly mutually exclusive, nor are they the only ones to guide governments and policy makers. A nation may be oriented simultaneously to more than one of these viewpoints or may abandon a position only to return to it later.

Dependency and Underdevelopment

The problems of dependency in Latin America are complicated by the inadequacies of most developing areas. Although industries have been established in the leading countries during the last several decades, basically, the dilemma remains; that is, too little income in too few hands. We may outline a few of the major problems.

First is the concentration of the national economy in one or two resources.[13] In eleven countries, for instance, coffee is a critical export, and in four (Colombia, Costa Rica, El Salvador, and Guatemala) it is the principal legal item. Also, various nations depend mainly on a single mineral or metal for their revenue from the outside world, such as tin in Bolivia.

Beyond the legal, traditional monoculturalism is the production and traffic of drugs. A number of countries are deeply involved in this economy. For instance, the growing of coca is a primary means of survival for peasants in Bolivia and is supplemented by Peru and Ecuador. The coca is shipped into Colombia, where the drug traffic has distorted the integrity of most sectors of the state and society. As Colombians remind us, this commodity supplies the needs of U.S. citizens.

The perils of dependency on specialization in one or two primary products, whether official or unofficial, are obvious. For one, the usual financial risks are associated with speculation and price fluctuations. A drop of one cent per pound in the price of coffee can amount to several million dollars per year in Brazil.

Second is the staggering difference of income between developed and underdeveloped areas (as seen in Table 1.1) and between rich and poor within each nation. This problem together with a dependency status vis-à-vis Western and oil-producing nations make for a continuing depressed economy.

Third is the demographic structure. With a high—although declining—birthrate (twenty-five per thousand population) over one-third of Latin Americans are below what is considered as the age of economic productivity. Low educational attainment, shortage of occupational skills, and isolation of a large portion of the population from the urban industrial complex complicate the task of raising the gross domestic product (GDP). Even allowing for enormous national differences—such as between two relatively rich countries like Argentina and Venezuela (with vastly different economies) and countries such as Bolivia, Honduras, and Haiti at the lower end—the entire area is underdeveloped.

A correlate of dependency is a situation of colonialism in view of the neoimperialism of the world's dominant nations—principally the United States—after World War II. In turn, this dynamic produced an internal colonialism whereby trade and capital flows, the labor force, and financial systems within each nation are subordinate to certain demands of the elites, usually in the capital.[14] Often this new power elite represents a symbiosis of industrialists and agriculturists.

Industrialization, Income, and Modernization

In broad historical terms the Latin American economy may be characterized as having two stages: The first is the period of *crecimiento hacia afuera* or a growth toward the outside world in which exports were supplied to the outside world in return for industrial goods. This phase began to change in the 1930s, when a *crecimiento hacia adentro* began—an economy oriented toward import substitution. For instance, in Brazil from 1929 to 1937 imports declined by 23 percent and industrial output increased by 50 percent. By the 1960s, Latin Americans were debating the respective merits of the dependency theory and the modernization theory. The economy has shown irregular growth with periods of stagnation, particularly from the 1960s to the 1980s. Certain countries, for example Chile, fare better than Brazil. Others (Peru for one) have had catastrophic economies. Brazil's growth rate represented a loss from 1981 to 1983, but reached a high of 8.3 in 1986. The attempts of national governments and international agencies to push forward investment and industrialization meet with only partial success.

The low rate of economic development in the immediate post–World War II period can be traced to various barriers in the sociopsychological climate and the institutional structure. For one, deployment of skills and the employment structure were too rigid. Traditionally, the *jefe*, along with the managerial elite, tended to avoid contact with labor. Manual work had to be detailed to a person below one's own status. The preference of the university student for law or philosophy as opposed to engineering was a case in point. This pattern changed in the 1960s as engineering and business careers increased. Also, from colonial days to the present, immediate profits have been the goal. Entrepreneurs desire a quick return on their investment. Consequently, long-term planning, acquisition of capital goods, and industrial expansion became subordinate to the future-oriented economies of Europe and North America—not least, because of low personal incomes, the mass market is weak in most Latin American countries.

Capital formation is another serious factor in industrialization. Basically, the shortage of capital derives from the limited income within the Latin American agricultural and extractive economy. Its products command a meager return on the international market as compared to manufactured goods from abroad, which sell at higher prices since value is added to the product. Capital shortage also results from the failure of the wealthy to invest in their own country. Moreover, the oligarchy pays few taxes on its profits, which are traditionally derived from agriculture. More important, upper-income groups have little confidence in their own country, and their wealth finds its way to bank accounts in New York and Zurich.

A critical aspect of capital formation is the sharp disparities in income levels. The upper 5 percent of Latin Americans receive roughly one-third of the national income, much of which ends up in foreign banks. As a means of combating this continuing problem, reform governments attempt income redistribution, collectivization of landed estates, unionization, and stimulation of employment. Since little progress has been made on a progressive income tax and variations of the value-added tax only deepen the disparity of income, the tax structure remains highly problematic.[15]

A correlate of the shortage of capital and the disparity of income is a continuously spiraling price level. Inflation is chronic in most of South America and to a lesser extent in Meso-America (Mexico and Central America). Over the past several decades, several South American countries have had a rate of more than 30 percent inflation per year (Peru had 400% inflation in August 1990 and until 1994 Brazil was not far behind). One reason for the cheapening of currency is government's encouragement of economic growth by underwriting new industry. This tendency causes an unbalanced budget since more money flows into the national economy than is received in taxes. Governments borrow from the national treasury or the central bank in order to cover their deficits. Also, the large volume of imports places a drain on the slender domestic financial resources. An adverse balance of payments is no less a serious aspect of inflation in view of the declining value of Latin American goods on the world market, further complicated by the increased costs of oil and other imports.

The Entrepreneur, the Social Setting, and a Global Economy

As implied previously, Latin America suffers from a shortage of entrepreneurs, although less today than in the past. Through most of history, commercial and industrial enterprises were secondary to the agricultural and extractive economy. When several Latin American countries began to industrialize in the late nineteenth century, foreigners usually played the leading role. In other words, migrants rather than the older oligarchy launched industries, although once these were successful the older aristocracy moved in. In view of the legacy of Spanish feudalism, the operations of the marketplace had an ambivalent status as compared to the more genteel career of cultivating the land.

A formidable impediment to development and modernization is the domination of what is called the North as opposed to the South—the "haves" versus the "have-nots"—or the dependency situation of Latin America. Indeed, the explanation lies in what is known as the *world dependency* model. In this world-capitalistic system, one differentiates between a core, a semiperiphery, and the periphery. The distinction is somewhat arbitrary as the economic structure of each country is in almost constant change and the degree of dependency consequently varies. In other words, modernization is precarious in a climate of subordination of one economic area to another. As a relevant example, in the 1970s Brazil entered a period of considerable industrial expansion, but by the end of the decade the growth was over—buyers simply were not there. Discontinuities in the local, national, and international markets were evident.

In spite of these problems, economic progress was impressive until the depression of the late 1970s and the 1980s. During the 1950s, Latin America and the United States had an almost equal growth rate. But between 1960 and 1980 the rate of economic growth was nearly twice as high for Latin America than for most industrial nations and for all other developing areas. During those two decades steel production multiplied almost sixteen times, automobile production ten times, and so on.[16] This growth was positive for both industrialists and workers, but in these years migrants poured into the cities by the thousands, yet only a fraction found employment. Today most nations follow more rational, if painful, economic policies, especially the stabilization programs of the IMF and related agencies. Debt, interest rates, and inflation continue to haunt both producer and consumer, and massive poverty continues.

The Crisis of the 1980s and Its Aftermath

International events of the last two decades drastically compounded the economic situation. It may be noted that in 1970 the total external debt of the Third World was $100 million but by 1988 it was $1.3 trillion.[17] During the fuel crisis of 1973–1974, the Third World OPEC (Organization of Petroleum Exporting Countries) demanded a higher return for oil from wealthier nations, and ideology about the status of natural resources entered a new phase. Along with Middle Eastern nations, oil producers such as Venezuela and Mexico decided to join OPEC. As a result, several countries experienced an adverse balance of payments. Brazil, Argentina, and others had to adjust to not only the higher cost of fuel, but also to the inflationary economy and the recession that plagued most of the Western world. In Latin America, borrowing became a means of economic growth. In 1982, after OPEC lowered the price of oil, Mexico and Venezuela, as well as Brazil, Argentina, and Peru, had huge debts as the expectation of economic growth and profits failed to materialize.[18] The early 1980s became frenzied as international banks were asking for interest payments that reached 23 percent! As these payments could not be met, further loans were made. However, these banks and the IMF demanded an economic restructuring, including austerity programs which had overwhelming effects on the Latin American economy and drastic restrictions on imports. Food shortages became ever more acute for the lower classes already locked in poverty. For instance, in Lima the amount of labor hours required for a kilo of rice rose seven times between 1980 and 1984; in Mexico subsidies for basic foods were ended in 1986. Massive unemployment increased throughout Latin America.[19] These economic policies create another kind of havoc as countries (Argentina, Brazil, and Mexico, among others) may pay 5 percent or more of their GDP in order to pay off foreign debt. In Venezuela, the GDP dropped 25 percent between 1981 and 1989.

The 1991 Gulf War brought a brief recovery to oil-producing countries, but structural problems remain. In 1992, Brazil experienced a monthly 30 percent inflationary rate. Similarly, Mexico and other countries found themselves unable to rectify trade deficits and pay off their international debt. In the end, economic change resembles a zero-sum game—a winner is balanced by a loser.[20] In reality, the world economic system from the core to the periphery is showing signs of decline. Consequently, colonialism, if of a different kind, still remains the fate of the developing world.

The advanced countries have intensified industrialization over the last two generations. Because of the bleak economic atmosphere of the 1980s, most Latin American nations encourage privatization and individual initiative. Chile led the way in this neoliberal, free-market–oriented renaissance. Since the mid-1980s, Mexico has tried to sell off its nonprofitable public corporations, a program accelerated by President Salinas de Gotori. The present regimes in Brazil and Argentina, among other nations, are attempting to reduce government monopolies. Even more marginal countries such as Bolivia, Ecuador, and Peru are moving toward neoliberalism. In part, it has been an "antistatist consensus among the local bourgeoisie."[21] In deference to European and North American banks, the IMF pressures nearly every government to divest their nonprofitable business operations.

Competing Ideologies and the Economic Future

A related aspect of stimulating a satisfactory climate for the entrepreneur is the particular economic ideology. The climate of economic development shifted back and forth between quasi-feudalism and the new industrialism. Most nations move at an irregular pace to the left and to the right. Cuba is the only country to break definitively with the Western economic world. In the 1950s, Guatemala, Bolivia, and Brazil—and Chile in 1970—swerved to a collectivist economy, only to be pulled back by a rightist regime, often prompted by U.S. intervention. The *sandinistas* in Nicaragua moved to the left after the overthrow of Somoza in 1979 but reached a compromise regime in 1990. The middle class added its weight to the upper class in permitting military regimes in these countries, the most devastating being Brazil in 1964 and Chile in 1973 (both returned to civilian rule in 1985 and 1989, respectively). In a different direction, in the 1940s Mexico chose the path of an "institutionalized" revolution—a government-sponsored industrialization, a form one might label as dual capitalism.

Despite its unhappy profile, it is too soon to make a final judgment about the socialist regime of Cuba.[22] Unquestionably, the Marxist regime attained a number of breakthroughs, including universal education, medical services, and a degree of economic equality unique to the Americas.[23] However, with the breakdown of the Soviet Union, aid was withdrawn. Beyond the intransigence of Fidel Castro himself, the grim reports on food and vitamin deficiencies might move the United States to remove its economic embargo and arrive at a compassionate rapprochement. Even though Castro has made several concessions, hard-liners among the Miami Cuban lobby appear to have the clout to forestall any change in Washington. Among the advanced nations, the United States stands alone in its opposition to Cuba, even though it now has ties with its one-time enemy Vietnam.

For various reasons, the Latin American economy calls for basic restructuring. The proposal of import substitution as a means of resolving underdevelopment did not prove to be a satisfactory avenue of revitalization. Neoliberal policies hold a promise, but at an enormous price. Latin Americans still suffer from the frustration of an unfulfilled need system. The lower and middle classes are trapped in an economic web created by agrindustrialists (if not an agrarian oligarchy), corrupt political regimes, and a debt-ridden economy. In the 1990s, one reads of 25 percent unemployment in Panama, 70 percent of the population living in poverty in Guatemala, 8.5 million tons of food imported yearly into Mexico, a decline of 3 percent in the GDP in Peru, and the share of household income being spent on food nearly tripling since 1970 in Venezuela. Gross inequalities in income have to be reduced—the economic advances of the 1960s and 1970s produced greater income disparities than what existed before, and data of the sluggish 1980s reveal the same. Avenues of economic growth must be found, notably in the private sector. As suggested, Chile may offer the most promising scenario. The GDP rose 6 percent in 1991 and 9.7 percent in 1992. Inflation declined 26 percent in 1990, 22 percent in 1991, and 13 percent in 1992.[24] Once more, Latin America is turning toward a policy of *hacia afuera*, as the adoption of NAFTA symbolizes, even though the consequences are far from clear, especially for Mexico.[25] Everywhere in Latin America a larger portion of the population must be involved in significant economic production and services beyond their present role in an outmoded agricultural or protoindustrial economy.

POLITICAL PROCESSES

Economic disparities are at the root of Latin America's underdevelopment. Yet political events are both the cause and effect of a regressive economy. Also, political institutions vary even more than economic processes. To some extent economic models have their corresponding political theories. Also, national governments display a wide divergence in style, stability, and sensitivity to the needs of the people. The linkage between economics and politics is not always clear. A positive relationship is often assumed to exist between democratization and economic development. One problem with this comparison is the failure to agree on what makes an economy healthy. No less problematic is the vagueness in defining a democratic government.

Is democracy a viable form of government for developing areas? Most social scientists say yes. We may debate whether the democratic process is effective for advanced societies, not least the United States in view of its parochial priorities, gridlock, seemingly unlimited political funds, and electronic media underwritten by special interests. In Latin America contradictions are even more apparent than in Europe and the United States. A country may move from a democracy to authoritarianism and later return to democracy.

Latin America displays divergent political climates; consequently the correlation between socioeconomic progress and "democracy" is remarkably shaky. For instance, Argentina, traditionally the most advanced economically of all twenty republics, experienced a military coup in 1930, the Perón dictatorship from 1946 to 1955, military rule again in 1966, a brief return to Peronism in the early 1970s, and rule by the generals again in 1976. The failure of the military in the disastrous Malvinas/Falklands war in 1982 eased the way for a return to democracy in 1983. Uruguay remained a showcase of representative government until 1973 when economic deterioration and political violence brought on authoritarian rule.

Similarly, Chile was a highly articulate democracy for a half century, but polarization intensified during the Allende period (1970–1973), ending in a relentless military dictatorship. Going along with the trend in Latin America, Chile returned to the democratic ledger in 1989. As of 1996, Peru is the only nation under authoritarian rule, with rumblings of instability and the use of arbitrary power in Guatemala, Haiti, Paraguay, and others. But all these nations are verbally committed to the democratic process, or at least regularly scheduled and "free" elections. The lengthiest record of voting and other civil rights belongs to Costa Rica, which abandoned the last vestiges of authoritarianism in 1948. Over the long term, Uruguay has an impressive record of democratic expression, except for its unhappy military excursion from 1973 to 1985. Venezuela, since the downfall of Pérez Jiménez in 1958, has enjoyed a pluralistic political apparatus, disturbed though it was by a brief military intervention in 1992 in regard to a failed presidency.

Mexico represents a special case. As political power was vested in only one party, the nation has been described as a "manifest democracy," or possibly a "benevolent dictatorship." Its economy is marked by a mix of capitalism and welfare orientation. The official party, the PRI (Institutionalized Revolutionary Party), embodies four major groupings—the peasantry, the workers, segments of the middle class, and economic elites. The prospects for the survival of this "democratic" arrangement appears favorable, but dissonance surfaces in rural areas.[26] The most dramatic episodes were the 1968 riots of university students and the restlessness of *campesinos* in 1976. What had been largely facade opposition parties became very active in the 1980s, and in the presidential election of 1988, had the votes been accurately counted, Carlos Salinas de Gotari probably would not have been elected president. The 1994 election was more closely monitored, but questions remain as to the integrity of victorious PRI.[27] Consequently, the party and the government have been forced to change their policies through the last decade in both image and substance in order that the power system can remain intact.[28] In the mid-1990s, the Chiapas revolt, assassination of the leading presidential candidate, revelations of widespread corruption within the presidency, and the fall of the peso remind Mexicans of the tenuousness of their sociopolitical structure.

As a comparison to the relative stability of the Mexican government structure, it is worth examining the cyclic behavior of most Latin American governments. When the Alliance for Progress was launched in 1961, only three (Haiti, Dominican Republic, and Nicaragua) of the twenty republics were assigned to the authoritarian ledger. Subsequent decades saw the twilight of the Camelot dreams of hemispheric partnership and well-established democratic regimes. More apparent were the vicissitudes of economic development, especially inflation, trade barriers, and the failure of economic growth to match population growth. Gradually through the 1960s and 1970s all but three governments (Colombia, Costa Rica, and Venezuela) moved into the dictatorial range or one-party rule. As military governments failed to resolve the horrendous economic problems, later intensified by heavy indebtedness, the elites and middle classes opted for a return to democratic rule, to which the generals or other authoritarian leaders reluctantly or not so reluctantly agreed. The pattern of these cycles and their transfer of power vary from country to country.

Political life in Latin America would seem to be in chaotic change. At the same time, it shows signs of continuity. *Personalismo* (the cult of the individual leader), *caudillismo* (reverence for the party head, often a military chieftain), and the *cuartelazo* (the barracks revolt) as institutions have declined dramatically. The political fabric is often in a state of transition with the emergence of new ideological movements and new party groupings, even though these are occasionally refurbishments of an older doctrine. In particular, the authoritarian form of government seems to ebb and flow. That is, the term "dictatorship" is a variable one. Certain countries were almost permanently relegated to a decadent and stagnant political structure, such as Nicaragua with the Somoza dynasty (1934–1979), Paraguay with its perennial General Stroessner (1954–1989), the Dominican Republic with Trujillo (1931–1961), and the still more primitive autocracy of the Duvaliers in Haiti (1946–1986). An archaic, despotic order can finally give way to change, even though exceptions persist, as in post–Duvalier Haiti. All this raises the question of whether conflict theory is correct in assuming that politics is an explanation of how violence is patterned. Even in a democracy, the political process is essentially the interplay of conflicting interest groups.

One facet of authoritarian regimes is the shift in style from those of yesteryear to those of the last decade. General Getúlio Vargas of Brazil (1930–1945) and Juan Perón of Argentina (1946–1955) based their raison d'être on a kind of *corporatism* or special sociopolitical ideology. However different their styles, both men, especially Perón, cultivated a doctrinaire and ritualistic structure vaguely reminiscent of Mussolini's Fascism in Italy. Even more than Perón, Vargas had to cater to the middle class.[29] The dictatorships of the 1970s and 1980s, at least in Brazil and Chile, came into being because the previous regime was perceived as failing to offer a viable social order, notably in regard to the economy. Consequently, the new military regimes were geared to fashion an economic machine. However, violations of human rights are well documented, if to a declining degree, as concern with legitimacy becomes more salient. Corporatism, both open and closed, still prevails. On the whole, Latin America is moving toward a more predictable bureaucratized political process. Sudden veerings toward the right or left are rare; civil life is relatively routinized.

Military regimes vary in their attitudes toward civil liberties but usually are concerned with building at least a facade of legitimacy and enfranchisement. Still, can we come to a meaningful generalization about their content and style? For example, Chile and Haiti hardly could be more different in their cultures, yet the two military rulers, Augusto Pinochet and Francois Duvalier, were remarkably similar in their skills of divide and conquer.[30] Possibly midway between two models—the old and new military rule—is a blend of ad hoc and planned government which eventually topples a corrupt and often inept regime. Yet as an attempt to remove the errors of a predecessor, the new order falls into the same errors and cannot relinquish power once habituated by it. Two particularly regressive examples of a military–civilian mix are El Salvador and notably Guatemala, in which an agrarian elite still resists land reform by use of military or paramilitary means. In both countries, military operations, including the murder of six prominent Jesuit priests in El Salvador in 1990, were led by units trained in a U.S. counterinsurgency program.

In common with other developing areas of the world, Latin America is caught between an urgency for change on one side and traditionalism on the other. Because economic growth is at a higher level than in the Near East, parts of Asia, or Africa, democratic processes are judged to be more advanced as compared with the continual insurgency of these less politically mature areas.

Too often writers apply to these societies developmental norms and goals more relevant to their own society. During the Cold War, the United States somehow assumed that Latin American countries would desire to align themselves with a Pax Americana. As Rómulo Betancourt, former president of Venezuela, pointed out a generation ago, these nations are committed to a policy of neither West nor East but remain part of the Third World.[31] Although the influence of the United States still looms throughout the area, particularly in Mexico and Central America, Latin Americans are struggling to assert their sovereignty and to somehow find an accommodation to an ever more complex international network. Increasingly since the 1970s, Europe and Asia have made political and economic inroads in Latin America.

Socialization, Social Movements, and the Institutionalized Climate of Politics

A variety of societal factors surround the political process. For instance, literacy rates are reported to vary from approximately 95 percent in Argentina and Uruguay to 75 percent in Brazil and 29 percent in Haiti—percentages that fail to distinguish between functional and nonfunctional literacy.[32] Consequently, political socialization is rudimentary for several countries, notably in rural areas. Since the urban masses are more politicized they are becoming aware that decisions at the polls can affect their needs and wants, as a study of a Lima shantytown shows.[33]

The duality of a rigid power system and a changing urban society poses a basic contradiction and instability in Latin American political life. Revolutionary tendencies appeared relatively early in several societies, Mexico being the first in 1910. For example, the rise of the urban proletariat in Chile during the 1920s culminated in a major change in the power relations of that country for more than a generation, creating a decisive impact on further democratization of its society. In today's unstable world of developing nations, political commitment assumes an urgency unfamiliar to the more "mature" countries. In addition to the remnants of the *caudillo* cult, local traditions can be a barrier to change. This parochialism is giving way to industrialization, urbanization, educational expansion, and a faint degree of restratification, as with Chile since 1989.

What is apparent today is a number of social movements, both violent and nonviolent, as a means of urging social change.[34] Impatience with the slow response of governments to social needs has led to various improvizations to effect social change, both in the rural and the urban scene. These movements range from uprisings in the countryside to discontent in the urban setting, whether by underpaid workers or socially conscious university students. They have risen in recent years because of growing awareness of pressures and disturbances in the global economy. The degree to which these movements influence "cultural meanings and identities" for individuals in or outside the movement relates to the extent a movement affects various institutions, particularly the government.[35] Perhaps most striking among social movements is the insurgency of the Shining Path (*Sendero Luminoso*) in Peru, of which we shall see more in Chapter 4. It is significant that Nicaragua, after the successful revolution against Somoza in 1979, established the Sandinista socialist regime and since the election of Violet Chamorro in 1992 is making the transition to a "compromise" administration. This arrangement is marginally successful in working toward *concertación,* or a national dialogue in order to find and implement a workable economic program.

Another force making for political participation is a diffusion of Western cultural features among the Indians and recently acculturated *mestizos, ladinos,* and *cholos,* as will become clear in Chapter 5. A related factor is secularization and the transformation of the Roman Catholic Church. This shift was perceptible well before this century, but the ecumenical movement of the 1960s, along with awareness of social dislocations, brought about a broader outlook among the segments of the clergy. With the papacy of John Paul II, a more conservative stance has set in. It is uncertain whether the Church can respond successfully to the challenges of the present social order.

Because of the effects of industrialization, urbanization, and restratification, the middle class became more visible after World War II, especially after 1960. The older elites no longer have a monopoly of power; rather they must share it with the managerial–professional sectors and increasingly with the lower middle class. Also, military officers, even in the higher grades, are predominantly of middle-class origin, and more recently, skilled workers are moving closer to the fulcrum of political power. In other words, traditional elites have to share power with nonelite groups.

As in many parts of the world, the climate of politics is never very far from the effect of the economy. New politicial forces are at work—often grassroots expressions that grow into social movements. In the case of Ecuador, populist movements arose as a result of the insensitivity of the economic elites to the effect of a declining export market and a growing external debt on wage earners.[36] Similarly in Uruguay during the military dictatorship a high rate of inflation with a sharp decline in real wages set the stage for a return to democratic rule.[37]

The Advent of Nationalism

Even though nationalism has been redefined—with wider groupings such as NAFTA—it still preoccupies Latin America. Gradually what became in several countries a negative self-image, or an ambivalence in self-perception as in Argentina, was transformed into a "positive national identity," sometimes by pride in an ethnic heritage—European for Argentina and indigenous for Mexico.[38] Earlier the processes of communication, intra- and interregional contact were too rudimentary. Beginning with the war of independence, programs of national integration were viewed as the key to development. However, the building of a national consciousness is mostly a product of the twentieth century.

Nationalism was deeply ingrained among many Mexicans, as evident in the struggle against such episodes as the Texan uprisings of the 1840s and the French occupation in 1863. It was also intensifed in the Mexican Revolution. The static social system of President Porfírio Díaz had to end before Mexicans could become conscious of the social and political forces of the modern world. With the awareness of a crisis Mexicans came together more than ever before in a common cause. Consequently, a generation after the fall of Díaz in 1910, a nation-state was created. In other words, however much indigenous loyalties may be incorporated into the process, nationalism appears to be partly an outgrowth of modernization. Education, modern transport, and interregional and international trade all tend to favor a sense of national belongingness. For instance, in Colombia only since the 1950s *antioqueños* began to look upon themselves as *colombianos* (perhaps New Yorkers or Texans may still be uncertain as to whether their identity belongs first to their region or to the nation). The overwhelming dominance of foreign powers drove Mexicans toward nationalism. Similarly, Castro whipped up his own brand of nationalism because of pressures from the colossus to the North.

The factors surrounding nationalism emerge from various sources, as they do in most parts of the world. The rise of a middle class played an indispensable role in creating national unity. Yet the expression of nationalism is by no means confined to this class. After all, the middle classes are rooted in diverse groupings—the armed forces, proprietors, and intellectuals, among others. These sectors agree only in their conviction that the national government should become a major medium for social and economic change. In addition, the individual's specific cultural setting has its effects. For instance, according to a survey of Mexican medical students, graduates of bicultural (Mexican-American) schools are significantly less ethnocentric than graduates of monocultural ones.[39] Spontaneous situations are also relevant. Even the wild enthusiasm of the soccer match can be a means of raising nationalist fervor.[40] The drug war that the United States brought to several Latin American nations indirectly fostered nationalism. As another instance, the ill-fated 1982 Malvinas/Falkland attack was largely the desperate attempt on the part of the generals to assert Argentine nationalism against a British colony, as well as to furnish legitimacy to their arbitrary rule. The intermittent border conflict between Peru and Ecuador represents another example of the struggle for national identity.

Nationalism becomes a rallying point for those segments of the population who are marginal to the national community. Frontier settlements in the Mato Grosso in Brazil or Aymara villages in Bolivia are largely removed from national identity for reasons of physical or sociopsychological distance. Even within the urban enclaves, wealthy landowners living in the capital identify with a world outside Latin America—Paris, New York, or Miami. At the other end of the urban scene, the slum or shanty dweller who has just fled the countryside is too preoccupied with his or her survival to identify with the larger society. In other words, factors inhibiting politicization also retard nationalism. Finally, one may hypothesize that familism, regionalism, social disorganization, and authoritarianism lead to various ideologies and not necessarily to nationalism.

The Political Structure

In the shifting scene of Latin America, political parties are more diverse and less stable than in the United States or Northwestern Europe. Countries differ in the degree to which parties are dominant actors, as in Colombia, Costa Rica, Mexico or Venezuela, or fairly marginal as in Haiti, Paraguay, or Peru, where the executive branch (or the military) may be all-important. The other countries lie somewhere between these extremes.[41] Because of conflicting sectors and the range of personal followings, proliferation of parties is greater. Social movements increasingly foment much of the political processes. On the whole, political parties tend to be ephemeral and noninstitutionalized. Faced as they are with hostility on the part of the opposition government, limited finances, primordial organization, and inadequate grassroots, many parties function on an ad hoc basis. Sometimes they originate only on the eve of an election. With the ebb and flow of political fortunes, survival is tenuous, and leaders may go into hiding or exile. A party may disappear altogether, but the same ideology or leadership reappears under a different label with a somewhat altered set of goals and slogans. In multiparty countries, survival risks are especially high. To survive in any country a party must have a certain amount of power capability or political efficacy. It must have the potential of meeting broad social and economic purposes and be capable of arousing support in significant areas of the power structure, not least the armed forces, even though the military is less restless than it was in the 1960s and 1970s.

The structure varies from a one-party or two-party system to a multiplicity of parties. As implied, perhaps the most paradoxical case is Mexico. As the official party, the PRI permits the existence of facade parties, which have become increasingly independent. The PRI is more a testimonial to national consensus than to a functioning democracy, but until the 1980s—if we omit the late 1960s—major interest groups perceived their needs as reasonably fulfilled. However, 1994 was a critical year in view of the revolt in Chiapas and the challenge to the PRI in the August election.

A two-party system traditionally operated in Colombia since the 1850s, as it did for many decades in Honduras and Uruguay. But in several Latin American countries, notably Argentina and Chile, the plurality of political parties is roughly similar to the situation of Western Europe. In Argentina, the Socialists and especially the Radicals, although split, have been leading contenders in the alternation of civilian and military governments. With alliances and fissions new party groupings emerge; however, since 1930 the nation has experienced dictatorship as often as democracy. Seemingly, party diversity does not assure mass political involvement. In Chile, a relatively stable party structure continued despite a pattern of shifting alliances. The 1970 election was a contest between (1) the Nationalists (the right), (2) the Christian Democrats (the center), and (3) the Popular Unity coalition of Socialists, Communists, and dissident elements of the Radicals (the left). In this three-way election, the left won with little more than one-third of the ballots. With the return to democracy in 1989 after the Pinochet military rule, the basic opposition was between the rightist National Renovation Party (PNR) and the left-center *Concertación por la Democracia*.

Until the 1964 coup, more than a dozen parties in Brazil represented the range of sectional and class interests tinged with a certain *personalismo*. Yet only four of these were serious contenders for power. The most important were the relatively conservative Social Democratic Party, the even more traditionalist National Democratic Union, the Brazilian Labor Party, which was closely identified if not altogether dominated by Getúlio Vargas until his suicide in 1954, and finally, the Social Progressive Party sponsored by the São Paulo politician Ademar de Barros. When democracy returned to Brazil after military rule (1964–1985), the leading party became the PMDB (Brazilian Democratic Movement Party). However, the inability of President José Sarney to move the economy forward provided an opening for the Social Democrats, the Liberal Front party, and others in 1989 to elect a relative newcomer, the young, vibrant Fernando Collor de Mello, who to most Brazilians seemed less charismatic after he was elected. He was forced to resign in 1992 because of alleged corruption on the part of himself, his family, and cronies. Competing pressure groups, a relatively weak party structure, a deeply entrenched clientelism, along with the diverse ethnic and regional cultures hardly provide for a stable democratic process in Brazil. A "fragmented partism" was especially evident after 1985.[42] Then Brazil turned the corner as the election, through a coalition of Liberal Front and the Social Democratic parties, brought the distinguished social scientist Fernando Henrique Cardoso to the presidency in 1994. A lowering of the inflation rate and a compromise between capital and labor suggest that basic change is on the horizon.

Since World War II, a distinction arose between traditionalist parties with their roots in the historic position of upper-class interests and newer parties oriented to the needs of a growing middle class or members of the commercial, professional, and higher-level labor organizations. Traditional parties often represent a range of sectional and class interests tinged with a degree of *personalismo*. Beyond the traditional parties is what was once called "the new center." This grouping includes the Christian Democrats, who were in power in Chile from 1964 to 1970, and in Venezuela the Social Christian Party (COPEI). In a number of countries, this type of party developed after World War II and found its inspirations in liberal Catholic doctrines ranging from the 1891 papal encyclical to Vatican II (1962–1965).

In the same vein but without a religious connotation are the "national revolutionary parties." These also strive for the end of colonialism, agrarian and fiscal reform, improvement of the underprivileged classes, and expansion of education. In international relations, they periodically favor cooperation with the United States. But as compared to the conservative and centrist parties, they were often favorable to the Soviet Union. Neutralism was a favorite theme in Brazil's National Democratic Union (UDN), which elected Quadros and Goulart in the early 1960s. Similar but of differing coloration are Acción Demócrata in Venezuela and the National Liberation Party (PLN) in Costa Rica. In another direction Peru's APRA (American People's Revolutionary Alliance), founded and led for more than a generation by Haya de la Torre, is now opposed by new rivals, most significantly Cambio (Change) '90 that ushered in Alberto Fujimori as president.

Whether parties are left or right, innovative or traditional, democratic or authoritarian, the locus of power is traditionally in the executive. This focus in the executive is often referred to as *presidentialism*. The origins of a strong executive derive from several factors: the historic authoritarianism of Spain, the supremacy of headship in the Inca and other pre-Columbian cultures, the nature of the constitution, a kind of charisma or personality cult associated with a number of leaders in the past, and a clientelism, which is in few places as well institutionalized as in Mexico.[43] As another exhibit of presidential power, he or she in situations of emergency may declare an *estado de sitio* (state of siege) and dismiss the legislature. Only several countries (notably Chile, Colombia, Costa Rica, Uruguay, and Venezuela) have a relatively strong legislative branch, but events in other countries are moving toward increased power for the legislature, the 1992 downfall of Collar in Brazil being a case in point.

There is, then, no specific pattern of Latin American governments either from a substantive or stylistic viewpoint. Also, models designed for one purpose may not serve another. Apparently, in the eyes of some observers, when a government wants to make the harsh decisions demanded by economic modernization, the luxury of a democracy becomes a dubious option.

Power is the essence of the political process. Various groups contend for this precious commodity. Probably the most fundamental division is between power as belonging to a few elites or to a pluralistic constituency. Also, many neo-Marxists regard power as the "reproduction of inequality."[44] That is, a number of societal segments are struggling for dominance. Unquestionably, the Latin American scene would support this contention, if less tragically today than a half century ago.

A Concluding Note

This discussion has been oriented toward a few critical issues, such as colonialism, nationalization, modernization, development, political socialization, and the aim and style of government structures. The interrelationships of the political to other areas of the social order will appear in the chapters ahead. For one, how can politics influence various issues like population growth? How do political climates vary between city and countryside and influence the rise of new movements, including populism? Do ethnic and class identities relate to the political sphere? What is the interplay of institutional roles and political attitudes? For instance, student protest against the establishment has a long heritage. The outcry of the clergy is a more recent trend.

Despite fluctuations between popular and dictatorial rule, in most countries a kind of stability persists. As one instance, the PRI in Mexico has veered between corporatism and populism for more than a half century.[45]

Liberals and Conservatives have alternated in their domination of Colombian political life since the mid-nineteenth century—in a fairly stormy fashion for most of that period but more orderly since the late 1950s. The various political labels throughout most of the hemisphere may dissolve, but a drastic change in the power structure seems unlikely.

One factor that may be predictive of success is the solidity of democratic institutions. Pertinent to the Southern Cone countries and Brazil is the lengthy experience of Chile and Uruguay (despite their lapse in the 1970s and 1980s) with representative government as compared to the history of a less stable democratic process in their two large neighbors.[46] Whether future governments can maintain a democratic system is a fundamental question, but more to the point is whether governments, democratic or not so democratic, can deliver to their people an equitable distribution of income, adequate employment, or a measure of civil rights. We shall return to these problems in Chapters 9.

NOTES

1. Mary T. Gilderhus, "Got a Gringo on Their Shoulders: U.S. Relations with Latin America," *Latin American Research Review* 31(1): 189–210 (1996).

2. World Population Data Sheet (Washington, D.C.: Population Reference Bureau, 1996).

3. Larry Diamond and Juan J. Linz, "Introduction: Politics, Society, and Democracy in Latin America," in *Democracy in Developing Countries*, vol. 3, *Latin America*, ed. Larry Diamond, Juan J. Linz, and Martin M. Lipset (Boulder, Colo.: Riemer Publishers, 1989), 1–58.

4. Ernest A. Duff and John F. McCamant, *Violence and Repression in Latin America* (New York: Free Press, 1976), 136.

5. Susan Calvert and Peter Calvert, *Argentina: Political Culture and Instability* (Pittsburgh: University of Pittsburgh Press, 1989), 20–22.

6. Charles Wagley, *An Introduction to Brazil*, rev. ed. (New York: Columbia University Press, 1971), 29–85.

7. Julian Steward, *The People of Puerto Rico* (Urbana, Ill.: University of Illinois Press, 1956).

8. Sergio G. Roca, ed., *Socialist Cuba: Past Interpretations and Future Challenges* (Boulder, Colo.: Westview Press, 1988).

9. Arturo Uslar Pietri, *La Otra América* (Madrid: Alianza Editorial, 1974), 221–233.

10. Celso Furtado, *Ecomomic Development of Latin America* (New York: Cambridge University Press, 1970).

11. Werner Baer, "Social Aspects of Latin American Inflation," in *Latin America: The Crisis of the Eighties and the Opportunities of the Nineties*, ed. Werner Baer, Joseph Petry, and Murray Simpson (Champaign, Ill.: University of Illinois Press, 1991), 45–57.

12. Barbara Geddes, "The Politics of Economic Liberalization," *Latin American Research Review* 30(2): 195–214 (1995).

13. Latin American Center, *Statistical Abstract of Latin America* (Los Angeles: University of California, 1995), 640–644.

14. John Walton, "Urban Hierarchies and Patterns of Dependence in Latin America: Theoretical Bases for a New Research Agenda," in *Current Perspectives in Latin American Research*, ed. Alejandro Portes and Harley L. Browning (Austin: University of Texas Press, 1976), 43–69.

15. Richard M. Bird, "Tax Reform in Latin America: A Review of Some Recent Experiences," *Latin American Research Review* 27(1): 7–36 (1992).

16. Abraham F. Lowenthal, *Partners in Conflict: The United States and Latin America in the 1990s*, rev. ed. (Baltimore: Johns Hopkins University Press, 1990), 10.

17. Seamus O'Cleireacain, *Third World Debt and International Public Policy* (Westport, Conn.: Praeger, 1990), 3.

18. Hector Silva Michelina, *América Política: Económica de la Democracia* (Caracas: Editorial "José Martí," 1986), 142–146.

19. Susan George, *A Fate Worse Than Debt* (New York: Grove Press, 1988), 121–139.

20. Daniel Cheriot, *How Societies Change* (Thousand Oaks, Calif.: Pine Forge Press, 1994), 90.

21. Catherine M. Conaghan, James M. Malloy, and Luis A. Abugattas, "Business and the 'Boys': The Politics of Neoliberalism in the Central Andes," *Latin American Research Review* 25(2): 3–30 (1990).

22. Jorge F. Pérez-López, "Bringing the Cuban Economy into Focus: Conceptual and Empirical Challenges," *Latin American Research Review* 26(3): 7–54 (1991).

23. Julie Feinsilver, *Healing the Masses: Cuban Health Policies at Home and Abroad* (Berkeley: University of California Press, 1993).

24. Felipe Agüero, "Chile: South America's Success Story," *Current History* 92: 130–135 (1993).

25. Alain Touraine, "From the Mobilizing State to Democratic Politics," in *Redefining the State in Latin America*, ed. Colin I. Bradford, Jr. (Paris: Organization for Economic Cooperation and Development, 1994), 45–65.

26. Carmen Nava N., "La Democracia Interna del Partido de la Revolución Mexicana (PRM): El Problema de la Supresión de los Consejos Regionales," *Revista Mexicana de Sociología* 50(1): 157–166 (1988).

27. Philip L. Russell, *Mexico Under Salinas* (Austin: Mexico Resource Center, University of Texas, 1994).

28. Michael W. Foley, "Agenda for Mobilization: The Agrarian Question and Popular Mobilization in Contemporary Mexico," *Latin America Research Review* 26(2): 39–74 (1991).

29. N. Werneck Sodre, *Evolução Social do Brasil* (Porto Alegre: Editora da Universidad do Rio Grande do Sul, 1988), 87–88.

30. David Pion-Berlin, "The Armed Forces and Politics: Gains and Snares in Recent Scholarship," *Latin American Research Review* 30(1): 147–162 (1995).

31. Rómulo Betancourt, *Hacia una América Latina Demócrata e Integrada* (Caracas: Editorial Senderos, 1967), 143–145.

32. Latin American Center, *Statistical Abstract of Latin America* (Los Angeles: University of California, 1995), 231.

33. Susan C. Stokes, "Politics and Latin America's Urban Poor: Reflections from a Lima Shantytown," *Latin America Research Review* 26(2): 75–101 (1991).

34. Rafael Guido and Otto Fernández, "El Juicio al Sujeto: Un Análisis de los Movimientos Sociales en América Latina," *Revista Mexicana de Sociología* 51(4): 45–54 (1989).

35. Paul L. Haber, "Identity and Political Process: Recent Trends in the Study of Latin American Social Movements," *Latin American Reserch Review* 31(1): 171–188 (1996).

36. Luis Verdesota, "Los Mitos Sociales y la Democracia en el Ecuador," in *Consejo Latinamericano de Ciencias Sociales, Movimientos Sociales en el Ecuador* (Quito: CLACSO-ILDIS, 1986), 13–62.

37. Carolyn Craven, "Wage Determination and Inflation in Uruguay: Regime Changes," *Journal of Developing Areas* 27: 457–468 (1993).

38. Jeffrey W. Barrett, *Impulse to Revolution in Latin America* (New York: Praeger, 1985), 189–195.

39. Erwin H. Epstein and Catherine A. Riordan, "Bicultural Preparation and National Identity: A Study of Medical Students at a Mexican University," *Mexican Studies* 5(2): 239–248 (1989).

40. Neil Larsen, "Sport as Civil Society: The Argentinean Junta Plays Championship Soccer," in *The Discourse of Power*, ed. Neil Larsen (Minneapolis: Institute for the Study of Ideologies and Literature, 1983), 113–128.

41. Ronald H. McDonald and J. Mark Ruhl, *Party Politics and Elections in Latin America* (Boulder, Colo.: Westview Press, 1989), 3–4.

42. Scott Mainwaring, "Political Parties and Democratization in Brazil," *Latin American Research Review* 30(3): 177–187 (1995).

43. Martin C. Needler, *Mexican Politics: The Containment of Conflict* (New York: Praeger, 1982), 89–91.

44. Anthony M. Orum, "Political Sociology," in *Handbook of Sociology*, ed. Neil J. Smelser (Newbury Park, Calif.: Sage Publications, 1988), 393–424.

45. Viviane Brachet-Márquez, *The Dynamics of Domination: State, Class, and Social Reform in Mexico 1910–1990* (Pittsburgh: University of Pittsburgh Press, 1994).

46. Scott Mainwaring, "Democracy in Brazil and the Southern Cone: Achievements and Problems," *Journal of Interamerican Studies and World Affairs* 37: 113–173 (1995).

Chapter 2

Social Systems, Values, and Roles

The purpose of this chapter is to establish the framework within which I am operating; that is, the present discussion introduces the chapters that follow. Ethnic relations, the class structure, rural and urban societies, and social institutions are among the components of a cultural or a national system. The functioning of any society must be analyzed in both macro- and microperspectives. Systems and subsystems involve individuals and groups, statuses and roles, ideology and social movements. Specifically, the social scientist is committed to analyze how the behaviors and values of selected individuals, groups, and organizations affect the actions of other persons and systems. The search for what kinds of behaviors elicit—and hopefully explain—other behaviors or events has a lengthy tradition in the behavioral sciences.

THE THEORETICAL SETTING

As one approach, functionalism (along with systems theories) reached its height in the 1950s and 1960s as a means of understanding how societies operate. A great deal of significant research emerged from this approach. Still, functionalism had only marginal interest in conflict and no satisfactory explanation for crises. A related problem is the role of the individual as opposed to organizations. For example, a functionalist might explain the role of the Roman Catholic Church in Latin America as providing a sense of meaning for or, more critically, an escape from an imponderable social order, a rationalization of or an occasional check on the evils of the political and economic order. But functionalism does not answer the question how the Church endured for three centuries before its power was questioned. That is, the functionalists never satisfactorily resolved the problem of how the individual actor behaves in the social order.

Opposed to functionalism are the conflict theories. Most conspicuous is Marxism with its bipolaristic viewpoint of the exploiters and the exploited, which still has relevance possibly more for developing than for advanced nations. Other conflict theorists from Georg Simmel to Rolf Dahrendorf and Lewis Coser analyze the causes, texture, and effects of conflict, including its direct and indirect contribution to a group or organization—solidarity as well as the possibility of change. In other words, conflict does not necessarily mean the breakdown of a society but rather its reshaping, as events in Latin America show.

In the search for explanatory hypotheses for the more elusive cause-and-effect relationship, this book does not assume a Marxist viewpoint. Neither does it reject the dependency model as presented in Chapter 1, nor does it necessarily favor a traditional capitalistic solution. In other words, my position reflects Marxist theory in the importance of economic variables as well as a political ideology in giving attention to the socioeconomic needs of the people. As both classical Marxists and neo-Marxists assert, opposing economic groups promote conflict and revolt. I share the belief that conflict theory offers an indispensable key to understanding Latin American—and probably most—cultures. Social class, ethnicity, and political behavior are only a few of the areas of conflict. Indeed, the structure of society is based on an interrelation of conflict and cooperation as the central government and a local community painfully work out over decades a modus operandi in governance.[1]

In a somewhat different vein, it is useful to explore Immanuel Wallerstein's theory that national economies are intricately interlocked as explained in his theory of a world-system.[2] Over the last hundred years, international economics and politics have moved to what has been labeled "globalization." Moreover, with the end of the Cold War we have entered a phase of uncertainty for many issues, among them: multiculturality, civil rights, an ethnic revolution, a global media system, environmental reform, and in the case of Latin America, the fate of Marxism and post-Marxism.[3] It can argued that events—political restructuring and financial stagnation—at the periphery of the world-system during the 1980s was a reaction to the convulsive happenings in the core nations—breakup of the Soviet empire and the economic recession of the capitalist powers.[4] More to the point, as Latin America along with the rest of the world moves into the twenty-first century, new technologies and relationships must be recognized. As most nations are competing for limited markets, they must accept to some degree the reality of global interdependence.[5]

The framework of the following chapters, where relevant, will borrow primarily from two general viewpoints. One is *functionalist* or *equilibrium* theory, as suggested above. That is, the system responds to stresses and maintains stability by adjusting to changing conditions and needs. The functional approach posits some inequality in the society and allows for incremental change to make corrections. *Exchange* theory with its emphasis on costs and rewards and comparison level may be subsumed in a broad sense under functionalism. As an example, in Latin America—and in most of the world—labor groups enter into a trade-off with industrialists, each side reckoning its gains and losses, generally with the advantage going to the owner–capitalist rather than the worker.

The other approach is the *conflict* model, which views society as composed of autonomous structures. Conflict theory sometimes assumes the Marxian method of the dialectic in order to point out opposing power structures. Or, in a broader perspective, the state, economic, and other sectors use various resources in forming coalitions to achieve their goals. The conflict process involves a number of coercion techniques including belief systems.[6] Both the functionalist and conflict paradigms are useful in analyzing social processes in Latin America. The conflict model has special relevance to those countries that underwent a revolution—Mexico, Bolivia, and Nicaragua—and to the brutal struggles in Central America in the 1980s.

Besides the conceptual aspects of stability and change there are also sociopolitical horizons. Or put more directly, can one anticipate that Latin American societies, notably their political systems, will find a middle ground between the two extremes of populist ideologies on one side and conventional ideas and practices on the other? Nearly all social scientists believe that the economic order is capable of significant change. For most observers, change means modernization. However, one problem with modernization theory is that societies do not necessarily move according to a neat linear development. As with all advanced or semiadvanced societies, Latin America has a limited set of options for altering its social institutions. In a Weberian context, it appears that the majority of actors, whether as individuals or groups, act according to what seems to them to be rational means and ends.[7] Without drifting into the murky waters of the free will–determinism controversy, one could assume that degrees of freedom in the various strategies are available to Latin America. However, at this point our explanatory goal is a more limited one: simply a search for selected relationships of cause and effect.

The search for understanding is a challenge for all social scientists as well as for change agents in general. Understanding must precede prediction, and control lies well beyond the province of any ethically responsible social scientist. Understanding itself is a demanding task as one works through the intricacies of an unfamiliar culture. The sociologist is no better equipped to broach the analysis of continuity and change than is the anthropologist, social psychologist, political scientist, or historian. Sociology is simply *one* of the relevant perspectives, and one that depends on the contribution of other social scientists. Still, more than other behavioral sciences, sociology is concerned with explaining social behavior, institutions, values, and norms in developing and advanced cultures.

The Power Structure, Societal Change, and the Individual

Most societies are goal-directed: They are moving toward given ends or purposes. They also have a power structure. Power is a commodity shared between society and individuals. Power relates to authority and legitimacy. For most persons in any society, power is limited—in Latin America less so than in most developing areas, but more so than in other parts of the Western world. The nature of goals and the ability of the individual to maneuver, of course, differs remarkably within and between nations. The segments of any society have varying resources and power. Indeed, one aspect of change is *resource mobilization*, which depends on the legitimate use of power. For instance, rural society is, as compared to urban, limited in its visibility and its access to power as concerns economic and government structures.

As implied in Chapter 1, a salient factor is income inequalities. Before the turn of the century, stirrings of discontent surfaced among the more advanced nations such as Argentina, Chile, and Uruguay. Mass frustration was both the cause and effect of the Mexican Revolution of 1910–1917, which resulted from a strong state which had ceded much to foreign powers and ingratiated themselves with an "exporting bourgeoisie." In subsequent years, social observers urged continuation of the revolution through effective social movements.[8] Unsuccessful challenges to the system have occurred in both less and more advanced countries, as for instance to varying degrees in the Bolivian revolution of 1952, the Chilean experiment of 1970, and the Nicaraguan *concertización* after 1979. The most far-reaching overthrow of an older order was the establishment of a Marxist-oriented regime in Cuba in 1959.

Moderate and not-so-moderate attempts to change the older order have more often met with failure than success. Even when the climate of change was in the air, a projected overhauling of the economic and political power structure brought forth regressive regimes in Brazil in 1964, in Argentina in 1966 and 1976, in Uruguay and Chile in 1973, and in Peru in 1968 and 1990, to recapitulate a painful catalog. In these and other countries, populist sentiment precipitated socioeconomic reforms, but when the political apparatus moved too far, military rule was ushered in. In other words, traditional authoritarian rulers may consent to share power with a change-oriented regime, yet when maneuvers to the left are perceived as a threat to entrenched interests, the president will likely be asked to pack his or her bags. When the rules of the game are violated—for example, when a coalition of labor unions and reformist intellectuals aspire to be an equal contender rather that a recipient of power—the right regroups its forces. Moreover, in view of a drift toward conservatism and privatization in recent years, new forms of improvisation are appearing in social movements as case studies in Argentina and Brazil show.[9]

Often the fulcrum lies with members of the middle class, who will counteract if property rights are challenged or inflation is out of control. No less than other actors, Latin Americans can be alarmed by the threat of uncertainty. The middle class is seemingly more frightened by the left than by the right. It is hardly surprising that cross-national comparisons document the correlation between life satisfaction and per capita income. Other psychological effects are also evident. For instance, in a comparison of some twenty advanced nations, Argentina had the lowest index in faith in others ("most people can be trusted") and, along with South Africa and Portugal, the lowest average income level.[10] As another instance, at the beginning of the Belaúnde Terry presidency in 1963, Peruvians were optimistic about their future, but with the failure of that administration to produce results, satisfaction profiles took a dramatic downturn.[11]

Finally, individuals perceive their universe through the series of events, both macrosocial and microsocial, that befall them. Beyond the physical needs of survival is the ego-value. The social system must to some degree maintain or restore the person's self-satisfaction. But more pressing issues concern much of the Third World, its constant anxiety about hunger, illness, or violence has led to a desperate search for charismatic leadership on one side or a retreat into apathy as another "solution."

SOCIALIZATION AND VALUES

The parameters of any culture are defined by the socialization of roles, values, and norms. This socialization usually takes place in social institutions, which society has found indispensable for its survival—for instance, the economy, family, school, and church. The significance of these institutions vary markedly between cultures—the family, for instance, looms large for Latin Americans. Even though the early years are most critical, socialization takes place throughout the life cycle in a variety of environments. Social class and ethnicity are among the factors influencing both values and interpersonal relations.

Surrounded by an institutional structure from childhood to adulthood, the person responds to a complex of values and acquires a set of roles. Implicit in the role structure are both instrumental and expressive dimensions. The *instrumental* role encompasses power and economic relationships. The *expressive* role pertains to a wide spectrum of interpersonal relations ranging from warmth and affection to aggression and violence. These dimensions transcend cultural boundaries, yet in any complex society they almost constantly undergo change. They remain more separate in Latin America than in most areas of the Western world. As an example, gender roles, which reflect the traditional instrumental–expressive axis, remain relatively intact, except for the more vibrant urban areas. Still, in the wake of industrialization and urbanization, role patterns have been modified. Instrumental options are redefined with the changes in mobility channels and occupational outlets. Also, expansion of education, however short of its goals, has not only offered upward mobility but has also transformed societal norms and values, whether through new definitions of Catholicism, the spread of Pentecostalism, exposure to new technologies, exploding mass media, and the varied contacts the urban setting offers. In the view of one critic, Latin America suffers fundamentally from the dilemma of Catholic insistence on ceremonial norms with minimum concern for public morality.[12] Obviously, a similar judgment might be made about other parts of the world. The total role repertory is not always brought into scrutiny, but both expected and enacted roles tend to become less rigid when influenced by mobility within the system or migration to the city. The urban migrant in Latin America may remain as much an isolate as he or she was in the countryside, and no less exploited.

Are Value Orientations a Meaningful Concept?

Values are usually more implicit than are roles. Along with attitudes, they bear the stamp of the subculture: male or female, young or old, urban or rural, rich or poor. Some values transcend these subcultures; others do not. Values differ among nations; for instance, *machismo* has remained fairly strong in Mexico, but is less so in Chile.

Although a less fashionable activity than a generation ago, the search for value orientations is a means of assessing culture. The major problem is method. Even though empirical studies appear, as in Díaz-Guerrero's study of the sociopsychological bases of Mexican culture,[13] attitudinal approaches to nationalism in Brazil and Mexico,[14] or the relationship of personal values and role behavior in Peru,[15] most analyses rely largely on impressionistic data. One question is how to discriminate between themes dominant in the culture and those that are variant or alternative. This question involves several aspects: How are values defined in different contexts? What is the degree of commitment to given values? How deeply are the values expressed in overt behavior? Mere lip service to a value becomes at most a culture ideal, with little transfer into action. Also, the distinction between *explicit* and *implicit* values is as relevant to Latin America as elsewhere. One attempt to resolve these problems of analysis involved the use of projective techniques in the study of a Mexican village.[16] In addition, other studies of attitudes through in-depth interviews and panel techniques have given a more penetrating analysis of political values.[17] In contrast, appraisals resting on philosophical interpretations of history pose particular problems with verification, however intriguing the explanations may be.[18]

Inconsistencies in values are universal. One thinks of the shibboleths among many North Americans regarding personal freedom. For example, we in the United States pride ourselves on commitment to personal freedom, yet we often show an unyielding conformity, whether in the upkeep of our front lawn, being seen in the right place, or orthodoxy in political beliefs. In similar contradiction, Latin Americans talk of the integrity of the individual's rights and yet passively accept an authoritarian government in an advanced country, such as Argentina. The legal institution offers an example of this ambivalent approach to values. As an example, the adoption of a law in Latin America on, say, social welfare or land tenure is passed off as the "solution" to a problem, but once enacted the law is all too seldom implemented. Richard M. Morse characterizes Latin Americans, Brazilians in particular, as having a more flexible value system than North Americans: "In the United States the imputation that a person or group is 'un-American' carries a clear set of meanings, while in Brazil the term 'un-Brazilian' would be something of a puzzle."[19]

A Value Model

Possibly most cited among the value orientations regarding Latin America are those of John P. Gillin.[20] These have markedly changed as the society has undergone modernization and urbanization, yet a few of them may still stand as reference points or Weberian ideal types. Among these values are (1) *personalismo*, or belief in the self as a unique entity, with *machismo* and *caudillismo* as variations; (2) *familism*, or the solidarity and sacredness of the family; (3) sense of hierarchy, or the acceptance of vertical structures as found in the class system and political authority (the subordinate in an office dares not trespass on the authority of his or her superior); (4) *materialism*, or the orientation toward the practical or concrete over the theoretical, as with the preference of real estate over stocks and bonds; (5) transcendental values, which are complementary to materialistic values as found in the strong commitment to the aesthetic (the business man or politician who writes poetry can still retain his *macho* image); (6) emotion as fulfillment of the self—that is, avoidance of rationalism and giving vent to feelings and intuition, as revealed in the world of fiestas, storytelling, jokes, music, and dancing; and (7) a sense of *fatalism*, or the "lottery syndrome."

These values are, of course, not unique to Latin America. Nor are they to be considered as other than tentative statements. For example, in regard to fatalism, workers and especially peasants display a certain degree of passivity, but when economic conditions become impossible, defiance and revolt are the result. Or the peasant may choose to exit from the system; that is, migration to the city.[21] Values are conditioned by the region, social class, and personality of the individual. They are also shaped by a long history of intervening cultures based on varied ethnicity and ideologies. One has only to consider the complexity of Spanish culture with its blend of Christian, Islamic, and Jewish traditions, much of which was superimposed on various indigenous societies in the New World.[22]

Attitude research supports a higher presence of familism and hierarchy or subordination as values among Hispanics as compared to non-Hispanics.[23] However, at this point we return to fatalism, which is seen in a variety of behaviors—flirtation with death in the bullring, the contest of one motorist with another, the absence of helmets among cyclists, or the nonchalant daring of pedestrians (including myself) crossing an intersection against a signal. In another sphere, I recall my fascination while living in El Salvador with movie audiences as they identified with the vicissitudes of the protagonists on the screen. Reactions were markedly more salient than what one encounters in Europe and North America.[24] Tragic and comic become an arbitrary distinction, whether for the moviegoer or the lover. Fate appears as tragedy, or comedy, or even farce, depending on the spectator's educational level. Possibly the carnival of Rio de Janeiro embodies the ultimate transfiguration of fatalism as a kind of "ritual journey," merging exhibition and restraint, hierarchy and equality, dream and reality.[25] This fatalism assumes a dualism, as it does in many cultures—God and the Devil, good versus evil, love and hate. Moreover, fatalism is woven through with mythology. As reported in a study of the Cauca Valley of Colombia, among the indigenous even more than mestizo cultures a belief in "magic and rite can strengthen the critical consciousness that a devastatingly hostile reality forces on the people in plantations and mines."[26] However, fatalism and its variants differ sharply for region, ethnicity, gender, and social class. Nor is the United States exempt from fatalism, myth, and magic, as illustrated by the wide appeal of pseudo-psychology in astrology and the like, along with the staggering rise of state lotteries and gambling since the 1980s.

The interrelationship of value clusters is seldom consistent. *Personalismo* contradicts the sense of hierarchy; the materialistic is opposed to the transcendental. Possibly more than with most of the West, inconsistency becomes the norm. Latin American culture seems only marginally oriented to the rationalist-empirical approach that has characterized Western thought since the seventeenth century. In this connection, popular culture, which assumes different forms and appeals in different ways to both middle and lower classes, tends to emphasize the mystical over the rational. The ethos is often based on a blending of the indigenous culture with the dominant European culture. As the folk culture is transformed by electronic media, new values emerge.[27]

Other interrelationships are suggested in this value paradigm. The duality of materialism and spiritualism is well established in Western culture, especially in its religious belief system. It has been argued that Latin Americans more than West Europeans express contradictory values. But almost any society has the problem of bringing together the traditional and the bureaucratic-technical, as noted in an account of the transition from old to new in a provincial Argentine community:

Cars and horsecarts sharing streets, modern appliances lying protected under a layer of newspapers with ads for Florida's Disney World, rock music blaring out the door behind a man drinking maté, unisex clothes from the used American clothing store being worn by a stereotypical macho campo man—these are the daily reminders of the complex relationship between tradition and modernity. This is a culture that accepts innovation but largely on its own terms. . . . For all of the limitations put on this world by the perceptions of its own inhabitants and its particular situation on the edge of Western civilization, it is a complex society. Indeed, a society that functions through personalism, good will, and a sharing of individual expertise in different areas is really no less complex than a society that functions primarily through bureaucracies and laws.[28]

According to data from modernization scales, Latin Americans—more than Europeans and Anglo-Americans—tend to be rigid in cognitive norms and classify the world into sharper categories, as shaped by educational and other subcultures. In this context, scores for the "uncertainty avoidance index" (UAI) are relevant. Scores for Latin American samples from several nations ranged from 76 to 87, whereas among U.S. samples the scores averaged 46. In other words, Latin Americans avoided uncertainty, preferring explicit rules, a hierarchical structure, and familistic norms.[29] As another case in point, gender relations are more separate than in most Western cultures. Octavio Paz asserts that the male expresses a heightened masculinity in order to compensate for the sense of inferiority he feels.[30] Farther south, according to one observer, the cult of the Argentine gaucho in his nomadic life rejects romantic love and glorifies maleness.[31] It has been suggested that the fervor and nationalistic flavor of the Mexican Revolution received an impetus from the machismo represented by such heroes as Emiliano Zapata and Pancho Villa.[32] In sharp contrast is the cult of virginity traditionally assigned to the female. Still, this gender duality shifts with subcultures. With a background from pre-Columbian, European, and African sources and more recently the impact of the "big brother" to the North, any dichotomy would be an oversimplification for Latin America. The concept of *mestizaje* or the blending of indigenous and European cultures complicates any classification of values.

Is the pattern of value orientations in part a compensatory reaction to what is described as a sense of inadequacy on the part of Latin Americans? Probably not, despite statements to the contrary. The cult of *personalismo* may be an example since Latin Americans occasionally regard themselves both collectively and individually as offering a unique gift to the world. According to one observer, a feeling of inferiority has been visible even in a large national culture like Brazil.[33] Ideas trickled in from abroad from the late nineteenth century to the twentieth century but were generally given a Brazilian stamp.[34] Several writers find a disjunction between the European and indigenous in Latin America both a liability and an asset in establishing a cultural identity. The feeling about *mestizaje* is surrounded by a degree of ambivalence.[35]

Another symptom of this compensatory reaction is the ambivalence, if not hostility, that Latin Americans understandably feel toward the materialism of the United States, preferring their own values based on either indigenous or European cultures. As one instance, they point to the comfort they feel in their familistic society as opposed to the mass culture of the United States with its vast impersonal shopping malls. This attitude has been intermittently voiced since the beginning of the century when the "big stick" was the image of the United States.[36] For instance, an analysis of leading Latin American newspapers found that articles on culture from Europe were more than twice as likely to be published than were those from the United States.[37] Consequently, despite the diffusion of material culture from the United States, ambivalence continues about its value themes. The political front offers another source of discontent. Anxieties about the effects of NAFTA on workers and the California voters' acceptance in 1994 of Proposition 187 (a measure to deny education and medical service to aliens) served to alienate Latin Americans, particularly Mexicans from their northern neighbors.

Culture, Values, and Their Assessment

The Gillin value themes are cited as a kind of cultural core, yet the search for themes has been unending. The present discussion will confine itself to a few of the more frequently cited value orientations.

A remarkable aspect of the Latin American value structure is its communicative style. For the European and North American, notwithstanding a number of semantic gaps, language usually has reasonable correspondence to the referent in the outside world. In Latin America, the orientation is slightly different. In certain sectors, language becomes a matter of communicating what the speaker (or often the receiver) would like to believe. Américo Castro implies that this expansive tendency is found in Spanish thought because of the heroic stature of men and events from the eleventh to the sixteenth century. In "opposition to the principle inherited from Greece that reality is what is presented to the sense organs, the Spaniard sustained the principle that reality is what he felt, believed, imagined."[38] This difference suggests the traditional preference in Spain for the mystical rather than the scientific. Reportedly, this marginal interest in science and technology still remains in Latin America. Of the 263,072 science articles published in the world in 1984, only 1 percent were from Latin America.[39]

Possibly the Hispanic penchant for the mystical is a hangover from the Arab culture; the Near East (and even much of Asia) perceives language as designed to veil the nature of reality more than to disclose it. Or more accurately, the communicator wishes to please the recipient. This argument breaks down if one looks at the Madrid of post-Franco Spain or at the major cities of Latin America today. Nor can citizens of the United States find validity in their communication based on sound bites, whether hawking a commercial product or a fragment of political ideology.

A quite different but recurrent theme, one that reflects the fatalism syndrome, is the importance given to death. An analysis of poetry finds twice as many references to death as in a comparable sample of North American poetry.[40] The penchant for making cookies and the like in the shape of skulls for All Soul's Day in Mexico is an example. One may question whether in a society marked by a high, though declining mortality rate, the notion of death evokes possibly less—or more—anxiety than in the more secure environment of "developed" societies.

A related theme is the tendency to violence on the part of Latin Americans. Social philosophers who support this viewpoint point to strikes, revolutions, and the relatively high rate of homicide in several countries. Victor Alba notes the complexity of the problem:

The Latin American is not more violent than other men—in many places, especially in regions with a large Indian population, he is probably more resigned, passive, and pacific than the generality of men—but the society in which he lives often leaves him little with which to defend his interests and rights. (It is not insignificant that there has never been a pacifist movement in Latin America or the use of non-violence for political ends. Gandhi was never a popular figure in Latin America.)[41]

It would be absurd to accuse Latin Americans of excessive violence when we realize that the area has taken to international aggression far less than other parts of the world. One could make the case that historically the United States surpasses Latin America in violence if one were to catalog the events surrounding the Civil War, the Western movement, labor unionization, or military ventures, not to mention the rate of homicide in contemporary urban life. At the same time, with a variety of structural ills to be righted, Latin Americans have followed a cult of violence. Sociologists speak of *violencia institucionalizada*.[42] Violence is often revolutionary, geared to either the left or right, often led by middle-class intellectuals.[43] Che Quevara in Cuba and Bolivia, the Shining Path in Peru, and death squads in El Salvador, Guatemala, and other countries bear testimony to a tradition of violent social intervention. Others would argue that a certain degree of violence, at least in threat if not in actuality, is inevitable in any capitalist system, whether by the state or the entrepreneur.[44] However, socialist regimes do not preclude the use of violence.

To what degree are these value orientations a product of a Spanish feudalistic past? After all, both Spain and her colonies missed much of the intellectual Renaissance, the French Enlightenment, and the scientific revolution of the eighteenth and nineteenth centuries. Nor is it clear to what extent Ibero-American value themes derive from the indigenous past. The passivity and intransigence attributed to certain Native American societies possibly relate to a sense of fatalism.

This discussion must be viewed in the context of the changes taking place in Latin America in the direction of rationality. Technology transfer, for example, is occurring in practically all countries. Computers, automation, telecommunications, and new personnel procedures have been a medium of introducing Latin Americans to a new kind of rationalism.[45] Brazil is only one of several nations in which a new generation of technicians, engineers, and scientists is transforming approaches to business, industry, education, and other spheres, even though problems such as balance of payments may place restrictions on the degree of diffusion.[46]

Again, any scheme of value orientations is highly tentative. Increasingly, sociologists and other behavioral scientists turn to empirical research in order to test the validity of these constructs. In a related frame of reference, hypotheses have been constructed regarding a modal personality within a national culture. For instance, do test scores (whatever they mean) of Mexicans tend to cluster on a specific trait or value, which may correspond to a bell-shaped curve? How different will the modal point be for them as compared with those of Argentines, Germans, or Anglo-Americans? The search for value orientations overlaps with this identification of personality patterns characterizing national, regional, occupational, and educational subcultures. Brazil is only one of several nations where regional differences appear more in the lower class, whereas the middle class tends to cultivate certain attitudes and values according to national norms.[47]

We may summarize several qualifications to be applied to the study of value themes. First, any list of value orientations may be regarded as a set of hypotheses to be tested. Second, a given list of values also applies in some degree to other Western—or even Eastern—countries. Certain values are presumably dominant in Latin America, whereas in other cultures they operate as possible alternatives. Third, they are not altogether consistent. In no culture do values approach a perfect integration. Marked national, regional, and individual variations occur in the particular constellation of the values. A catalogue of several value themes hardly exhausts the Latin American cultural core.

So often cultural values become mere descriptions or worse, stereotypes. Anglo-Americans are all too often accustomed to project on to Latin Americans such epithets as "violent," "corrupt," "inefficient," or other unfavorable qualities. Interestingly, North Americans are now aware that these characteristics are not so far from home. The ubiquity of weapons and homicide rates are a national tragedy. Or witness the "What's in it for me?" attitude, make-believe public relations, litigation, political payoffs, and PAC (Political Action Committee) contributions. Personal responsibility, meticulousness, or even an efficient mail service are not exactly relics of the past, but many observers are wondering if the "system" is working—whether family breakdown, mass media, failure of schools, or a growing hedonism are the problems. Nor are we conscious of the rapidity with which Latin America is changing.[48] Shopping malls, McDonalds, and a wave of evangelical Protestantism testify to a transformed landscape.

Finally, if we are to assess any value profile we would have to return to the question of what constitutes Latin America over time. The term "Latin" may cover a number of variants. Puerto Ricans in New York, French Creoles of Louisiana's bayous, or Mexican Americans in Los Angeles may be as much or more "Latin" than the inhabitants of southern Brazil or Chile, or the African Americans of Bahia and Panama City. In reference to Latin America itself, one cannot ignore the spectrum of historical antecedents, indigenous sources, and class, educational, and occupational hierarchies. As a case in point, peasants as an occupational group embody a relatively conservative set of attitudes. Even this statement would have to be conditioned by variations represented in the range of Native American and mestizo-peasant economies with their differing perspectives toward the universe. One has also to reckon with the impact of information processing. Mass communication has changed the values and attitudes of individuals and groups even in the rural area. For instance, the introduction of television to an isolated community in the Amazon led to more socializing as the medium is shared with neighbors. Although *telenovelas* enjoy a wide audience in the village, political events are not ignored. The direction of national leadership is questioned, class consciousness—and conflict—becomes aroused, and other sociocultural changes are likely.[49]

ROLE DIMENSIONS AND SOCIAL CHANGE

Values are fundamental in socialization. Equally so is the allotment of roles, which are shaped by the quality of interpersonal relations, nature of social organization, and the immaterial culture in general. Roles relate to the value and norm structure. We have already mentioned the matter of instrumental and expressive roles and values. Roles are also linked to age, gender, and other subcultures.

Although the functionalist "pattern variables" of Talcott Parsons are criticized as being too simplistic, they are still as relevant for Latin Americans as for other areas of the developed and underdeveloped world. At least, they are possible models by which societies and social systems can be assessed.[50] For one, the particularism–universalism axis defines an actor's obligations to the persons with whom he or she interacts. *Particularism*, or the dependence on kinship and friendship as a means of defining role obligations, is more entrenched in Latin America, whereas *universalism*, or the rationalist-bureaucratic order, possibly carries more weight in northwestern Europe or the United States. Studies of how individuals perceive social situations show Mexicans to view close personal or family ties as important, whereas North Americans are generally oriented to broader social relationships. (Significantly, migrants to the United States shift gradually to a less particularistic outlook.) As an example, it is not unusual to find members of the boss's family employed in the same office, even in a fairly bureaucratic setting. Members of international organizations find Latin Americans to be more concerned with personal relationships in business and other transactions. Cronyism or use of the *palanca* (lever) in finding one's way upward is even more institutionalized in Latin America than in other parts of the Western world.[51] In this connection, criteria of universalism are less scrupulously maintained in a society oriented to *ascription*, in which roles and norms remain somewhat rigid and mobility is limited. In contrast, the mobile society of the United States is achievement-oriented, even though inhabitants of Montevideo or Mexico City may well place more stress on achievement than would those in rural North America. As compared to the invariable demands of certain preliterate cultures, Western society, including Latin America, demands only marginal compliance with role prescriptions. If we allow for marked differences among individuals and families, universalism and achievement are less salient than particularism and ascription.[52]

In contrast to the needs of a postindustrial society, bureaucratic role conformity is supposedly more relaxed in Latin America, or more accurately stated, bureaucracy rests more on tradition than on rational criteria. According to common stereotypes—which are hardly trustworthy—the student is not expected to explore knowledge too deeply and the factory worker is only marginally concerned with quality and quantity or production and is paid accordingly. In reality, Latin Americans work very hard in view of their economic return and resulting malnutrition. In this context, Latin Americans may in reality be among the more productive workers of the world.

Can the Latin American social structure, then, be described as particularistic-ascriptive?[53] This axis relates to the variable of self-orientation versus collectivity-orientation. Latin Americans tend to be subjectively involved; a Mexican study implies that the self-as-actor is relatively un-concerned with others.[54] One hears in Latin America variations of *yo primero, mi familia segundo, lo demás tercero* (me first, my family next, the others third). My own impression is that in part the failure of the Chilean collectivist experiment under Allende was the difficulty of bring-ing about a sustained cooperative effort in an individualistic society. However, after 1960 Cuban society was collectivized with reasonable success. In view of the almost universal "What's-in-it-for-me?" theme characterizing North Americans in the 1990s, it would be difficult to make a case for self-orientation on the part of Latin Americans.

Value orientations also refer to the political scene. As another indica-tor of the particularist, ascriptive, and self-orientation, Gabriel A. Al-mond and Sidney Verba found in their study of five national cultures that Mexicans (as compared to samples in Britain, Italy, West Germany, and the United States) tend to perceive themselves as being the least in-volved in national decision making.[55] Even though the methodology of the study posed some problems of validity, subsequent research has not contradicted their findings.[56] Moreover, in a cross-national survey, Ar-gentines and Mexicans were alienated politically as compared to samples in Europe and the United States, more than twice the number of respon-dents agreeing with the statement that "the entire way our society is or-ganized must be changed by revolutionary action."[57] Many other factors beyond self- and collective-orientation are involved in political commit-ment. Cultural and subcultural factors are substantial. To promote po-litical awareness would be more difficult in Paraguay than in Uruguay, in Haiti more than in Mexico. On the whole, a stratified society seldom augers well for the transfer of the self to the collectivity.

Conclusions: Power and Decision Making

As the rate of social change accelerates in Latin America, a crucial ques-tion is: How are decisions made? At least three aspects are relevant to this question: (1) What are the sources of power and where are they lo-cated? (2) How is power shared with other parts of the society? (3) How is power transferred into decisions and how are they implemented? These questions go beyond this chapter or even the entire book. Some atten-tion to this question will be given in Chapter 9, but in this chapter we may introduce the general problem of decision making. In the following chapters, we shall be analyzing the processes of decision making, power, and social change in various environmental and institutional sectors.

More than once these first two chapters have noted the difficulty of finding a satisfactory means of channeling frustration and discontent. Even in a relatively free society, dissatisfaction finds few outlets. Conse-quently, repression and violence are most acute during periods of eco-nomic stagnation or when a rise in economic activity is abruptly slowed down. As frustration moves from micro to macro levels (from the individual to societal dimensions) and relevant organizations assemble sufficient power, revolutionary social change becomes possible.[58] Among the likely outcomes are domestic violence, government crisis, social movements, or guerrilla warfare. The end result may be instability, and the consequent mobilization often means a movement to the left or to the right; but the new equilibrium may not be a solution to the problem. Alternately, the result can be a constructive rearrangement of the power structure with economic benefits to a wider distribution among the people. The probability of a favorable outcome has not been too promising, yet the mid-1990s offer more optimism than ever before.

In attempting to resolve social frustration, the problem is once again of how the government is to share power with other segments of the society. To cite an example, by 1940 Mexico institutionalized the revolution with a mix of welfare and capitalism. But after World War II the political elites became more conservative, even though they recast revolutionary rhetoric with an occasional return to reformist zeal in order to reassure the urban and rural proletariat of the PRI's earlier promises and future accomplishments.[59] As with several other countries, leadership in Mexico has fluctuated between two groups, people- and welfare-oriented politicians versus impersonal technocrats. After the financial crisis of the 1980s, the technocrats were in the upper hand, as illustrated by Carlos Salinas and his attempt at revival of the economy, along with financial favors to kin and cronies.

Ideally, the most effective means of assuring greater democratic decision making would be the transition toward a pluralistic society. At present, various power contenders—peasants, workers, intellectuals, and the new managerial elite—are too far apart to launch an assault on the establishment. We return to the case of Chile as relevant, although not necessarily typical. During the 1960s, the Christian Democrats under Eduardo Frei were gradually moving toward a welfare state but within the context of established property rights. This disequilibrium gave rise to Unidad Popular, placing Allende in power in 1970. Even if it had been less inept, the Allende regime had slim chances of assembling the power to placate the right or center. Almost inescapable was the 1973 coup, orchestrated in part by the CIA, initiating the most tragic phase of Chilean history in this century.

In no area of the world is democracy truly secure, nor is it inevitably the solution for socioeconomic development, but in Latin America the equilibrium in political processes is especially uncertain. That Latin Americans are struggling in that vast area represented by both development and underdevelopment may itself underlie the uneven course of political decision making. Even so, the political profile of the twenty republics in the mid-1990s offers a degree of optimism for the future.

NOTES

1. David Nugent, "Building the State, Making the Nation: The Bases and Limits of State Centralization in 'Modern' Peru," *American Anthropologist* 96: 333–369 (1994).

2. Immanuel Wallerstein, *The Politics of the Capitalist World Economy* (Cambridge: Cambridge University Press, 1984).

3. Roland Robertson, *Globalization: Social Theory and Global Culture* (Newbury Park, Calif.: Sage Publications, 1992), 20–59.

4. Albert Bergeson, "Regime Changes in the Semiphery: Democratization in Latin America and the Socialist Bloc," *Sociological Perspectives* 35: 405–413 (1992).

5. Dennis Pirages, *Global Technopolitics* (Pacific Grove, Calif.: Brooks/Cole Publishing, 1988).

6. Hubert M. Blalock, Jr., *Power and Conflict: Toward a General Theory* (Thousand Oaks, Calif.: Sage Publications, 1989).

7. Barry Hindess, "Rationality and Modern Society," *Sociological Theory* 9: 216–229 (1991).

8. D. E. Davis, "The Sociology of Mexico: Stalking the Path Not Taken," in *Annual Review of Sociology*, vol. 18, ed. Judith Blake and John Hagan (Palo Alto, Calif.: Annual Reviews, Inc., 1992), 395–417.

9. Juan Carlos Gorlier, "Democratización en América del Sur: Una Reflexión sobre el Potencial de los Movimientos Sociales en Argentina y Brasil," *Revista Mexicana de Sociología* 52(4): 119–152 (1992).

10. Ronald Inglehart, *Culture Shift in Advanced Industrial Society* (Princeton, N.J.: Princeton University Press, 1990), 37.

11. Lawrence V. Stockman, "Modernization Research in Culturally Segmented Societies: A Peruvian Experience," in *Directions of Change: Modernization Theory, Research and Realities*, ed. Mustafa O. Attir, Burkart Holzner, and Zdenek Suda (Boulder, Colo.: Westview Press, 1981), 233–248.

12. Glen C. Dealy, *The Latin Americans: Spirit and Ethos* (Boulder, Colo.: Westview Press, 1992).

13. Rogelio Díaz-Guerrero, *Psychology of the Mexican* (Austin: University of Texas Press, 1975).

14. Joseph A. Kahl, *The Measurement of Modernism: A Study of Values in Brazil and Mexico* (Austin: University of Texas Press, 1968) and Alex Inkeles and David H. Smith, *Becoming Modern: Individual Change in Six Developing Countries* (Cambridge, Mass.: Harvard University Press, 1974).

15. Luis G. Flores and Ralph F. Catanello, "Personal Value Systems and Organizational Roles in Peru," *Journal of Social Psychology* 127: 627–638 (1987).

16. Erich Fromm and Michael Maccoby, *Social Character in a Mexican Village: A Sociopsychoanalytic Study* (Englewood Cliffs, N.J.: Prentice-Hall, 1970).

17. José A. Silva Michelina, *The Illusion of Democracy in Dependent Nations* (Cambridge, Mass.: M.I.T. Press, 1971).

18. An example is Zavier R. deVentós, *The Hispanic Labyrinth: Tradition and Modernity in the Colonization of the Americas* (New Brunswick, N.J.: Transaction Publishers, 1991).

19. Richard M. Morse, *New World Soundings: Culture and Ideology in the Americas* (Baltimore: Johns Hopkins University Press, 1989), 144.

20. John P. Gillin, "Some Signposts for Policy," in Council on Foreign Relations, *Social Change in Latin America Today* (New York: Random House, 1960), 14–62.

21. Susan Eckstein, "Power and Popular Protest in Latin America," in *Power and Popular Protest: Latin American Social Movements*, ed. Susan Eckstein (Berkeley: University of California Press, 1989), 1–60.

22. Enrique A. González Ordosgoití, *Diez Ensayos de Cultura Venezolana* (Caracas: Editorial Tropykis, 1991), 18–25.

23. Gerardo Marín and Harry C. Triandis, "Allocentrism as an Important Characteristic of the Behavior of Latin Americans and Hispanics," in *Cross-Cultural and National Studies in Social Psychology*, ed. Rogelio Díaz-Guerrero (Amsterdam: North Holland, 1985), 85–104.

24. Lest one be too critical of Latin American audiences, it must be recalled that subtitles are used far more in Latin America than in the United States or Europe, where dubbing is more the trend. This tolerance of foreign speech indicates a fairly urbane approach. We may note also that the level of the press and other mass media in major cities is in some cases more sophisticated than in other parts of Latin America. One has only to compare the daily newspapers of Bogotá and Cali or of Santiago and Concepción with those of Boston and Spokane.

25. Roberto DaMatta, *Carnivals, Rogues, and Heroes: An Interpretation of the Brazilian Dilemma*, tr. by John Drury (Notre Dame, Ind.: Notre Dame University Press, 1991), 102–115.

26. Michael T. Taussig, *The Devil and Commodity Fetishism in South America* (Chapel Hill: University of North Carolina Press, 1980), 232.

27. Chuck Tatum, "From Sandino to Mafalda: Recent Works on Latin American Popular Culture," *Latin American Research Review* 29(1): 198–214 (1994).

28. Kristin Hoffman Ruggiero, *And Here the World Ends: The Life of an Argentine Village* (Stanford, Calif.: Stanford University Press, 1988), 169.

29. G. Hofstede, *Culture's Consequences: International Differences in Work-Related Values* (Thousand Oaks, Calif.: Sage Publications, 1984).

30. Octavio Paz, *The Labyrinth of Solitude* (New York: Grove Press, 1961).

31. Julio Mafud, "El Machismo en la Argentina," *Nuevo Mundo* 16(October): 72–78 (1967).

32. Ilene V. O'Malley, *The Myth of the Revolution* (New York: Greenwood Press, 1986).

33. Charles Wagley, *An Introduction to Brazil*, rev. ed. (New York: Columbia University Press, 1971), 278–279.

34. William Rowe and Vivian Schelling, *Memory and Modernity: Popular Culture in Latin America* (New York: Verso, 1991), 161–168.

35. Ofelia Schutte, *Cultural Identity and Social Liberation in Latin American Thought* (Albany: State University of New York Press, 1993), 121–127.

36. A penetrating analysis of the United States as seen by the Latin American is found in the often-quoted *Ariel* of the late-nineteenth-century Uruguayan intellectual José Enrique Rodó (Austin: University of Texas Press, 1988).

37. Robert Buckman, "Cultural Agenda of Latin American Newspapers and Magazines: Is U.S. Domination a Myth?" *Latin American Research Review* 25(2): 134–155 (1990).

38. Américo Castro, *The Structure of Spanish History* (Princeton, N.J.: Princeton University Press, 1954), 613.

39. Constantin von Barloewen, *Cultural History and Modernity in Latin America* (Providence, R.I.: Berghan Books, 1995), 145.

40. Gillin, "Some Signposts for Policy."

41. Victor Alba, *The Latin Americans* (New York: Praeger, 1969), 44–45.

42. José Joaquín Salcedo G. et al., *América Latina: La Revolución de la Esperanza* (Bogotá: Publicaciones Violeta, 1990), 57.

43. Michael Radu, *Violence and the Latin American Revolutionaries* (New Brunswick, N.J.: Transaction Books, 1988).

44. Anthony Giddens, *Social Theory and Modern Sociology* (Stanford, Calif.: Stanford University Press, 1987), 174–177.

45. Manuel Sadosky, "Some Aspects of the Problem in Latin America," in *Faith and Science in an Unjust World*, vol. 1, ed. Roger L. Shinn (Philadelphia: Fortress Press, 1980), 96–104.

46. Fábio Stefano Erber, "Science and Technology in Brazil: A Review of the Literature," *Latin American Research Review* 16(1): 3–56 (1981).

47. Wagley, *Introduction to Brazil*, 111–117.

48. Fredrick B. Pike, *The United States and Latin America* (Austin: University of Texas Press, 1992), 342–350.

49. Richard Pace, "First-time Televiewing in Amazônia: Television Acculturation in Gurupá, Brazil," *Ethnology* 32: 187–195 (1993).

50. Richard Münch, "Parsonian Theory Today: In Search of a New Synthesis," in *Social Theory Today*, ed. Anthony Giddens and Jonathan H. Turner (Stanford, Calif.: Stanford University Press, 1987), 116–155.

51. Lecia Archer and Kristine L. Fitch, "Communication in Latin American Multinational Oganizations," in *Communicating in Multinational Organizations*, ed. Richard L. Wiseman and Robert Shuter (Thousand Oaks, Calif.: Sage Publications, 1994), 75–93.

52. Marín and Triandis, "Allocentrism"; Lorand B. Szalay and Rogelio Díaz-Guerrero, "Similarities and Differences between Subjective Cultures: A Comparison of Latin, Hispanic, and Anglo-Americans," in *Cross-Cultural and National Studies*, ed. Díaz-Guerrero, 105–135.

53. Seymour M. Lipset, "Values, Education, and Entrepreneurship," in *Promise of Development: Theories of Change in Latin America*, ed. Peter F. Klarén and Thomas J. Bossert (Boulder, Colo.: Westview Press, 1986), 39–75.

54. Rogelio Díaz-Guerrero, *Psychology of the Mexican* (Austin: University of Texas Press, 1975), 35.

55. Gabriel A. Almond and Sidney Verba, *The Civic Culture: Political Attitudes and Democracy in Five Nations* (Princeton, N.J.: Princeton University Press, 1963), 90.

56. Ann L. Craig and Wayne A. Cornelius, "Political Culture in Mexico: Continuities and Revisionist Interpretations," in *The Civic Culture Revised*, ed. Gabriel A. Almond and Sidney Verba (Boston: Little, Brown, 1980), 325–393.

57. Inglehart, *Culture Shift*, 39.

58. James S. Coleman, *Foundations of Social Theory* (Cambridge, Mass.: Harvard University Press, 1990), 483–491.

59. Viviane Brachet-Márquez, *The Dynamics of Domination: State, Class, and Social Reform in Mexico 1910–1990* (Pittsburgh: University of Pittsburgh Press, 1994).

Chapter 3

Population Dynamics

The demography of Latin America is unique in the world. Not only its rapid growth but also its socioeconomic advance will make the area ever-more important in the international power structure. When Columbus arrived on American soil, North America (Canada and the United States) possibly had six million inhabitants, and Latin America perhaps twenty million—with some estimates being much higher.[1] Despite the tremendous decline of population in the sixteenth century, Latin America remained larger than North America until the middle of the nineteenth century when the flow of immigrants and natural increase gave the latter a decisive lead. After the middle of the twentieth century, Latin America again became the larger of the two; 475 million in 1995, as opposed to 295 million in North America.

Latin America's accelerated growth rate is due to a rapidly falling death rate after 1940. Because of this demographic revolution, Latin Americans will outnumber Anglo-Americans by nearly two to one in the year 2010—an event with far-reaching implications for power relationships within the hemisphere.

Aside from its growth, several features distinguish Latin American demographic processes and structure:

1. A great divergence in population concentration and growth—the burgeoning population of Middle America and most of South America, including Brazil, the slightly slower growth countries such as Chile and Colombia, and the almost stationary population of Argentina and Uruguay. However, by the 1980s the birthrate was declining in nearly all countries.

2. A sharp demarcation between urban and rural population, with an unprecedented migration taking place from the rural hinterland to the city.

3. An age profile distinctly different from Europe and the United States—a majority of persons under 22 years old, and a comparative scarcity of the aged. This preponderance of the young or economically dependent is a factor making for slow economic growth. It is debatable whether age structure is relevant to the revolutionary fervor endemic in Latin America, but the underrepresentation of adults hardly encourages political stability.

Other differences that set off Latin America from most of the Western world are a large proportion of single persons, low educational services, and a relatively high (although declining) ratio of males in primary economic pursuits.

Demographic processes have decisive consequences for the shape of any society. Population growth and decline respond in both a micro and a macro fashion to cultural systems and the social and psychological needs of the group and individual.[2] For instance, economic activity has reciprocal effects with the demographic profile.[3] In this chapter, we are concerned with the role of fertility, mortality, and migration in the growth and distribution of population. The validity of demographic data is no greater than the accuracy of the reports by the government and other agencies. Also, because of the threat of overpopulation, we will want to consider how the birthrate can be lowered.

GROWTH AND DISTRIBUTION OF POPULATION

As the drop in the death rate was not matched by a comparable fall in the birthrate, Latin America grew rapidly after 1940, with some reduction of its pace beginning in the 1970s. This spurt is in marked contrast to the first three centuries of European occupation. In 1825, the population was estimated to be 23 million, increasing twenty times to 465 million in 1994, as shown in Figure 3.1.[4] A tripling of the population during the nineteenth century must be compared with a quintupling during the first seventy-five years of this century. If the prediction of a population of more than 550 million by the beginning of the twenty-first century proves to be valid, the area will have grown ten times since 1900.

Latin America represented 5 percent of the world population in 1920 and 9 percent in 1990, and it occupies 15 percent of the total area of the inhabited continents of the world. With a density well less than that of the world average, it is little wonder that overpopulation was not a major source of concern until the 1970s. Latin America's rate of growth was, until the 1960s, leading the world. In the 1950s, it was 2.7 percent; in the 1970s, 2.8 percent. Although the birthrate began to slacken in the 1970s, the population will continue to increase for several decades. Currently, the annual growth rate is 1.9; only Africa is higher. The number of young

FIGURE 3.1
Estimated Population of Latin America from 1825 to 1994 (In Millions)

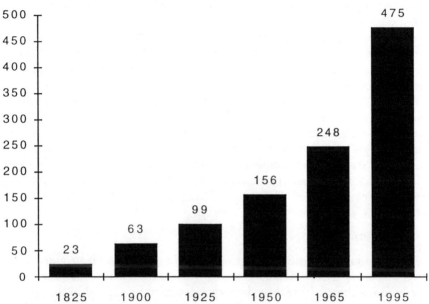

Sources: América Latina y Desarrollo Social (Santiago: Centro para el Desarrollo Económico y Social de America Latina, 1965) and World Population Data Sheet (Washington, D.C.: Population Reference Bureau, 1994).

people entering the fertility cycle means a population growth into the next century. In Latin America, population pressure on resources is rapidly becoming acute. Because of climate, topography, and resources, neither industrialization nor land reform is likely to solve the overconcentration of people in some areas and their comparative absence in others.

Rapid growth is not an entirely recent phenomenon, but spurts in the past resulted more from immigration. For instance, Argentina increased in population by 1,000 percent between 1870 and 1960, as compared to the United States' growth of 500 percent during the same period. In both instances, the growth shifted from immigration to natural increase, after 1914 in the United States, and later and more gradually in Argentina. Now the Americas depend almost exclusively on natural increase for population growth.

Variations in the natural increase are also startling. Most of Central America (except Costa Rica and Panama) is just under 3 percent, whereas Argentina (1.3%) and Uruguay (0.8%) roughly equal the United States' rate of 0.7 percent and far surpass Europe's 0.1 percent. In view of these differing rates, Latin America's population may be divided into three demographic types:

Type 1. Slow growth countries in which birth and death rates have reached relatively low levels, and consequently a low natural increase, below 1.5 percent per year. Significantly, Argentina and Uruguay have high urbanization and relatively high educational levels. Mortality and fertility probably have not yet reached the maximum in their downward trend in Chile and Cuba, but the growth rate is at 1.6 and 0.7 percent, respectively.

Type 2. Moderate growth areas, 1.5 to 2.4 percent, are in most of Latin America, including Brazil and Mexico. (The rate in Costa Rica fell from 3.6 in 1960 to 2.4 percent in 1990.) In these countries, a limited decline in the death rate is gradually combined with decreasing fertility. Natural increase is accelerated when the mortality decline sharpens. The growth rate is roughly 2.1, but is anticipated to move toward that of type 1.

Type 3. Areas of rapidly declining mortality with slowly changing fertility yield a rapid growth rate, above 2.5 percent per year. Most of Central America along with Bolivia and Paraguay are in this cycle.

Distribution of Population

An outstanding feature of Latin America's population is its clustering. Every country except El Salvador and the Caribbean has vast spaces virtually uninhabited. In reality, density rates must be viewed in the framework of economic and social variables—arable land, living space (persons per room), or degree of interaction and communication. Especially important are the available capital, technology, and per capita output.

Density rates are very unequal by nation and region. In a 1989 report, El Salvador had 247 inhabitants per square kilometer, whereas Bolivia had only 7. Brazil, with 17, was below the average 21 for all of Latin America.[5] Regional differences abound within each nation. The Amazon basin, or half of Brazil, is occupied by scattered Indian tribes and a few river towns. Its outer reaches have far less than one person per square kilometer. Almost two-thirds of Brazil's population inhabits the southeast; two states, Minas Gerais and São Paulo, contain one-third of the total population. It is the area with the highest agricultural production, and includes the industrial triangle of Rio de Janeiro, São Paulo, and Belo Horizonte. A second cluster of population is along the northeast coast, Bahia being the third most populous state in the country. Similarly, over half of Mexico's ninety million are found in the Mesa Central, one-seventh of the national territory. Half of all Argentines belong to the province of Buenos Aires, one-tenth of the national territory.

The overall distribution of Latin America's population shows clusterings in coastal areas and in the highlands. In the intermontane valleys, soil and climate are favorable for subsistence farming—the occupation of one-third or more of the population in most countries. The

Amazon basin, the desert areas of northern Mexico and South America's west coast, much of the *altiplano*, and the tip of the continent are generally uninhabitable under present conditions, and probably will be for a long time to come. The only exceptions are agricultural oases and areas rich in mineral deposits. On the whole, population pressure is not yet severe, but a few areas, notably El Salvador, are at the explosive stage. Also, land availability is among the factors setting limits to fertility and future natural increase.

An interesting connection exists between natural barriers and political boundaries. One only has to consider the demographic pressure in the Caribbean islands, with some of the highest densities in the world. Puerto Rico at 352 inhabitants per square mile would be at a crisis stage were it not for industrialization, migration to the mainland, and an incipient decline in the birthrate. In Central America, striking differences in density appear between the five countries. Although volcanic soils permit a large population in coffee cultivation and subsistence farming in El Salvador, it has been nearly impossible for peasants (especially after the 1969 war) to cross the border into Honduras and Nicaragua, both relatively underpopulated.

Contrasts are sharp even within the same country. In Guatemala, the rugged highlands with a scarcity of arable land are overpopulated, whereas the Petén, the northern portion constituting one-third of the country, is home to only 1 percent of the population, even though it supported a heavy population in the Mayan period. Road development and malaria control are necessary if the region is to reach its potential. Also, the Pacific coast region is underdeveloped. For traditional Indian societies, which constitute more than half of Guatemala's population, migration is not an easy process. Chile represents another case of centrality and marginality. Both the northern and southern portions have an average density of less than one person per square kilometer, and of its fourteen million people, over 90 percent live within the central quarter of the country (300 miles north and south of Santiago). National integrity might be strained if it were not for this clustering of the population.

Demographic Processes

Population growth or decline of any society is the result of three factors: fertility, mortality, and migration. The rapid growth rate (1.9% annually) is in antithesis to the colonial period. For instance, the population of Peru declined 35 percent between the arrival of Europeans in 1530 and the beginning of the national period in 1825, although these estimates are difficult to substantiate.[6] But areas with small indigenous populations increased during the same period, Argentina by 300 percent. In the nineteenth century, a few countries showed tremendous gains, almost entirely due to immigration: Uruguay increased thirtyfold and Brazil tenfold. As no meaningful census took place in Latin America before 1900, these estimates of population must be considered as tentative.

FERTILITY PATTERNS

The history of most developing societies indicates a decline in mortality usually preceding a decrease in fertility. The advance in GNP generally accompanies the decline in reproduction.[7] The drop in fertility in Latin America since 1960 shows marked variations between and within countries as to when and how deeply this change has taken place. Mobility aspirations within the middle class and segments of the working class lower the aspirations toward a large family.

Fertility is measured by various means. The most common, if not the most valid, is the *birthrate*, which refers to the number of live births registered per 1,000 population. As seen in Table 3.1, fertility differs from high-rate countries (Bolivia, Guatemala, Honduras, and Nicaragua) to low-growth-rate countries (Cuba, Argentina, and Uruguay). What was reported as an increasing birthrate early in this century could simply be more adequate birth registration.[8] It appears that birthrates remained relatively constant in most countries for the first two-thirds of this century. Only Argentina and Uruguay had rates comparable to those of Western Europe. Chile, too, showed a decline, from 44.5 in the early 1900s to 21.0 in 1995.[9] This difference is attributable to the European character of these countries, higher availability of birth control information, a more permissive Catholicism, differing values placed on the size of the family, and greater hope for upward mobility. Declining fertility is also related to several socioeconomic and psychological factors: industrialization, urbanization, middle-class status, literacy level, and future orientation.

The variables underlying fertility are, of course, complex. Hypotheses revolve around short- and long-term effects, nuclear and extended family needs, reference groups, intergenerational survival, and sociocultural values, among other factors. New norms gradually become established as to the family size desired. Fertility models revolve around a cost/rewards equation. According to the investment model in the developing world, parents may "expect to receive more wealth from their children than they will give to them."[10] Age at marriage or at cohabitation, duration of the union, and postpartum practices are also fundamental to understanding fertility.[11] In addition, socioeconomic variables as well as a number of personal experiences, including the rate of infant and child mortality, enter into decision making. Rural rates are above urban rates, but even among the rural, fertility varies for the type of agriculture. High-density and high-production areas are different from low-density and low-output ones, where the labor of children may be less critical.[12]

TABLE 3.1
Fertility Rates and Life Expectancy

	Birth Rate 1970	Birth Rate 1995	Natural Increase 1995	Life Expectancy 1995 M	Life Expectancy 1995 F
Argentina	22	20	1.2	69	76
Bolivia	24	31	2.6	58	62
Brazil	40	26	1.7	64	69
Chile	25	21	1.6	72	76
Colombia	27.5	27	2.1	69	72
Costa Rica	32	26	2.2	74	79
Cuba	30	14	0.7	73	78
Dominican Republic	40	29	2.3	66	70
Ecuador	39	29	2.3	65	71
El Salvador	42	32	2.6	65	70
Guatemala	43	36	2.9	62	67
Haiti		35	2.3	55	58
Honduras	45	34	2.8	66	71
Mexico	45	27	2.2	70	76
Nicaragua	41	33	2.7	62	68
Panama	34.5	22	1.8	71	75
Paraguay	33	34	2.8	66	71
Peru	36	29	2.1	64	68
Uruguay	22	18	0.8	69	76
Venezuela	37	26	2.1	69	75
United States	16	15	0.6	74	79

Sources: Demographic Yearbook, 1975 (New York: United Nations, 1976), 520–522; World Population Data Sheet (Washington, D.C.: Population Reference Bureau, 1996).

The rate at which fertility decreases is, in part, a measure of modernization, but it is not necessarily directly correlated to industrialization and urbanization. Many couples have a notion about the number of children they wish to have. Fertility declines emerge from informal—and sometimes formal—planning.[13] For instance, fertility decreased in Costa Rica in the 1960s; this decrease represents a greater fall than that of Mexico and Brazil and far outranks the other Central American republics (except Panama, which has traditionally had a lower birthrate than most of Latin America). In Colombia, the drop in the annual rate of natural increase from nearly 4 percent in 1960 to 2.5 percent in 1973 was due partly to the decline in mortality, but the number of children for the average married woman fell from 7.3 to 4.1 in the same period.[14] Similarly, in Mexico the total fertility rate (TFR) declined from 6.7 births per woman in 1970 to approximately 4.0 in 1986.[15] As we shall see later in the chapter, family planning is related to these changes.

Variations in Fertility

Differential fertility is found throughout Latin America, as noted in Table 3.1. A number of variables involve social status. Education operates as a deterrent to fertility. In a cross-continental study, the effect of education in reducing the birthrate was more evident among Latin Americans than among Africans and Middle Easterners.[16] The wife's education is more predictive than the husband's.[17] According to a Brazilian study, this relationship exists for both the number of children desired and those actually born. Further, education appears to have a stronger effect in the city than in the country.[18]

Several variables affect urban fertility. For one, education provides access to mobility—and to contraception. Aspirations toward upward mobility are generally conducive to a lower birthrate, as a survey of Central American migrants shows.[19] Also, a higher number of single women are found in the city. Although a less important factor than education in determining fertility, employment of women is predictive. Too, the specific setting of employment is significant. For example, in one study "live-in" domestics had a lower birthrate than those who lived out, as employers prefer single or childless women for this role.[20]

As compared to urban areas, the *unión libre* or consensual union is more prevalent and stable in the rural areas; also, children are more desired. A survey of Costa Rican fertility trends suggests that male dominance in rural areas may be one cause of the higher birthrate.[21] In urban areas, where employment is an option, work involvement and birth control may be both cause and effect of fertility. Yet, whatever the environment, urban or rural, fertility depends on a variety of cultural, sociopsychological, and economic variables. In regard to that point, nearly all Latin American countries recorded a drop in the birthrate during the Depression of the early 1930s.[22]

Still other variables influence fertility. Regarding the rural birthrate, studies point to the factor of land ownership, which has operated both negatively and positively on fertility. The fear of dividing the terrain upon inheritance discourages couples from having large families, even though anticipation of children's labor can encourage fertility, as with the *ejido* system in Mexico.[23] Evidence from northern Argentina implies that sedentary agricultural workers have higher fertility than do migrant laborers.[24] Ethnic differences are another determinant of fertility. It is difficult to detach race from social status, employment, and the geographic setting. For instance, in Guatemala and southern Mexico, Maya women have more children than do *ladinos*, but ethnicity overlaps with social class.[25]

Moreover, regional variables overlap with ethnicity. The upper-status Spanish and mestizo populations of the rural coastal area in Andean countries have a higher birthrate than Indians in the severely impoverished *altiplano*. Altitude may adversely affect sperm production. However, one has to be wary of data regarding differential fertility. Interpretations of the supposed effects of altitude in Peru have been questioned.[26]

Social Factors and the Individual

Presumably, regional cultures and psychological factors influence fertility. Patterns of breastfeeding and infant and child mortality rates are significant. Breastfeeding tends to prevent the return of menses.[27] At the same time, breastfeeding appears more often among women who attend educational programs about health care and family planning, again indicating the interlocking of variables affecting prevention of conception.[28] In addition, a negative correlation is found between breastfeeding and infant mortality. After the death of an infant or a child, the mother may try to compensate this loss by opting for another pregnancy. In two countries, Colombia and Costa Rica, contraceptive practices were reduced after the death of a child.[29] A study of Brazil, particularly the Northeast, found neonatal death to be related to a lack of spacing. Consequently, breastfeeding and contraception continue to be encouraged.[30] Moreover, for most of Latin America the rural birthrate is one-third higher than the urban. Better medical facilities and disease prevention tend to lower the maternal and infant mortality. A wider distribution of these programs could reduce somewhat the urban–rural differential.

Our catalog of variables surrounding fertility is hardly exhausted. An analysis of Mexican data points to a high sex ratio (the numerical balance of men over women) as positive. Yet indices such as higher income and female participation in the labor force also contribute to low fertility.[31] A Paraguayan study points to the positive effect of an urban setting, higher educational level, and the stability of the relationship on the usage of contraception.[32]

According to Colombian demographers, the migration of women to the city is a factor in declining fertility.[33] Among the modernizing effects of the city are absence from the home through employment, heterogeneity of social influences, the mass media, and educational opportunities. Also, contraceptives and abortion are more available than they are in the countryside. Data from a rural community in Chiapas, Mexico, reveal the intricacy of factors determining fertility—religious restraints, degree of fatalism, perceived need of children in the immediate and distant future, and anxiety about abortions, among others.[34] Later in the chapter we shall return to the question of fertility and contraception in connection with population policy and control.

MORTALITY AND ITS SIGNIFICANCE

As stated earlier, the primary factor in the demographic revolution overtaking most of the world during the twentieth century is the shift from a high death rate to one that ranges from moderate to low. Even before the turn of the century, a slight decrease in mortality occurred as slavery ended in Brazil and Cuba. The death rate has fallen more rapidly in Latin America than in Southeast Asia, the Middle East, or Africa. In the thirty years between 1940 and 1970, Latin Americans attained a decline in the death rate comparable to what Europe accomplished in nearly one hundred years, yet life expectancy is markedly higher in the advanced Western countries. As with fertility, explicit comparisons cannot be made, as statistics for rural areas in most transitional countries are unreliable. However, estimates place most Latin American countries as having approximately 7 deaths per 1,000 population. Among the exceptions are Bolivia, with a reported death rate of 10, and Haiti, with 12. As an advanced country, Uruguay at 10 is high, but it has an older population. Moreover, Uruguay has more accurate reporting.

Life expectancy data are not always reliable, based as they are on the registration of deaths and in relation to the latest census returns. Peasant subcultures are not always included in this type of data, hence life expectancies for countries with large Indian populations are especially inaccurate, even though registration has improved in recent decades. Once more, we are struck with national and regional differences, as seen in Table 3.1. For example, we may place reasonable credence in the estimate for life expectancy for Argentine males at 69 years of age and females at 76, but 59 and 62 respectively in Bolivia may be on the generous side.[35] Longevity has increased in all Latin American countries over the last four decades. Consequently, the gap today is not as staggering as formerly when compared with the life expectancy of 72 for males and 79 for females in the United States. The advanced nations have nearly reached a ceiling in life expectancy, especially for the first half of the life course, but developing nations have a greater potential, again with gender differences.[36]

Several observations are in order: First, life expectancy is increased if we omit the effect of infant mortality. In 1990, the infant mortality rate (the number of deaths under one year of age per 1,000 live births) was a "high" of 69 in Nicaragua and 122 in Haiti, a "low" of 17 in Costa Rica (and 10 in the United States). Roughly half of the difference of thirteen years in life expectancy between Costa Rica and Guatemala is accounted for by the higher mortality rate for children under 5 years old.[37] Even in an advanced nation, say Argentina, life expectancy is increased three years for both sexes if it is determined at the end of the first year rather than at birth, and this difference is still greater for the less developed countries.

Second, the availability of medical care varies greatly. In 1988, Uruguay had nearly nine times the physicians per capita as did Guatemala, although for nurses the ratio was nearer to two to one between the two countries. Brazil with 852 doctors and 1,005 nurses (and nurse aides) per capita was fairly typical for Latin America.[38]

Third, the fall of the death rate has meant a huge population increase, but one that should taper off. It is more difficult to extend life expectancy from 60 to 70 years than from 50 to 60, and the transition from 70 to 80 would be even more difficult, as mortality trends have shown in advanced countries.

Culture, subcultures, and biology affect mortality as well as fertility. First of all, the difference in life expectancy between men and women is roughly five years in most Latin American countries, as compared to seven years in the United States. In Latin America, as in many parts of the world, the female is not as vulnerable as the male to forms of personal disorganization and violence. Probably the most plausible explanation for the women's relatively higher mortality (as compared to other Western areas) is questionable medical care, especially before and after childbirth. Only since 1920 has the large sex differential appeared in the industrialized countries. Yet even in an advanced nation, irregularities occur. A Buenos Aires survey in the 1980s revealed that induced abortions are a major cause of death for women in the childbearing years.[39]

Other factors include social class and urban–rural and regional variation; but again, caution in interpreting the data is important. Studies show one of the most dependable predictors of longevity is educational level. Underlying this factor is a structuring of the economy, which facilitates advances in public health and literacy.[40] Mortality is reported as high in many cities, but correction is seldom made for age differences between urban and rural areas. Also, deaths are reported for place of occurrence instead of residence, and are not systematically registered in outlying areas. Largely because of better health facilities, mortality is significantly lower in the city. Income remains a factor in mortality, but less so than it was before the 1940s. Because of differences in lifestyle, the relation between per capita income and mortality is variable, being especially uneven for Colombia and Mexico.[41]

Region and ethnicity also influence mortality. In colonial times the highlands were freer of disease than were the coastal areas, but a number of factors came into play, such as labor conditions and harsh treatment of the indigenous population.[42] For the present, data from Mexico are revealing. The northern states have lower death rates, specifically from infectious, parasitic, and digestive diseases, but higher death rates in circulatory diseases and neoplasms. Generally, states sending immigrants to the United States have lower mortality.[43] Similarly, in Brazil the states of São Paulo and Rio Grande do Sul have higher life expectancies than states of the Northeast or even Guanabara (Rio de Janeiro). Life expectancy for Rio Grande do Sul in 1980 was 70.6 years, but in Ceará in the north it was 47 years.[44] These regional differences result from societal processes.

Consequently, the death rate at all ages taps a number of interrelated factors. This is notably the case in countries with a sizeable indigenous population. Most striking in a sample of villages in Guatemala is that infants and children under 5 years old account for 50 to 70 percent (depending on the region) of the mortality.[45] Infant and child mortality is influenced by ethnicity, urban–rural residence, parental education, and sanitation (sewage disposal), among other items. *Ladinos* living in Guatemala City are especially favored.[46]

Indexes of Death

The principal causes of death contrast acutely with those of the advanced nations. Even allowing for inadequate reporting, gastric and intestinal disorders and pulmonary infections lead the list. Most inhabitants of underdeveloped countries hardly live long enough to enjoy the distinction of dying from circulatory disorders or cancer. However, the data are not clear. The causes for many illnesses are unknown; consequently, cardiac disorders, among others, may be underrepresented.

In several Latin American nations, statistics regarding causation are weakened by the use of folkloric terms and practices along with insufficient knowledge concerning the indexes of disease and death.[47] Although individual countries vary, Central American statistics point to diseases of early infancy as the most frequent cause of death, followed by pneumonia, and gastritis and enteritis third. Yet for over one-fifth of deaths, the causes are unknown. In Mexico, coronary diseases lead, followed in order by accidents, malignant neoplasms, intestinal infections, diabetes, influenza and pneumonia, and homicides.[48] The statistics on infant and child mortality have shown scanty improvement, and as with adult mortality a number of factors are interrelated. A report from Chile showed that even in a slum setting certain inputs—better education of mother and midwife, breastfeeding, and basic sanitation procedures—can bring down the rate of infant and child mortality.[49]

MIGRATION

The third process underlying population change is far less an influence in the total national population, but can markedly affect the distributional aspects of population. Migration is a major force from the Rio Grande to Patagonia. As a process it may be more complex than fertility and mortality, since it is relatively voluntary. People have no control over their birth and little over death, but in most instances they determine if and when movement to another area is desirable or mandatory. In other words, migration is selective as to what segments of the population change their location and for how long. In view of these movements of people, one may speak of *net* migration—how many individuals enter or leave a country, region, or city.

Internal Migration

People may move from one rural area to another, but more often they move to the city. This trek is universal but endemic in most developing countries, and Latin America has a longer tradition of urban concentration than Africa or even Southern Asia. This enormous cityward migration occurs because resources in the rural areas can no longer support the population. More women than men flee to the city from the countryside. They also tend to be younger than the men. The specific pattern differs with locality. Service-oriented Rio de Janeiro attracts more females, but industrialized São Paulo appeals to male migrants.

Nearly 70 percent of migrants to Brazil's metropolitan centers came from smaller urban areas.[50] On the other hand, in Mexico industrialization attracts mainly peasants to the city, notably since World War II. Other stimuli also foment this movement. For example, in Colombia, nineteen cities have passed the 200,000 mark; several of these owe part of their growth to rural *violencia* in the 1950s. Cali, for instance, more than doubled its population in that decade by drawing *campesinos* from the countryside. Bogotá and Medellín continue to grow despite their high rate of drug-related violence. Presumably between one-half and two-thirds of the growth of major Latin American cities is a result of immigration rather than natural increase.

In Brazil, the trek is not only to the cities and coffee *fazendas* of the south, but to Goias and Mato Grosso in the west, and migration has not lost its momentum. Whether to a coastal city or to emerging agricultural areas of the Paraná basin, migration reinforces the southeast more than ever as the center of Brazil's population. In Brazil, the causes of this migration are more "push" than "pull": the desire to flee areas caught in intermittent natural catastrophes such as droughts of the sertão, floods in the north, or abandonment of regions where resources have become exhausted by exploitation, as in Minas Gerais and Bahia in the central and eastern parts of the country. In all Latin America the city offers a labor market, yet industrialization does not advance proportionately with migration. Nevertheless, the city is an escape from inhospitable features of the rural milieu. Health, educational, and recreational goals can be as powerful a magnet as the labor market.

Gender and Age

Although migration to the city is predominantly by women, it is the men who go to the coffee plantations of the South, the irrigation projects and pioneer settlements of the West, and the construction sites of the trans-Amazon highway. Occasionally, whole families migrate, as in the flight from the Northeast, particularly during the disastrous droughts of the 1950s. In Brazil, three times as many men as women are involved in migration, which is primarily to agricultural areas. Cityward migration is rising but is more likely a second generation event.

A survey of the migration patterns in Colombia follows the profile of most countries.[51] Migration involves primarily the young and unmarried. In 1970 migration to rural areas accounted for 36 percent of the total migration in the country and primarily attracted males. However, as mobility for the above-average educated male is meager in rural areas, he finds his best opportunities in the city. As work for women is limited in the country, they are drawn to the city. Whether male or female, the migrant's educational level may be less than the average of the host city, yet income differences are partially equalized within a few years. As in Brazil, most migrants reach a higher status than what they would have realized had they remained in their original habitat.

Motives and Spatial Patterns

The nature of this trek from North to South in Brazil has not changed over the last half century; only the volume has increased with the growth of population. New highways, improved roads, and more trucks and buses have widened the avenue of escape for the *sertanejo*. In a sense, migration may be described as both intragenerational and intergenerational mobility, both horizontal and vertical. In other words, migration is a major means of social mobility. After five years, migrants tend to have higher incomes than nonmigrants in the locality of origin. In one survey, a sizeable minority, with wide variations, depending on the point of origin and arrival, found their income to be higher than for the natives of their adopted area.[52] Sons of peasants who move to the colonies and plantations of the South may find employment in the mills and factories of the city. Not for all migrants is the move a success; a third or so return to the Northeast. Beginning with the 1970s, the Western movement was accelerated, and the Amazon basin became another goal both for exploiter and colonizer—with serious ecological consequences to the tropical rain forest.

Once again, migration assumes a variety of forms regarding its stages and distances. For more than a century, migrants moved from a rural area to a smaller center and then to a larger one. The concept of "intervening opportunities" accounts for the urge to move on to a new horizon. Studies in Chile and Guatemala underscore this finding. Mexican rural migrants to the United States tend to move to a small town, often not too far from the border, before they take on this greater leap.[53] An interesting relationship between earnings and distance is also found in

Mexico. As economic conditions improved somewhat in the 1970s, the threshold for migration rose. States with the highest income levels accounted for the largest outmigration. For migrations up to 340 miles, higher-origin earnings discouraged migration; beyond that distance these same earnings prompted migration. Movement was more manageable when one had the necessary resources and the goal was primarily Mexico City or north of the Rio Grande. Workers with higher income were best able to undertake a major move.[54] A duality in migration also appears in other countries such as Chile. The more educated a woman was, the more likely she was to choose a smaller city than Santiago. Possibly she found greater opportunities and preferred to be closer to her home.[55]

Other questions remain about the meaning of migration for the individual actor. One may look at this question in the context of social change. What are the costs of modernization to society and the individual? How much is the migrant reacting to push or pull pressures? Does migration result in the individual improving his or her status? We will return to these questions in Chapter 8 in connection with cityward migration. A partial answer is found in a comparison of migrants and nonmigrants in a Bahia sample which shows few significant differences in mental health, even though the migrant experiences frustration and marginalization.[56]

International Migration

In our twentieth century, population movements across nations take on vast proportions. Areas of high density have encouraged people to find less crowded areas. The incorporation of Latin America in the world economy inevitably makes for the recruitment of labor from one area to another.[57] Not only does economic expansion drive people to seek a newer arena, but political oppression demands escape routes. These migrations were not impervious to the Cold War, which dominated nearly half of this century. The United States is directly and indirectly an actor in this development.

The Past and the Present

Immigration has played a major role in Latin America, not only during the colonial settlement, but intermittently up to the present. In the late nineteenth century, the exodus was out of Europe to Argentina, Brazil, Chile, and Uruguay. The wave of twelve million immigrants to these countries began after 1880 and continued in a heavy stream until 1914. Arrivals in Latin America dwindled during the 1920s and 1930s, and rose again for a brief spurt after World War II. Of the total recorded immigration to Latin America, approximately four million were from Spain, more than four million from Italy, and almost two million from Portugal; the remainder were Germans, Poles, and a dozen other nationalities, including some three hundred thousand Japanese who went primarily to Brazil. After World War II, Italians led in a wave of immigration to Argentina, Brazil, and Venezuela. Since the 1970s, movement over borders generally has involved other Latin Americans.

Argentina has stood first in Latin America since the 1870s as a recipient of some eight million immigrants, of whom 48 percent remained. Italians numbered three million, Spanish two million, and Germans and Eastern Europeans accounted for most of the remainder. In 1900, a quarter of Argentines were foreign born; in 1914 they outnumbered natives by two to one in the provinces of Santa Fé, Córdoba, and Buenos Aires. Historically, immigrants arrived in three principal waves: (1) the 1800s, broken off by political and economic difficulties of the 1890s; (2) from 1903 to 1914 corresponding to the heavy tide of immigrants to the United States; and (3) during the 1920s, when migration from Italy, which was then entering the Fascist period, began to swell.[58] Also, Congress's adoption of quotas in 1923 nearly ended the immigration of Italians to the United States. With the Depression of the 1930s, immigration to Argentina, as well as to other countries, was reduced to a trickle of what it had been. In 1980, Italians constituted 36 percent and Spaniards 29 percent of the 2.6 million foreign-born residing in Argentina.

Although the first wave of immigrants to Argentina was largely agriculturists, by 1900 immigrants were operating urban factories. After the turn of the century, sons of immigrants were turning to commerce. Gradually, business elites feared encroachment by this upwardly mobile generation, in addition to new immigrants who were better educated than earlier arrivals. Immigrants at the bottom of the social scale were even more threatening to the ruling class, as they brought in a variety of European ideologies from syndicalism to anarchism. By the outbreak of World War I, restrictions on immigration were proposed.

As the second largest host nation, Brazil received between 1884 and 1957 no less than one and a half million from Italy and Portugal each, with smaller numbers from Spain, Japan, Germany, and Russia. These six nations accounted for over three-fourths of the 14.7 million immigrants who came to Latin America during these years. As in Argentina and the United States, immigration never regained the importance that it had before World War I. Consequently, the proportion of foreign-born drops with each census.

Changing Patterns

As European immigration slowed, immigrants came from other South American countries, to Argentina for instance. Whereas Europeans preferred the large urban centers, especially Buenos Aires and Mendoza,

South American immigrants are almost equally divided between urban and rural areas. The number of immigrants varies with the political and economic climate of both Argentina and neighboring countries In 1980, the foreign born included over 750,000 from Argentina's five closest neighbors, of which the largest group (35%) were from Paraguay. Consequently, the north (Gran Chaco and Mesopotamia) was showing an unprecedented population growth.[59]

Immigration was once primarily an Argentine and Brazilian affair; today the flow of Europeans, Caribbeans, and Asians is more widely distributed. Panama opened its doors to many workers from the Antilles and elsewhere. As with Argentina, Venezuela has been a desired nation, notably because of its prosperity before the oil crisis in 1973–1974. Under an open-door policy, Venezuela admitted immigrants who selected that country in an uneven movement depending on the economic and political conditions which fluctuated during the postwar period. For instance, in 1953, 140,000 migrants, largely Italian and Spanish, were admitted, but only one-third chose to stay. The desire for change of status in a new environment, and one of growing prosperity, was counterbalanced by cultural differences, a monotonous climate, and the need to reestablish family ties in the homeland. Not all immigration to Latin America is contemplated as permanent.

By the 1980s, over half of a million Colombians had moved into Venezuela, perhaps half of them illegally. As the two economies are highly uneven, discrimination in wages, housing, and gender has been widespread.[60] However, with economic decline the problems of adjustment became no less an issue.[61] As conditions in Colombia began to offer a more hospitable environment, skilled and professional cadres were the most willing to return to their native country.[62] In most countries, the bulk of immigration is unskilled labor, not only across Latin American borders, but even regarding the traditional immigration from Spain and Italy into Argentina, Brazil, and more recently, Venezuela.

As international migration decreased over the last generation, the character of the movement also changed to include a greater variety of backgrounds, skills, and goals. According to a study of Paraguayan samples, migration is often temporary, of short distance, and based on the search for schooling as well as work.[63] With the emergence of Latin America out of an almost purely agricultural economy, opportunities expanded, and Europeans found a wider assortment of occupational and entrepreneurial roles. Immigrants have played the major role in the socioeconomic advance of most Central and South American nations. No one visiting San Salvador, La Paz, or Asunción can fail to notice the technical, commercial, and cultural leadership of European minorities. Germans have been the dominant foreign group, but the French, Italians, Spanish, and Eastern Europeans are important in industrial, scientific, educational, and artistic life. The Lebanese, along with other Middle Eastern and Asian immigrants, are leaders in commercial life from Santiago and São Paulo to Central American capitals.

Political and Economic Forces

Latin American migration, of course, reflects political forces. Along with Anglo-America, Latin America has a long history of accepting refugees seeking a better life. For example, Argentina accepted—almost uniquely among Roman Catholic nations—thousands of Jews between 1880 and 1914. Its role during the crisis imposed by Nazism in the late 1930s was markedly less progressive, but then neither was the record of the United States or Britain very humanitarian.[64] A few smaller countries offered German Jews a haven during the critical year of 1939. Ironically, with the return to dictatorial rule in most countries in the 1970s the only escape for many Latin Americans was immigration to Europe, the United States, or the few democratic regimes in the region. This was not a totally new movement; Paraguayans were fleeing Stroessner, as the Nicaraguans had fled the Somoza regime.

One of the largest flows out of Latin America was the middle-class and professional refugees from Cuba in the early 1960s. They were welcomed in the United States since victims (or malcontents) of Communist-oriented regimes were given favored status as compared to refugees from rightist governments. Following the U.S. intervention in Central American republics, notably El Salvador and Guatemala, victims found access to the United States more difficult. Consequently, many sought refuge in Mexico. In 1990, some two hundred thousand Latin American refugees, principally Guatemalans and Salvadorans, found asylum in another country, notably Mexico and the United States.[65] The Meso-American situation has been consistently turbulent. Between 1985 and 1989, refugees in Mexico doubled, and in Costa Rica the number of refugees rose from 16,800 to 278,600.[66] Guatemala and Honduras also showed marked increases of refugees, primarily from El Salvador and Nicaragua.

In the early 1990s, Haitians were increasingly seeking asylum in the United States but were rejected by the White House and Congress, in response to the economic recession and political expediency, not least by pressures from Cuban Americans in Miami. Again, in selecting political refugees a differential equation applies according to ideological needs, not excluding racial prejudice. During the Pinochet regime (1973–1989), Chileans were fleeing to various republics in this hemisphere as well as to Europe. Guerrilla movements are another problem. Some two hundred thousand refugees were forced to leave their homes because of the Shining Path in Peru, and whole villages became ghost towns.[67]

Probably a larger wave of immigrants is motivated by economic pressures and what is anticipated as greater opportunities abroad. Access is shifting as economic conditions and political philosophies evolve. The Mexican American situation is a case in point.[68] Since the 1920s the flow of migrants from south of the Rio Grande has followed the winds of economic and political realities. After an ambivalent status in the 1920s and 1930s, Mexican workers were welcomed under the *bracero* program in 1942 in order to assume lower-status work in agriculture during World War II. The agreement continued with the Mexican government until 1964, ending the special relationship of an open-door policy for Latin America. Under the 1965 immigration act, a reduced number of work permits were granted and the "wetback" became both symbol and reality. Whether legal or illegal, immigration offered the trade-off between transfer payments on one side and exploitation on the other.[69] A review of Mexican immigration points to the difficulty of documenting the flow of immigrants. It appears that the number of immigrants is a function of the community's networks. If the area has a long history of outmigration the possibility of further exodus is enhanced. The distribution and quality of disposable agricultural land is another variable, not only in size but in the type of tenure, landless or small landholder.[70]

Another aspect of migration is the *maquiladora* program. American entrepreneurs locate their plants along the Mexican side of the border and thereby escape the "Mexicanization" requirements of the central part of the country. Most of these are textile or assembly plants that largely employ women at a wage set by the Mexican government.[71] Bordertowns from Tijuana to Nueva Laredo are the target of migration from areas far from the border. The enactment of NAFTA will likely expand this process, but hopefully with an improvement in wages and working conditions.

International immigration assumes an almost hierarchical form. Jewish refugees from the Third Reich in 1939 found only the less developed nations open—Bolivia, the Dominican Republic, and Ecuador, among others. In the postwar period, these immigrants looked forward to moving to a major Latin American nation like Argentina, then to the United States, and a number succeeded in this progression. During the 1980s and 1990s, Haitians were crossing the border into the Dominican Republic while the more mobile Dominicans immigrated to the United States. In other words, the most economically depressed nations send their less poor across the frontier, replacing those who had moved on.[72]

THE STRUCTURE OF POPULATION

Demographic processes are the dynamics of population; the profile of the population describes its characteristics. Influencing most social behaviors, including demographic events, are several factors: composition of the working force, racial distribution, and literacy levels, among others. As ethnicity and social status appear in later chapters, this section focuses on the sex and age structure. Although changes in population—fertility, mortality, and migration—are more significant for understanding a given society, structural characteristics are also necessary for social planning.

Sex Ratio

In all societies, males outnumber females in the early years of life. The sex ratio (the number of males divided by the number of females, multiplied by 100) is approximately 105 at birth. By age 48, males and females tend to be equal, with variations for different societies. Sex ratios for Latin American nations are approximately 100, or slightly higher than in the advanced nations but markedly lower than in India and Nationalist China, where female mortality is greater. Countries with a history of immigration have a lower sex ratio as immigration slows down. For instance, Argentina in 1947 had a ratio of 105.1, but in 1990 it was 99.8. The low sex ratio of Paraguay in 1950 (95.6) was the result of the disastrous Chaco War of the 1930s and the civil war of 1947.[73] Degenerative diseases affect men more than women. Even so, by 1989 the ratio in Paraguay was reported to be 98.0. However, most countries were in the average range; Brazil had a sex ratio of 99.4 and Mexico 99.6, as compared to the U.S. ratio of 94.8. Possibly because of underenumeration of females, Guatemala in 1988 at 102.1 had the highest sex ratio, whereas El Salvador was the lowest at 96.1, reflecting male emigration and interpersonal violence.[74]

The sex ratio varies not only by country but also by region. Since women are attracted to the city for domestic service and to a lesser extent for clerical positions, cities have a lower ratio of males. Men tend to remain with agriculture and extractive industries. The low sex ratio of the city corresponds to the situation in Europe and North America but in contrast to Africa and Asia, where migration to the city is a male phenomenon. In the African city jobs are largely confined to commerce, construction, and industry. In contrast to Latin America, there is almost no middle class to support servants, nor is female employment prevalent.

Age Ratio

The age structure is an obvious index of the economically active population. As Latin America is a universe of the young, a high dependency is reflected in the statistics for all but a few nations. In 1989, the average age for Brazil and Mexico was 21 and 19 years, respectively, but for Argentina it is 28 years and for the United States, 29 years. According to a 1996 estimate, 35 percent of the Latin American population are under 15 years of age, and 5 percent are 65 and over. The respective percentages for the

United States are 22 and 13.[75] This high clustering in the early years arises from the difference between a country in rapid growth with a high birthrate and later periods with a more stabilized population, as shown in Figure 3.2. At the same time, one must be cautious in interpreting age data, since people between 30 and 50 tend to report their age lower than it is.[76] This tendency disproportionately raises the ratio of the young and old. Despite some distortion, data point to a high dependency ratio in most countries; indeed, nearly twice what it is in the United States, which itself is changing demographically. Because of a relatively small number of persons between 20 and 65 in Latin America, roughly half of the population must support the other half. The problem is no less complicated by low employment. The question remains whether the labor market can be expanded so that adults may assume responsibility for maintaining high dependency loads.

Regional differences inevitably appear. In Brazil, the state of Sergipe on the northern coast has an excessive proportion of the aged since young people have left the area over the past few decades. But for nearly all Latin America, the ratio of persons over 60 is the lowest of the Western world.

FIGURE 3.2
Youth Ages 15 to 24 in Mexico's Population Age Pyramid: 1980, 1990, 2000

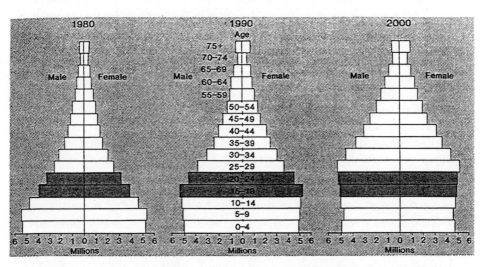

Source: *Proyecciones de la Población de México y de las Entidades Federativas 1980–2010* (México, DF: Consejo Nacional de Población and Instituto Nacional de Estadística, Geografía ed Informática, 1985), as published in Thomas W. Merrick, Population Pressures in Latin America (Washington, D.C.: Population Reference Bureau, 1991), 47.

FUTURE GROWTH AND NATIONAL POLICY

Today the areas of demographic transition are ever more noticeable because of diffusion from centers of low natural growth to neighboring countries. Fertility norms in Argentina and Uruguay have been spreading northward and from the United States southward. But despite this transition, Latin America will continue to grow. Indeed, as the second most rapidly growing part of the world, Latin America and the Caribbean is expected to increase from its 1996 estimated population of 486 million to 584 million by the year 2010, and 678 million in 2025, if one estimates medium growth; this latter figure is more than three times the area's population of 1950.[77] Brazil has overtaken Russia to become the fifth most populous nation of the world (after China, India, the United States, and Indonesia). Mexico is predicted to be more than 100 million by the turn of the century. Despite the danger of making population projections, every indication points to large increases in this hemisphere.

With a density of only about one-half of the rest of the world, this increase in itself is not serious for Latin America. With scientific agriculture and wider distribution, most nations could feed more people than they do at present. However, the present diet, by health standards, is inadequate both in caloric intake and protein level. Only Argentina reaches the three thousand calorie average daily intake (the United States is 3,600) and sufficient protein consumption.[78] Only in El Salvador and several Caribbean islands are densities sufficiently high to inhibit further growth, since all arable land is already under cultivation, and not at a very efficient level. Another issue is the sustainability of economic resources and the ecology.[79] Pollution, acid rain, and other environmental problems accompany intensive urbanization and poor industrial planning.

The problem of overpopulation lies rather in the growth rate in relation to the economy and a relatively severe dependency level. With a rate of natural increase at 1.9 percent per year (the average for Latin America), a nation must invest 4 to 8 percent of the national income in economic expansion annually in order to maintain a constant productivity level per worker. Most international loans or domestic savings are required simply to continue the status quo. Countries with population growth of 2.0 percent or more are unable to move ahead when their GNP is advancing at little above that rate. Peru is among those with negative economic advance; however, by 1994 a dramatic upturn was visible—a decrease of 15 percent in inflation and economic growth of 13 percent.[80] The sheer problem of trying to build classrooms and recruit teachers in order to raise the status quo of less than 75 percent literacy in several countries to say, 90 percent, becomes questionable. Those Latin American nations, such as Guatemala, which may double their populations by the year 2020, are at more of a disadvantage than was the United States when it doubled its population between 1860 and 1900, a change resulting as much from immigration as from natural increase. Most immigrants who arrived in North America had been schooled or had acquired a skill relevant to an industrializing economy. The receiving nation gained an advantage which would not have been possible if it assumed the entire burden of education and training.

Various questions remain: Will the rate of economic growth keep pace with population? With the declining birthrate, the outlook is less pessimistic than a decade ago; yet, a severe problem is the slow rate of increase in food production—only 2.5 percent per year during the 1980s. Although this rate is higher than population growth, at least half of Latin Americans suffer from malnutrition. Can birthrates be brought down still further over the next generation? Will death rates also continue to fall? Decline in mortality has been less controversial than the decline in fertility. The birthrate will probably continue its decline. In the more backward countries, the transition will be slower.

Significance of Modernization

Expansion of education, industrialization, and urbanization can mean better diets and health practices, which might temporarily enhance fertility. Technological advances imply a relationship between population increase and economic growth. The evidence is still inconclusive.[81] For the world as a whole, the correlation is approximately zero. In this context, two general viewpoints are relevant: the neo-Malthusian and the structuralist.[82] The *neo-Malthusian* insists that population outdistances resources, inhibits savings and investment, and produces a disproportionate age profile with a high dependency load. On the other hand, *structuralism* emphasizes the poor distribution of wealth rather than population growth. In this connection, we must distinguish between short-range and long-range effects of modernization. Rural migrants may accept the technology of the city, but when deep attitudes and sexual mores are concerned, change can be threatening. Family-planning facilities attempt to restructure values as well as provide specific techniques.

Aspirations and Ideology

In the 1960s, Latin Americans became aware of the "population explosion," but with marked ambivalence. Traditionally, they thought of large empty areas to be filled, population size as determining national power, and the sacred rights of procreation. The influence of the Roman Catholic Church, although changing, is still relevant, especially during the conservative papacy of John Paul II. Also, for many years Latin Americans felt that their low prestige was partly a reflection of a sparse population, outnumbered as they were by both Europeans and North Americans. In the 1930s, the Mexican demographer Gilberto Loyo expressed the fear that Mexico would be permanently isolated from the world power system unless the nation were to grow rapidly to meet the challenge of Anglo-Saxon civilization.[83] In the 1970s, Loyo became a leader in the family-planning movement.

Until the 1970s, government spokesmen in Latin America supported intellectuals, economists, and physicians who had a laissez-faire attitude about demographic pressure and its socioeconomic effects. However, disquieted by the poverty of large families, they looked upon this misfortune as a transitional phase, rationalizing that the difference between two and five children is a relative one. This sentiment was seemingly shared by rural peons, particularly the male, living in his *choza* (hut). Whatever the size of his family, he was poor and without status; he might as well be rich in the size of his household. The spouse or *compañera* was seldom consulted. These attitudes shifted as family planning seeped into rural culture.

On the whole, the clergy is ambivalent about family planning. A survey of elites in Brazil revealed an extreme opposition on the part of bishops to divorce and especially abortion, but only a mild antipathy to birth control. At the same time, they were far more conservative about all three issues as compared to a sample of other elites.[84] The Vatican continues to exert pressure on contraceptive measures, as shown by its attitude in the 1994 Cairo population conference.

Opposition to family planning comes from within Latin America as well as from abroad. Voices vary from the moralist position on the privacy of family decision making and from those who wish to promote economic growth by ensuring a large labor supply and a potential market for goods. Similar to the black protest against birth control in the United States, Latin Americans interpreted the contraceptive ideology as a racist attempt to preserve a European or Anglo-Saxon dominance of the hemisphere. Marxists continued to view the family-planning movement as a distraction from the real problem of changing the nature of society. A serious blockage of the family-planning movement came from the United States during the Reagan administration and once again with the 1995 Republican-controlled Congress.

Planning and Control

According to most observers, the only likely solution for the problem of economic development is an accelerated program of birth control. Industrialization, urbanization, and improved agriculture are in themselves not sufficient to reduce fertility since their effect is too slow and other factors are involved. Most fundamental in the judgment of many Latin American demographers is a significant educational program focused on both the public and key personnel in strategic institutions, especially government.[85]

Attitudinal Base and Subcultures

Underlying any program of birth control is the value one places on family planning; the role of the wife more than of the husband is critical. Data from other countries, the United States for example, show more ambivalence on the part of the father than the mother as to the desirability of a third child.[86] Social class, which is related to educational level, is not an entirely consistent variable in determining aspirations about family size in certain parts of the Third World; however, it is a predictor in Latin America. In addition, employment leads to delay in marriage and to child spacing.

Contraception: Method and Choice

Quite apart from modern contraceptive techniques, an important factor in reducing fertility is, of course, motivation. It is relevant that in the late nineteenth century, Europeans reduced their birthrate by means of the douche, condom, and coitus interruptus. Family planning has not been of sufficient saliency in Latin America, at least among the rural lower class, to establish a climate of fertility control. Communication between spouses may not be sufficiently articulate to address the question of the desired number of children.

As compared to Africa, where only 17 percent of the women use contraception, Latin America at 41 percent compares favorably but lags the world average of 55 percent.[87] Specifically, the percentage of married women using contraceptive methods reportedly ranges from 68 percent for Costa Rica to less than 30 percent for most of Central America, with Brazil at 66 percent and Mexico at 53 percent (only 7% for Haiti).[88] In Mexico between 1976 and 1987, reported contraceptive practices on the part of women rose from 30 to 53 percent, with an increase of sterilization among females from 9 to 35 percent (males from 0 to 2%), the pill declining from 33 to 18 percent, and the IUD remaining roughly the same at 20 percent. No drastic change appeared in the use of condom and vaginal methods. The use of casual or traditional methods such as rhythm, withdrawal, and abstinence dropped from 21 to 15 percent.[89] Because of its simplicity, low cost, and ease of usage, the IUD in its variations is likely to be the most promising method among rural women despite its medical risks. Sterilization is also widely used in several countries.

Summing Up

As family planning began to take shape in Latin America in the late 1960s, a number of governments remained ambivalent, if not actually hostile. By the mid 1970s, a new attitude was visible. Perhaps the most dramatic shift was in Mexico. Although private facilities existed, the contraceptive movement remained in limbo, especially in view of the election of Luis Echeverría in 1970 as president. But as he became convinced of the dangers of overpopulation, he reversed his strong pronatalist policy in 1972. By 1976 the Mexican Social Security Institute was offering family planning services in 133 clinics, which were to be expanded in future years. Too, as with other Latin American countries, the United Nations and International Planned Parenthood Federation, along with a host of other agencies, were dispensing birth control information and materials. The Roman Catholic Church, which traditionally has something less than a congenial relationship with the government, prefers the voluntary aspects of the program. Still, as elsewhere, the clergy stresses responsible planned parenthood rather than categorically opposing the birth control movement.

One reason for the neglect of population policies is the priority governments attach to more pressing issues, whether averting economic disaster or staying in power. The efforts of increasing education and the mass media (including soap operas on the advantage of spacing children) as well as stressing consumerism and individualistic values has considerable payoff.[90] In this connection, nearly all governments have moved toward official recognition of the problem. After wavering in its stance on controlling population growth, Brazil joined the majority position at the World Population Conference in Bucharest in 1974. Argentina represents possibly the most doctrinaire nation in its pronatalist policy, especially during its dictatorial regimes.[91] In 1974, the government forbade by executive decree the dissemination of birth control information and closed existing facilities. Yet, as with its neighbors, a high abortion rate in Argentina—estimates indicate that from 15 to 35 percent of pregnancies are terminated—indicates little consensus between government and the individual in regard to the significance of birth control.

Prospects for the Future

With a program of population control now launched, the rate of natural increase will continue to fall in Latin America. But it seems unlikely that most of the area can, in this century, reduce its natural growth rate to the low level now found in temperate South America (1.6% in Chile, 1.2% in Argentina, or 0.8% in Uruguay). As has been pointed out earlier, the variables surrounding fertility are not altogether predictable. Improved health standards, a continuing decline of the death rate, and indices of economic development are not necessarily accompanied by lower fertility. Mortality will probably continue to decline in Latin America. With increased life expectancy and an accelerated reduction in fertility, Brazil, for example, is predicted to have a population of 180 million by the year 2010 and 200 million by 2025.

On the whole, the population profile of Latin America should become more homogeneous over the next half century, even though disproportionate rates of increase will continue to exist. That is, Mexico, which in 1930 represented one-sixth of Latin American population, will be one-fifth by the turn of the century. Brazil will continue to be one-third, and Argentina, which was one-tenth in 1930, will be a mere sixteenth in the year 2000.

Other kinds of changes are foreseeable. With the increase of urbanization and a more crowded landscape, outmigration will be even more a reality than at present—for years Mexican emigration to the United States has been a significant response to overpopulation in Mexico. The degree of demographic pressure will depend on the ability of Latin America to support itself in food production and distribution. The agricultural situation, which will be explored in Chapter 4, is not promising, but revolutionary advances are a possible option. Already the Green Revolution has brought improvements in farming techniques. Scientists have been concerned with potential breakthroughs, ranging from developing new marine reserves and breeds of grains to the possibility of synthetic fertilizers.

A NOTE ON ECOLOGY

No discussion of demography would be complete without mention of environmental policy. Although the developing world, including Latin America, bears less guilt than the industrial world, misuse and plundering of the natural environment is serious. For example, the state of São Paulo has only 3 percent of its original forests.[92] In Haiti, more than one-fifth of the forests are now denuded, with such far-reaching soil erosion that human habitation is no longer possible.

In Latin America, exploitation of the natural environment is the basic ecological issue. Tropical forests were once nearly one-tenth of the world's surface but have been reduced by nearly 25 percent over the last generation.[93] Undoubtedly, the most widespread loss is occurring in the Amazon. Developers cut hardwood for the world market, and subsistence farmers turn to slash-and-burn, grow crops for a few years, then allow the land to lay fallow. Population pressure means a constantly shorter period for forest regeneration. The situation is complicated further by highway construction which began in the 1970s, accompanied by land speculation, cattle ranching, and exploration for minerals, all promoted by generous tax allowances. According to studies of the Amazon region, tropical forests reduce the level of carbon dioxide and counteract the loss of ozone.[94] By 1991, ozone holes in both the northern and southern hemisphere became a grim reality. Government intervention in the form of commercial exploitation seems all the more ironic in view of the precarious existence of aborigines and long-term settlers. Despite the poverty of nutrients in the soil and the toxicity of many plants, the native population is attuned to the limitations of the ecosystem.[95]

Various dangers threaten the ecosystem. A number of areas present serious problems of subsistence and are in special need of environmental protection. The Catinga and specifically the *sertão* of northeast Brazil suffer from disastrous droughts and misguided agricultural use, as have the North American Great Plains and the African savannahs. An intricate root system binds the soil into a fairly erosion-resistant structure, but drought and overgrazing leads to deterioration.[96] Moreover, in its frontier expansion large parts of Brazil go through a cycle of "intensive attraction–stagnation–expulsion," lasting perhaps thirty to thirty-five years in Paraná, twenty to twenty-five years in Maranhão, and ten to fifteen years in the Amazon.[97] On another front, the Contra attacks in Nicaragua were destructive of the environment as are the drug wars in the Andean nations, notably Colombia, not to mention the pursuit of drug producers and distributors by the United States. Basically the problem is one of overpopulation and exploitation of the ecosystem.

A pressing problem is to make the power brokers—bankers, corporate heads, and the government elites—aware of the ecological crisis.[98] It is not to say that there is no public concern with these problems. "Green" parties are found in Brazil and Mexico. With its profits from oil, Venezuela was in 1976 the first Latin American country to enact relevant legislation. Movements in several countries are trying to stem the tide, but they are limited by gaps in strategy and ideology between idealistic groups and the political–economic structure. When federal and local governments are inactive, small landowners can cooperate effectively in informal controls in order to prevent deforestation and mining operations, as reported for portions of the Ecuadorian Amazon.[99] As another complication, social movements in Latin America generally focus on survival needs, whereas in the more "advanced" societies the stress is on "postindustrial contradictions."[100] However, developments in Latin America, including population growth, are causing an ever larger number of individuals and governments to be aware of the need for ecological reform.

Conclusions: The Interrelationship of Demographic Variables

Demographic and environmental processes function reciprocally. Besides the crucial role of demographic processes in the present and future of either developed or underdeveloped areas, one cannot escape the interface between population and the total ecological and societal structure. Demography must be viewed in the context of a chain reaction. The processes of fertility, mortality, and migration are integrally related to the unfolding of biological, economic, and sociopsychological factors, all of which are undergoing almost constant change.

Population trends are, then, more a dependent than an independent variable. Fertility, for instance, reflects societal facilitators and inhibitors surrounding marriage, decision making about marriage, the nature of communication between spouses, the perceived benefits and costs of having children, and the range of communication in marriage or consensual unions. Similarly, mortality is shaped by a set of factors: income levels, availability of health facilities, proneness to violence, and, of course, age structure of the population. Migration, too, represents a matrix of decisions: different kinds of migratory flow, each responding to educational level, career structure, and economic opportunities. Other variables include countermigration or reverse flow, internal versus external migration, and homogeneity or heterogeneity in the population of the exit or entry point. The level of economic development, not only the potential for industrialization but the technology of agriculture, are relevant. Mechanization of agriculture is sending an even greater wave of rural inhabitants to the cities.

Population and Development

Economists point out that high population growth produces an ample supply of workers, low wages, and large profits, at least as compared to low population increase. However, demography is not the whole story. Ideally, investments should be at least 15 percent of the annual GNP in order to assure future growth.[101] But in underdeveloped countries economic growth can demand a high social cost—low wages, deferment of educational goals, and other belt-tightening measures.[102] Even with advanced nations, the birthrate and migration have fluctuated in industrial and postindustrial eras. Nor is economic prosperity, or even stability, assured by a controlled population growth, as the case of Uruguay, among other nations, demonstrates. At least industrialization, urbanization, and education make the shift from ascription- to achievement-orientation more probable. For one thing, this change suggests less familism and deference to kinship.

The movement away from traditionalism also permits the confronting of a larger range of options in residence, occupational choice, and lifestyle. The individual is introduced to a more varied institutional fabric, in which mobility, urban location, and contractual relationships are the order. The inescapable result will be regional differences and the tentativeness of predicting future population trends. Government can play a critical role in stimulating health and housing.[103] Unfortunately the depression of the 1980s reduced the possibility of meeting these needs. For example, only three countries (Argentina, Brazil, and Panama) reported a significantly greater expenditure on health in 1987 than they had in 1980, and several countries were spending markedly less than the earlier amount.[104] The one secure prediction is that Latin America will be wrestling with the problem of a growing population without an adequate infrastructure for some decades.

NOTES

1. Censuses of aboriginal population were made long after European diseases had taken their toll. Consequently, the Western Hemisphere could conceivably have had a population of one hundred million. Henry F. Dobyns, "Estimating Aboriginal American Population: An Appraisal of Techniques with a New Hemispheric Estimate," *Current Anthropology* 7(October): 395–416 (1966). A more detailed account is found in Williams M. Denevan, ed., *The Native Population of the Americas in 1492* (Madison: University of Wisconsin Press, 1976). The epidemics of the sixteenth to the eighteenth centuries were especially disastrous, but improvement occurred with the introduction of a smallpox vaccine in the first decade of the nineteenth century, David J. Robinson, ed., *Studies of Spanish American Population History* (Boulder, Colo.: Westview Press, 1981).

2. David Coleman, "Population Regulation: A Long-Range View," in *The State of Population Theory*, ed. David Coleman and Roger Schofield (Oxford: Basil Blackwell, 1986), 14–42.

3. Alberto Palloni, Kenneth Hill, and Guido Pinto Aguirre, "Economic Swings and Demographic Changes in the History of Latin America," *Population Studies* 50: 105–132 (1996).

4. *América Latina y Desarrollo Social* (Santiago: Centro para el Desarrollo Económico y Social, 1965), vol. 1, 242.

5. Latin American Center, *Statistical Abstract of Latin America* (Los Angeles: University of California, 1995), 4.

6. Federico Debuyst, *La Población en América Latina: Demografía y Evolución del Empleo* (Brussels: Estudios Sociológicos Latinoamericaos FERES, 1961), 15–19.

7. Loraine Donaldson, *Fertility Transition: The Social Dynamics of Population Change* (Cambridge, Mass.: Basil Blackwell, 1991), 9.

8. Thomas McKeown, *The Modern Rise of Population* (New York: Academic Press, 1976), 152–153.

9. Armand Mattelart, *Manual de Análisis Demográfico* (Santiago: Centro para el Desarrollo Económico y Social de América Latina, 1964), 397; World Population Data Sheet (Washington, D.C.: Population Reference Bureau, 1996).

10. Marian F. Zeitlin et al., *Nutrition and Population Growth: The Delicate Balance* (Cambridge, Mass.: Apt Associates, 1982), 62.

11. Lorenzo Moreno-Novarro, "Fertility Change in Five Latin American Countries: A Covariance of Birth Intervals," *Demography* 24: 23–36 (1987).

12. Ester Boserup, "Shifts in the Determinants of Fertility in the Developing World: Environmental, Technical, Economic and Cultural Factors," in *The State of Population Theory*, ed. Coleman and Schofield (Oxford: Basil Blackwell, 1986), 239–255.

13. Etienne van de Walle, "Fertility Transition, Conscious Choice, and Numeracy," *Demography* 29: 487–495 (1992).

14. Harold D. Nelson et al., *Colombia: A Country Study* (Washington, D.C.: Government Printing Office, 1983), 82.

15. "Mexico's Population: A Profile," *Interchange* 16, no. 2 (1987).

16. Peter N. Hess, *Population Growth and Socioeconomic Progress in Less Developed Countries* (New York: Praeger, 1988), 128.

17. John Cleland and German Rodriguez, "The Effect of Parental Education on Marital Fertility in Developing Countries," *Population Studies* 42: 419–442 (1988).

18. Nelson do V. Silva et al., "An Analysis of Reproductive Behavior in Brazil," *Further Analysis Series*, no. 6 (Columbia, Md.: Institute for Resource Development, 1990).

19. Nancy Moss, Michael C. Stone, and Jason B. Smith, "Fertility among Central American Refugees and Immigrants in Belize," *Human Organization* 52: 186–193 (1993).

20. Murray Gendell, Maria N. Maraviglia, and Philip C. Kreitner, "Fertility and Economic Activity of Women in Guatemala City, 1964," *Demography* 7: 273–286 (1970).

21. Carlos Denton and Olda Acuña, "Población y Desarrollo en Costa Rica," Report of the Population Division, no. 39 (New York: United Nations, 1984).

22. O. Andrew Collver, *Birth Rates in Latin America* (Berkeley: Institute of International Studies, University of California, 1965), 34–36.

23. C. Shannon Stokes and Wayne A. Schutzer, "Access to Land and Fertility in Developing Countries," in *Rural Development and Human Fertility*, ed. Wayne A. Schutzer and C. Shannon Stokes (New York: Macmillan, 1984), 195–215.

24. Robert Benencia and Floreal Forni, "Conductas Demográficas Diferenciadas entre Pobladores Rurales de Santiago del Estero," *Revista Paraguaya de Sociología* 29(83): 19–42 (1992).

25. John Hollan, "The Fertility of Maya and Ladino Women," *Latin American Research Review* 20(2): 87–103 (1985).

26. Benjamin Spencer Bradshaw, "Fertility Differences in Peru: A Reconsideration," *Population Studies* 23(March): 5–19 (1969).

27. Deborah Guz and John Hobcraft, "Breastfeeding and Fertility: A Comparative Analysis," *Population Studies* 45: 91–108 (1985).

28. Halvor Gille, "Policy Implications," in *Reproductive Change in Developing Countries*, ed. John Cleland and John Hobcraft (New York: Oxford University Press, 1985), 273–295.

29. Barbara Sena Mensch, "The Effect of Child Mortality on Contraceptive Use and Fertility in Colombia, Costa Rica and Korea," *Population Studies* 39: 309–327 (1985).

30. Sain L. Curtis et al., "Birth Interval and Family Effects on Postnatal Mortality in Brazil," *Demography* 30: 3–43 (1993).

31. Daniel A. Seiver, "Recent Fertility in Mexico: Measurement and Interpretation," *Population Studies* 29: 341–354 (1975).

32. Edith A. Pantelides and Georgina Binstock, "Factores de Riesgo de Embarazco Adolescente en el Paraguay," *Revista Paraguaya de Sociología* 30(87): 171–186 (1993).

33. Carlos A. Patiño et al., *Pobreza y Desarrollo en Colombia: Su Impacto sobre la Infancia y la Mujer* (Bogotá: UNICEF, 1988), 63.

34. Debra A. Schumann, "Fertility and Historical Variation in Economic Strategy among Migrants to the Lacandon Forest, Mexico," in *Culture and Reproduction*, ed. W. Penn Handwerker (Boulder, Colo.: Westview Press, 1986), 144–158.

35. World Population Data Sheet (Washington, D.C.: Population Reference Bureau, 1996).

36. Timothy B. Gage, "Population Variation in Cause of Death: Level, Gender, and Period Effects," *Demography* 31: 271–280 (1994).

37. Arjun Adlakha, "Excess Mortality in Guatemala: A Comparison of Death in Guatemala and Costa Rica," paper presented at the 1990 meeting of the Population Association of America.

38. United Nations, *Statistical Yearbook for Latin America and the Caribbean* (Santiago: CELADE, 1991), 48–50.

39. Juan J. Llovet and Silvina Ramos, "La Práctica del Aborto en las Mujeres de Sectores Populares de Buenos Aires," *Documento CEDOS* (Buenos Aires: Centro de Estudios de Estado y Sociedad, 1987).

40. Ozzie G. Simmons, *Perspectives on Development and Population Growth in the Third World* (New York: Plenum Press, 1988), 164.

41. Samuel H. Preston, *Mortality Patterns in National Populations* (New York: Academic Press, 1976), 69–79.

42. Linda A. Newson, "Indian Population Patterns in Colonial Spanish America," *Latin American Research Review* 20(3): 41–74 (1985).

43. Benjamin S. Bradshaw, "Mortality in Mexico," in *Mortality of Hispanic Populations*, ed. Ira Rosenwalke (New York: Greenwood Press, 1991), 15–30.

44. *Anuário Estatístico do Brasil* (Rio de Janeiro: Directoria Geral de Estatística, 1990), 82.

45. John D. Early, *The Demographic Structure and Evolution of a Peasant System: The Guatemalan Population* (Boca Raton: University Presses of Florida, 1982), 182.

46. Michael R. Haines, Roer C. Avery, and Michael A. Strong, "Differences in Infant and Child Mortality and Their Change over Time: Guatemala, 1959–1973," *Demography* 20: 609–620 (1983).

47. Gery W. Ryan and Romero Martínez, "Can We Predict What Mothers Do? Modeling Childhood Diarrhea in Rural Mexico," *Human Organization* 55: 37–48 (1996).

48. Latin American Center, *Statistical Abstract* (1995), 165.

49. David H. Hojman, "Neoliberal Economic Policies and Infant and Child Mortality: Simulation Analysis of a Chilean Paradox," *World Development* 17(1): 93–108 (1989).

50. Thomas W. Merrick, *Population Pressures in Latin America* (Washington, D.C.: Population Reference Bureau, 1991).

51. George Martine, "Volume, Characteristics, and Consequences of Internal Migration in Colombia," *Demography* 12: 193–208 (1975).

52. Milton da Mata et al., *Migrações Internas no Brasil* (Rio de Janeiro: Instituto de Planejamento Econômico e Social, 1973).

53. Wouter Hoenderos and Wim de Regt, "Migración y Ciudad Intermedia: Hildalgo del Parral, Mexico," *Revista Paraguaya de Sociologiá* 24: 86–106 (1987).

54. Michael J. Greenwood, Jerry R. Ladman, and Barry S. Siegel, "Long-Term Trends in Migratory Behavior in a Developing Country: The Case of Mexico," *Demography* 18: 369–388 (1981).

55. Joan M. Herald, "Female Migration in Chile: Types of Moves and Socioeconomic Characteristics," *Demography* 16: 257–275 (1979).

56. Naomar de Almeida-Filho, "The Psychosocial Costs of Development," *Latin American Research Review* 17(3): 91–118 (1982).

57. Nora Hamilton and Norma Soltz Chinchilla, "Central American Migration: A Framework for Analysis," *Latin American Research Review* 26(1): 75–110 (1991).

58. Vicente Vasquez-Presidio, *Estadísticas Históricas Argentinas*, vol. 2 (Buenos Aires: Ediciones Nacchi, 1976), 30.

59. James D. Rudolph et al., *Argentina: A Country Study*, 3d. ed. (Washington, D.C.: U.S. Government Printing Office, 1986), 105.

60. Ricardo Torrealba, "Mercados de Trabajo y Migraciones Laborales entre Colombia y Venezuela en el Contexto de la Crísis Venezolana," in *Las Migraciones Laborales Colombo-Venezolanas*, ed. Gabriel Bidegain Greising (Caracas: Editorial Nueva Sociedad, 1987), 121–147.

61. A. Pellegrino, "Colombian Immigrants in Venezuela," in *The Impact of International Migration on Developing Countries*, ed. Reginald Appleyard (Paris: Organization for Cooperation and Development, 1989).

62. Alcides Gómez Jiménez and Luz Marina Díaz, "Las Perspectivas de la Migración en el Contexto de la Crísis Económica: La Experiencia Colombo Venezolana," in *Migraciones Internacionales en las Americas*, ed. Ricardo Torrealba (Bogotá: Centro de Estudios sobre Desarrollo Económico, 1988), 65–79.

63. Tomás Palau Viladesau, "Modificación de Patrones Migratorios y Movilidad Transfronteriza en el Paraguay," *Revista Paraguaya de Sociología* 31(90): 113–128 (1994).

64. David Rock, "Ideas, Immigrants et alia in Nineteenth- and Twentieth-Century Argentina," *Latin American Research Review* 29(1): 172–183 (1994).

65. Jonas Widgren, "Movements of Refugees and Asylum Seekers: Recent Trends in Comparative Perspective," in *Organization for Economic Cooperation and Development* (Paris: OECD, 1993), 87–95.

66. *Population Newsletter*, June 1991, 6.

67. Robin Kirk, *The Decade of Chaowa: Peru's Internal Refugees* (Washington, D.C.: American Council for Nationalities Service, 1991).

68. Robert A. Pastor, "U.S. Immigration Policy and Latin America: In Search of the 'Special Relationship,'" *Latin American Research Review* 19(3): 35–56 (1984).

69. Judith Adler Hellman, *Mexico in Crisis*, 2d. ed. (New York: Holmes & Meier, 1983), 108–112.

70. Jorge Durand and Douglas S. Massey, "Mexican Migration to the United States: A Critical Review," *Latin American Research Review* 27(2): 3–42 (1992).

71. Maria P. Fernandez-Kelly, *For We Are Sold, I and My People: Women and Industry in Mexico's Frontier* (Albany: State University of New York Press, 1983).

72. Richard G. Bach, "Migration in the 1990s," in *The United States and Latin America: Beyond the Cold War*, ed. Jonathan Harlyn (Chapel Hill: University of North Carolina Press, 1992), 262–281.

73. Dennis M. Hamratty and Sandra W. Meditz, eds., *Paraguay: A Country Study* (Washington, D.C.: U.S. Government Printing Office, 1990), 63.

74. United Nations Fund for Population Activities, *Inventory of Population Profiles in Developing Countries of the World, 1988–89* (The Hague: Mouton, 1990).

75. World Population Data Sheet (1996).

76. Collver, *Birth Rates*, 13–14.

77. World Population Data Sheet (1996).

78. Latin American Center, *Statistical Abstract* (1995), 192.

79. Robert Costanza, "The Ecological Economics of Sustainability: Investing in Natural Capital," in *Population, Technology, and Lifestyle*, ed. Robert Goodland et al. (Washington, D.C.: Island Press, 1992), 106–118.

80. David S. Palmer, "'Fujipopulism' and Peru's Progress," *Current History* 95(February): 70–75 (1996).

81. Samuel H. Preston, "The Social Sciences and the Population Problem," in *Demography as an Interdiscipline*, ed. J. Mayone Stycos (New Brunswick, N.J.: Transaction Publishers, 1989), 1–26.

82. Merrick, Population Pressures, 37–40.

83. Gilberto Loyo, *La Política Demográfica de México* (Mexico, D.F.: Editorial La Impresora, 1935).

84. Peter McDonough and Amancy de Souza, *The Politics of Population in Brazil* (Austin: University of Texas Press, 1981), 33–34.

85. Centro Americano de Demografía, *Docencia en Población en América Latina* (Santiago: CEPAL, 1989).

86. Brenda D. Townes et al., "Birth-Planning Values and Decisions: Preliminary Findings," in *Population Psychology: Research and Educational Issues*, ed. Sidney H. Newman and Vaida D. Thompson (Washington, D.C.: Center for Population Research, 1976), 113–130.

87. Peter J. Donaldson and Amy Ong Tsui, *The International Family Planning Movement* (Washington, D.C.: Population Reference Bureau, 1990), 20.

88. Latin American Center, *Statistical Abstract* (1995), 195.

89. W. Parker Mauldin and Sheldon J. Segal, "Prevalence of Contraceptive Use: Trends and Issues," *Studies in Family Planning* 19(6): 57–65 (1985).

90. Charles F. Westoff, "International Population Policy," *Society* 32(4): 11–15 (1995).

91. Susana Novick, *Política y Población: Argentina 1970–1989* (Buenos Aires: Centro Editorial de América Latina, 1992), 29–31.

92. Jorge Wilhelm, "Metropolitización y Medio Ambiente," in *Estilos de Desarrollo y Medio Ambiente en América Latina*, ed. Oswaldo Sunkel and Nicolo Griglo (Mexico, D.F.: Fondo de Cultura Económica, 1986), 9–40.

93. Richard J. Tobin, "Environment, Population, and Development in the Third World," in *Environment Policy in the 1990s: Toward a New Agenda*, ed. Norman J. Vig and Michael E. Kraft (Washington, D.C.: CQ Press, 1990), 279–300.

94. Cheryl Simon Silver and Ruth S. Defreis, *One Earth, One Future: Our Changing Global Environment* (Washington, D.C.: National Academy Press, 1990), 118–119.

95. Emilio F. Moran, "Human Adaptive Strategies in Amazonian Blackwater Ecosystems," *American Anthropologist* 93: 361–373 (1991).

96. John Stewart and Holm Tiessen, "Grasslands into Deserts?" in *Planet Under Stress*, ed. Constance Mungall and Digby J. McLaren (Toronto: Oxford University Press, 1991), 188–208.

97. Martine, "Volume, Characteristics, and Consequences," 192.

98. John O. Browder, "Deforestation and the Environmental Crisis in Latin America," *Latin American Research Review* 30(3): 123–137 (1995).

99. Thomas K. Rudel, "When Do Property Rights Matter? Open Access, Informal Social Controls, and Deforestation in the Ecuadorian Amazon," *Human Organization* 54: 187–194 (1995).

100. María Pilar García, "The Venezuelan Ecology Movement: Symbolic Effectiveness, Social Practices, and Political Strategies," in *The Making of Social Movements in Latin America*, ed. Arturo Escobar and Sonia E. Alvarez (Boulder, Colo.: Westview Press, 1992), 150–170.

101. Loraine Donaldson, *Fertility Transition: The Social Dynamics of Population Change* (Cambridge, Mass.: Basil Blackwell, 1991), 179–181.

102. Celso Furtado, "Underdevelopment: To Conform or Reform," in *Pioneers in Development: Second Series*, ed. Gerald M. Meier (New York: Oxford University Press, 1987), 205–227.

103. Donaldson, *Fertility Transition*, 199.

104. Latin American Center, *Statistical Abstract* (1995), 199.

Chapter 4

People and the Land

Less than one-third (29% in 1995) of Latin America's population is classified as rural.[1] Similarly, over one-fourth of the workers work on the land in one form or another as their principal occupation. Rural poverty is reported to be worse than urban poverty; income levels and welfare have deteriorated since the 1960s.[2] Cities are growing faster than the countryside, as has generally been true of human society since the classical civilizations of the Mediterranean. This urban pressure places demands on the agricultural sector which it is not always prepared to meet. The higher birthrate of the hinterland provides labor for trade, industry, and the civil service. Even for rural areas, population in Latin America is increasing at the rate of more than 1 percent per year, in spite of massive migration to the city.

As we have seen, populated areas, both rural and urban, are a small portion of the land expanse of the Western Hemisphere. A mere 5 percent of Latin America is cultivated, and if we include pasturage, only 25 percent of the total land surface has any relation to agriculture. The agricultural product is not keeping pace with the needs of the people. Ferment toward change and revolution is as much a product of the rural social system as of forces in the city. Even after implementation of land reform programs, more than 60 percent of the rural population in most countries are without land. In Mexico, which has had an agrarian reform program for some sixty years, more than half of the peasants are still landless. In 1940, with a population of twenty million, nearly all eligible peasants acquired land, but by 1990 the population had grown more than fourfold. Acquisition of land remains a major political goal.[3]

In other words, despite development in the urban sector, agriculture in Latin America remains largely in a semicolonial status. The area supplies food and raw material for Europe and, to a lesser extent, for North America, a relationship comparable to the one between the South and North in the United States during the last century. Manufactured items are imported in limited amounts from developed areas, with little effect on Latin America's own technology.

It is relevant to look at the agricultural systems of Latin America from the perspective of economic theories. One is *structuralism* and its emphasis on relationships between technology and productivity and on rigidities in the land tenure. Closely related is *dependency* theory, including the idea of internal colonialism and the history of import substitution. Another economic viewpoint is the hypothesis of an inverse relationship between farm size and productivity.[4]

In this chapter, besides looking at the problem of land tenure, I shall also examine types of agricultural systems and their respective technology and the arrangement of work statuses accompanying the hacienda system and its variants. This relationship leads us into the discussion of settlement patterns and the social values of peasants. I then turn to the political mobilization of the rural scene and the need for agrarian reform. Finally, I assess the rural situation in the context of the larger society.

THE HACIENDA SYSTEM AND ITS VARIANTS

Well into this century a dominant feature of rural life was the hacienda and its peculiar brand of feudalism. Historically, a kind of dependence and loyalty still characterizes the relationship between *patrón* and peon. Also, a form of solidarity evolved into an "open triangle." The openness refers at the base of the triangle to the lack of horizontal bonds between peasants, yet they are bound by economic and other needs to their landlord. This triangle is a kind of zero-sum game.[5] This model represents a pattern of uneven exchange based on power and coercion.

Even in relatively democratized countries, such as Costa Rica, remnants of latifundio remain. In Mexico, the system had immense economic and social implications, and despite the changes brought on by the Revolution, wealthy landowners remain today—not without their political influence. Until the fall of Díaz, peons who tilled the soil were confined to the hacienda. All decisions affecting their livelihood were subject to the will of the owner. The hacienda was self-sufficient, producing for its own needs; but because of the concern with profits surpluses found their way into the domestic or foreign market. The hacienda operated as a social system. That is, one or more villages might be found in the hacienda, isolated from the regional and national arena.

This system may be compared with the collectivized, if sharply hierarchical, ordering of agriculture in pre-Columbian civilizations. In the case of the Aztecs, the *calpulli*, or clans, had lands which were not individually owned but belonged to the clan as a whole, in addition to community fields of the village as owned by several clans. Before the Conquest, members of the nobility acquired rights to large landholdings—a fundamental change from the social order characterizing the early Aztecs.

The Aztecs and particularly the Incas made efficient use of the land with irrigation, crop rotation, and fertilizers. The system of land tenure and the type of control imposed from above facilitated the transfer of ownership from the New World priesthood and nobility to the Spanish conquistadors. The authoritarian structure of these empires was nearly ideal for the Spanish to impose their own version of feudalism, even though it had—unlike the Aztecs or Incas—capitalist overtones in its search for wealth.

The origin of the hacienda derives from the *encomienda* system as practiced in Spain and Portugal. In the New World, an important aspect of the *encomienda* was the right of the owner to use the indigenous population as labor. As approved by the Crown, Cortés and Pizarro distributed the holdings (land and Indians) of the native empires to their men, reserving large tracts for themselves. Cortés had claim to a concession of some 25,000 square miles, with a total of 115,000 people.[6] Sizeable tracts were even given to lesser members of these military expeditions, and small tracts (*caballerías* and *peonías*) were awarded the cavalry and foot soldiers.

In Peru, Pizarro lavishly bestowed *encomiendas* on his officers, a practice later forbidden by royal decree. In the late sixteenth century, recognition came to the *ayllus* of the Inca in the dense population of the Peruvian highlands, a number of native villages being relegated to the status of *reducciones*. At the same time, *comunidades* were recognized, encompassing many of the lands belonging to the Indians. The distribution of plots to family heads resembled the traditional Inca system. Indians still paid royal tribute and were subject to the *mita*, or forced labor. By 1550, Indians came under the *repartimiento*, a contract specifying hours and other conditions of labor, naturally to the advantage of the Europeans.[7]

By the nineteenth century, at least three basic agricultural tenure systems were firmly established. One, the hacienda—known variously as *fazenda* (Brazil), *estancia* (Argentina), *fundo* (Chile), *finca* (parts of Central America)—arose from the *encomienda*. The local community or hacienda itself consumed the cereals, beef, and occasional horticultural products, but as mining operations and urban life became established, a wider distribution occurred and exports were allotted to the nation and beyond. The pattern did not basically change until the middle of the twentieth century. With respect to the Peruvian scene, at least, the "community-hacienda model" functioned as an effective expression of "solidarity, cooperation, and consensus," or it could be interpreted as the system of an outdated elite exploiting the peasantry.[8]

The second type of the agricultural tenure system, the commercially-oriented *plantation*, had its origin in the Caribbean and Brazil, with commitment to an export market and slave labor. It extended to the lowlands of Middle America and the Andean countries, using indigenous labor, but this population resisted plantation work. Consequently, Africans were imported and a system of slavery survived into the nineteenth century. Plantations required a greater investment in capital and technology, but the hierarchical social system differed little from the hacienda. As the plantation represented more intensive agriculture, the settlement pattern in time became more concentrated. The owner lived in the *casa grande*, and to the rear a row of huts composed the slave quarters. As colonial society became more affluent and urbane, the owner might have a town house as well as the plantation house. Not until the twentieth century did the caste structure reach its twilight. As the "plantation complex" was primarily based on slavery, it could hardly survive beyond the nineteenth century. Indeed, the seeds of its destruction were in the democratic stirrings of the late eighteenth century.[9]

A third type of colonial agricultural system, the Indian *comunidades*, was usually found in the less productive areas, partly as a holdover of the indigenous land tenure.[10] These remained relatively free from Spanish occupation, as newcomers could not effectively control all areas under their domain. Other *comunidades* were relegated to the status of *reducciones* (designated and controlled areas or villages), where Indians were subject to work in the mines, or *obrajes*. Because of the severe conditions, many Indians in Peru chose to become laborers (*yanaconas*) on the haciendas. Certain *comunidades* were converted to municipal lands in which Indians had relatively freer range, but few completely escaped the labor draft.

Significant change occurred in the three systems during the first century after Independence.[11] Commercial farming appeared both in the more progressive haciendas and in the smaller plots belonging to Indians and mestizos. Crops became more diversified, and improvements in transportation and stabilization of economic life were achieved. In the middle of the twentieth century, rumblings about land reform stimulated changes in land tenure. Even the disintegration of some haciendas led to diversification, since new owners were forced to find different methods of cultivation or innovations in crops. Colonization, cooperatives, and other developments were to reshape, if only to a limited extent, the world of the peasant.

Because of its policy of forced labor, the hacienda system is generally described as feudalistic; yet, other observers of the system prefer to think of it as paternalistic. The sponsoring of fiestas was ritualized into an act of reciprocity, with their symbolic presentations of sacrifice, conflict, and renewal. For instance, mock fighting was balanced with interpersonal bonds such as the pseudo-kinship of the *compadrazgo* system. In other words, moral authority supplanted property relationships. At the same time, both sides had their defenses—the peasants could pilfer crops and the landlord could turn to violence to discipline rebellion.[12]

Patterns of Land Tenure

The hacienda system is, in reality, the dominant form of latifundio, the system brought from Rome through Spain and Portugal to the New World. The most obvious aspect of this latifundio is the extreme size of the holdings. For example, in Argentina, despite promises to urban workers, the anti-establishment fervor of Perón could not break this monopolistic situation. Another development is the frontier expansion, with massive colonization schemes, particularly in Brazil. Commercialization, technological input, and financial barriers to the small farmer have increased the size of holdings since 1970.[13]

The pattern of large estates extends from the Rio Grande to Patagonia. Most coffee production, which constitutes the major wealth of El Salvador, is from the *fincas* of some twenty families. At the southern tip of the continent, one Argentine–Chilean corporation owns one million hectares (a hectare is equal to 2.5 acres) with roughly the same number of sheep. In Brazil, 1.6 percent of owners control 37 percent of productive land, yet *fazendas* of under twenty hectares (or approximately fifty acres) account for half the nation's food crops.[14] Throughout Central America and the Andean countries, the latifundio is worked by sharecroppers or other variations of the *colono* system, only slightly different from the ancient Roman version.

What characterizes these large landholdings? The first characteristic is absentee ownership. Most owners spend only a few weeks or months per year in the *casa grande*. The need to enjoy urbane living, intervene in national politics, educate their children, travel abroad, and escape boredom all drive the owners to the capital or beyond—a villa or apartment in Lima *and* Paris, Buenos Aires *and* Rome, Cali *and* Miami. Second is supervision by an administrator, who runs the gamut from a professionally trained technician hired on a semipermanent basis to the constant turnover of a *mayordomo* on the more marginal estate. The system functions at the level one would expect of individual variations. The owners themselves have varying aspirations as to what productivity should be. A conservative rather than progressive outlook is common among large-scale owners, and consequently among administrators. Ownership and management are interlaced with other networks involving *caciques* (local chieftains), the patron–client relationship, and occasionally government intervention.[15] Third is extensive rather than intensive cultivation with a prodigious waste of land—with exceptions such as El Salvador and Puerto Rico. The fourth characteristic is a growing preference for export crops for cash profits, hopefully in foreign exchange, despite acute domestic needs for food. The fifth is a low rate of investment in capital equipment, crop cover, fertilizers, insecticides, and other improvements. Investment is usually directed abroad, or perhaps to the purchase of additional land, more recently in industrial enterprise. The final characteristic is road construction and transport focused on access to seaports. Connections with domestic market areas are neglected.

This feudalistic tenure system endures because of a number of factors, not least of which is the exploitation of the peasantry, and represents a pattern stretching from Central America into much of South America. The difficulty of securing land forced millions of campesinos into working for minimal wages. Attempts at unionization and forming cooperatives, as in the Amazon basin, have only marginal success.[16] Moreover, the landlord's monopoly of power finds its way into economic, political, and military coercion. The basic philosophy was well represented in Somoza's Nicaragua with its two aims for the economy: (1) the export of cash crops (which accounted for 70% of its GNP as compared to 10% in Mexico and 18% in Chile) and (2) a limited production of luxury goods for the upper class. Never was increasing the economic return or improving working conditions for the campesinos which would permit them to purchase manufactured goods among the options.[17]

The relationship of *patrón* and peon remains an unbalanced exchange, and often a violent one. Death squads have been documented since at least the 1970s, most notoriously in El Salvador and Guatemala, but also in other countries, including an advanced culture such as Uruguay.[18] Generally, such violent means usually are not necessary, as debt peonage or even sheer isolation renders the campesino powerless. In any event, as a national and an international economy emerged, the hacienda operation no longer operated as a discrete unit.

The Middle-Size Farm and Minifundio

If latifundia is the dominant form of land tenure, the family type of farm, usually between 30 and 100 acres depending on the type of farming, exists in several countries. These farms appeared mainly during the last century when land was cheap and where some variation of homesteading was available. They are still found, more often under conditions of political and economic stability. In Argentina, land acquisition was possible when tenants accumulated sufficient capital to purchase acreage from the owner, a process much more difficult after the turn of the century when the price of land, even when nonproductive, soared. The effectiveness of small- or middle-size farms is well documented. In several countries, they are reported to be at least three times more efficient in per capita food production than are the large ones.[19] Yet most countries, especially those to the political right, have little faith in the small, independent farmer, as was the case in Pinochet's Chile.[20]

Many middle-size farms are rented in parts of Argentina, Uruguay, and southern Brazil. In the state of São Paulo, sons of immigrants were able to lease land and maintain a standard of living significantly above the sharecropper level. A number of immigrant groups could buy land within a generation after their arrival, at least when the price of land was less prohibitive. The Japanese in São Paulo, the Italians in Mendoza in western Argentina, and the Germans in southern Chile represent models of the European farmer. In Cuba, two-thirds of all farms were under sixty-two acres prior to the Revolution.[21] The agrarian reform of the Castro regime has allowed this pattern of limited holdings to continue, if on a radically modified basis.

Various factors beyond the cost of land surround the question of farm size. Throughout Latin America, the gradual shift to mechanized farming requires a much larger unit in order to be efficient. This problem haunts land reform today, and some mix of the family plot and cooperative fields is one means of solving the dilemma. In this context, the question remains as to whether land becomes an end in itself or an instrumental value.[22] The independent farmer as well as the corporate entrepreneur are forced into a search for land, or the concept of the "moving frontier," as one finds on the Brazilian–Paraguayan border. But whether in settled or new areas, the risk of the choice of one or possibly two crops is often perilous.[23]

Only a minority of Latin America's rural population can be considered independent farmers. Perhaps four-fifths of the rural working population live either as wage workers on the haciendas or as sharecroppers who may also occupy tiny patches of land which dot the countryside. For others, the only contact with the land is their *chacra* or *parcela*. Even in a relatively advanced area such as Argentina, the size of farms varies widely. Small- and medium-size farms coexist with latifundio.[24]

Minifundio is the other side of latifundio. Indians and mestizos are relegated to less desirable hillsides and canyons, whereas the *hacendado* occupies the richer and more workable valleys and plateaus. In Latin America, 90 percent of the cultivated land belongs to 10 percent of the landholders, and 65 percent of all land is concentrated in 1.5 percent of the farms. The cause of this crazy quilt of small acreage alongside the basic system of the large estates is the product of several factors: (1) succession of family crises which lead to forced sale of properties; (2) necessity to subdivide holdings because of inheritance; (3) birthrate—the Maya in Guatemala illustrate how high fertility intensifies the trend to minifundio;[25] (4) squatters who occupy plots for subsistence purposes; and (5) erosion and soil depletion, which take their toll, shifting cultivation from one *parcela* to another. The more fortunate campesinos have solved the problem of minifundio by sharing two or three plots which together might mean efficient farming.

Costa Rica offers a somewhat more hopeful scenario than do the more regressive countries. Under legislative decree, land is more equitably distributed in order to reduce minifundio and squatting, discourage speculation in underutilized land, and raise food production. These measures have an ecological benefit as they reduce the movement of campesinos into *tierras baldías* (idle land).[26]

Commercialization and a Rural Proletariat

Industrialization usually threatens cash crops, export, and the hacienda system as well as minifundio. In several areas this process began in the nineteenth century, increased in the early twentieth century, and accelerated after 1950. Coffee production in Costa Rica is a case in point. After 1830, coffee production in Costa Rica was in high gear, as it was in El Salvador, Guatemala, and the state of São Paulo. After the revolution of 1948, Costa Rica, as with other countries, turned to import substitution.[27] The world price of coffee was dropping as production increased in Africa and other areas. Similarly, Mexico was giving less priority to agriculture. Many observers criticized this kind of search for profits as inimical to the individual farmer. Concern with an export market, failure to provide capital, and neglect of an infrastructure were viewed as violating the trust of the revolution.[28] For instance, Sinaloa farmers can make a profit twenty times greater by growing tomatoes for the U.S. market instead of producing corn for Mexico.[29] Reluctance about NAFTA in rural Michocán stems from the trend of U.S. companies to extend credit only to large-scale producers rather than peasant cooperatives.[30] In these commercial developments, the small operator and the local economy almost always lose.

This trend toward large-scale commercialization explains the increase in the size of land holdings since 1970, even though the public theme is land reform programs for the peasant. The well-connected entrepreneur can tap credit which is seldom available to the small operator. This tendency seems to be nearly universal in Latin America. A report from Goiás in Brazil indicates a growing polarization in the 1980s between *patrão* (boss) and *peão* (laborer), who are bound in a contractual and litigious relationship.[31] An analysis of the microeconomics of small farmers in three countries points to increased poverty as a result of a booming export market since the 1980s. In this process, a competitive market and the rising cost of land means more sharecroppers are driven from their occupation. Although the situation is perhaps worse in Chile and Paraguay than in Guatemala, the findings demand a shift in policy in all three.[32]

As Merilee Grindle sums up the change apparent by the 1970s as a "new dualism." For the small farmer there were "extension services, infrastructure, and green revolution technology." For the large commercial farmers there appeared "various forms of production aid, credit, and extension."[33] A species of modernization had come to the rural scene, if a generation after the city.[34]

LAND TENURE AND FARMING OPERATIONS

Two different concepts underlie the problem of land distribution. One refers to the arrangement of tenure statuses, that is, *who* owns the land. The other is the question of the *size* of individual units. Of course, these problems are related. Still, two different factors of agricultural efficiency and social justice must be considered in any discussion of the present and future of land policy. Land monopolies unhampered by taxes remained the basic wealth of the nation, until at least the 1960s. This situation was threatened by protest and even violence for more than a quarter of a century. To understand the real significance of land ownership, it is necessary to analyze the *types* of tenure.

The renter is typical of certain areas where migrants are unable to break into the inherited land tenure. Although renters may have their own equipment, more often they rent it from the owner or from a renting agency. Credit facilities are still more difficult for the renter than for the owner. In renting, farmers have little sense of permanency, nor can they make rational plans. No less serious, the tenant's earnings rarely rise above a subsistence income with few means of investing toward future purchase of the property. Neither tenant nor landlord is likely to make any long-term capital investments. Finally, the cost of land has risen at a higher rate than farm productivity.

Then there are the squatters. As land titles are not well-defined, the definition of what constitutes illegal land occupation is arbitrary. In most of Latin America, a person occupying unfenced land for a given period cannot legally be ejected by the owner. In several countries, as in Paraguay, a relaxed view toward property pervades, and if unused, land should accommodate as many individuals as can maintain a subsistence. From 1930 to 1950, conflicts over property rights in Colombia between *colonos* (sharecroppers and squatters) and large landowners became a matter of national controversy. As violence pervaded most of the countryside from 1949 to 1958, the problem of legal claims assumed secondary importance. Squatters' claims still surface in agrarian reform proposals.

Variations of Work Systems

In a broad sense, farm laborers or *peones* (*jornaleros* is another term for farm laborers on a wage basis) constitute a variant of farm operators, especially as they may have their own *chacra* (plot). In the agrarian hierarchy, exceptions occur, as with those *colonos* hiring migrating laborers for work on their own parcel.[35] The distinction between *colono* and peon is a dubious one. Together they represent nearly one-sixth of Latin America's population and have in common a very low standard of living. As the inheritors of the Roman *latifundium*, they may live their entire life on a hacienda or plantation. *Colonos* purchase goods at the company store (usually by a coupon or token issued by the hacienda) and worship at the hacienda chapel. Members of their families serve the household in a number of ways—the appropriate time, plot, and specific subsistence crop the peasant may plant are all determined by the patron.

Even today, the relation between tenancy, sharecropping, and wage earning is at the convenience of the *hacendado*. When the price of crops is high, the owner may pay wages and make a great profit, especially as minimum wage laws rarely apply to agricultural labor. When the market is poor, owners prefer sharecropping in order to share their loss with colonos or peons. Almost all sharecroppers are likely to hire out during the slack season for wages or other types of remuneration—food for their family or a chance to find work for their children. Incurring of debts often makes the sharecropper, or for that matter the hired worker or tenant, obligated to his patron for years to come. In Brazil, the soaring land values of the 1970s curtailed the degree of sharecropping as wage labor became the norm. An examination of rural workers in Morelos, Mexico, found no sharecroppers; 53.5 percent were laborers; the remainder were small landowners or members of the *ejido*, a collective farm.[36] With the emergence of "agribusiness" in various areas, sharecropping has become one more phase of extension service. Extension agents may be part of a governmental aid operation, but more often they are provided by private firms, as a study in the highlands of Ecuador reveals.[37]

A more enlightened policy on the part of proprietors could raise the level of the *colono* and others who work the farm. Aid programs, whether from internal or international sources, can effect change in credit, technology, and marketing, but institutional impediments usually remain.[38] Productivity improves as workers are given incentives. For example, a Brazilian landowner in some areas provides land, money, water, and half the seed and buys the *colono's* product at the going price. Not until 1947 did Peru adopt legislation for the protection of both *yanacona* (the local term for *colono*) and owner. Under this Law of Yanaconaje, all contracts are written and the *yanacona* are free to sell their product in the market of their choice and be compensated for any labor rendered the proprietor. But the law is seldom enforced. With variations, this system exists in most Andean countries and Middle America, except where agrarian reform has led to adjustments. Exploitation was particularly severe in Bolivia, where in 1950 4 percent of the owners controlled 95 percent of the land. Mainly the Indians were exploited, but conditions improved marginally after the Revolution of 1952.[39] This situation is preferable in Chile, where *inquilinos* (tenants) are allowed grazing privileges on the *hacendado's* pastures.

Sharecroppers and agricultural laborers seldom find a solution to their dilemma. *Sertenejos* in Brazil may migrate to the South for higher wages, but should it be a good year in the Northeast, they may do better at sharecropping and selling the product at current market prices, which go further in an area of lower living cost than the wages they would receive in the South. In the more backward areas of several countries, they do not have this choice. Caught in the necessity of *colono* status, they hire out in their free hours or full time during the harvesting season to the landlord or another *hacendado*, receiving possibly the only cash they see during the entire year. Most of the year they grow subsistence crops of corn, manioc, or beans. Their sons may find little work as mechanization proceeds and eventually migrate to the newer areas of the country or follow the trek to the city. Increasingly, farm families depend on off-farm income, usually in the form of migration of males to other agricultural areas or to the city. Consequently, the responsibility for labor falls ever more on the female.[40]

Not all Latin American farmers fit into precise categories. As one instance, Indian *comunidades* still have their adherents who are primarily oriented toward cultivation on an extended family basis. As another development, especially since the 1950s, colonization schemes are generally of two types: One is the colony resulting from the opening up of an area of swamp clearance, a new irrigation system, or some other large-scale, government supported project. The other follows the nationalization or expropriation of a hacienda; the land can be opened to colonization by former *colonos* or a group of migrants, as provided by the agrarian reform law. The distribution of land varies from middle- to small-size family farms or is organized as a type of collective farming or a combination of the two. European and other colonists have practiced collective agriculture since the nineteenth century. Northern Mexico was the scene of several colonization projects for dissident religious sects—Mormons from the United States, Mennonites from Canada, and Molokoners from Russia. Colonization has been greatly implemented in the postwar world, although still largely as pilot projects.

AGRICULTURE, TECHNOLOGY, AND THE WORKER

Latin American agriculture is a fusion of New World and Old World methods. Spain was dependent on the hoe and rudimentary plow. Despite their advanced techniques of cultivation, the Inca and other pre-Colombian civilizations did not offer much better tools. However, the colonizers only partially adopted the sophisticated methods of irrigation and erosion control practiced by their vassals. Even today, the digging stick and the machete remain as principal tools on the mountainsides for the peasant on a precarious *chacra*. The hoe continues as a basic tool; the wooden plow has been giving way to one of steel.

Special methods of cultivation are adopted to regional needs. A prevalent method in tropical areas is the slash-and-burn, or the *roza*, system. This method of clearing generally occurs toward the end of the dry season in March or April for southern Mexico and Central America and during the opposite months in the Southern Hemisphere. The undergrowth is cut away by machete and trees are felled by axe, after which the area is burned. It is an inefficient process, despite the labor saved in clearing and killing weeds and noxious insects. The greatest drawback is the destruction of the humus and topsoil, which is followed by a leaching from the tropical rains. In order to allow for soil restoration, the farmer moves on to another area as the plots must be abandoned for three to four years, far short of the ideal of ten to fifteen years. Other problems associated with the *roza* system are unintentional burning of areas and hillside erosion and floods that only further complicate the problem of land shortage. Even though burning kills various kinds of parasites and aids nitrogen mineralization, erosion is the result. But the *roza* is the only system that makes sense to a peasant without modern equipment. Corn, beans, manioc, and squash—the staples of life—have been raised by this system for generations. Another primitive method is the riverbank system of irrigation. Because of the annual rise and fall of the river, inundation of the floodplain along the Amazon and, to a lesser extent, the São Francisco River in Brazil is widespread. Various tropical areas are adapted to flooding for the cultivation of rice—a basic part of the Latin American diet.

Mechanization has made a number of areas productive; for instance, the cotton culture on the Pacific Coast of Central America. These projects have brought a movement of people from the highlands to the once desolate and unusable lowlands. Mechanization, beginning with windmills and reapers and advancing to tractors and combines, made possible the enormous wheat production of the Argentine pampa. It is a slow process and barely perceptible in most countries. The South of Brazil only reached in the 1970s the stage of development of the American Deep South in the late 1930s, but this statement must be qualified by the usual caveat in regard to local variations. It is debated whether mechanization of farming, which has only appeared in the more progressive regions, is worthwhile in view of its threat to farm labor, already a surplus commodity. For most *colonos* and small landowners, the choice of tractor or advanced plow becomes an academic matter as long as the campesino is forced into marginal lands. The technological decision is made regardless of the pattern of land ownership or tenancy.

Developmental Programs

Government aid programs and nongovernment organizations (NGOs), whether foreign or domestic, occasionally attempt to introduce new techniques to the farmer. Often the goal is to move from the low surplus productivity to commercial agriculture. For instance, in Minas Gerais a study of peasant participation in the Rural Development Program initiated in 1980 focuses on such problems as land concentration and the transition from a familistic economy to wage labor. Strategies include means of decision making and cooperation in several ventures, ranging from the purchase and use of tractors to the role of unions. Success depends on local factors and the effectiveness of the particular leader or of the team trying to affect change or create a community consensus. Obvious limits are imposed by the lack of resources as well as the clash between capitalist and peasant demands.[41]

Community development assumes various forms. One is the effort to establish community stores in order to enhance local feelings of belonging and cooperation, provide better and cheaper food, and introduce rationalized marketing operations. These goals stand in contrast to the traditional company- or family-run enterprise. Also, the success—or failure—of the project is related to the size of the community.[42] In a broader context, the improvement of rural institutions can come through community action, as in the work of the Colombian sociologist Orlando Fals Borda and his team providing education and morale-building, decision-making, and planning techniques. Five communities in Mexico, Colombia, and Chile reached higher levels of food production than they had before the arrival of the change agents, which illustrates the effectiveness of a grassroots approach. For instance, in El Cerrito in northern Colombia 120 families were unable to defend their rights in the collective use of the 2,500 acres the Colombian Institute of Agrarian Reform (INCORA) had awarded them. As advisors recruited from rural organizations in the region worked with committees from the collective, pressure on relevant government agencies was intensified. In other words, the change process involved consciousness-raising along with coordination of the internal and external relations of the community.[43]

Community development may take a variety of forms. Occasionally, a shift in the economy has positive effects. A comparison of two neighboring communities in western Guatemala revealed a more progressive attitude as agricultural production moved toward a national rather than a local market. Acquisition of entrepreneurial skills, exposure to the Spanish language, and conversion to Protestantism were also evident.[44]

Work Patterns

For peasants who remain in the hacienda tradition, work obligations involve a specific employer–employee or landowner–tenant relationship. The *patrón* and the *colono* have a reciprocal obligation set by tradition. The Bolivian arrangement is reminiscent of the Peruvian pattern described earlier and still remains in many sectors. The *patrón* must furnish each *colono* a plot of cultivable land (*sayana*) on which he can build a house with what materials are available. The parcel is demarcated for different crops: barley, potatoes, and corn. The *patrón* must provide pasture rights for that area not under cultivation, and the plot must be large enough to accommodate some livestock, at least a donkey or an ox. Likewise, the *colono* has certain irrigation rights if the water is not needed by the *patrón*.

Subsistence agriculture has the minimal consolation of self-employment, but the hired worker, especially if a migrant, is traditionally considered as lowest of all *agricultores*. Working for someone else is somehow undignified, but norms are changing; outside employment is more common. Moreover, work in the field is usually a family affair. The wife's tasks overlap with those of the husband in the exhausting process of planting, weeding, cultivating, and harvesting, depending on the crop and the locality. Separate roles can be assigned; in the Amazon basin, the man is responsible for clearing the field under the *roza* system, but the planting is shared between the spouses.

Group labor is found in most agricultural areas, if to a decreasing extent over the last generation. The nature of most primitive economies depends on reciprocal labor of one variety or another as illustrated in more backward agricultures. Reciprocal or group labor has given way to wage labor, but a number of enterprises still depend on cooperative work, either on a reciprocal or exchange basis. For example, the slash-and-burn operation and house construction are group activities. Another variation is on the Brazilian *fazenda*, where squatters offer a day's work for use of the land.

Reciprocal labor can be either exchange or festive. *Exchange* presumes an equal amount of labor to be shared between the two parties, whereas with *festive* labor the host provides food and drink as a part of the payment. Festive labor is designed to meet a special need, such as building a house in the Colombian village of Aritama—always an occasion for merrymaking and joking. In addition, the occasion offers the opportunity to break down old feuds; a personal enemy may use the occasion to indicate his willingness to end the hostility. Refusing to participate is the peasants' means of making known their desire to continue the animosity.[45] In the Peruvian Amazon, exchange labor is primarily used in emergencies or for irregular tasks. Peasants must consider a number of inputs in the decision to go beyond family members for their labor needs. Exchange labor is preferred to festive because of such costs as feeding the workers. In the case of cash crops, wage earners or *jornaleros* are generally chosen.[46]

Festive labor or work parties often introduce a kind of competition, but more stress is on the aspects of social participation. Music and dancing may climax the project of the work party. Also, unpleasant tasks are less forbidding when performed in a group setting. But inflation takes its toll; festive labor declines with the cost of food and liquor, which have risen at a higher rate than the cost of labor. Yet, the ability to provide these commodities can be a means of status.

Exchange labor continues to function when it is mutually agreeable to two parties; it is, of course, not gratuitous since, as with any service, it must be returned in kind. With increased commercialization of crops, most laborers prefer payment in wages. But exchange and festive labor cater to the needs of heavier labor loads, as during the harvest season. The survival of reciprocal labor in Latin America emphasizes its Gemeinschaft character and isolation from urban bureaucratic processes. Exchange of labor also implies a position of equality between peasants.

Unions and the Changing Nature of Peasantry

With commercialization and industrialization of agriculture, unionization of the peasantry becomes an intermittent or unstabilized reality. In most countries, unions have an ambivalent status depending on the political climate, democracies being more hospitable than authoritarian regimes. The case of Costa Rica is one variation. As democracy evolved after the quiet revolution of 1948, unions advanced and receded in the wake of governmental shifts. Co-optation is a recurrent theme. Landless peasants hoped for the benefits of agrarian reform, but the Instituto de Desarrollo Agrario (agrarian development) failed to deliver. Direct action by land invasion was the peasants' answer. In the 1980s, the Unión de Pequeños Agricultores (Union of Small Farmers) arrived at a rather cozy arrangement with the government. Consequently, when demands and grievances were not met the most successful stance became one of *crisis creation*, with highway blockages as one form of dislocation.[47] In some instances, tolerance of unions is a means of forestalling land reform. At least in Mexico, where agrarian reform has been a rallying cry since the Revolution, promises are more evident than achievements. Unions are a key instrument of the PRI, which severely limits their bargaining power for land or wages. Government interest in the campesino fluctuates widely—strong support by Cárdenas in the 1930s, López Mateos in the 1960s, and Echeverría in the mid-1970s, but lip service has been the reality for most of the postwar period. By the 1980s, even the rhetoric virtually disappeared, as we shall see later in the chapter. Social welfare, especially for the urbanites, replaced social justice for the peasants.

Peasantry in developing nations is becoming increasingly proletarian. Whereas historically peasants focused on their family and their land, the rural worker of today, at least in Latin America, is forced to migrate periodically or permanently and is oriented predominantly by wages.[48] The virtual removal of the peasants from the marketing process and their loss of feelings of belonging to a given community are indices of partial or complete disorganization as regional and national economies are modernized.[49]

THE SOCIAL WORLD OF THE CAMPESINO

It has long been known that the rural person belongs to a parochial and structured world. Early in this century, Ferdinand Toennies conceptualized the Gemeinschaft and Gesellschaft models to account for the differences between the rural and urban universe. Sociologists have adopted still other distinctions; for instance, the sacred and secular, traditional and rationalistic. To some extent, Durkheim's concept of mechanistic and organic societies hinges on this paradigm.[50] Compared to the urban environment, the rural, as implied in Chapter 2, shows greater familism, restricted cognitive structures, orientation toward the past, and boundary maintenance. These characteristics are documented for a number of transitional societies. The "particularistic-ascriptive attributes" of Latin American culture hinge on domination of the rural elements in its historical development. Orientation to family, kin, and the village or hacienda is a product of a static, nonurban society, one now undergoing extensive, if somewhat abrasive, change. Innovations in methods of cultivation, food habits, and medical aid all show resistance to change, much as they did in the remainder of Western culture a century ago.

Since the level of living, education, circulation of mass media, and access to the city have differentiating effects, some observers have reservations as to whether the rural–urban dichotomy has validity in view of the urban penetration of the hinterland; yet even in North America differences are found between town and country.[51] The boundary is sharper in Latin America, where the agricultural scene displays different kinds of social organization. We have already noted the influence of the type of land distribution—the family-size farm as opposed to latifundio. For instance, because of its rigid stratification, the hacienda community places less importance on education than does a community of small landholders. It is difficult to assess to what degree the campesino is or is not adjusted to this traditional social structure, but migration to the city points to the dysfunctionality of rural life, both in material resources and lifestyle.

In view of the background of Hispanic-American civilization, both Old World and indigenous features, feelings of isolation—and hostility—

are predictable. In the case of Mexico, at the time of Díaz, haciendas were autonomous structures in which peasants could hardly consider any item they touched as their own. Most communal lands and native Indian villages which survived the colonial period and early republic eventually passed into the hands of large landowners. The situation changed, but a corporate structure replaced the *hacendado*. Whether in the "old" or the "new" rural society, peasants cannot escape the knowledge that the locus of control lies beyond them.[52]

These conditions can produce negativism or, more likely, a stoical outlook toward the world, but individual reactions are not always predictable. Further, the routine of work and bleakness is broken by fiestas and *chiche* (a cheap liquor). Fiestas follow or surround crisis events, marriage, birth, and death as well as the day of the patron saint. In the highlands of Morelos, Mexico, fiestas and an occasional carnival provide a means of social solidarity and relief from monotony and frustration, but they also relate to the agricultural cycle—the beginning and end of the rainy period, cajoling the gods to protect the crops from either deficient or excessive storm, and so on. The fiesta, as implied in the discussion of festive labor, represents reciprocity and the exchange of goods and indirectly fosters a degree of community solidarity.[53] Fiestas, particularly in the Andes, also assume a mystical significance in integrating human beings and their life cycle with the processes of nature, notably fertility and the assurance of crops.[54]

Peasants display a remarkable capacity for tolerating the impossible. For instance, an anthropologist reports that in the aftermath of the 1970 earthquake at Callejón de Huaylas in the Peruvian Andes, tragedy was somewhat eased by various adaptive techniques—mutual aid and even an improvised sense of humor.[55] Moreover, peasants are not necessarily "conservative inhibitors of change," but can make rational decisions regarding ecological and societal changes around them, as an intensive study of Quinua in Ayacucho, Peru, shows.[56] In this community, new labor techniques, education, and the advent of Protestantism were among the change agents.

Still, apathy, intransigence, and final resignation remain. In Costa Rica and El Salvador, I studied attitudes about the present and past along with projections toward the future. A somewhat stoical if pessimistic attitude was expressed by most respondents. Farmers, no less than other occupational groups, reflected the ambivalent feeling toward work found throughout Latin America. In many villages, physical labor is associated with poverty. "Successful" persons, in this case, farm owners, have others perform their work for them. In other words, they have the good fortune (*la suerte*) to manipulate others. This categorization was reflected in my El Salvador study of attitudes toward upward mobility. To the question "What is most important to ensure success in life, being lucky or working hard?" the rural sample selected "being lucky," whereas the urban middle class sample was more inclined to choose "work" and the urban lower class sample was uncertain. In El Salvador, only one-fourth of the villagers and campesinos thought the world would be a "happier place in twenty years" (26% as compared to 43% in the urban sample). Daily wages at less than a subsistence margin, high infant mortality, and lack of political demographic processes were tacitly accepted as the nature of things, as one interviewee expressed, *"lo que Díos manda"* ("it is God's will"). If internal protest was felt, it was not overt, as it was not healthy to verbalize discontent outside the confines of the anonymous— and superficially democratic—atmosphere of the city. The rural Costa Rican sample showed less passivity, but in both countries the urban population was less inclined toward fatalism and resignation.

This sense of isolation and apathy is changing somewhat in view of greater mobility through better communication, transportation, and sociopolitical movements. A no less important issue is how to improve rural schools. Finally, television is introducing urbanism. In Brazil, this innovation acculturates tribal groups as well as the general rural population, with a marginal impact on political consciousness.[57]

Isolation, Locality, and Settlement Patterns

Dispersion of settlements in rural life with a minimum of interpersonal contact can be isolating, yet the norms are less confusing than those in the urban realm. A variety of labels exist in the designation of groupings identified within the rural scene. Classification of locality can be made on the basis of social relationships, as applied to Argentine farmers: (1) neighborhood with fairly close interpersonal contacts, (2) trade centered in the community, village, or small town with various social networks, and (3) an open dispersal of association with little interpersonal orientation—houses being too widespread to constitute a neighborhood or a well-defined community.[58] *Estancias* engaged in livestock production could conceivably constitute any one of these three types as determined by the size of the estate. Cereal farming, horticulture, and sugar plantations represent somewhat smaller units, occasionally constituting a village. More often, farm dwellings are dispersed as in the United States.

A survey of several Latin American countries suggests a threefold classification as based on ecological considerations, more related to Western cultural patterns. First, as a major settlement type in Europe, the *village* only partially took root in the New World. The agricultural village developed where indigenous influences remained or where houses were grouped at some distance from the *casa grande* on the hacienda. In certain areas undergoing agrarian reform, the *collective*, or aggregations of people and land, is larger than a farm but smaller than a village.[59] Second, the *line* village became accepted in Brazil as colonization programs favored this form of settlement. Elsewhere, line villages also took shape along transportation arteries or a natural boundary, likely a riverbank or lake front. Third, scattered farmsteads are the dominant form of settlement in Brazil, Argentina, Cuba, Paraguay, and most Andean countries. Only in parts of Middle America does this form give way to the village settlement. As in North America, farmers prefer to live on the land they cultivate, not least because it eliminates the problem of transportation from home to field. In view of the necessity of subduing a continent and clearing a terrain, the settlers preferred direct access and claim to their own lands.

As implied above, a recurring process throughout the Americas is frontier and colonization projects, spontaneous or planned. The Mexican government has organized a number of agricultural communities in connection with land reform. Most Andean countries have moved in this direction to varying degrees. With its vast lands to the west and north, along with its boom psychology, Brazil probably offers the most extensive array of colonies, some growing into cities, others abandoned as mines or crops fade out. Rivalries may occur, such as between a spontaneous colony and a government- or corporation-sponsored project.[60] The Cardoso government has not yet been able to end the violence the land- owners impose on landless families.[61]

Locality Groupings and Their Significance

In all human life, except perhaps for migratory peoples and frontier outposts, community affiliations appear. In most agrarian societies, twenty to forty families may constitute a community. Not least, this primary group includes mutual aid, as in the Brazilian work party, or *mutirão*. The homogeneity of occupation and lack of basic class differences favor a community spirit, despite the grouping of diverse strata from free farmers to peons. Evidence from Costa Rica points to an emergence of community in given villages, where residents are challenged by innovations in cultivation.[62]

Any classification of locality designations varies somewhat from country to country. Official designations most likely use the label *municipio*, something between the township and county concept, to describe administrative units. The head or center of each of these units is known as *cabecería municipal*, a term roughly equivalent to the county seat. Clusters in most municipios are designated according to size or to local jargon as *pueblo, aldea, villarrio*, and *caserío*. Above the municipio level is the state (*estado, provincia*, or *departamento*, depending on the usage in the particular country).[63] In many administrative aspects, the locality is responsible to the national government, which often fails to fulfill its legal obligations.[64] However, law enforcement, social services, and sometimes education are often on an ad hoc basis.

Resources in the *municipios* are frequently insufficient to make available essential services. One problem is the small size of the *municipio*, which often has a population of less than ten thousand, which means no secondary school, hospital, or credit union. Unfortunately, a clear cut designation between local and national authority is lacking.[65] Expansion of roads and vehicular traffic is another facet in this problem of the ineffectiveness of the *municipio*. Similar to the country government in the United States, the *municipio* is a cultural lag in the twentieth century. Most serious is underemployment in these primordial urban centers.

The Local Economy

The restricted economic life makes for a parochial village or small town. This situation is especially common in societies with large Indian populations, but a localized economy characterizes most of rural Latin America. The *casa grande* of Brazil, the village markets of Central America and the Andean nations, and the subsistence farmers of most countries document how remote the peasant is from the economic processes of the modern world. In fact, these peasant economies characterized Europe at the origin of Western capitalism. Can a peasant economy exist side by side with an industrial system? Not all authorities agree regarding the healthiness of this kind of a dual society. Yet in the marketplaces of southern Mexico, Guatemala, the Caribbean, and in most Andean nations, peasant and mercantile economies meet. As with the paternalistic hacienda, the market represents a primitive stage of capitalism.

The village market is transitional between the city and the barter economy of Latin America's indigenous and colonial past. The market is itself highly traditionalistic. In Mexico, for example, the precise day of the week for the market may be determined by Aztec or pre-Aztec customs. During the nineteenth century, regional markets in Peru involving both peasants and large-scale merchants with products ranging from textiles to liquors were well-developed.[66] Until the 1960s, each village had its specialty. Basic economic processes such as the law of supply and demand are readily observable, whether in Chichicastenango, Guatemala, or Otovalo, Ecuador. Bargaining is an established practice. In view of the limits of price controls, tax injunctions, and demands of the middle man, the market is more in the tradition of a free economy than is the operator of a retail store in town.

The market entrepreneur is usually a woman, who aside from her economic motives finds the market serving social and recreational functions. Escape from the *choza*, stimulation of the crowd, and fascination of the bargaining process are among the attractions. Despite a slim volume of trade, many women sit by their wares the entire day. Bargaining usually becomes more flexible toward the end of the day; the client may obtain her or his item at a lower price, sometimes with a bit of by-play in the negotiation.

As practiced in an Ecuadorian Andean village, bartering permits peasants to exchange one product for another in order to assure food for the family table. A peasant woman may buy a can of fish in one market, move to another market, and exchange it for an *arroba* of potatoes, finally exchanging it for sour oranges, which she sells singly at the corner of the square in another village. The public clearly distinguishes between articles for use and those for exchange value: "Any peasant makes a clear distinction between the economic sphere of family subsistence and the sphere of the market."[67] Exchange at the market is also conditioned by a number of networks, including both real and fictive kinship. A study of the marketplace in northeast Brazil found trust and reciprocity essential to the exchange process.[68]

The two economies, local and national, become more intimately associated if one judges by the display of items and invasion of tourist wares. At present, the marketplace can no longer escape factory products, whether *aguardiente*, patent medicines, matches, or fireworks, whether in Peru or Guatemala. Also, fluctuations in the international price of coffee, sugar, or wool are reflected in the amount of trade in the weekly market transactions. It is possible that the local market is slowly passing from the Latin American scene. As a carryover from the Mayan and Aztec past, it is continually caught in intraregional and national demands which are chipping away at its indigenous character. A study of the Guatemalan market scene shows that a number of vendors, males as much as females, are escaping their rural community. The capital city is perceived as too dangerous and the villages economically unrewarding. Consequently, a town such as Antigua might offer at least a precarious income with some social stimulation. Reciprocity with the other vendors may provide a meal, a room, or other services through a kind of barter.[69]

The economic universe of the peasant still reflects a background of a more primitive system of barter and at the same time a desire for independence. A money exchange is gradually evolving, but it is conditioned by the degree of politicization that exists and by the peasants' reluctance to simply exchange their serf-like position for one of being a wage proletarian. Most important, a monetary system has less symbolic value for them than for the urbanite. This attitude has been changing with the expansion of credit facilities, unionization, agricultural labor, urban contact, horizontal and vertical mobility, all of which emerged with the advent of agrarian reform, however incomplete the reform may be. Traditional patterns are giving way—irregularly, painfully, and somewhat violently and at quite irregular tempos in time and place—to rationalistic and secularized procedures.

AGRARIAN REFORM

Turning from land tenure, agricultural systems, and settlement patterns, we may examine the social values of campesinos and their feelings about certain aspects of social change. Changes in tenure and agricultural technology are fundamental for food production and its implications for demographic processes. In the final reckoning, food supply determines future levels of living and, indeed, human survival. Moreover, the economic return of the land is far below its potential, particularly when we realize that more than one-fourth of the working population in Latin American nations are engaged in agriculture.

The most articulate cry for reform often comes less from peasants than from city dwellers, especially the politicized. One reason for this anomaly is the lack of politicization of the peasant. Also, the urban housewife is aware of the rising cost of food brought on by the general spiral of inflation and by the shortage of agricultural products. The increase in population has sharpened the picture. Further, labor unions and the more militant political parties have compassion for the campesino, believing that once this concession is wrung from the elite, other kinds of reforms will be easier to obtain. Peasants are now more conscious of a number of pressures, among others, the scarcity of land and the necessity of dividing their property among their sons. Attitudes about given feudalistic practices have become more polarized.

The oligarchy meets this demand for land reform with an assortment of emotional resistance and threats. Consequently, land reform is a critical political issue in nearly all countries. Nearly every government has adopted land reform measures, whether implemented or not. Six countries (Bolivia, Chile, Cuba, Guatemala, Mexico, and Nicaragua) have turned at one time or another to revolutionary land policies. Since Mexico was the first of these, we will examine its history.

Mexico's Ejido System

Probably the Mexican Revolution of 1910 received its greatest impetus from the demand for land reform. Although Francisco Madero convinced the urban intelligentsia of the need for overthrowing Porfirio Díaz and democratizing Mexico, it was Emiliano Zapata who inflamed the peons with the cry for land. As a consequence, the 1917 Constitution provided for the distribution of land to peasants along the lines of the *ejido*. The *ejido*—an extension of the *comunidad* principle—was based on the collectivized agricultural communities of the Aztecs. Beginning in 1934, President Lázaro Cárdenas restored or granted more land than all his predecessors or successors. These lands were largely from expropriated haciendas as well as new lands brought under irrigation. More often they were in the north of the country or the extreme south; however, almost every state had its share of *ejidos*.

After World War II, the Mexican government favored industrialization and private agriculture, but in 1963 President López Mateos decided to strengthen colonization. Several projects were established in 1964 along the Gulf Coast in the state of Vera Cruz by which sale was made to some 700 families who had moved from the desert areas of the North. By 1969, nearly sixty million hectares had been distributed to 2,525,811 families, ten times more than the next most generous countries, Bolivia and Cuba.[70] The presidency of Luis Echeverría initiated a remarkable degree of rural social change as he rekindled the aspirations of the Revolution. With this inspiration, land invasions occurred in several states in 1975 and 1976. In addition, over six hundred *ejidos* were collectivized. After the economic disaster of the late 1970s and particularly the 1980s, government paternalism toward *ejiditarios* (occupants of the ejidos) was largely suspended. Nonetheless, in 1980 Mexico initiated an ambitious program for rural development, the Mexican Food System (SAM), which provided for increased production of staples in areas of sufficient rainfall—a policy of aiding the campesinos but infused with sizeable portions of agribusiness. The two-year program was successful. However, it is difficult to know whether the higher production of maize and beans, for example, was a result of favorable weather conditions or of the SAM program or what might be the ideal mix of capitalism and peasant production.[71]

Collective farming is reported to be roughly equal in productivity to private operations. In either case, it falls below the norms of the advanced world. Productivity per agricultural worker is one-twentieth of what it is in Canada or the United States. More than 6 tons of corn are produced per hectare in Canada as compared to 1.7 in Mexico.[72] Other statistics further document the difference.

One accomplishment of collectivization is the virtual disappearance of the hacienda from central Mexico, even though corporate agriculture produced a new economic elite. With the growth of the rural population and the slowing down of agrarian reform, landless peasants are as numerous as when Cárdenas initiated the *ejido* system.[73] Between 1950 and 1985, more than five million people migrated from rural areas to urban centers or to the United States. A 1982 analysis of a Michoacán village found 47 percent of families involved in internal migration, 70 percent of the families going to the United States, with an average of 2.8 members per family.[74] These statistics reveal something of the limitations of agrarian reform, whether of governmental decree or individualistic capitalism. Finally, the impact of NAFTA may produce an exodus of one to two million campesinos to the cities and to the United States.[75]

Chile: Reform and Revolution

Despite its history of democratic principles, Chile has long been a country marked by latifundio. On the *fundos*, the *patrón* transformed

Araucanian captives and *encomienda* Indians into *inquilinos* (tenants) who had little more status than the Peruvian *yanaconas*. Even as late as 1966, the *latifundistas*, who were 2 percent of the rural population, received more than one-third of the total income.[76] The situation in Chile is not atypical of what occurred in Latin America—the slow agricultural growth as one cause of economic stagnation. As population grew faster than agricultural production in the 1950s and 1960s, food prices rose higher than other commodities, becoming a major cause of inflation. More than any other sector, food imports upset the balance of payments. The plight is further aggravated by the large surplus of agricultural labor. Even if allowance is made for peak seasonal demands, at least one-fifth of the rural labor force is economically nonproductive because of mechanization.

Agrarian reform evolved in the late 1960s in the form of the *asentamento*, or a production-cooperative organization for three years, with revision of the form of landholding to be decided by majority vote of the members.[77] Most projects tried to maintain a balance between collective and individual plots in order to avoid the disaster of minifundio. At a horticultural project I visited in Puente Alto, only ten miles from Santiago, the members were more concerned with their own plots than with the collectively cultivated area. This attitude may have been a function of the particular type of agriculture. Throughout the Frei regime (1964–1970), CORA (Corporación de Reforma Agraria) made surveys of *fundos* to determine levels of productivity and the possibility of nationalization. Guidance and resources were available to the campesinos as they made the transition from *inquilino* to proprietor. With the Allende socialist regime (1970–1973), this process was accelerated with a massive scheme of expropriation.

As many of the chroniclers were also its advisors, it is difficult to assess the accomplishment of the Pinochet dictatorship in the area of agrarian policy.[78] Of the some 5,800 *fundos* expropriated before the coup against Allende, over 3,800 were restored, in part or in full, to their former owners. Although the military regime was committed to modernization and "neoliberal" economic policies, the government intervened on the side of the *fundo* owners with loans and a protective tariff. Economically the new system worked, but not without human cost. Between 1981 and 1986, per capita food consumption dropped 5 percent in calories and 20 percent in protein.[79] The economic profile of the campesinos was hardly more favorable. With the process of *descomposición*, or proletarization, most of them became wage earners without access to their own land.[80]

The Balance Sheet

One can hardly catalog all the land reforms of the hemisphere, but a few additional comments are in order. A principal goal of the Cuban

Revolution was redistribution of land. The government confiscated most sugar estates by 1961, and, in some instances, payment was made. The policy represented a compromise between individual parcelization and the collective farm. Under the First Agrarian Reform, 40 percent of the land fell to state ownership; 60 percent was privately owned. The Second Agrarian Reform shifted to a 70/30 ratio in favor of state ownership.

As the largest food producer and a country with the greatest latifundio, Brazil is understandably the most critical candidate for agrarian reform. The fragmentary reform of the Goulart period (1961–1964) was shattered by the 1964 military coup. The return to the latifundium was especially noticeable after 1970, at which time small farms had a percentage share similar to what they had had in 1960.[81] Brazil has striven to solve its minifundio problem by frontier expansion. As the country moved toward nonmilitary rule, an agrarian law was passed in 1985 providing for aid to small farmers and wage workers. Still, a study of a northern sugar zone points to the weakness of the unions in urging implementation of the law.[82] In the South, no less than in the North, the struggle for land and equitable working conditions continues.[83] Observers of the Brazilian scene feel that "no programmatic consensus" has appeared among the change agents or in parliament itself. The election of the rightist but ill-fated Collar de Mello in 1990 gave temporary strength to the latifundists.[84] In the 1994 electoral campaign, agrarian reform was once more a central issue, and remains so today.

A familiar litany applies to the rest of the hemisphere. For instance, in Ecuador the 1964 law served little else than to abolish the feudal system of *hausipango*. Limits were set on the maximum size of landholdings, but the norms were extremely flexible.[85] Also, in both the *costa* and the *sierra*, productivity was only marginally increased. Elimination of the estates meant that the offspring of peasants had little chance of obtaining land. Consequently, migration to the towns was inevitable.[86] In Bolivia, by 1980 more than half of the redistribution of terrain went to only 3 percent of the relevant population. With no significant reduction of *minifundismo*, 85 percent of the peasants who left the altiplano did so because they had no land.[87] Even in areas undergoing truly revolutionary change such as Nicaragua, only a fraction of the peasants were able to own land.

Agrarian Reform and Orientation to Change

Demand for land reform and revitalization of agriculture is a rallying cry in nearly all developing areas of the world. In Latin America, as elsewhere, agrarian change is necessary in order to prevent malnutrition. Fundamentally, land reform has been in two directions: first, colonization projects on government or reclaimed land; and second, redistribution of the existing tenure system. Often no fundamental change occurs in either process. More than occasionally, land reform is superficially interpreted as involvement with agricultural extension or the establishment of credit and various technical facilities. Precisely what is meant by land reform must be defined by each government before any significant changes can be made.

Research in rural areas pinpoints factors predisposing to attitude change. In a study of six Colombian communities, modernism as well as achievement motivation were linked to educational status, exposure to mass media, contact with urban centers, and farm productivity.[88] In analyzing agrarian reform in the Dominican Republic, certain sociopsychological characteristics—for instance, feelings of reciprocity, group homogeneity, cohesiveness, and leadership—could be more important in productivity than soil quality, pricing, and market availability.[89] It is not always clear as to what is cause and effect in these relationships. More strategic than the effect of communication is the structural relationships in rural society. Farm workers in the contractual setting are more sensitive to the need for change. A high degree of subordination between worker and manager is not conducive to change.

The government has to consider the economic and psychological costs of reform. Unfortunately, most reform laws are short-range in their objectives. Long-range plans are usually geared to basic land reform. A government initiating agrarian reform must integrate the program with the total economy. Questions must be raised as to the possibilities for nonagricultural employment, realities of moving population, and availability of cultivable land. Nor have governments given adequate attention to the psychological aspects of change. Innovations are decreed without preparing peasants for the adjustment they have to make in their farming methods and personal lives.

Still other problems surface, such as changes in tax structure, but more important is the necessity of linking specific measures in agrarian reform with the more basic problem of agricultural development. All too often, land reform is accompanied by a drop in production. Farm credit, marketing facilities, and price supports are relevant, along with the technical assistance an agriculturalist must have. In order to meet its needs of food production, Mexico's land reform program offers few solutions to the problems of exchange rates, price stabilization, crop insurance, and labor-intensive technology.[90] The failure of agrarian reform to resolve problems of rural distress has led to a sense of deep frustration in most of Latin America. Consequently, aggressive social movements and guerrilla warfare arose during the 1960s. In summary, the basic problem is the unwillingness of the landed aristocracy to make concessions. In several instances, compromise results in agrarian change. For example, Costa Rica's coffee oligarchy was threatened by the Great Depression, loss of exports during World War II, and a rising populism. In return for certain political and economic advantages, the growers accepted a restrained agrarian reform.[91]

Other issues also are relevant in rural development: (1) lack of an adequate technology for the small farmer—too often the machinery is directed toward the commercial, large-scale enterprise; (2) inappropriate leadership and counseling, with little attention to the complex interplay of production and consumption; and (3) inadequate organization among the peasantry, that is, paternalistic dependency and control.[92] Many problems remain, such as improving land registration and titling, the rural worker's lack of access to new areas of informal (and even formal) labor, and establishment of more cooperatives. In view of restricted government budgets, NGOs are playing an ever larger role in the countryside.

MILITANCY IN THE COUNTRYSIDE

It is said that cities are the birthplace of revolutions. Latin America is partially an exception. Campesinos are on the move, in recent years most visibly in Mexico and Peru. Unrest in rural areas, as much as intellectual ferment in the city, produced the Mexican Revolution. Emiliano Zapata was forced into battle by unrest among the landless, and Pancho Villa gathered support from rural dissidents in the north. Rural violence is usually interlaced with the political and economic climate of the nation.

In a number of countries, especially Brazil, Colombia, Peru, Venezuela, and Bolivia, guerrilla warfare has at one time or another become the response to social injustice. Not all movements directly involve peasants, but they have the support of a rural proletariat. Most movements aim their strategy at capturing allegiance from disenfranchised agrarian segments. The Cuban Revolution had only limited support from campesinos until 1958, the last year of the campaign.

Both the rural and the urban scene display violence, as in the Tupamaros or the Movement of National Liberation in Uruguay, which in the 1970s brought the end of personal and social freedom to perhaps the most politically sophisticated country in the hemisphere. Whether urban or rural—and more often it is rural—violence derives from the structure of conflict. Fundamentally it is a breakdown in trust.[93] The actors have implicitly explored other means of resolving differences. Frustration, rumor, belief systems, and leadership—especially charismatic as in Castro and Che Quevara—enter into the drift toward violence and revolution. Some Latin American observers suggest that violence may be an extension of machismo.[94] As in other parts of the world, guerrilla warfare is inspired by ideologies, whether Leninism, Maoism, or other exotic variants, but infused with nationalism, including the idea that the problem lies beyond the frontier, often the United States.[95] Nevertheless, this xenophobic perception is not without a base in reality.

The Colombian *violencia* from 1948 to 1957 is a special case. Primarily it was a "limited" civil war (it cost over two-hundred thousand lives) fought between vendetta-like elements of the two principal political parties, Liberal and Conservative. The war gained momentum from the campesino's frustration at the intransigence of rural social institutions. It is significant that the cataclysm occurred in those parts of Colombia where latifundio was most deeply entrenched, although influences of social dissent in the city were not far away. *La violencia* did not affect the commercial plantation areas along the coast or in the south. After 1957, this peculiar form of guerrilla tactics based on political motivation shifted more to social banditry, but both participants and victims continued to be essentially of rural birth and upbringing.

There is another side to the Colombian scenario; for one, the existence of several independent republics, most notably the community (*vereda*) of Viotá, which continues as a center of agrarian revolutionary activity. Also, guerrilla movements arose, especially as the two parties moved closer together, neither of them truly representing the "forgotten man." Particularly active in the rural scene and among university students were the Fuerzas Armadas Revolucionarias de Colombia, which had its origin in *la violencia* of the 1950s and 1960s.[96] Two movements that began in the 1960s are the Frente Unido del Pueblo (People's United Front) and the Ejército de Liberación Nacional (Army of National Liberation). These guerrilla movements are often the product of disaffected urban elements, but receive support in the hinterland. Both leaders and followers occasionally cooperate with drug lords as an expression of anti-establishment feeling.

In Central America, guerrilla warfare is almost legendary. After the peasant uprisings in El Salvador during the Great Depression, the Martínez dictatorship ruthlessly imposed a state of terror with the massacre of over 25,000 peasants in 1932. After his fall in 1944, the country was quietly ruled by a government subservient to the interests of the coffee barons.[97] In the 1970s, landless peasants launched a civil war that was to last until the truce of 1992. In Guatemala, the National Liberation Movement arose as rural entrepreneurs seized more Indian communal lands in the 1960s. Counterinsurgency troops, with help from the United States, were responsible for the death of over 30,000 peasants. By 1977, U.S. aid was suspended by President Jimmy Carter, only to be renewed by Ronald Reagan in 1981.[98] Violence toward the campesinos continued through the 1980s. An especially complex political and economic struggle took place throughout the 1980s in Nicaragua after the fall of the Somoza empire. The United States became even more involved in the Contra war against the Sandinista government than it was in the repressive regimes of El Salvador and Guatemala. Much of Central America's militarization—directed mainly toward peasants—was encouraged by the United

States. Even Costa Rica was reportedly warned that any economic aid from the United States was contingent on the formation of an army.[99]

In the 1960s, the Peasant Leagues of Brazil gained major visibility, particularly in the Northeast. In reality, the Ligas arose in the 1940s among the Northeast sugar plantations, but their strength increased when Francisco Julião became leader of the landless peasants against the landlords. As a result, both the Brazilian government and United States agencies became concerned with the crisis of the Northeast. Although Julião had a checkered political past, he was no exception to the Brazilian political tradition of combining extremist thought with a recognition of practical realities. In fact, peasant unionization spread south. As a result, wage earnings rose in the 1970s, but inflation made the increase meaningless. As mobilization of the countryside continued, death squads in 1985–1986 murdered approximately five hundred peasants and their supporters—lawyers and priests.[100]

In regard to rural insurgency, probably no struggle in Latin America equals the intensity of the Sendero Luminoso (Shining Path), a Maoist movement that began in 1980 in the Upper Huallaga Valley of Peru. Composed of both peasants and young urban middle-class intellectuals, the movement is committed to violent insurrection. Its appeal is not difficult to understand in a country where more than 70 percent of the population live below the poverty line and are alienated from political parties.[101] The movement operates as a "magnetic promise" of moving beyond the cruelties of everyday life in Peru, probably more for women than for men.[102] The Sendero is in part the consequence of economic decline and the vacuum created by the loss of traditional social controls with the advent of agrarian reform.[103] A serious aspect of the Sendero movement is the counterinsurgency program, which has led to gross violations of civil liberties. Another contretemps was the *autogolpe* of President Alberto Fujimoro, which discouraged international economic cooperation. Internally, the government needs, among other measures, to restore democracy, implement development programs, and slow down the drug traffic because these measures would reduce the resources that underwrite the Sendero.[104] By 1994, measurable progress was made in subduing the movement, with the capture of Sendero's head, Abimael Guzmán, and the master computer files—a factor in the 1995 reelection of Fujimoro.

In the 1970s, various governments were giving mostly lip service to land reform and Fidel Castro's popularity was waning in the hemisphere (as was an awareness of the implications surrounding agrarian socialism in Cuba). Campesinos remain divided in their opinion as to whether more moderate agrarian reform programs could solve their problem.

However intolerable the status quo or the violence, factionalism, and potential corruption of the Left, many observers believe this disorganization would permit a more favorable climate for change than does the present mix of capitalism and quasi-feudalism. In the ultimate judgment, is rural violence functional or dysfunctional? Whether peaceful change can be effective depends on the probability of both urban and rural populations perceiving the causes of poverty in the countryside and its relationship to the national and global market. One aspect of the problem is the relative decrease in the rural population as compared to the urban. Governments, as in El Salvador, are less concerned with political pressure from outside the city.[105] Also, one may ask, Can discontent and protest be channeled into a realistic—and hopefully successful—plan of reform and its implementation? Of course, each country or region has its own profile of productivity and profits and their distribution which can vary with domestic and international market conditions. "Collective defiance" is only likely when the sociocultural climate permits it.[106]

CONCLUSIONS: LATIN AMERICA AND THE WORLD

I have stressed the importance of agricultural societies in the formation of Latin America and the crisis it now faces. Without more attention to food production and distribution, parts of Latin America may not escape the famines we identify with Africa. Any health improvement program has to reckon with the crisis of increasing longevity and population. Sufficient food supply can come only through increased technology or bringing more areas under cultivation. In addition there are the problems of forest cover, slash-and-burn, mineral depletion, sewage, and other forms of environmental contamination, which have implications well beyond this hemisphere. More attention will have to be given to the long-term consequences of policy options concerning basic resources.

In the improvement of agriculture, the Rockefeller Foundation has played a role for more than a quarter of a century in improving corn, wheat, beans, and other crops in Mexico and a dozen other countries. More comprehensive are the United Nations teams in nearly all Latin American countries with similar aims, in addition to studying rural life in general. These and other agencies have often been more constructive in their policies and practices than have the short-range attacks of national governments.

In assessing the agricultural situation, one can hardly escape its relationship to a global economy. Depending on their situation, the actors in this scheme have the choice of revolution, unions as pressure groups, passivity, or other responses. Risk taking is inherent in any option. Possibly more than any other Latin American nation, Mexico is wrestling with its reversal of the land reforms dating from the Revolution. In its need to relieve food shortages, Mexico may no longer support the cultivation of marginal lands. Rather, with NAFTA, products from the grain belt of the United States will be traded for fruits and vegetables from

Mexico's Northwest. One can only imagine the effect of these changes on poor farmers—increased migration to the city for some, and for others soil depletion and deforestation as inefficient farming and grazing continue.[107] In part, the Chiapas revolt was triggered by the fear of imported corn and the effect it would have on local farmers. Similar scenarios will probably haunt other nations.

The forces of change are at hand. Even the most rigid *hacendados* are aware that they are in a twilight zone, forestall as they may the hour of their decline. A number of owners are instituting changes in their estates, if for no other reason than to increase their own profits. New and better agricultural schools are producing technicians, and they have an unmistakable impact. From the other side, peasants are increasingly conscious of their rights in contemporary society, even Latin American style.

NOTES

1. World Population Data Sheet (Washington, D.C.: Population Reference Bureau, 1996).

2. Merilee S. Grindle, *State and Countryside: Development Policy and Agrarian Politics in Latin America* (Baltimore: Johns Hopkins University Press, 1986), 7.

3. Clarissa Hardy, *La Tierra y los Campesinos: La Confederación Campesina* (Mexico, D.F.: Editorial Nueva Edad, 1984).

4. Peter Dorner, *Latin American Land Reforms in Theory and Practice* (Madison: University of Wisconsin Press, 1992), 14–21.

5. Peter Singelmann, *Structures of Domination and Peasant Movements in Latin America* (Columbia: University of Missouri Press, 1981), 11–21.

6. Nathan L. Whetten, *Rural Mexico* (Chicago: University of Chicago Press, 1948), 91.

7. Jack A. Licate, *Creation of a Mexican Landscape* (Chicago: Department of Geography, University of Chicago, 1981), 127.

8. Benjamin S. Orlove and Glynn Custred, eds., *Land and Power in Latin America: Agrarian Economies and Social Processes in the Andes* (New York: Holmes & Meier, 1980), 21.

9. Philip D. Curtin, *The Rise and Fall of the Plantation Complex: Essays in Atlantic History* (Cambridge: Cambridge University Press, 1990).

10. John Rex et al., *Raza y Clase en la Sociedad* (Paris: UNESCO, 1978), 203–204.

11. Arnold Bauer, "Rural Society," in *Latin America: Economy and Society 1870–1930*, ed. Leslie Bethell (Cambridge: Cambridge University Press, 1989), 115–148.

12. Mark Thurner, "Peasant Politics and Andean Haciendas in the Transition to Capitalism: An Ethnographic History," *Latin American Research Review* 28(3): 41–82 (1993).

13. George Martine, "Frontier Expansion, Agricultural Modernization, and Population Trends," in *Population, Food and Rural Development*, ed. Ronald D. Lee et al. (New York: Oxford University Press, 1988), 187–203.

14. N. Patrick Peritore and Ana K. Galve Peritore, "Brazilian Attitudes toward Agrarian Reform: A Q-Methodology Opinion Study of a Conflicted Issue," *Journal of Developing Areas* 24: 377–406 (1990).

15. Luis Roniger, *Hierarchy and Trust in Modern Mexico and Brazil* (New York: Praeger, 1990), 66–72.

16. James D. Hay, "Re-generazión del Proletariado: Cambio Social en la Frontera Amazónica," *Revista Paraguaya de Sociología* 27(77): 99–116 (1990).

17. John Brohman, "Prerevolutionary Nicaraguan Agricultural Development," in *Studies of Development and Change in the Modern World*, ed. Michael T. Martin and Terry R. Kandal (New York: Oxford University Press, 1989), 216–244.

18. Singelmann, *Structures of Domination*, 69.

19. Frances Moore, Richard Lappe, and Joe Collins, "Food First," *The New Internationalist* 42: 5–9 (1976).

20. Lowell S. Jarvis, *Chile Under Military Rule: From Reform to Reaction* (Berkeley: Institute of International Studies, University of California, 1985).

21. Lowry Nelson, *Rural Cuba* (Minneapolis: University of Minnesota Press, 1950), 134.

22. Juan Martinez-Adler, *Haciendas, Plantations, and Collective Farms: Cuba and Peru* (London: Frank Cass, 1977), 29.

23. John F. Wilson, James Diego Hay, and Maxine L. Margolis, "The Bi-National Frontier of Eastern Paraguay," in *The Human Ecology of Tropical Settlement in Latin America*, ed. Debra A. Schumann and William L. Partridge (Boulder, Colo.: Westview Press, 1989), 199–237.

24. Leopoldo J. Bartolomé, "European Colonists in the Argentine Subtropics: The Development of a Specialized Family-Farm System in Misiones," in *The Human Ecology of Tropical Settlement in Latin America*, ed. Schumann and Partridge (Boulder, Colo.: Westview Press, 1989), 133–171.

25. John D. Early, *The Demographic Structure and Evolution of a Peasant System: The Guatemalan Population* (Boca Raton: University Presses of Florida, 1982), 75.

26. Carolyn Hall, *Costa Rica: A Geographical Interpretation in Historical Perspective* (Boulder, Colo.: Westview Press, 1985), 201.

27. Lowell Gudmonson, *Costa Rica Before Coffee: Society and Economy on the Eve of the Export Boom* (Baton Rouge: Louisiana State University Press, 1985).

28. Arturo Warman, "El Problema del Campo," in *México Hoy*, 2d. ed., ed. José Ayala et al. (Mexico, D.F.: Siglo Veinte, 1980), 108–120.

29. Moore, Lappe, and Collins, "Food First."

30. Lois Stanford, "Transitions to Free Trade: Local Impacts of Changes in Mexican Agrarian Policy," *Human Organization* 53: 99–106 (1994).

31. Carlos Rodrigues Brandão and José R. Ramalho, *Campesinato Goiano* (Goiânia: Editora da Universidade Federal de Goias, 1986).

32. Michael R. Carter, Bradford L. Barham, and Dina Mesbah, "Agricultural Export Booms and the Rural Poor in Chile, Guatemala, and Paraguay," *Latin American Research Review* 31(1): 33–65 (1996).

33. Grindle, *State and Countryside*, 188.

34. Hugo F. Wiener, *Cambios en la Estructura Social del Campo Peruano* (Lima: Instituto de Apoyo Agrario, 1987), 15.

35. Herbert S. Klein, *Haciendas and Ayllus* (Stanford, Calif.: Stanford University Press, 1993), 164.

36. Guillermo de la Peña, *A Legacy of Promises: Agriculture, Politics, and Ritual in the Highlands of Mexico* (Austin: University of Texas Press, 1981), 109.

37. L. Van Crowder, "Extension for Profit: Agents and Sharecropping in the Highlands of Ecuador," *Human Organization* 50(1): 39–45 (1991).

38. Bruce F. Johnston et al., *U.S.–Mexico Relations: Agriculture and Rural Development* (Stanford, Calif.: Stanford University Press, 1987).

39. Fernando Calderón, "Los Pueblos Quechua y Aymara en la Formación de la Sociedad Boliviana," in *Raza y Clase en la Sociedad Postcolonial*, ed. John Rex et al. (Paris: UNESCO, 1978), 197–207.

40. María E. Gisbert, Michael Painter, and Mery Quitón, "Gender Issues Associated with Labor Migration and Dependence on Off-Farm Income in Rural Bolivia," *Human Organization* 53: 110–118 (1994).

41. João Maros Alem and Leda M. Benevello De Castro, "Peasant Participation in an Integrated Rural Development Program: Minas Gerais," in *Research in Rural Sociology and Development: Third World Contexts*, vol. 3, ed. Harry K. Schwarzweller (Greenwich, Conn.: JAI Press, 1987), 41–64.

42. Jan L. Flora and Cornelia Butler Flora, "Peasant Consumer Stores as Community Development: The Colombian Case," in *Research in Rural Sociology and Development: Third World Contexts*, vol. 3, ed. Harry K. Schwarzweller (Greenwich, Conn.: JAI Press, 1987), 103–125.

43. Orlando Fals Borda, *Knowledge and People's Power* (New Delhi: Indian Social Institute, 1985).

44. Liliana R. Goldin and María E. Saenz de Tejada, "Uneven Development in Western Guatemala," *Ethnology* 32: 237–252 (1993).

45. Gerardo Reichel-Dolmotoff and Alicia Reichel-Dolmotoff, *The People of Aritama: The Cultural Personality of a Colombian Mestizo Village* (Chicago: University of Chicago Press, 1961), 257.

46. Michael Chibnik and Wil de Jong, "Agricultural Labor Organization in Ribereño Communities of the Peruvian Amazon," *Ethnology* 28: 75–96 (1989).

47. Leslie Anderson, "Mixed Blessings: Disruption and Organization among Peasant Unions in Costa Rica," *Latin American Research Review* 26(1): 111–143 (1991).

48. B. R. Roberts, "Peasants and Proletarians," in *Annual Review of Sociology*, vol. 16, ed. W. Richard Scott and Judith Blake (Palo Alto, Calif.: Annual Reviews, 1990), 353–377.

49. Andrew Pearse, *The Latin American Peasant* (London: Frank Cass, 1975), 94–99.

50. Emile Durkheim, *The Division of Labor*, tr. George Simpson (New York: Macmillan, 1933).

51. Michael M. Bell, "The Fruit of Difference: The Rural–Urban Continuum of a System of Identity," *Rural Sociology* 57: 65–82 (1992).

52. Herbert M. Lefcourt and Rod A. Martin, "Locus of Control and the Rural Experience," in *Rural Psychology*, ed. Alan W. Childs and Gary B. Melton (New York: Plenum Press, 1983), 151–168.

53. John Monaghan, "Reciprocity, Redistribution, and the Transaction of Value in the Mesoamerican Fiesta," *American Ethnologist* 17: 758–774 (1990).

54. L. Nicole Bourque, "Developing People and Plants: Life-Cycle and Agricultural Festivals in the Andes," *Ethnology* 34: 75–87 (1995).

55. Barbara Bode, *No Bells to Toll: Destruction and Creation in the Peruvian Andes* (New York: Scribner's, 1989), 57–70.

56. William P. Mitchell, *Peasants on the Edge: Crop, Cult, and Crisis* (Austin: University of Texas Press, 1991), 198–200.

57. Richard Pace, "First-Time Televiewing in Amazônia: Television Acculturation in Gurupá, Brazil," *Ethnology* 32: 187–204 (1993).

58. Carl C. Taylor, *Rural Life in Argentina* (Baton Rouge: Louisiana State University Press, 1948), 275.

59. Richard T. Forman and Michel Gordon, *Landscape Ecology* (New York: Wiley, 1986), 295.

60. Judith Lisansky, *Migrants to Amazonia: Spontaneous Colonization in the Brazilian Frontier* (Boulder, Colo.: Westview Press, 1990).

61. Diana J. Schemo, "Violence Growing in Battle Over Brazilian Land," *New York Times*, April 21, 1996, p. 12.

62. Leslie Anderson, "Alternative Action in Costa Rica: Peasants as Positive Participants," *Journal of Latin American Studies* 22: 89–113 (1990).

63. Marshall Wolfe, "Rural Settlement Patterns and Social Change in Latin America: Notes for a Strategy of Rural Development," *Latin American Research Review* 1(Spring): 5–50; 15 cited (1966).

64. Dario L. Restrepo, "Cartografía de la Descentralización: Emergencia, Actualidad, e Indefiniciones," *Revista Interamericana de Planificación* 105(27): 7–22 (1994).

65. Emiliano Ortega R., "Estructura Territorial del Estado y Ruralidad," *Revista Paraguaya de Sociología* 30(87): 125–151 (1993).

66. José Deustua, "Mining Markets, Peasants, and Power in Nineteenth-Century Peru," *Latin American Research Review* 29(1): 29–54 (1994).

67. César Fonseca Martel, "Peasant Differentiation in the Peruvian Andes," in *Peruvian Contexts of Change*, ed. William W. Stein (New Brunswick, N.J.: Transaction Books, 1985), 124–162; 144 cited.

68. Timothy J. Finan, "Market Operations and Market Performance in Northeast Brazil," *American Ethnologist* 15: 694–707 (1988).

69. John Swetnam, "Migratory Patterns in a Guatemalan Market," *Ethnology* 29: 261–270 (1990).

70. Latin American Center, *Statistical Abstract of Latin America* (Los Angeles: University of California, 1995), 43.

71. Alan de Janvry and Ann Vandenman, "The Macrocontext of Rural Development: A Second View of the U.S. Experience," in *U.S.–Mexico Relations*, ed. Bruce F. Johnston et al., 83–109.

72. Luís Pazos, *La Disputa por el Ejido* (Mexico, D.F.: Editorial Diana, 1991).

73. Bruce F. Johnston, Cassio Luiselli, and Clark W. Reynolds, "An Overview: Asymmetry and Independence," in *U.S.–Mexico Relations*, ed. Bruce F. Johnston et al., 1–12.

74. Irma Adelman, J. Edward Taylor, and Stephen Vogl, "Life in a Mexican Village: A SAM Perspective," *Journal of Developing Studies* 23: 1–24 (1989).

75. Michael W. Foley, "Privatizing the Countryside: The Mexican Peasant Movement and Neoliberal Reform," *Latin American Perspectives* 22(1): 59–74 (1995).

Movement and Neoliberal Reform," *Latin American Perspectives* 22(1): 59–74 (1995).

76. Ronaldo Munck, *Politics and Dependency in the Third World: The Case of Latin America* (London: Zea Books, 1984), 182.

77. Dorner, *Latin American Land Reforms*, 38.

78. Patricio Silva, "Agrarian Change under the Chilean Military Government," *Latin American Research Review* 25(1): 193–205 (1990).

79. Sergio Gómez and Jorge Echeñique, *La Agricultura Chilena: Las Dos Caras de la Modernación* (Santiago: FLACSO/AGARIA, 1988).

80. Rigoberto Rivera A., *Los Campesinos Chilenos* (Santiago: Academia de Humanismo Chileno, 1988), 274–275.

81. Martine, "Frontier Expansion," 197.

82. Anthony W. Pereira, "Agrarian Reform and the Rural Worker's Unions of the Pernambuco Sugar Zone, Brazil 1985–1988," *Journal of Developing Areas* 26: 169–192 (1992).

83. Avril Scherer-Warren, "Los Trabajadores Rurales en el Sur de Brasil y la Democratización de la Sociedad," *Revista Mexicana de Sociología* 50: 243–259 (1988).

84. N. Patrick Peritore and Ana K. Galve Peritore, "Brazilian Attitudes toward Agrarian Reform: A Q-Methodology Opinion Study of a Conflictual Issue," *Journal of Developing Areas* 24: 377–406 (1990).

85. David W. Schodt, *Ecuador: An Andean Enigma* (Boulder, Colo.: Westview Press, 1987), 84.

86. Michael R. Redclift and David A. Preston, "Agrarian Reform and Rural Change in Ecuador," in *Environment, Society, and Rural Change in Latin America*, ed. David A. Preston (New York: Wiley, 1980), 53–63.

87. Miguel Urioste, *Segunda Reforma Agraria* (La Paz: CEDLA, 1987), 147.

88. Everett M. Rogers, *Modernization among Peasants: The Impact of Communication* (New York: Holt, Rinehart and Winston, 1969), 265–267.

89. Carrie A. Meyer, *Land Reform in Latin America: The Dominican Case* (New York: Praeger, 1989).

90. John R. Heath, "Further Analysis of the Mexican Food Crisis," *Latin American Research Review* 27(3): 123–145 (1992).

91. Anthony Winson, *Coffee and Democracy in Modern Costa Rica* (New York: St. Martin's Press, 1988).

92. Alan de Janvry and Ann Vandeman, "Macrocontext of Rural Development," 84.

93. Hubert M. Blalock, Jr., *Power and Conflict: Toward a General Theory* (Thousand Oaks, Calif.: Sage Publications, 1989), 146–147.

94. Roger Lancaster, *Life Is Hard: Machismo, Danger, and the Intimacy of Power in Nicaragua* (Berkeley: University of California Press, 1992), 247–248.

95. Michael Radu, *Violence and the Latin American Revolutionaries* (New Brunswick, N.J.: Transaction Books, 1988), 8–10.

96. Jonathan Hartlyn, *The Politics of Coalition Rule in Colombia* (Cambridge: Cambridge University Press, 1988), 191.

97. Patricia Parkman, *Nonviolent Insurrection in El Salvador* (Tucson: University of Arizona Press, 1988).

98. Michael McClintock, *The American Connection: State Terror and Popular Resistance in Guatemala*, vol. 2 (London: Zed Books, 1985), 66.

99. Robert G. Williams, *Export Agriculture and the Crisis in Latin America* (Chapel Hill: University of North Carolina Press, 1986), 187.

100. Susan George, *A Fate Worse Than Debt* (New York: Grove Press, 1988), 147.

101. Orin Starn, "New Literature on Peru's Sendero Luminoso," *Latin American Research Review* 27(2): 212–226 (1992).

102. Orin Starn, "Maoism in the Andes: The Communist Party of Peru: Shining Path and the Refusal of History," *Journal of Latin American Studies* 27: 399–421 (1995).

103. Philip Mauceri, "State Reform, Coalitions, and the Neoliberal *Autogolpe* in Peru," *Latin American Research Review* 30(1): 7–37 (1995).

104. David S. Palmer, "Peru, the Drug Business and Shining Path: Between Scylla and Charybdis?" *Journal of Interamerican Studies and World Affairs* 34: 65–83 (1992).

105. Mitchell A. Seligson, "Thirty Years of Transformation in the Agrarian Structure of El Salvador, 1961–1991," *Latin American Research Review* 30(3): 43–74 (1995).

106. Susan Eckstein, "Power and Protest in Latin America," in *Power and Popular Protest*, ed. Susan Eckstein (Berkeley: University of California Press, 1989), 1–60.

107. Steven E. Sanderson, "Mexico's Environmental Future," *Current History* 92: 73–77 (1993).

Chapter 5

Ethnic Relations

Even more than Anglo-America, Latin America represents racial diversity. Only parts of Asia and Africa show a wider spectrum of ethnic types. Moreover, when compared to South Africa, India, the Middle East, or even the United States, Latin America enjoys a degree of ethnic harmony unique in today's world. One recalls the often-repeated generalization that in Latin America race is an economic and cultural rather than a physical phenomenon. Again, one tends to gloss over certain realities. For Peruvians or Brazilians, the situation is more complicated than simply identifying race with class.

The purpose of this chapter is to examine the status of racial groups in the various countries and how ethnic characterizations developed in the social structure and to attempt to answer the following questions: What are the criteria in identifying race? How did stereotypes arise? To what degree can the individual change his or her ethnic status? What explains the prejudices found in most if not all countries? What are the implications of an interracial society and its significance to the world scene?

Historical Factors

Historians say that the North American chose to exterminate the Indians, the Latin American to exploit them. However oversimplified this statement, it tells something of the differing development of the two societies. Not only were the Indians of Meso-America and the Andean region more numerous, they were also more highly developed than those who awaited the colonizers from Britain and northwestern Europe. The history of the black more than of the Indian bears a resemblance to the North American past, since the plantation culture from Williamsburg to Bahia was based on the institution of slavery. What the black and indigenous had in common was their status as chattel. Currently, both experience discrimination, which has its roots in their caste position during colonial times.

Slavery showed marked regional diversity as it spread to nearly every part of the Americas. Two value systems emerged as the result of different cultural systems: first, the Anglo-Saxon heritage in the South of the United States and in the Caribbean, and second, the development of the Iberian New World. First of all, Spain and Portugal were themselves characterized by a feudal system even more deeply entrenched than that of northwestern Europe. Consequently, it was no accident that a stratified society developed from the hegemony superimposed by the conquistadores. Slavery was institutionalized in Spanish feudalism.[1] However, this caste society changed more in the colonial and early national period than did the U.S. South. Since the society included masses of Indians as well as African slaves, a multiracial structure evolved, and it exists to this day. To the three groups composing the society—white, Indians, and Afro-Americans—were added other strains as the result of miscegenation.

The Spaniards, who were comparatively tolerant of sexual relations with natives of the New World, looked favorably on marriage with the Indian nobility. Cortés's officers married among remnants of the Aztec aristocracy. Several reasons account for this acceptance of interracial liaisons. For one, the infusion of Moorish blood into the southern Iberian peninsula occurred for several centuries before Columbus. As prominent Spanish and Portuguese families married into the Moorish elite, little stigma was attached to people of darker complexion. In fact, prejudice was more directed to cultural and particularly religious differences in this transition from Spanish to Moorish and back to Spanish domination, which labels of Mozarab and Morisco indicate.[2] Racial purity was seemingly of minimal concern to the conquistadors in the New World or to their successors. Moreover, migration to the New World was over 75 percent male. Even in the less tolerant racial climate of the United States, nearly 90 percent of the Afro-American population show the effects of three centuries of miscegenation.

Still another reason for miscegenation was the sexual attractiveness of the nonwhite female, especially the Afro-American and mulatto. As implied above, miscegenation began in the first days of colonization. During the sixteenth century, Indians were increasingly replaced by blacks, who numbered about one-fourth of the population by 1600. Yet of the 1950 Brazilian population, 62 percent were white, 26 percent were mixed, and 11 percent were African, though these terms are relative. It is significant that the *Anuário Estatístico do Brazil* no longer carries any direct reference to race, even though the census bureau operates according to a fourfold racial classification based on color.[3] In Mexico, *mestizaje* was well-established by the end of the colonial period, when 31 percent of the population were mestizo, 60 percent were Indian, and the remainder were either European or African.[4] Over the next century and a half, the percentage of mestizos doubled. Racial boundaries cannot be very firm when mixture characterizes a large portion of the population, even though miscegenation did not completely break down caste relationships.

Also influencing the different development of race relations in the two Americas was the system of slavery. Despite its extreme harshness, the institution of slavery existed in a more flexible atmosphere in Latin America than in the United States. Brazil especially had a more liberal policy than did the Caribbean or the old South in regard to manumission. This policy offered the possibility of mobility for Latin American slavery. Afro-Americans could occasionally enter the skilled trades and the clergy. Visitors to Brazil during the nineteenth century reported an increasing number of freed slaves, and by the end of the slave trade in 1850, more than half the slaves were already free. A census in 1872 found one and a half million slaves; by the emancipation in 1888 a half million were in slavery.[5] This is not to argue that conditions for slavery were good; on the contrary, in Iberian America they were abysmal—mortality was significantly greater than for the slaves of the United States.

Most important, the end of slavery arrived without the violence that North America experienced. Despite the gross inequities of slavery in Brazil, it was predominantly an adaptation of medieval feudalism to the New World. Peoples who accepted a harshly stratified social system did not feel compelled to rationalize slavery according to the Biblical notions of the need for racial hierarchy and purity.

Slavery did not come to a sudden end in most countries. Manumission began in the eighteenth century, but slavery lingered on through most of the nineteenth century. For instance, the socioeconomic structure of Colombia, at least in the traditional city of Popayán, involved a dual society of aristocrats and slaves. Even though the Law of Cúcuta proclaimed abolition in 1821, the institution did not end until 1852.[6]

Religious ideology also shaped the differing race ideology of the two Americas. By 1530, the crown and especially the Church urged a more lenient policy toward Indians, however remote the influence of these institutions may have been to adventurers and *hacendados* from the Valley of Mexico to the Rio de la Plata. Bartolomé de las Casas was the outstanding, but not the only, cleric who preached a Christian philosophy in the treatment of the nonwhite. As the colonists wanted the wealth produced by the toil of the Indians, the churchmen wanted their soul. Perhaps the most ambitious promoters of this movement were the Jesuits, who established mission stations in Mexico, Brazil, and Paraguay for the purpose of training the Indian in Christian dogma as well as in the values and skills of Western culture. At first, instruction was attempted in the Indian languages, but Spanish—and Portuguese—increasingly became the vehicles, which in turn accelerated Hispanization of the Indian. In areas with a high density of Indians, this policy was less successful; languages like Quechua, Aymara, Guaraní, and Mayan remain to this day. In the Amazon basin, the Jesuits adapted a European script to Tupí as a kind of lingua franca that has continued to exist among a number of tribes until this century.

In the long run the Church had limited success in converting natives; at best Christian rituals and beliefs were fused with indigenous practices. Whatever the idealism of the Church fathers, efforts of the colonists to enlist the natives in the working of the mines and plantations contradicted the purposes of the Church in its tolerance toward Indians. In regard to Afro-Americans, during the early colonial period the Church was not convinced that they had souls, but by the early seventeenth century conceded that they did.

On the whole, the Roman Catholic Church seemed to be more concerned with the welfare of the nonwhite than were Protestants in the U.S. South, possibly because of the greater economic dependency of Latin Americans, both lay and clerical, on Indians and Afro-Americans. The heightened missionary zeal on the part of the Catholics may also explain the difference, but in North America the attitude resulted more from the Calvinist orientation to the Old Testament doctrine of ethnic superiority. Because of a lack of centralized authority, the Protestants were more sensitive to the policy of the local church community. On the whole, British America was more of a racist society than was the Latin world.[7] This ideological difference does not exempt Catholicism from a history of exploitation in its relationships with nonwhites. However, its emphasis on the faith as embracing all people is significant when viewed against the separatism underlying the history of Protestantism, which is manifest not only in the diversity of sects but also in its basic tenet whereby human beings are individually and directly accountable to the Deity.

These fundamental differences in beliefs about racial superiority and in institutional values, particularly between Protestantism and Catholicism, are relevant to the different racial ideologies in the two Americas. According to the statistics available on such indexes as number of beatings and mortality, possibly the Latins were more cruel than their Northern counterparts, but the emotional reaction to slavery was more the desire for exploitation and profit than a kind of racial judgment.

After the end of slavery, the justification for a racial hierarchy turned to sources beyond economic needs. In varying forms, ranging geographically from Mexico to Argentina, an ideology maintaining that white or

European blood has an inherent superiority emerged. This belief was especially evident from the late nineteenth into the early part of the twentieth century, when theories of racial purity were current in Europe and North America.[8] For example, Venezuela offers an example of most of the Americas in proclaiming a "myth of racial democracy," which under the surface displays a more complex situation.[9]

REGIONAL VARIATIONS

Each region has its own pattern of race relations. No society exists in a static situation. It may be recalled from Chapter 1 that a broad ethnic classification can divide Latin America into at least four groups: (1) countries in which a mestizo population dominates; (2) countries overwhelmingly European in character; (3) countries with conspicuous Indian groupings, generally inhabiting the highlands; and (4) Portuguese America and the Caribbean with their African admixture. I shall examine the ethnic background of a few typical areas as follows.

Mexico

The Indians were decimated in Mexico during the early colonial period. Of perhaps twenty million inhabitants living at the time of the arrival of Cortés, barely one million had survived the epidemics of smallpox, measles, influenza, and other European diseases by 1650. Perhaps more tragic than this demographic process was the effect of the conqueror on the indigenous social system. The status of the Indian declined with the loss of his lands to the *encomienda* system and to forced labor in the *repartimiento*. Even in the protective climate of the *comunidad* at least 4 percent of the males were required to toil in public works and on farms or in mines. The Jesuits, often inspired by utopian principles, were not alone in their efforts to establish Christian communities, but the demands of the *encomiendero* bypassed these efforts. Thus, except for occasional instruction by the Church, Indians were relegated to an obscure position for the remainder of the colonial period, although they were never brought into slavery. In fact, the high mortality rate and the idea of the Indian as unfit for certain types of hard labor led to the importation of Africans in the late sixteenth century, a practice abandoned well before the end of the colonial period; yet the number of Afro-Americans was roughly 25,000 on the eve of Independence. Even today, some 10,000 are found along the Pacific Coast in the states of Oaxaca and Guerrero, and at least ten times that number have some African blood.

Since not more than 25 percent of European immigrants were women, miscegenation was taken for granted. By the end of the eighteenth century, the number of mixed bloods was surpassed only by Indians, who had begun their long climb back to numerical preponderance after they acquired some immunity to European diseases. Until Independence all nonwhites were considered *castas*, according to an elaborate scheme based on the type of mixture and social status:

I. *Peninsulares* (or more vulgarly, *gachupines*): natives of Spain

II. Creoles: pure descendants of *penisulares* born in Mexico or prominent mestizos who bought certificates of blood purity

III. Persons of mixed blood, including:

    1. Mestizo: born of one Spanish and one Indian parent

    2. Castizo: born of one mestizo and one Spanish parent

    3. Spaniard: born of one castizo and one Spanish parent

    4. Mulatto: born of one Spanish and one black parent

    5. Morisco: born of one Spanish and one mulatto parent

    6 to 16. Eleven different labels based on the mixture of Spanish, mestizo, mulatto, morisco, and so on

IV. Indians: pure-bloods

V. Negroes: pure-bloods[10]

The increase of the mestizo population along with the permutations of mixtures made the system of *castas* unworkable by the late colonial period. Moreover, for the early revolutionary leaders independence meant the end of a tight hierarchical society.

The century following independence brought vast change to the indigenous population. In the nineteenth century, Mexico and other Latin American regimes were opting more for private property rather than the communal principle. Under President Porfirio Díaz, the *comunidades* were handed over to the haciendas, many of which came to be foreign-owned. The restoration of the Indians to their rightful heritage in national life was a major aim of the Revolution. At that time it was estimated that more than one-third (37%) of the nation was Indian, as opposed to 43 percent who were mestizo and a mythical 20 percent white.[11]

Following the Revolution, the view that Indians should be fully integrated and assimilated into the national culture clashed with the new view of protection of the Indians. The most militant protectionism came with the Cárdenas regime (1934–1940). Beginning with the 1940s, especially during the Alemán administration (1946–1952), the goal became one of national economic growth rather than correcting social injustices.

Of Mexico's forty-nine million inhabitants over the age of five in 1980, more than one million were described as either monolingual or bilingual speakers of an Indian language. Other estimates place the figure much higher.[12] But the Indian biological influence is, of course, even greater than the linguistic, since at least 85 percent of the Mexican population is estimated to be of more than half Indian origin. Even those who claim purely European ancestry are often from traditional families which are conveniently unaware of an Indian ancestor in the colonial period. Indians of Mexico still conform to tribal distribution, that is, Aztec remnants in the North and Mayans in Yucatan and the South, with several other groups, notably Tarascans in Michoacán and Zapotecs and Mixtecs in Oaxaca. Acculturation has been taking place rapidly in this century, with individuals and even whole villages abandoning their *jacales, huaraches*, and original languages as they become absorbed into the occupational and economic world of the dominant majority. Until the Revolution, both in the South and the North, whites and mestizos looked on the Indians as a convenient target for exploitation.

Ethnic cultures are thought of as different. The Indian tends to be group-oriented, whereas the mestizo is self-assertive.[13] Over the last generation, these different social worlds have partially accommodated each other socially and economically. The borderline between mestizo and indigenous is increasingly arbitrary.[14] With fairly rapid social change in Mexico, Indians are caught between different cultures and subcultures. In the 1950s, members of the Mazahua, a tribe in central Mexico, began searching for work in agricultural areas in order to support their families. As industrialization encroached on these areas they were drawn into work in competition with mestizos. This conflict is reflected in the school as well as in employment. The Mazahuas who are unable to find a niche in the mestizo world return to their traditional occupations in the villages; or they develop a new identity, known as *Concheros*, turning to their indigenous roots, including Aztec dances and other rituals performed in greater Mexico City. This experience of the Mazahua illustrates the ambivalent ethnic policy of the Mexican government in recent decades.[15]

A striking case of an indigenous culture defiantly experiencing conflict is that of the Mixtec in Oaxaca.[16] Many of its members migrated to the north of Mexico and the United States, where on both sides of the border they are exploited more than mestizo migrants. Both in their original setting and their new home they resist complete acculturation through various ceremonials. They "find themselves collectively identified by the predominant mestizo population in Mexico as 'other' members of a minority and a despised one at that."[17] This inferior status led to the development of an ethnic identity and a political activism by forming a union.

The 1994 uprising by the Zapatista National Liberation Army (EZLN) made public the sad profile of the Chiapas Indians. A caste situation exists between the mestizo and Indian cultures in Chiapas; north and south of this line class and caste very according to the locality. Chiapas has for decades been the poorest state in Mexico. At least 30 percent of its 3.2 million inhabitants are illiterate and 32 percent speak only an indigenous language. The *caciques* (feudal land barons) use violence to evict the Indians from their lands, all in a state comfortably in the hands of the PRI until 1994.[18] The accord between the government and EZLN in 1996 may bring some acknowledgement of civil rights, but improvement of living conditions is another question.

The influences of the Aztecs and Mayans are important in Mexican life. Indian communities still inhabit the escarpments and valleys of the Sierra Madre Occidental and Oriental as well as the highland communities of the South. Isolation and traditionalism prevent many of them from being incorporated into the greater Mexican society, but Mexico's industrialization would seem in the future to make for further Westernization of its indigenous population. These cultural differences are what make Mexico's ethnic relations of interest, since, except for Chiapas, racial discrimination no longer exists as a serious problem; that is, if the Indian accepts the majority culture. The problem remains as to the degree of recognition or even understanding the PRI brings to indigenous communities. NGOs are attempting to encourage greater involvement of the local citizens in decision making.[19] Consequently, it is questionable if the purposes of the Revolution have been fulfilled, or whether racial democracy except for certain enclaves is accepted.

Central America

The most striking ethnic profile in Central America is found in Guatemala, where Indian and *ladino* (an Indian or mestizo who has assumed some aspects of Western culture) live side by side, if in different universes. The varied traditions of these indigenous societies are well known, as costumes and marketplaces are major tourist attractions. However, behind the rich color of these Indian villages are a number of serious problems in medicine, health, employment, and education. Historically, the Ubico dictatorship gave little recognition to the integrity of Indian communities, but the Arévalo regime in 1944 set about rectifying the abuses. For one thing, the *municipio* became autonomous, and the community could elect its own officials. These reforms were slowed down by the overthrow—with CIA intervention—of President Arbenz in 1954.

Race relations in Guatemala might be described as a dual or parallel structure that varies according to locality. Although Indians produce nearly all of Guatemala's food supply, they have little role in the general economy. The land is owned by the traditional monopoly of wealthy *ladinos*. Few Indians are encouraged to participate in *ladino* occupations, and educational opportunities are similarly restricted. This structure is in a continuous process of change as Indians living on the margin of ladino culture undergo the process of *ladinoization*. Despite their heterogeneity, *ladinos* look upon themselves as superior, more because of cultural traits than physical features. They live in the more desirable area around the central plaza, whereas Indians occupy the periphery of the village or town. Commercial and social relationships between the two communities are limited and strained. In Alta Verapaz, *ladinos* control access to the outside market and therefore determine what Indians receive for their coffee crop. Even in the local market, they establish the price they are willing to pay.[20] The Indian defers to the *ladino*, whom he addresses as *señor*, or *Usted*; the *ladino* in turn uses *tu* to the Indian.

The degree to which Indians may alter their status depends on the community, but even more on individual resources. The young are more successful than the old in making this adjustment. Unlike skin color and physical features, dress and language are relevant factors, since movement into the *ladino* stratum is accomplished by means of achieved rather than ascribed criteria. Among the value and attitudinal shifts is the degree of acceptance of orthodox Catholicism (or Protestantism) as opposed to a more syncretized version. Individual personality may count as much as environmental and chance events. Besides being deeply attached to the village and to kinship, Indians are involved in a more or less self-sufficient economy. Consequently, they have little compulsion to enter into the national society toward which they feel somewhat alienated. They are often penalized by the *ladino* culture; for example, labor legislation offers little benefit and vagrancy laws are enforced against them disproportionately.

In view of the political fluidity experienced by Guatemala for the last generation, the future status of Indians is questionable. They have been victimized by the reign of terror in the countryside since the 1980s, when landholders with military support carried on mass killings and torture. The situation is complicated by a rising population in the north central area of the country. Indians suffer more than mestizos, although they have occasionally come together in their guerrilla struggle against the military.[21] The role of the U.S. military in training personnel for the death squads is not lost on the Latin American public.[22] In this context, over 150,000 indigenous Guatemalans have been forced to find refuge in Mexico (20,000 in Chiapas), adding to the fierce struggle for limited resources.[23] Generally, *ladino*–Indian relations are similar to the equilibrium between mestizo and Indian in Mexico prior to the Revolution of 1910. It is the large proportion, 53 percent, of Indians in Guatemala that makes the problem a far-reaching one. Even though upward mobility from Indian to *ladino* will continue as occupational lines become less rigid, the highland Indian communities are not likely to change greatly for another generation.

Aside from Guatemala, only fragments of Central America's indigenous past remain; however, prejudice toward minorities continues. In a few pockets of Honduras and Nicaragua, native languages are still used. As with all Central American republics (with the exception of El Salvador, which faces only the Pacific), a large Afro-Caribbean population has populated the eastern areas. Of Honduras's five million inhabitants, one-sixth are ethnics; of these, 70 percent are African, and 30 percent Indian. The Indians especially are isolated and face a desperate search for employment as they migrate from their inland location to the coast, where their relationship with the *ladino* population remains precarious.[24] In Nicaragua during the near half century of Somoza rule (with connivance by the United States), the Miskito Indians on the Atlantic side of the country experienced discrimination and exploitation.[25] Later, conflict also occurred with the Sandinistas; the Miskitos, partly because of the influence of Moravian missionaries, held to an "Anglo affinity" and anti-Marxist attitude.[26] By the late 1980s, conditions improved as the Sandinista government permitted them to have more autonomy in their economy.[27] Yet a certain degree of snobbery remains toward Miskitos and blacks as they are both considered to be backward.[28] One negative effect of the Contra war was suspicion on both sides about the role of the Miskitos. However, by the end of the Sandinista rule, self-pride and political revitalization was evident.[29] El Salvador retains almost nothing of its *pipil* past. In the 1930s, the Martínez dictatorship persecuted and obliterated several indigenous communities. Although communities like Izalco and Panchimalco retained a few reminders of the pre-Spanish period well into this century, mostly a mestizo character prevails.[30] By the nineteenth century, Costa Rica shattered what few Indian tribes remained.

Hispanic South America

Various ethnic patterns characterize the countries of South America. In Colombia and Venezuela, blacks and mulattoes are an important constituent of the coastal population, unlike the Indians who are in isolated tribal enclaves extending from the Amazon to the Chocó and Guajirá. Consequently, these societies play almost no role in national life. In the Andean countries, slavery and the eradication of African culture as well as the *encomienda* system paved the way for segregation and discrimination into the twentieth century.[31] Over 200,000 Paez and Guambiano Indians in southwest Colombia have been struggling for the restitution of their *resguardos*, which were illegally seized in the postcolonial period. Generally, the indigenous population rejects Western culture, as in the case of the Motilones, a tribe of headhunters found in a remote area of the Columbia–Venezuela border.

In contrast to these essentially mestizo nations are Peru and Ecuador, where feeling between Indians and *cholos* is polarized. Ecuador, Peru, and Bolivia represent a strong tradition of New World culture, as illustrated by the Quechua-speaking Peruvian Indians, who still hold on to the language, agricultural technology, and social and religious beliefs of the Inca empire. Because of the limited number of Spanish overseers, Indian societies were able to survive despite being raided for work parties.

The gulf between mestizo and Indian is no less great for much of the Andean region than for Guatemala. One subtle difference can be made between *cholo* and meztizo or *ladino*. The *cholo* speaks some Spanish but adheres to the cultural traits of his or her folk society, whereas meztizos or criollos primarily belong to European culture, even though they may know their native language. Social status is the major criterion determining race, since physical factors have little to do with racial designation of the *colon* or *yanacona* on the hacienda. Stereotypes are freely affixed to Indians for their supposed lack of incentive, suspiciousness, and addiction to coca and alcohol.

In approaching the history of European–Indian relations, the case of Peru is instructive. Whereas Spain attempted to superimpose a caste structure, relationships after Independence developed more according to the need of the economy—the market, productivity, and occupations, and so on all determined the boundary between Indian and "criollization" (*criollo* referring more or less to the equivalent of ladino in Guatemala).[32] Indians have maintained their identity but have been exploited from the colonial period to the present, which encourages their adherence to the Sendero Luminoso.

Because of political and social changes of the twentieth century, Indians, even in Peru, can scarcely be considered a caste. Movement to the city produces an ever-expanding *cholo* and criollo society as the language and the lifestyle change with migration. Moreover, Indian militancy in the peasant syndicates means that the ethnic class structure is in a state of flux. The effect of community development as represented by Vicos in Peru and other projects is also indicative of the potential for change. The experience of Peru and its neighbors only underscores how meaningless the biological concept of race is. Social more than physical factors determine ethnicity. It should also be mentioned that African admixtures in Peru serve as a reminder of the use of slave labor in the coastal plantations of colonial times. Manumission occurred there as in Brazil; Lima had a black ghetto well into the nineteenth century.[33]

In Ecuador, despite an Indian majority, Afro-Americans represent approximately one-fifth of the population. Their arrival in Ecuador is subject to controversy, but shipwrecks account for a contingent by the end of the sixteenth century. Also, Jesuits imported a number to work in their plantations. In the Chota Valley, the Spanish language was affected by African elements, as was Portuguese in some areas of Brazil.[34] Today in several areas, as in the community of San Lorenzo in the northwestern part of that country, blacks occupy a lower rung of the social ladder than does the mestizo, who has a highly variable status.[35]

Still other patterns are visible in South America. Bolivia also had a dual society until at least the 1952 revolution. Both Quechua and the Aymara Indians struggle against an inhospitable physical environment. Also, settlers in the lowlands encroached on their traditional territory. However, mestizos and *cholos* are roughly 30 percent of the population. Consequently, Indians may well have the balance of political leverage in Bolivia. It is impossible to assess the eventual social and political power of indigenous cultures, but they are hardly likely to lose their distinctiveness in Ecuador, Peru, or Bolivia. Because of separate languages, ways of life, and lack of intermarriage, a boundary still separates *cholos* and Indians.

Chile and Paraguay portray other variations. Chile has some 100,000 Araucanian Indians or Mapuches, as they are generally called. Successive seizures of their land intensified their poverty. The Christian Democrats in the 1960s reversed this process, only to see the regressive policy of Pinochet suspend the progress that had been made. Today, the Mapuches generally remain in a self-contained agricultural society, which is diminishing somewhat in size because it is surrounded by a more dynamic environment. Mere vestiges are found in Chile of other indigenous groups, such as the handful of Alakalufs in the extreme south, who fish in the waters of the fjorded coast and trade their products with coastal vessels. Paraguay has in one sense the most vibrant Indian heritage, as the lingua franca of most Paraguayans is Guaraní, even though the nation is essentially mestizo. The few Indians who maintained their way of life had, until the end of the Stroessner dictatorship in 1989, to obey a curfew law if they visited the capital Asunción. Still, the democratic regime has not protected indigenous groups such as the Enxet from exploitation, nor has it recognized their land rights.[36]

Argentina prides itself on being the most purely white country other than Canada in the hemisphere. Yet, according to one report, as late as 1869 the country had 80,000 Indians, 15,000 blacks, 120,000 mulattoes, and 1,315,000 mixed as opposed to 350,000 whites.[37] Even with the addition of several million Europeans during the last one hundred years, the country can hardly be as pure as claimed by its people, who have hurled at Brazil, especially during the Perón era, such epithets as that "Nigger country." Similar statements are heard in upper-class circles in Chile in reference to its own Indian minority as well as to Peru or to Bolivia.

Even within the white community, ethnic divisions are found. Whether in Buenos Aires or Santiago, the descendants of English and Germans are bilingual, yet gather at their respective country club. Similarly, private schools are usually referred to as American, British, French, German, or Italian. In addition, various traditions, such as "high tea" or the Anglican church, assure allegiance to their European—or in this case—English past. Another segment of the European population throughout Latin America is the Jewish community.[38] Argentina has the largest, with nearly 300,000 members, and Brazil the second, with over 100,000. The migration began in the late nineteenth century when they were escaping the pogroms of Eastern Europe, and a second wave followed the advent of Nazism. Although most Jews are involved in the commercial and professional world, they established no less than a dozen agricultural communities at the turn of the century. Antisemitism appears sporadically in Argentina. On the other hand, in the more ethnically diverse Brazil a number of Jews have occupied political posts.

Brazil

Compared to the United States or the Union of South Africa, Brazil appears to be a model multiracial society. In fact, Brazilians usually prefer the term "color" to "race" as it embodies their image of race as a continuum from black or African to white or European.[39] This characterization is hardly valid, but it does underline the Latin American formula that race is a class concept rather than a physical category. No legal boundaries exist, but occupational, residential, and social patterns are correlated with skin color. The belief that Brazil is a racial democracy is comparable to the myth of the self-made man in the United States.[40]

Brazil derives from four kinds of population: (1) the Portuguese colonists; (2) indigenous tribes, many of whom were virtually enslaved in colonial times; (3) Negro slaves brought over from Africa; and (4) mixed strains, from the *mamelucos* of the first Portuguese and Indian mixing to the *pardos* or white–Negro mixture of today. The majority of Indians remained relatively free and inaccessible during the first half century after the discovery of Brazil, but thousands were pressed into labor during this period. The high death rate of Indians led to the importation of Africans at the middle of the sixteenth century. From that time to the end of the slave trade in 1850, over three million Africans (if we exclude the extravagant estimates that go to sixteen million) were brought to Brazil. Until about 1750, life expectancy on arrival in Brazil was perhaps five years, the system being built on the necessity for constant replacement. The importation was about 90 percent male; however, the reservoir of slaves was minimally increased by reproduction.[41] Men and women were usually separated at night in order to prevent pregnancies as it was not considered economical to rear slave children, not least because infant and child mortality was high.[42]

The degree of indulgence toward racial types bears a regional stamp. The presence of African blood is itself of little interest since discrimination is based on shifting, ambivalent modes of behavior.[43] Lighter complexion and less coarse features favor occupational entrée, social relationships, and intermarriage. Still, only small differences were found between mulattoes and blacks in income, which was only half of the income of whites in both 1960 and 1976.[44] Unlike the United States, where one Afro-American grandparent would make one a black, it is not ancestry but physical appearance and social status that become the relevant criteria. São Paulo has the southernmost concentration of *pretos* (blacks), and their undefined, ambivalent position is reminiscent of the color line in the North of the United States before the advent of black militancy in the 1960s. In the 1930s, the city witnessed movements for Afro-Brazilian rights like the Frente Negra Brasileira. Even in the more permissive atmosphere of postwar Brazil, the *preto* did not attain the educational, occupational, and social advantages of the whites.[45]

The north–south axis remains a subtle but significant factor in race relations. Recife in the North encourages intermarriage, usually the darker male finding a lighter wife; only in the white upper class are marriage lines racially drawn. Social life generally cuts across racial boundaries.[46] Rio experiences large-scale migration and limited mobility of blacks into white-collar positions. As with the more conservative areas of the Northeast Coast, the upper class is reluctant to accept *pessoas de côr* (colored persons). Still, it would be difficult to find overt discrimination. Similarly, São Paulo, with only 11 percent nonwhite in the population, has no formal discrimination in public places (housing, transportation, cinemas, hospitals, etc.); yet, Afro-Brazilians are subtly discouraged from entering barber shops or restaurants. Civil service employment is open to all, but promotion of blacks is doubtful, and few are found in management positions.

Even though Brazil represents one of the highest approximations of racial democracy to be found in the world, it is impossible to speak of race equality. Comparison with the ethnic structure of the United States is more appropriate today than it was a generation ago.[47] The economics of color remains, conditioned though it is by a whitening process. The older saying at Bahia, "*Quem escapa de branco, negro e*" ("Who can't be a white man is a Negro") was replaced by "*Quem escapa de negro, branco e*" ("Who isn't a Negro is a white man").[48] In fact, because of a bleaching process by marital selection the pure black is less conspicuous. In any case, the darker man with money becomes whiter, and the less affluent *pardo* becomes a *preto*. Because of a sliding scale, with only the very black or dark relegated to an outgroup, a "black identity" is difficult to develop. Nonetheless, a number of black organizations appeared in the 1970s. Also, a "black soul movement" emerged in the *favelas* (slums).[49]

It is not easy to divorce race relations from politics. Although no official discrimination occurred after the establishment of the Republic in 1889 (the nation had one black as president, Nilo Pecanha in 1909–1910), political climate is itself a relevant variable. Progress in advancing the status of the nonwhite was most visible during the Kubitschek and Goulart regimes. The military dictatorship in 1964 had different priorities. President Geisel did not have a single black in his cabinet, and relations between Brazil and the Union of South Africa became warmer. With the shift to democracy in 1985, racial barriers again broke down. Industrialization, urbanization, and migration are three important processes making for the movement to a racially equalitarian society. Nonetheless, in the 1980s Afro-Brazilians—and women—were still experiencing discrimination in occupational status and income.[50] The final solution to the problem can come only with a full social and economic democracy.

TOWARD A CLASSIFICATION OF ETHNIC PATTERNS

Throughout Latin America, patterns of integration and segregation are complex, with marked differences between countries. Nonetheless, a tentative categorization is possible:

1. *Actively integrative.* Probably more than any other Latin American country, Mexico, at least officially, has insisted on the incorporation of the Indian into its national culture, Chiapas notwithstanding. Indeed, the *indigenista* movement is not altogether consistent in its attempt to preserve the Indians' culture, but at the same time it tries to make them fully functioning members of the society. With a greater problem than Mexico, Bolivia turned to integration after the 1952 revolution, however uneven the results became.

2. *Quasi-integrative.* Despite social and economic barriers, Brazil, notably in the North, has a permeable racial structure. In view of the integration of the Guaraní culture, Paraguay also belongs to this category. Colombia, Venezuela, and, to a lesser extent, three of the Central American republics (El Salvador, Honduras, and Nicaragua) are characterized by both a preponderantly mestizo population and minimal racial prejudice, even if they fall well short of northern Brazil. As with most Latin American nations, social advantages remain with a small ratio of pure or almost pure whites. However, urbanization and the rise of the middle class make ethnic differences less conspicuous.

3. *Quasi-prejudicial.* Argentina, Uruguay, Costa Rica, Panama, and Chile to different degrees offer a European character and way of life. Though probably below the level of overt prejudice found in the United States, these countries exhibit a latent hostility toward nonwhites.

4. *Dualistic.* Guatemala, Ecuador, and Peru are examples of a semicaste structure. Especially in Peru, the relations between Indians and mestizos are in a state of flux, and perhaps in the end will move in the direction of Mexico.

Not all regions or subcultures fit within this classification. Also, a number of nations constitute special cases. The Caribbean, for example, has its own variants. Cuba changed from a predominantly black population— 60 percent in the early nineteenth century—to the present when less than one-third of the population are black or mulatto. Segregation has been sharply evident for most of Cuban history. Despite its promises to the contrary, the Castro regime has not completely eradicated the social or even the economic forms of discrimination, especially as African Cubans are underrepresented in the higher echelons of the Communist Party.[51] Other variants include Haiti, with an almost totally African population in which mulattoes enjoy economic and social domination. In the Dominican Republic, whites and mestizos are in a superior position over those of African background. Rarely in Latin America is skin color unrelated to socioeconomic status.

THE STATUS STRUCTURE

After this broad look at the historical and regional aspects of race relations, we may examine the social and psychological aspects of ethnic discrimination and prejudice: How are ethnic categories defined? How do they function? To what degree can they be changed?

What Is Race?

The North American is accustomed to explicit categories defining race in terms of physical terms and ancestry, whereas in Latin America the concept of race is more variable, since it primarily involves sociocultural criteria. It is often said that a person with similar physical characteristics might be labeled a mulatto in Brazil, a black in the United States, and possibly a mestizo in Mexico. For instance, to define a person as an Indian or a *ladino* depends on the language she or he speaks, where and how he or she lives, and other aspects of social behavior.

The question of what constitutes an Indian is especially arbitrary in Mexico. Indians are most clearly identified when they live in a self-contained tribal group, whereas at the other end of the scale dress or language may be the only identifying characteristic. Perhaps as safe a means as any is to ask individuals how they classify themselves. On that point, an experiment in Brazil found that when the choice on a questionnaire was between *pardo* (dark brown) or "white," people of mixed race tended to choose the latter or occasionally the former, but if *morena* (dark or tan) was offered, many of them preferred this identification.[52] Seemingly, self-identity and semantics have much to do with race relations.

The task of distinguishing between Indian and mestizo or *ladino* becomes tantalizing in southern Mexico and Guatemala when we attempt to erect special criteria, which may vary from one community to another. Many Indians who live near *ladinos* learn at least a limited amount of Spanish. Surnames are usually changed on *ladinoization*, but not in all communities. Dress is variable according to the type of employment or the level of local pressure. The *jacal* or hut is another sign; still, acculturated Indians occasionally prefer this type of housing. Indians often live on the periphery of the community, but as they rise occupationally they filter into the area near the plaza. Similarly, although Indians are more concerned with the supernatural and revere a number of sacred objects and places, this difference thins out in biracial communities that are more or less integrated.

The Problem of Terminology

The nomenclature of race can likewise become elaborate and often inconsistent. We have already referred to the pedantic classification of colonial Mexico. Not everyone in Brazil can be placed neatly into precise categories, but they do function as convenient reference points, as when one might say a person is *bem preto* (really black).

The term "Negro" generally is not used since it has negative overtones, and refers to an "African" or "foreigner." Yet *meu negro* (my Negro) can be interpreted as a very affectionate expression, at least in Bahia, even as used by whites when speaking to other whites, between lovers, or in deference to another person.[53] The expression harks back to the endearment to the blacks associated with the *casa grande* subculture. At the same time, over the four centuries since the arrival of Africans in Brazil, terms have taken on negative as well as positive associations.[54] Among the labels for the Luso–African are *boçal* meaning newly arrived but also "crude," and *ladino* referring to "astute" or "cunning."

An analysis of Cuzco, Peru, reveals an elaborate terminology in defining ethnic groups. Occasionally, the official nomenclature suggests economic and political ideology, such as after the 1968 coup the government chose to rename Indians as *campesinos*. This Marxist touch found favor among various leftist groups. The mestizos, who occupy a privileged position in the community, are labeled variously *la crema, los ricos,* or less often *los blancos*. More often they refer to themselves as *los vecinos,* the "neighbors" or "town burghers." Someone who looks especially white or foreign is called a "gringo," and if of dubious morals, a "hippy." The jargon applied to the Indians of the Amazon includes *selváticos* (the forest people) or *salvajes* (the savages). These terms and a variety of similar ones take on special meanings and statuses. In Guatemala, these elaborate or at least subtle distinctions still occur; for example, the *ladino* can be a "declassé creole." The term "mestizo" only appeared after 1960.[55] Most societies have a hierarchical structure based in part on ethnicity. Generally, boundaries have become more flexible in recent decades. Yet, equalized opportunity, to what point it exists, is different from the reward structure, which ends as a zero-sum game, since education, skills, and other means of access have never been equalized.[56]

Prejudice and Stereotypes

The language of color is only one element reflecting prejudice. Latin Americans are not unique in ascribing lower status to women, children, Protestants, and, occasionally, foreigners. Attitudes of the mestizo or ladino toward the Indian in Peru, Guatemala, and southern Mexico are similar, although intimate social relations often make for a complex set of relationships. For example, the rape of servant girls by *ladinos* in the Chiapas highlands is rationalized as a means of improving the Indian blood. Casual sexual liaisons and concubinage are widespread, but few marriages occur. Commercial transactions are at the advantage of the *ladino*, shopkeepers often cheat Indians, and social etiquette is based on the superior position of the *ladino*. Transportation reflects the same pattern. The Indian pays second class fare for standing room on a truck while the *ladino* for the same fare has a seat on a bus. Wage rates are similarly adjusted downward for Indian labor. All these differences are rationalized according to a hierarchical social order based on supposedly innate superiority and inferiority.

Nor are stereotypes confined to nonwhites. Polish immigrants to the state of Paraná in Brazil were identified by those who preceded them as "prone to alcoholism, excessively religious, always blond, inclined to prefer rough physical (and hence intellectually inferior) labor, given to cohabitation with Negroes."[57] It required three generations to transform these Poles into Brazilians. As with any racial ethnic stereotype, this dislike of the Pole served those who feared competition in the search for security and upward mobility. Distinctions between individuals are based on the "domination–subordination relationships" surrounding the labor market and access to power, whether in regard to the black, the Indian, the Japanese, or the Pole. As elsewhere in the world, the nonwhite of lower class is subject to prejudices of a "self-fulfilling prophecy." As a consequence, Indians often accept the stereotype placed on them by the mestizo or white. Whether or not they rebel, and in rare instances they do, they are unable to change the stereotype.

Stereotyping is not always negative. Despite conditioning of race relations by class and other considerations, the Afro-Brazilian, and especially the mulatto, have an ambivalent status in Brazil because of the Portuguese tolerance of darker complexion and the traditional dependency of one racial group on another. Moreover, the question of sexual attractiveness is relevant. According to Donald Pierson's study of race attitudes in Bahia, the *morena* is an ideal type of femininity with her dark brown eyes and hair, often wavy and curly, and coffee-like complexion. When confronted with a questionnaire item as to their marital choice, 80 percent of the students of both sexes preferred the *moreno* or *morena* to the white or black.[58] This stereotyped response reveals an esthetic feeling as well as the idea that the *moreno* typically exhibits strong affection and sexuality. Also, two-thirds of Brazilians are racially mixed. Both whites and blacks are minorities within their national culture.

Stereotypes permit us to establish boundaries between groups. We differentiate a category that remains as a label in our memory. Whether favorable or unfavorable, stereotypes provide a means of categorizing individuals into groups. We can then make predictions about their behavior. These stereotypes are necessary for us to process the barrage of social stimuli impinging on our sense organs. Of course, as the social scene undergoes change, older stereotypes may not serve and new ones have to be created. Guatemalan society was once divided into *ladino* and *indio*, but the 1944–1954 socialist regime shattered the caste structure. Gray areas appeared; that is, some persons did not fit neatly into a given category. New labels—or old ones with new meaning—such as mestizo had to be created to permit differentiation. In other words, as used over the last few decades the term *mestizo* has come to cover the person in a "conceptual middle ground."[59]

Class Variables

The relationship of social class to color remains fundamental to all multiracial countries, but the relation is not necessarily clear. For instance, the Afro-Brazilian occupies the lowest rungs of the socioeconomic ladder. In a study of university students, upper- more than lower-class subjects were inclined to have negative stereotypes but were more tolerant in their social norms and reported behavior—possibly a reflection of paternalism in the upper class and competitiveness in the lower class.[60] Yet middle-class *paulistas* have generally appeared to be more psychologically threatened when equality is granted to blacks in schools, professions, clubs, and other domains not traditionally open to them. In São Paulo, blacks are encouraged to enter the rear of apartment houses and use the "service" elevator rather than the elevator labeled as "social." Neither the city council nor the Union of Housekeepers has been successful in ending the practice.[61] In much of Brazil, factors of social status, appearance, and demeanor are probably more important than skin color.

Similarly, in rural areas, social class is intertwined with race. Even in the Peruvian Amazon one cannot escape one's ethnic origins with upward occupational mobility.[62] In some instances it is difficult to determine what is cause and effect, as in several Argentine villages where the indigenous members of the population occupy lower status—one more example of self-fulfilling prophecy.[63] Status differentials seem to be at the core of prejudice and discrimination. Status and accompanying power gives the individual access to more options in the economic and other relevant markets. However, there is disagreement about the relevance of status attainment as an explanation of racial prejudice.[64]

Color, Mobility, and Interethnic Marriage

As implied previously, in Guatemala the social structure is moving from a dualistic society to a kind of class system as interethnic mobility increases. Today, the relationships between Indian and *ladino* appear like strata within a partially integrated system, even though minimal social interaction occurs between the two groups. It is relevant that *ladinos* themselves belong to several socioeconomic levels ranging from landowners to workers, and the more affluent Indians are at least equal in status to the lower strata of *ladino* society. Indeed, according to a study of two communities, in the more affluent San Pedro Sacatepéquez, an Indian might live better than the average *ladino* in San Marcos.[65] Similarly in Peru, the possibility of upward mobility is threatening traditional ethnic barriers. It depends on the observer's perspective whether she or he perceives ethnic stratification as a dichotomy or a continuum. If the society is undergoing a high rate of acculturation, the term "caste" is no longer applicable.

For most Indians, Afro-Americans, and mestizos, the problem of upward mobility remains, yet the phenomenon of passing would hardly have meaning for a society in which race is subordinate to class criteria. At the same time, a long-term tendency toward whitening of the skin in Brazil is the result of European immigration, greater survival rates of whites over blacks, and multiple sexual contact of white males with nonwhite females. *Embranquecimento* (whitening) has been the ideal of many blacks who mate with whites in order to have lighter offspring. According to an analysis of intermarriage, the much higher rate of intermarriage in northeast Brazil may be more the result of propinquity than tolerance.[66] As the marriage market depends on the pool of candidates, the availability of whites in the North (and blacks and mulattoes in the South) is limited.

Presumably, the psychological mechanisms appearing in the research literature in the United States are relevant to the Latin American scene. That is, despite the more liberal attitudes of recent years, the whites continue to cling to nonracial—or racial—factors that allow them to rationalize their antipathy to nonwhites.[67] For instance, among the staff of a Bogotá transnational oil company, an Afro-American with a graduate degree is usually referred to as that "negrito."

Interracial marriage reflects the restructuring of racial lines. Intermarriage in countries with Indian population is rare, though white males carry on exploitative sexual activities. Indeed, servant girls of whatever race are vulnerable throughout Latin America, either at the call of the *patrón* or as a training episode for his son. Even though marriage generally reflects status needs and family considerations, intermarriage is increasing in a number of places. In Recife, Brazil, it has been extensive for many decades, whereas in the village of Cruz das Almas it is a more recent phenomenon. As in the United States, marriage occurs most frequently between the nonwhite male who is occupationally mobile and a female a shade lighter than himself. Intermarriage is a symptom of the more open mobility of the blacks that emerged after the end of slavery. The rate of intermarriage in Brazil began to decline in the mid-1970s.[68] The explanation may lie in changed perception of mobility channels or the emergence of black consciousness. Moreover, the crossing of racial boundaries is more prevalent in the lower class, whereas in all strata of the U.S. South, caste norms still discourage crossing of the threshold.

PREJUDICE AND SOCIAL CHANGE

The complexity of ethnic prejudice calls for a multifactor approach. Analysis of the cause of attitudes and behavior involves the historian, the economist, the anthropologist, the psychologist, and the legal specialist as well as the psychiatrist and sociologist. Investigations in the United States point to the institutional supports of prejudice within the socio-economic system, such as legal segregation, job discrimination, and the appropriateness of a given marital candidate.

In Latin America, prejudice is not usually of high salience and can be unlearned when it is recognized that nonwhites meet a dominant need of the community. It would seem to follow that in Argentina, Uruguay, and Chile, with relatively few nonwhites, prejudice is widespread, whereas in countries where Europeans are at most 10 percent of the population, strong racial bias is most evident in the aristocracy and older middle class. Prejudice is not, however, confined to any social class. In a broader context, we may look upon societies as undergoing fairly constant change, whether slow or rapid. People must adopt new situations, and their perceptions are readjusted accordingly. These new perceptions include the changing images of ethnic groups. During periods of rapid social change, racial tensions are related to "perceptual defense." When individuals perceive their world as no longer predictable, they look upon members of a racial outgroup as threatening. Moreover, racial attitudes are difficult to change if the individual's or group's self-interests are in any way threatened.[69]

In the Western Hemisphere, reassessments have tended to be more inclusive in recent years; still, progress is not universal. As an instance, Peruvian intellectuals speak of the irrational fear of *limeños* who see their values and their city under attack by Andean peasants.[70] The resilience of the society and its members to accept ethnic varieties is, of course, an outgrowth of the structure of the society. The distinction has been made between disparate plural societies which are characterized by parallel ethnic groups with rigid boundaries, as in pre-1994 South Africa, as opposed to the more open pluralistic societies. As the society moves to more acceptance or even homogeneity, another problem appears; that is, many ethnic groups struggle to retain their cultural identity.[71]

Industrialization and Its Consequences

As implied previously, race relations are affected by the process of modernization. Technological and other innovations break up traditional belief systems and offer individuals the opportunity to get acquainted with each other. On the other hand, processes such as industrialization and urbanization usher in changes to a society that may bring out latent conflicts between groups: The shift from traditional plantations to corporate agriculture, as in Costa Rica, makes for more stereotyping of blacks and mestizos. However, stereotyping is less severe than in Panama, presumably because of a more liberal political policy and wider educational possibilities.[72]

Brazil furnishes an example of the effect of industrialization on racial attitudes. With the end of slavery, former slaves began to move into the emerging cities, only to find most avenues of employment closed to them but open to the newly arrived European immigrants. World War I did provide an occupational arena for blacks, but only at the unskilled level. Industrialization around the period of World War II offered Afro-Brazilians better job opportunities at the very time that unionization was approaching the high-water mark. Blacks were absorbed gradually into the urban proletariat. Although large factories now accept blacks, placement for them is more difficult in the smaller establishments, especially those owned by immigrants who see no need for accepting the nonwhite. Also, they may have their own obligations to the foreign-born community. In a survey of seventy-four metropolitan areas in Brazil, industrialization promoted access of nonwhites to blue-collar jobs, but their acceptance in white-collar work was still limited. The lack of an Afro-Brazilian middle class is relevant. Further, the government "does nothing to protect its citizens against racism"; consequently, employers are free to discriminate.[73]

Whatever the strides of the last half century, the employment situation is a variable one. Afro-Brazilians are often forced to depend on rumor in order to determine what opportunities actually exist. Fear of rejection, whether real or imagined, becomes one more burden to them in their attempt to repair their self-image. Various rationalizing and compensatory outlets are the result. As Fernandes notes, the insecurity the black experiences leads to feelings of self-destructiveness and social isolation. "Little by little, young people are forced to accept two truths: one which affirms and one which negates racial democracy."[74]

Afro-Brazilians—or other ethnic groups—are not psychologically prepared for the rationalized society they find in the urban scene or the insecurity in the mushrooming *favelas* of Rio de Janeiro and other cities. The processes of abolition, industrialization, and urbanization are not completely integrated into the Brazilian culture pattern. For one thing, acceptance of the black in the workplace does not follow into most social settings, any more than it does in the United States. As slavery gradually gave way to a system of retainers, blacks and whites still held to their tradition of paternalism. This tendency lingered in the *fazenda* and *engheno* cultures, but as they moved into the urban *favela* culture the migrant *pretos* felt alienated toward the white bureaucratic society and found refuge in cultism, sports clubs, and other pursuits available to them in the metropolis. Industrialism does not solve the problem of racial differences but may change their character.

Modernization and industrialization can also introduce the seeds of prejudice when the migrant crosses national and cultural boundaries. One historical example is the importation of West Indians or *chombos* as labor during the building of the Panama Canal early in the twentieth century. The *chombos* were to remain only for the period of construction; consequently, an agreement was reached with the United States to ensure their repatriation. Panamanian shopkeepers, however, came to depend on them for business. The World War I period, beginning the year the Canal was completed, provided a rich employment market. As West Indians were a surplus in the 1920s, fierce competition for jobs revived the native Panamanians' prejudice, which became intense during the Depression years of the 1930s. During World War II, *chombos* again were wanted and the Constitution of 1946 gave citizenship, with immigration continuing into the postwar period.

Actually, prejudice is not based on simply physical characteristics, since the Panamanian black is generally darker than the West Indian, but the latter is stereotyped as having thick lips, coarse features, and an ungainly physique. Nor are class considerations a critical point, as the West Indian or *chombo* is better educated and has achieved middle-class status. Rather, it is a matter of cultural difference—British tradition, different food and dress, and use of English. As second- and third-generation *chombos* have become Panamanians, tensions are less marked.

Change and the Social Structure

As a pluralistic society, Latin America is held together—in contrast to India, Southeast Asia, the Middle East, or South Africa—by the bonds of language, religion, and a common past. Nonetheless, slavery and indentured labor produced strain. Ironically, the end of slavery in Brazil did not create upward mobility for the Afro-Brazilian, whereas after the breakup of slavery in North America blacks slowly and painfully began to move up the socioeconomic scale. In Brazil, feeling is less polarized between whites and blacks, not least because race is a matter of shades of color.

In analyzing how discrimination is related to the structural and functional aspects of the specific society, we turn again to the social status and work patterns of different ethnic groups in Panama.[75] The position of these groups varied with the particular economic needs with which they could supply their society as well as their bargaining power within the social structure of the Canal Zone and the Republic of Panama, which has been economically dependent on the Zone. During the building of the Canal prior to 1914, the need for technological skills favored American and European workers, whose feeling of superiority over the darker-skinned Panamanians and West Indians consequently increased. Thus remuneration came to be based on two types of workers, the U.S. or "gold roll" and the local or "silver roll." The differential was functional to some degree as the Americans contributed their needed skills to developing the economy and also became acclimated to a tropical area. After the completion of the Canal, the pay differential continued since it had become structural as American technicians now had a vested interest in staying in the Canal Zone because of higher benefits they received as opposed to what awaited them in their homeland. These built-in rewards for the Anglo-Saxon caused considerable tension among the natives who were disadvantaged in the Zone.

A new functional period began around World War II when increased job opportunities became available to both Panamanians and West Indians. A Congress of Industrial Organizations (CIO) affiliate organized the "silver" workers at the same time that new recruits were brought into the "gold roll." This new equilibrium favored more equitable race relations. A moderate degree of tension continues and is complicated by the transitional period regarding the status of the Canal. Today, both white North Americans and West Indians are resented for cultural and linguistic reasons. In other words, nationalistic aspirations influence ethnic relations. The color line is of secondary importance, since Panamanians regard themselves as a mestizo nation. The upper class has some sense of superior ancestry, but for most of the population, racial purity is a meaningless concept.

The Institutional Fabric and the Individual

Just as ethnic attitudes inevitably affect, and are affected by, economics and politics, so are they likewise structured by other social institutions. First of all, racial attitudes are acquired in the socialization process within the family. The school setting itself provides a basis for the strengthening of racial attitudes. Although education in Brazil is committed to the idea of racial equality, the white or *branco* is favored. Peer groups also influence this tendency. Children and adolescents are surrounded by a system of rewards for those with lighter skin, extolled though the *moreno* may be in song and poetry. Education is also a means of mobility. Ethnic groups improve their occupational chances in those social settings where they have access to schooling. For instance, Bolivia provides a greater opportunity for upward mobility than does Guatemala.[76]

Even the Church has subtle effects on the status of nonwhites. For many Catholics, African cultism in the *preto's* religious beliefs and practices account for this negative reaction. Since overt discriminatory practices became inappropriate, it is doubtful today that Church officials would let their private beliefs enter into relations with clergy or lay members of their parish or diocese. In fact, the Roman Catholic clergy in the Amazon is a force in resisting exploitation by Brazilian entrepreneurs.[77]

Nor is the government apparatus free of prejudice. Until recently, the military favored whites for officer training. The Brazilian navy was criticized for its color prejudice because prior to 1960 no more than ten mulattoes had ever been chosen as officer candidates. Adverse publicity led to some relaxation of the criteria for the selection. It is still claimed that the Brazilian Foreign Service has its preferences: Whiteness of the skin is a basis of selection. Moreover, tests for the foreign service school are generally held in the capital so that those with sufficient means for travel have an advantage. For most of Latin America, candidacy for public office has recently attracted more mestizos. It is significant that Mexico and Bolivia, having undergone revolutions, exhibit relatively less prejudice, even concerning elite positions.

With few exceptions, the institutional structure favors the dominant group. Voluntary associations, among other arenas, display preference for the white. Anyone visiting a Latin American country club notes that European appearance is somehow the mark of admission, whether by selection machinery or simply by income level. In Brazil, the hierarchy of clubs is graded formally by the color continuum. In Bahia, Rio de Janeiro, or São Paulo, individuals shift their club membership as they advance in social status. Peer group associations often resemble a game of musical chairs. One chooses guests for a dinner party or even fellow spectators at a soccer match according to one's mobility aspirations. A number of voluntary associations have a civic character. The União dos Homens de Côr (Association of Colored People) is roughly equivalent to the traditional role of the NAACP before it became activist. For the most part, however, the black must advance as an individual since group pressure is only now beginning to assume some militancy. Similarly in Colombia, blacks are challenging attitudes about the "invisibility" of blackness. In some instances they work with indigenous groups on the political front and were successful in adding a clause to the 1991 Constitution recognizing the "multiethnic and plural" nature of the republic.[78]

The Role of Conflict

Racial prejudice basically appears as a value judgment resulting in the categorization of a given ethnic group, often in the form of a stereotype. At the same time, prejudice and discrimination are deepened by conflict, either in the external situation or in internal or unconscious processes. A person perceives a threat in the presence of an unacceptable individual or group, or she or he may have deep-seated hostility as a result of some incidents in her or his total experience.

Frustration is productive of conflict and aggression. This chapter has catalogued a number of sources of frustration to nonwhites in the Latin American scene. Bureaucracy, poverty, inflation, poor housing, and inadequate diet would only begin to tell the story. Competition is, of course, a form of conflict. As in the United States, ethnic populations, Indian and *ladino*, are forced to compete in the same markets. The migrant to the city often competes in the labor market with the urban lower class, who already have a foothold in the proletarian ladder.

Frustration and strain seldom find their way into overt race conflict, although exceptions are to be found. An example is the hostility between the strongly ethnocentric Yaqui *comunidad* in Sonora, Mexico, and the surrounding mestizo culture.[79] The Yaquis' dislike for the Yoris, as their acculturated neighbors are called, is a means of keeping their own culture relatively intact. Rural isolation in these *ejidos* helps to maintain suspiciousness of others. The frustration of the Indians rarely takes the form of violent action; rather they acquiesce to their inferior position, except when they are activated in the peasant leagues and the like. Conflict is more likely to be expressed at the verbal level.

One cause of hostility toward the outgroup is the fear of *loss of control*. In its extreme form, this concern of the white ruling class about holding on to power has led to violent incidents, mostly in the past. One such incident was the mass murder of some 2,500 Indians in El Salvador by the dictator Martínez in 1932. The surviving Indians in the region gave up some of their culture in order to avoid being the targets of an outraged government. This type of violence, reminiscent of the tactics of Díaz a generation earlier toward Indian and mestizo miners who were on strike, is a throwback to the depravities of the colonial era. Only in a few primitive areas, such as rural Haiti with its lack of modern communication, can a regressive government resort systematically to large-scale violence; elsewhere public authorities would be vulnerable to attacks from both within and outside the nation.

In the contemporary scene, social relationships between *cholo* or *ladino* and Indian reflect concern with power, albeit in a nonviolent fashion. The new rights given to Guatemalan Indians in the Arévalo and Arbenz regime magnified these fears. As long as Indians have only a marginal relation to the sources of power, they have no alternative but to accept the hegemony of the *ladino* and white and remain in their self-contained socioeconomic community, at least until revolutionary change moves the society in a different direction, as in Chiapas in 1994.

ETHNIC SURVIVAL AND THE
INDIGENISTA MOVEMENT

In Latin America, one sees two possible developments in respect to its ethnic groups. One path is integration. In other words, governments might move toward a relatively homogeneous, or at least a harmonious, society with two goals: (1) to encourage conformity to the society and provide the individual with the tools to proceed in his or her advance and (2) to reduce possible friction between ethnic groups and the larger society. The other option is the insistence that the indigenous societies maintain their own cultures and attempt to educate the public to respect these differences. There are arguments both for homogenization and for the protectionist policy of pluralism. In part, the argument derives from the view of the indigenous culture. The integrationist sometimes assumes a Social Darwinist viewpoint that primitive cultures must move to a higher order, which may mean the disappearance of less resourceful tribes. On the other hand, the preservationist viewpoint may err on taking a Rousseauesque view of the native as a romantic, almost childlike figure.[80] Occasionally, the two concepts—integration and indigenous pluralism— are fused. Political movements in Mexico, Peru, and Bolivia glorify an indigenous past, yet turn to Western culture for most of their innovations. Lip service is paid to the uniqueness of the American spirit with the fusion of the various races as the goal.

We may examine a few of the protectionist attempts to deal with the problem. In 1948 the Mexican government established the National Indigenous Institute (INI), which played the principal role in giving both impetus and implementing programs to solve problems of the Indian community. Besides acting as guardian of Indian affairs, the Institute carries on research as well as instruction of the indigenous population. It established a number of centers in various parts of the Republic, the most important one being at Las Casas in Chiapas, which provides training with stress on the native crafts and language. Its role in language instruction may be self-defeating as the end-result is exploitation when Indians move into towns and become a means of cheap labor, usually in the informal economy. The INI does not seem to be able to prevent capitalist invasions, as for instance the threat of logging to both the Lacandón Maya and the Huicholes in the Sierra Madre.

The most widespread destruction of the indigenous population occurs with Brazilian tribes. Of 230 tribes existent in the year 1900, 87 were extinct by the 1960s. Although this process of attrition has occurred since colonization, it was slowed down by Mariano da Silva Rondon, who organized the Indian Protection Service (IPS) in 1910. He spent years of feverish activity in rescuing the Indian from the encroachment of the armed forces and other threats. The leaders in the IPS who followed in Rondon's footsteps were caught in the conflict between their goals and the ambitions of miners, cattlemen, highway builders, and others who continued in the tradition of Brazilian boom psychology. The IPS's aims for a gradual assimilation of the indigenous population were hardly advanced by the military regime of 1964. A new wave of scandals of exploitation and extermination was revealed in 1968 when the Amazon basin and the New West were further carved up for the exploitation of ruthless developers. The government also authorized the establishment of more than one hundred cattle-ranching projects involving some one million hectares with the result of partial extermination of the Xavante tribe.[81] As a result, the government established FUNAI (National Indian Foundation) with the idea of integrating the indigenous population into the greater society and at the same time providing a degree of autonomy. Several parks have been established to assure protection, but the battle continues with the capitalist world; nor has FUNAI been able to find the resources to maintain a sound ecological environment either for the tribes or for national needs.[82] Attacks against various tribes have continued into the present as the tragic slaughter of Yanomanis by gold miners in 1993 documents.

Generally, provision for the indigenous population has been pitiful compared to the involvement of the Canadian and U.S. governments, notwithstanding the questionable outcome of their policies. One may cite various examples: In Argentina, remnants of fourteen tribes live on public lands or in national parks with neither title to their lands or hunting rights. In Chile, on the Bio Bio River near Concepción the traditional territory of the Pehuenche tribe is threatened by the construction of hydroelectric plants. Decisions are never simple. In both Chile and Argentina, the Mapuche have to decide to work with or against the government in their attempts to establish a nation of their own.[83] At the same time, the Sendero Luminoso in Peru threatened with death Quechuas who refused to join their movement. Indians in Colombia have suffered several massacres at the hands of drug traffickers.

On the other hand, an outgroup may use violent means to press its demands on the more affluent and conservative elements in the society. Through the years a number of tribes from Guatemala to Brazil returned in kind the violent means used by business interests against them. Peasant leagues, including the Sendero Luminoso of Peru and guerrilla warfare in Guatemala, are directed against the inequities of the society. This type of activity could in the broadest sense be a means of liberating the racially disenfranchised. These movements usually have mestizo leadership and in most instances involve various ethnic groups and indigenous tribes pitted against entrepreneurs and land-hungry frontiersmen, especially in Brazil.

THE PRESENT AND THE FUTURE

This chapter presents the relationships of the various racial strains in Latin America. The discussion has emphasized historical, sociological, and psychological factors in the patterns of acceptance and rejection. I have not attempted to focus on the cultures of indigenous societies, nor on the extensive contributions that certain races have made to the historical development of the society, as, for instance, the heritage the African has given to the religion, art, music, and folklore of Brazil. Rather, I have hinted at the significance of given ethnic groups, whether of minority or majority status, on the social relationships within the society. For example, the *cholos* of Peru have become local and occasionally national leaders pressing for social change. However, Indians are still removed from decision making in the society.

The ethnic conflicts of Latin America are rooted in the competition for the limited goods and resources of these various societies. In most countries, descendants of Europeans hold the power but are gradually forced to share their resources with mestizos. With the possible exception of Bolivia, Indians are very marginal competitors for the commodities of the society. In Brazil, blacks and other ethnic groups have an uneven status. Despite these various inconsistencies, Latin America is saved from the worst marks of prejudice when we think of Africa, the Middle East, or even the Western world. Its more severe problems lie in the nature of the economy and the political process. That the first citizens of the New World were of mixed blood did much to prevent the development of a social pyramid based on color per se.

The emphasis of this chapter is on both the fluidity and rigidity of ethnic relationships, linked as they are to the concept of class. Hopefully, as status differences can be reduced by a more equitable distribution of wealth, economic growth, and the strengthening of the middle class, we may anticipate an easing of the barriers existing today between whites, mestizos, Afro-Americans, and, possibly to a lesser extent, the Indians. In a society undergoing industrialization and shifting occupational roles, ethnic boundaries usually, but not always, tend to diminish. For the present, conflict seems to be as evident as accommodation.

NOTES

1. Jorge Palacios Preciado, "La Esclavitud y la Sociedad Esclavista," in *Manual de Historia de Colombia*, vol. 1, ed. Jaime Jaramillo Uribe (Bogotá: Instituto Colombiano de Cultura, 1978), 304–346.

2. John Hawkins, *Inverse Images: The Meaning of Culture, Ethnicity and Family in Postcolonial Guatemala* (Albuquerque: University of New Mexico Press, 1984), 31–32.

3. Peggy A. Lovell, "Race, Gender, and Development in Brazil," *Latin American Research Review* 29(3): 7–35 (1994).

4. Charles Wagley and Marvin Harris, *Minorities in the New World* (New York: Columbia University Press, 1958), 57.

5. Octavio Ianni, *Origens Agrárias do Estado Brasileiro* (São Paulo: Editora Brasiliense, 1984), 229.

6. D. R. Murray, "The Slave Trade and Slavery in Latin America and the Caribbean," *Latin American Research Review* 21(1): 202–215 (1986).

7. Alan Watson, *Slave Law in the Americas* (Athens: University of Georgia Press, 1990).

8. Richard Graham, ed., *The Idea of Race in Latin America, 1870–1940* (Austin: University of Texas Press, 1990).

9. Winthrop R. Wright, *Café con Leche: Race, Class, and National Image in Venezuela* (Austin: University of Texas Press, 1990), 127–131.

10. Nathan L. Whetten, *Rural Mexico* (Chicago: University of Chicago Press, 1948), 51–52.

11. Gonzalo Aguirre Beltrán and A. Ricardo Pozas, "Instituciones Indígenas en el México Actual," as cited in Wagley and Harris, *Minorities in the New World*, 60.

12. Pierre Beaucage, "La Condición Indígena en México," *Revista Mexicana de Sociología* 50(1): 191–203 (1988).

13. Erwin P. Grieshaber, "Hacienda-Indian Community Relations and Indian Acculturation: An Historigraphical Essay," *Latin American Research Review* 14(3): 107–128 (1979).

14. Scott Cook and Jong-Taick Joo, "Ethnicity and Economy in Rural Mexico: A Critique of the Indigenista Approach," *Latin American Research Review* 30(2): 33–59 (1995).

15. Lourdes Arizpe, "Cultural Change and Ethnicity in Rural Mexico," in *Environment, Society, and Rural Change in Latin America*, ed. David A. Preston (New York: Wiley, 1980), 123–134.

16. Carole Nagengast and Michael Kearney, "Mixtec Ethnicity: Social Identity, Political Consciousness, and Political Activism," *Latin American Research Review* 25(2): 61–91 (1990).

17. Ibid., 87.

18. Lucy Conger, "Mexico: Zapatista Thunder," *Current History* 93(March): 151–120 (1994).

19. Luis Fernández and Jonathan Fox, "Mexico's Difficult Democracy: Grassroots Movements, NGOs, and Local Government," in *New Paths to Democratic Development in Latin America*, ed. Charles A. Reilly (Boulder, Colo.: Lynne Rienner Publishers, 1995), 179–210.

20. Richard N. Adams, *Crucifixion by Power: Essays on Guatemalan National Social Structure, 1944–1966* (Austin: University of Texas Press, 1970), 202.

21. David Stoll, *Between Two Armies in the Ixil Towns of Guatemala* (New York: Columbia University Press, 1993).

22. Juan C. Zuarte, *Forging Democracy: A Comparative Study of the Effects of United States Foreign Policy on Central American Democracy* (Lanham, Md.: University Press of America, 1994).

23. June Nash, "The Reassertion of Indigenous Identity: Mayan Responses to State Intervention in Chiapas," *Latin American Research Review* 30(3): 7–41 (1995).

24. Manuel Chavez, "Las Areas Culturales en Honduras," in *Honduras: Panorama y Perspectivas*, ed. Leticia Salomón (Tequilicigalpa: Centro de Documentación de Honduras, 1989), 201–241.

25. Bernard Nietschmann, *The Unknown War: The Miskito Nation, Nicaragua, and the United States* (New York: Freedom House, 1989).

26. Charles R. Hale, *Resistance and Contradiction: Miskito Indians and the Nicaraguan State, 1894–1987* (Stanford, Calif.: Stanford University Press, 1994), 202–205.

27. Carlos M. Vilas, *State, Class, and Ethnicity in Nicaragua* (Boulder, Colo.: Lynne Rienner Publishers, 1989).

28. Roger N. Lancaster, "Skin Color, Race, and Racism in Nicaragua," *Ethnology* 30: 339–351 (1991).

′ 29. Philip A. Dennis, "The Miskito-Sandinista Conflict in the 1980s," *Latin American Research Review* 28(3): 214–234 (1993).

30. Alejandro D. Marroquín, *Pachimalco: Investigación Sociológica* (San Salvador: Editorial Universitaria, 1959).

31. Jaime Jaramillo Uribe, *Ensayos sobre la Historia Colombiana*, vol. 2 (Bogotá: Universidad de los Andes, 1990), 69–77.

32. Paul Gootenberg, "Population and Ethnicity in Early Republican Peru: Some Revisions," *Latin American Research Review* 26(3): 109–157 (1991).

33. Magnus Mörner, "The History of Race Relations in Latin America: Some Comments on the State of Research," *Latin American Research Review* 1(summer): 17–44 (1966).

34. John M. Lipski, "The Chota Valley: Afro-Hispanic Language in Highland Ecuador," *Latin American Research Review* 22(1): 155–170 (1987).

35. Norman E. Whitten, Jr., *Class, Kinship, and Power in an Ecuadorian Town: The Negroes of San Lorenzo* (Stanford: Stanford University Press, 1965), 892.

36. Stephen W. Kidd, "Land, Politics and Benevolent Shamanism: The Enxet Indians in a Democratic Paraguay," *Journal of Latin American Studies* 27: 43–75 (1995).

37. José Ingenieros, *Sociologia Argentina*, 1915, as reported in Carl C. Taylor, *Rural Life in Argentina* (Baton Rouge: Louisiana State University Press, 1948), 56.

38. Judith Laiken Elkin, *Jews of the Latin American Republics* (Chapel Hill: University of North Carolina Press, 1980).

39. Edward E. Telles, "Racial Distance and Region in Brazil: Intermarriage in Brazilian Urban Areas," *Latin American Research Review* 28(2): 141–162 (1993).

40. Emilia Viotti da Costa, *The Brazilian Empire: Myths and Histories* (Chicago: University of Chicago Press, 1985), 235.

41. Clóvis Monra, *Brasil: Raices do Protesto Negro* (São Paulo: Globa Editora, 1983), 133.

42. Thomas Sowell, *The Economics and Politics of Race* (New York: Morrow, 1983), 95.

43. Donald Pierson, *Negroes in Brazil: A Study of Race Contact at Bahia*, 2d ed. (Carbondale: Southern Illinois University Press, 1967), 127.

44. Nelson do Valle Silva, "Updating the Cost of Not Being White in Brazil," in *Race, Class and Power in Brazil*, ed. Pierre-Michel Fontaine (Los Angeles: Center for Afro-American Studies, University of California, 1985), 42–55.

45. João Camillo de Oliveira Torres, *Estratificação Social no Brasil* (São Paulo: Difusão Europeia do Livro, 1965), 215–222.

46. Octavio Ianni, *O ABC da Classe Operária* (São Paulo: Editora Hucitec, 1980).

47. Thomas E. Skidmore, "Biracial U.S.A. vs. Multi-racial Brazil: Is the Contrast Still Valid?" *Journal of Latin American Studies* 25: 373–386 (1993).

48. Pierson, *Negroes in Brazil*, 128–129.

49. Pierre-Michel Fontaine, "Transnational Relations and Racial Mobilization: Emerging Black Movements in Brazil," in *Ethnic Identities in a Transnational World*, ed. John F. Stack, Jr. (Westport, Conn.: Greenwood Press, 1981), 141–162.

50. Lovell, "Race, Gender, and Development," 30.

51. Enrique A. Baloyra and James A. Morris, *Conflict and Change in Cuba* (Albuquerque: University of New Mexico Press, 1993), 10.

52. Marvin Harris et al., "Who are the Whites?: Imposed Racial Categories and the Racial Demography of Brazil," *Social Forces* 72: 451–462 (1993).

53. Pierson, *Negroes in Brazil*, 139.

54. Octavio Ianni, *Escravidão e Racismo* (São Paulo: Editora Hucitec, 1978), 51.

55. Hawkins, *Inverse Images*, 66.

56. Ronald E. Reminick, *The Theory of Ethnicity: An Anthropologist's Perspective* (Lanham, Md.: University Press of America, 1983), 43–44.

57. Octavio Ianni, "Race and Class," in *Social Structure, Stratification, and Mobility*, ed. Anthony Leeds (Washington, D.C.: Pan American Union, 1967), 222–246, p. 233 cited.

58. Pierson, *Negroes in Brazil*, 381.

59. Hawkins, *Inverse Images*, 174.

60. Roger Bastide and Florestan Fernandes, *Ralacões Raciais entre Negroes e Brancos em Sao Paulo* (San Paulo: Unesco-Anhembi, 1955), 123.

61. Diana J. Schemo, "The Elevator Doesn't Lie: Intolerance in Brazil," *New York Times*, August 30, 1995, p. A4.

62. Michael Chibnik, "Quasi-ethnic Groups in Amazonia," *Ethnology* 30: 167–181 (1991).

63. Mario Tesler, *Racismo contra el Indio en la Argentina* (Buenos Aires: Editorial Corregidor, 1989).

64. Michael Banton, *Racial Theories* (Cambridge: Cambridge University Press, 1987), 121–126.

65. Hawkins, *Inverse Images*, 17.

66. Telles, "Racial Distance and Region," 159.

67. Samuel L. Gaertner and John T. Dovidio, eds., "The Aversive Form of Racism," in *Prejudice, Discrimination, and Racism* (San Diego: Academic Press, 1986), 61–90.

68. Fontaine, "Transnational Relations," 152.

69. Lawrence Bobo and James R. Kluegel, "Opposition to Race-Targetting: Self-Interest, Stratification Ideology, or Racial Attitudes?" *American Sociological Review* 58: 443–464 (1993).

70. William Rowe and Vivian Schelling, *Memory and Modernity: Popular Culture in Latin America* (New York: Verso, 1991), 103.

71. Charles F. Keyes, "The Dialectics of Ethnic Change," in *Ethnic Change*, ed. Charles F. Keyes (Seattle: University of Washington Press, 1981), 4–30.

72. María T. Ruíz, *Racismo es Algo Más que Discriminación* (San José: Editorial del Departmento Ecuménico de Investigaciones, 1988).

73. Edward E. Telles, "Industrialization and Racial Inequality in Employment: The Brazilian Example," *American Sociological Review* 59: 46–63 (1994).

74. Florestan Fernandes, "The Negro in Brazil Society: Twenty-five Years Later," in *Brazil, Anthropological Perspectives: Essays in Honor of Charles Wagley*, ed. Maxine L. Margolis and William E. Carter (New York: Columbia University Press, 1979), 96–114, p. 112 cited.

75. John Biesanz and Luke M. Smith, "Race Relations in Panama and the Canal Zone," *American Journal of Sociology* 57(July): 7–19 (1951).

76. George Psacharopoulos, "Ethnicity, Education, and Earnings in Bolivia and Guatemala," *Comparative Educational Review* 37: 9–19 (1993).

77. Charles Wagley, *Welcome of Tears: The Tapirapé Indians of Central Brazil* (New York: Oxford University Press, 1977), 289.

78. Peter Wade, "The Cultural Politics of Blackness in Colombia," *American Ethnologist* 22: 341–357 (1995).

79. Charles J. Erasmus, "Culture Change in Northwest Mexico," in *Contemporary Change in Traditional Societies*, ed. Julian H. Steward (Urbana: University of Illinois Press, 1967), 114–131.

80. Wagley, *Welcome of Tears*, 301–302.

81. Sheldon H. Davis, *Victims of the Miracle* (New York: Cambridge University Press, 1977), 114–119.

82. Debra Picchi, "The Impact of an Industrial Agricultural Project on the Bakairi Indians of Central Brazil," *Human Organization* 50: 26–37 (1991).

83. Estanislao A. Gacitua Mario, "Movilización e Identidad Etnica: El Caso Mapuche durante el Regímen Militar Chileno 1973–1988," *Revista Paraguayo de Sociología* 27: 71–95 (1990).

Chapter 6

Class Structure and Mobility

No subculture influences the individual's values and attitudes as much as does social class. Still, this sociological truism is occasionally questioned in as diverse areas of the world as Scandinavia and the postwar United States, where class lines were blurring, at least until the Reagan–Bush era. Income level, occupational status, education, and family background are potent factors in the shaping of behavior in any society. Social class is both cause and effect. One's lifestyle, which is determined by social rank, in turn creates the meaning of that rank or, in more professional jargon, socioeconomic class. If these generalizations hold for Western Europe and North America, they pertain even more so to Latin America. As it represents the most highly stratified society of the Western world (a possible exception is the United States with its concentration of wealth in few hands), Latin America is in a sense part of both the West and the Third World. The spindle-like pyramid of social class found in transitional societies is characteristic of nearly all of the twenty republics, with their small wealthy oligarchies, rising middle classes, and a large rural and an ever-growing urban proletariat.

A number of questions can be raised about the implications of social class in Latin America. First of all, what is social class? Numerous theories have wrestled with the meaning of stratification. In other words, can social class be defined and measured? To what degree are most individuals conscious of social class? How did class and caste evolve in Latin America? How many social classes can be found in urban and rural communities? Is class a continuum, or are there discrete classes? How do goals and values differ from class to class? What are the limits of social mobility? Finally, what is the significance of class position for the political and economic order and the future of the society? These questions are only suggestive, and no final answer can be given to most of them.

A CONCEPTUAL FRAMEWORK

Historically, the explanation of the class system evolved from a strict Marxist interpretation to various positions that either oppose or integrate functionalism and conflict perspectives. For Karl Marx as well as other classical economists such as Adam Smith and David Ricardo, property relationships are the fundamental axis in assigning individuals to their appropriate class. Further, since the primary concern in any society is to survive, the individual's position is related to the means of production. Consequently, a basically dual structure consists of an industrial elite (with the support of the bourgeoisie) and a proletariat, which represents two sides of "self-alienation."[1] Along with other areas of the world, Latin America fits rather well into this Marxian model. Alejandro Portes is only one of many analysts but is possibly the most articulate analyst of a neo-Marxian model.[2] There is little question as to the depth of Marx's analysis, but did he sufficiently comprehend the subtleties of elites in their control of a society and manipulation of culture?[3] Or putting the matter differently, he wrote before some of the more complex forms of control had appeared in the Western world.

Nearly a half century after Marx came the functionalist school led by Max Weber that focused on other variables but did not exclude conflict as a variable. Specifically, he emphasized wealth as well as power and prestige. In other words, the exercise of wealth and power determines the class structure. Further, one can acquire power and status through a number of avenues beyond ownership of property. Weber was particularly sensitive to the labyrinths of power and prestige as well as the inconsistencies of status.

Variations of the functionalist position include the notion that financial reward and status derive from the socially defined value of the roles we perform. In reality, the correlation between the prestige and the value of a given role performance is not too high; we may carry out certain services because they are self-rewarding. After all, the honor or status associated with a given occupational role may be more a function of its financial reward than its intrinsic value.

In combining a Marxian conflict approach and functionalism, Rolf Dahrendorf points to the importance of formal organizations in allocating status to given positions. The authority exercised by organizational elites determines the subordinate role of others.[4] Furthermore, stratification grows out of the norms as related to systems of power and authority, especially as expressed in interest groups.[5] Class conflict results in the struggle for scarce resources along with the perception of relative deprivation. Dahrendorf has been criticized for bypassing property and capital as the central ingredients in the class system. However, in our intricate, bureaucratic world both interpersonal and symbolic processes shape status. In complex societies it is difficult to account for differences in stratification and other structural differences without analyzing "the more micro- or individual-level processes that undergird them."[6] In this connection, studies of Latin America show a pattern with interlocking elites between the political and industrial order, as occurred in Brazil in the 1930s and in 1964.[7]

The more pluralistic a society, the more likely power is to be distributed on a broader basis, but stratification is inevitable. The shift from a caste society under medieval feudalism to the present fluidity of the status system does not preclude "class crystallization" as based on a variety of symbols of education, occupation, income, residential belongingness, and lifestyle.[8] Industrial societies display less concentration of status and prestige, especially as democratic societies move toward pluralism and the economy becomes more diversified. However, in any society a class structure is to be found as inequality is inevitable, at least from the functionalist viewpoint. Functionalists view inequality as the outcome of individual differences in abilities, values, and training, whereas the conflict theorists would assert that inequality is sustained by coercion and subterfuge. Latin America would seem to exhibit conflict more than functionalism.

The pursuit of a theory of social class occasionally takes place in the context of the blueprint for a society. Marxist theory is often used to promote a socialist regime, whereas functionalists tend to think of a market economy. The two systems often merge. As an instance, with its vulnerability to a world-system even a Communist regime (as in Cuba) is not impervious to market dynamics.[9] What, then, is the validity of theories on class? The questions may be premature, but we are probably better able to understand society when we have a meaningful theory of the social system, including social class.

Domination, exploitation, unemployment, or underemployment can occur in either a capitalist or communistic economy.[10] In both types of society, a class structure exists. No less meaningful than probing the economic basis of the society may be the decision to turn to a macro or a micro approach. Even this dual approach seems to involve a given theoretical perspective as the Marxist chooses a macro or a holistic viewpoint, whereas the functionalist leans somewhat more to the micro, with its emphasis on individuals. Dahrendorf, for example, thinks of class membership as a kind of role incumbency.

Theories of social class have played a conspicuous role in the models of social change. Ideologies of marginality, development, and class dominance have each had their day in court. Political movements and parties in their search for legitimacy must reckon with their position as to what social class or classes they represent. Because of the complexity of the class structure and the growing awareness to mass media, "ideologies of inequality" have been undergoing transformation.[11] Societal analyses of Latin America continue to turn to Marxist and neo-Marxist concepts. In most complex societies, sociopolitical conflicts now involve not only class but increasingly questions of gender, age, religion, community, region, and public policy. In Latin America, class location still looms exceedingly large as an independent variable, but the meaning and importance of class are undergoing change.

The Problems of Definition and Measurement

We may arbitrarily begin with Max Weber's definition of social class as (1) a "number of people who have in common a specific causal component of their life chances"; (2) this component offers opportunities for disposing of income; and (3) is exercised in "commodity or labor markets."[12] Other definitions, as we have seen, prefer a more explicit definition in relation to the economic system of production. Social class generally refers to a portion of the population who share a similar socioeconomic status and a roughly similar lifestyle as set off from other portions of the society who display a different income level and lifestyle, if we allow for overlapping as well as individual and subcultural differences. At the same time, concern for boundaries should not prevent us from thinking of class as a dynamic rather than a static concept. Class implies economic, ideological, and psychological dimensions. We may label class as a structure, but because it focuses on actors in various behaviors, class is also a process.

The crux of the problem is a delineation of a class structure. It is traditional to divide our classes into three broad categories of upper, middle, and lower, with a number of subdivisions or intermediate levels. Sociologists oriented to Latin America more often lean to the quasi-Marxist position. As shown in Table 6.1, Portes prefers an economically definable set of categories (essentially determined by sources of income), as in his designation of (1) a Dominant class which has control of both the means of production and control over labor; (2) a Bureaucratic–Technical class (Managerial, i.e., policy making and supervisory, consequently with power over labor); (3) a Formal Proletariat—protected to some degree by predictable wages; (4) an Informal Petty Bourgeoisie—irregular profits; and (5) an Informal Proletariat—casual wages or subsistence. These categories can overlap and change over time as seen in the Combined Dominant and Bureaucratic–Technical.[13] The distinction between the dominant and the informal petty bourgeoisie is quantitative, and often vastly so, even though both classes control the productive process and have authority over the labor of others.

Other Latin American observers prefer more orthodox, if rather elaborate, Marxian labels, as for instance, *gran burguesía, mediana y pequeña burguesías, proletariado estricto, semi-proletariado, sub-proletariado,* and *lumpen-proletariado.* The bourgeois levels are drawn from finance, industry, commerce, and agriculture, the upper proletariat is largely industrial and agrarian, and the bottom layer—the classically Marxian Lumpenproletariat—is borderline delinquent.[14] A more modest classification includes bourgeoisie, petty bourgeoisie, proletariat, and subproletariat.[15] These labels may or may not adequately deal with historical complexities, the differences between domination and exploitation, and the reality that classes are ultimately composed of individuals.[16]

TABLE 6.1
A Neo-Marxist and Quantitative Approach to the Latin American Class Structure

Country	Dominant 1980 (%)	Bureaucratic-Technical 1980 (%)	Combined Dominant and Bureaucratic Technical 1970 (%)	Formal Proletariat 1972 (%)	Informal Petty Bourgeoisie 1970 (%)	Informal Proletariat 1980 (%)
Argentina	----	----	9.5	59.0	9.7	23.0
Bolivia	0.6	5.7	5.7	3.3	4.8	56.4
Brazil	1.2	6.4	10.2	20.5	7.2	27.2
Chile	2.4	6.6	7.7	60.5	4.5	27.1
Colombia	0.7	4.3	6.6	12.9	15.7	34.3
Costa Rica	----	----	9.0	28.5	13.5	19.0
Dominican Republic	0.4	3.1	3.7	6.4	17.3	----
Ecuador	1.0	5.1	4.7	10.0	4.1	52.7
El Salvador	0.5	4.2	3.8	3.8	23.1	39.8
Guatemala	1.1	3.7	4.5	22.3	3.3	40.0
Haiti	----	----	----	0.0	----	----
Honduras	----	----	----	1.1	13.4	----
Mexico	----	----	7.7	15.9	11.3	35.7
Nicaragua	----	----	5.3	8.7	15.8	----
Panama	4.4	10.0	8.7	25.4	5.2	31.6
Paraguay	----	----	----	5.9	----	----
Peru	----	----	7.0	27.6	----	40.4
Uruguay	1.3	7.3	8.4	88.5	1.0	----
Venezuela	3.9	9.5	10.0	12.2	14.0	20.8

Source: Alejandro Portes, "Latin American Class Structures: Their Composition and Change during the Last Decade," *Latin American Research Review* 20(3): 7–39 (1985).

Any designation of specific strata must, of course, be viewed against the complexities of Latin American social structure. For one, I have already pointed to the tradition of a two-class system and the relatively late emergence of a genuine middle class. Too, sharp differences appear between rural and urban class systems, and for that matter, between conventional symbols of middle-class belongingness. The middle class still remains a tenuous phenomenon in the rural and semirural world, yet an intermediate category exists between upper- and lower-middle class. Three layers are also visible within the upper and lower classes. Certainly there is no final version of the class structure. For instance, Figure 6.1 illustrates the social structure of the Third World and refers to Latin America of earlier decades when rural outnumbered urban population.

The Portes framework provides a meaningful way to approach class from an economic and political viewpoint in its designation of dominant, bureaucratic–technical, bourgeois, and proletarian strata. This position is strengthened by recent research on the permeability of class boundaries in several industrial societies, where it was found that in cross-class friendships, boundaries based on property are less permeable than those based on authority.[17] However, certain behavior patterns such as residence, education, attitudes, and lifestyle are perhaps more adequately analyzed according to the more familiar labels of upper, middle, and lower.

A state of flux usually characterizes the Latin American social structure in those societies which have undergone revolution, industrialization, or both; only a few agrarian countries such as Haiti are relatively impervious to change. In Mexico, the middle class grew from 8 percent in 1900 to 17 percent in 1960 and the lower class fell from 91 to 82 percent (32% urban and 50% rural), with the upper class remaining at roughly 0.5 percent.[18] It is estimated that in 1980 approximately 6 percent were upper class, 31 percent middle class, and 63 percent lower class.[19] Possibly more important than the statistics are the changing concepts of material comforts or benefits and expected behavior for these classes as they expand or contract. For most countries, especially Mexico, Brazil, and Chile, it is possible to speak of a new and old upper and middle class. Diversification within the lower class, too, results from the migration of peasants to the city, where they confront industrial and related processes, however marginal they remain to this new world.

Criteria of Class

Only in a completely agrarian society are the boundaries of social classes inflexible. However open or closed a social class, its criteria include the following: (1) wealth and income, (2) cultural indexes—occupation, education, and lifestyle, and (3) ethnicity, although a less critical factor than in most of the Western world. As another factor, the relevant social re-

FIGURE 6.1
Class Structure of Latin America

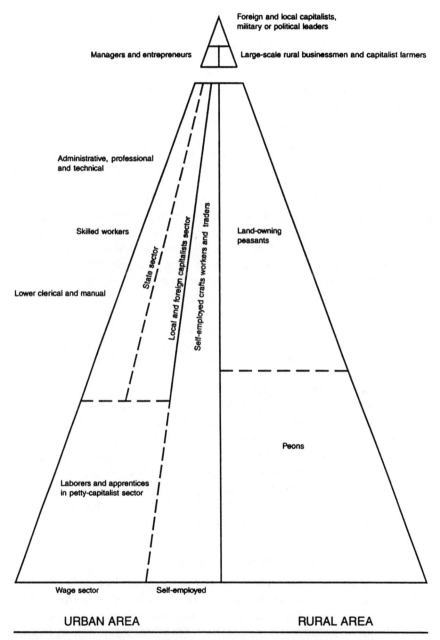

Source: Adapted from P. Waterman, *The Labouring Poor in the Third World* (The Hague: Institute of Social Studies, 1979), 18.

lationships and their implications include the acceptance by a *rosca* (clique) or a feeling of upward mobility. In the middle class, for example, the ability to impress others through imitation of upper-status norms may place the individual on the periphery of the next higher layer, or at least provide greater security in the present position. However, class position is always slippery; downward mobility is almost as predictable as upward.

Consequently, the symbols of class and mobility are not essentially different from those in other parts of the world, but local traditions make for specific nuances in defining status. Class differences, including inequality, can vary as compared to a bordering nation; for example, Costa Rica spends more than four times as much on social services per capita than do other Central American nations.[20] Further, the rise of a middle class in Chile, Costa Rica, and Uruguay was in no small part a product of their social security systems (which arose a generation before they did in the United States).[21] Generally, mobility is limited, as class barriers are fairly rigid. Moreover, a member of the vulnerable middle class may suffer more from transgressions or violations of societal norms than do members of other classes. The upper class are sheltered by their power, and the lower are already at the bottom. For all levels, class behavior is prescribed. In San Lorenzo, an Afro-American and mestizo community in coastal Ecuador, middle-class persons must never work with their hands, drink in saloons, or be seen at a marimba dance and cannot appear publicly without shoes, long pants, and a shirt.[22] Until recently, middle-class persons in Latin America hardly enhanced their status by carrying a package, being too much concerned with a servant's personal problems, or overpunctuality. It would seldom occur to a member of the upper class even to raise these questions.

Social scientists are far from agreement as to what norms or behavioral criteria constitute social class. Nor do Latin American anthropologists and sociologists concur as to specific criteria. Usually, Latin Americans have tended to use subjective and intuitive methods, probably inspired by nineteenth-century European social philosophers. American and European observers often assume that their own criteria about class could be superimposed on a different culture. The last few decades have seen a more systematic approach to these questions.

Self-Identification, Ratings, and Reality

If trained observers are sometimes in disagreement about the criteria of class, the man or woman on the street has no less difficulty. In the author's research in four Latin American cities, more than half of the subjects were unable to identify themselves in relation to the basic rubrics of low, middle, and upper class. Although in Bogotá the label "*clase popular*" was used in interviews in preference to the less desirable "*clase baja*," 66 percent of the lower-class sample preferred to identify themselves as "middle class" rather than as *"clase popular"* (people's or working class).[23] In view of ethnicity the class system can rarely be described as consisting of only three levels. When we turn to larger communities, the class structure becomes more involved. In Whiteford's study of Querétaro, Mexico, and Popayán, Colombia,[24] both cities at the time of the study hovered around the 50,000 mark and had a colonial past and a changing present, if not to the same degree. The familiar six classes were delineated according to the pattern of Warner's Yankee City,[25] ranging from upper-upper to lower-lower. (Querétaro had also a middle-middle class.) Undoubtedly at least three levels of a lower class might be found, and in some cities perhaps only one upper class is apparent, even though divisions in the class structure may surface as determined by the relationship to property and power as well as to lifestyle.

Using the three basic social classes as the framework, we my ask what percentage of the population is found in each class? At best, estimates can be made for the populations of various countries, and these percentages reveal something about the level of socioeconomic development. In order to provide objectivity, observers often prefer to approach the class structure in economic terms. For instance, according to a Brazilian study, "capitalists" in the broad sense constitute 8 percent, self-employed 29 percent, and salaried 63.5 percent of the working population. Significantly, the difference of income level between the upper level of self-employed and the working population was roughly eight to one.[26] These data are further complicated by regional differences and the extent of informal labor. Even in the more homogeneous and socialized atmosphere of Uruguay, a study of occupational categories found income differences between professional/white-collar and blue-collar of four to one for men, and three to one for women.[27] These figures apply to much of the Western world, even though they do not tell a great deal about the social class system.

The rural scene represents the gamut of the class system. Farm tenants and farm owner–operators are identified with all three classes. The technical, clerical, and administrative staff are likely to be either lower-middle or upper-middle class. At the apex, in Argentina at least, the *estancieros* traditionally represent the nucleus of the national elite.

Historical Development of the Class System

It is already clear from Chapter 5 that one variable affecting class is the racial identity of the individual, though race also involves many other factors. In certain countries, such as Brazil, ethnicity was historically the most important factor in social class.[28] Income level is an important determinant, more than it would be in Europe or perhaps North America, yet Latin Americans, when thinking in terms of class, respond to more criteria than simply ethnicity or the amount of wealth. Thus to understand the present class structure we need to review its development over the past four centuries.

The class culture was at its apex when the *peninsulares* (*chapetones* and *gachupines* as native Spaniards were more derisively called) held elite positions in the church and the economic system. Conquistadores and functionaries at all levels were seeking titles of nobility they could not secure in Spain. The question of who might speak to whom and the quality and quantity of titles, land, or jewelry could determine one's upward or downward mobility. In Mexico, a mere 70,000 Spanish-born inhabitants held sway over nearly one million creoles, both groups maintaining a social distance from the mestizos or *castas*, the Indians being assigned to a submerged position. Still, by the end of the eighteenth century a marginal middle class was visible in New Spain.[29]

The nineteenth century continued the hegemony of an agrarian elite based on the hacienda system. From Mexico to Argentina and Chile, landed wealth formed the foundation of the *gente de razón* (persons of reason or the privileged class). Toward the end of the century merchandizing and eventually industrial wealth became a basis for entree into the upper class.

The power structure in rural areas suggests that this oligarchical pattern has not been broken. In most of Iberian America an aristocracy of *latifundistas* occupy a universe separate from mestizo and Indian. They continue to occupy baronial structures, usually of a nineteenth-century tradition. Role behavior is largely oriented around kin and other networks that enjoy a similar way of life. In certain localities this prerogative is endangered by the national power structure, but in most areas the agrarian elite has been able to conserve its position.

THE UPPER CLASS

Any scheme for categorizing the class structure is arbitrary. Whatever its limitations, the tripartite system of upper, middle, and lower with its sublayers may be as useful as the Portes model. At least it signifies the traditional framework used by society.

The Traditional Upper Class

The upper class in most areas depends on the symbols of wealth, although *abolengo* (descent) may count equally. In other words, in any traditional locality it is nearly impossible to buy one's way into the upper class. Also, prestige assumes a number of subtleties. In Paraná, a river town in Argentina, a distinction is made between the *familias conocidas* (known families or the truly patrician families) and the *familias tradicionales*, who are often of greater antiquity in the community but may have lesser ties to the nation as a whole.[30] In Popayán, a Colombian provincial city, an important distinction separates the upper lineage or *clase por abolengo* from the nouveau riche or *arrivista*. Thus, throughout

Latin America kinship is of high priority and most elite families stress the consolidation of wealth and power. *Active* kinship is preferred to *fictive*; that is, blood relations are prior to *compadrazgo* (godparenthood) and marriages with first or second cousins are far from nonexistent. In a city oriented to the past, such as Popayán, concern with kinship becomes a preoccupation with family traditions, heirlooms, and continuity of residence, generally around the central plaza.

The traditional upper class has its own set of norms. Class belongingness is primarily a local affair, except for the relatively few families who belong to the national aristocracy. In the small community the upper class appears in its pristine form. Often only a few families have a variety of clothing, inside plumbing, servants, and other amenities. If they are large landholders, they can travel abroad and send their sons to European schools or in recent decades to the United States. In fact, *mozambismo* refers to the tendency of the Brazilian upper class to depreciate things Brazilian in deference to European sources, but after World War II a wider receptivity to innovations appeared in both the national and cosmopolitan scene.[31] Also, members of the upper class are insulated psychologically from the middle- and lower-class world. They are addressed by special titles, as for instance *o senhor* and *a senhora, meu patrão* (my lord), or *meu branco* (my white); older servants might use *Vossa Excêlencia*. Despite their support of the traditional family system, upper-class males can best afford to practice the ideal of *machismo*; supporting a mistress or having a series of sexual liaisons is a luxury not always available to the middle class. Social life assumes a particular style for the provincial upper class, as in the Club Popayán, albeit more the outlet of the male than of the female.

Upper-class life is carefully insulated from *lo démas* (the others). Their universe may include an apartment in Europe and a townhouse in the capital, with vague roots in the *estancia*. Not only are they necessarily indifferent to the welfare of the people, they seem unconcerned with the issues of the nation or the world. Their country exists mainly as the source of their income, and ever since the advent of Fidel Castro they transfer funds to a foreign bank. Vignettes of this class are a favorite subject for the novelist, as in the portrait of Don Eustaquio in Carmen de Silva's *Setiembre,* who flits from Buenos Aires to Paris in order to escape the crises of his native country.

Elites, Class, and Stability

The new upper class stands in contrast to the older privileged class, but the boundary is a slippery one. Elites, whose social status derives more from achievement than ascription, belong more to the emerging upper and upper-middle classes than to the traditional establishment. This process especially characterizes urban society; in Colombia, for example, the upper class by the 1980s assumed two variants, the economic and political.[32] The Mexican Revolution, along with industrialization and political favoritism, ushered new names into the national ruling elite, even though in a provincial city such as Querétaro several families still enjoy some status because of their antiquity. Presumably in many cities a given elite retains its dominance over generations, as was with the commercial elite in Oaxaca during most of this century.[33] Throughout Latin America, a number of prominent nineteenth-century families became semi-impoverished in this century and were reduced to middle-class status. This process is partly attributable to family size. A lower mortality rate throughout the life cycle and the necessity to divide an estate among a number of heirs are factors in an intergenerational loss of status. Poor judgment in investments is another problem; inflation plays havoc with individuals who have their fortunes in liquid assets. Few Latin Americans would be foolhardy enough to indulge in domestic bonds; rather they turn to New York or Zurich than to their home base for investments.

In some instances, marriage into the newer upper class staves off financial ruin and at the same time provides the *arrivista* with appropriate credentials. It is often necessary to find new recruits for the upper class by admitting through marriage attractive and university-educated young men from the middle class. Consequently, upward mobility is easier for the male than for the female. In several countries, notably Brazil, the landed gentry is seeking marriages with the industrial and banking elite. At the same time, 60 percent of the upper class marry endogamously, nearly one-third choosing members of the professions.[34]

The Forces of Change

Can one give a unified picture of the upper class? Consisting of rural and urban, old and new elements, it has no unanimous purpose or ideology. The new industrial elites are more sensitive to intellectual and social influences from abroad. Their sons more often than not receive a diversified modern education, turning to the newer curricula rather than the more traditional *facultades* of medicine, law, and humanities. Also, they are likely to attend foreign universities, many continuing into postgraduate study.

Will the upper classes eventually lose their political power? The answer appears to be negative, especially in rural areas, where they are entrenched. As the income tax is less institutionalized than in most of the Western world, their economic position is still unquestioned. There are several exceptions: In Cuba this class fled only to be replaced by a new elite; in Mexico a less complete and more gradual shift occurred after the Revolution; and in Uruguay both welfare ideology and a strongly European orientation made for a more modest upper class. In Nicaragua, the Sandinista revolution had no small impact on the upper class, many of whom went into exile or joined the Contras. Still, a study of the traditional families in the provincial cities of León and Granada found a number of the elites assuming positions with the new government.[35]

Finally, Latin American elites continue to change. Until the 1960s, political elites were almost universally drawn from the upper class. Later, decision making came to be shared with the middle sectors. According to an analysis of elites in Venezuela, political and cultural—but not economic—leadership is drawn from a middle class that is growing in power. In view of both the divergent backgrounds of these middle sectors and the complexity of problems to be resolved, consensus and commitment in these new elites may be limited.[36] An inability to adjust to a rapidly changing priority in needs and goals implies that new elites may be less successful than their predecessors in attacking the dilemmas inherent in a developing society. This impasse may leave power in the hands of the older elite or upper class—or may call for a new ordering of the power system, including the entry of new sectors, possibly from the urban or even the rural working class.

THE MIDDLE CLASS

The existence of a significant middle class in Latin America has been acknowledged only since World War II. As we have seen, the growth of a middle class is linked to the rise of industry—in the nineteenth century for countries such as Argentina, more recently for Brazil and other nations.[37] The class structure in larger cities was more complex than in smaller ones; the demarcation of the middle class in Buenos Aires did not really become clear until 1910.[38] However, the middle class has been implied traditionally in a number of terms such as *gente decente* and *gente de razón*, which are as likely to refer to the middle as to the upper class.

As Max Weber pointed out, the middle class are even more conscious of defining their boundaries than are the lower class. Moreover, the nature of the middle class is constantly changing with the advent of new technological breakthroughs (as in the diffusion of the computer) which call for high skills. Still other tasks amount to performing in a routine way what was once a complicated process, or one instance of "deskilling the middle class."[39] Terms such as the "middle sectors" only underscore the reluctance to accept the sociological notion of a class system. Furthermore, the reason for the ambiguous status of the middle class in Latin America is due not only to the recency of its emergence as a conspicuous segment of the population, but also to its relative ineffectiveness, at least until recently, in influencing decision making.

Although survey data in this area are risky, it is estimated that the middle class in Latin America represents less than 15 percent of the population in less developed countries, but up to 30 to 40 percent in the more advanced ones. Growth is particularly impressive in urban areas; 44 percent of the labor force in Caracas and 48 percent of Guadalajara were in white-collar occupations in 1988.[40] The relative size of the middle class has generally remained ahead of population growth. Between 1950 and 1970 the combined middle and upper class rose from 18 to 31 percent in Venezuela, but only 14.2 to 15.7 percent in Paraguay. Even in countries with a respectable history of economic growth such as Chile, the upper and upper-middle classes are reluctant to accept individuals moving up from the working class, and inflation limits the number of consumers who can enjoy a level of living commensurate with their level of employment.

Within the middle class one finds a continuum of occupations with varying educational and training norms. Indeed, the middle class is in large part the result of the expansion of occupational opportunities in this century.[41] At or near the top are the professionals (i.e., lawyers, doctors, engineers, architects, professors), all of whose incomes vary widely. Managers and merchants also range between middle- and upper-class position. The middle and lower spectrum of occupations in all areas contains the clerk, teacher, shopkeeper, and, in smaller towns, the artisan. A traditional distinction between middle and lower class is whether the work is primarily mental or manual. In an industrialized or welfare-oriented society, this barrier is not too fixed. Even in the period of Perón, blue-collar workers chose to change to suits and ties before leaving work in order to pose as members of the white-collar world.[42] Indeed, through much of the Western world, including Latin America, images of middle-class equalitarianism permeate the mass media. Also, reference groups—family, friends, and coworkers—give an illusion of middle-class belongingness, even if the reality is otherwise.[43]

Various indexes show a varied complexion of the middle class. The educational level differs a great deal. In rural areas, few in the middle class continue beyond the fifth grade, but in the city completion of secondary education and, for a minority, university education is increasingly expected. Income differences run an even greater gamut: At the upper end a breadwinner may receive ten times the income of a person at the lower limit of what might be considered as middle class. The situation is complicated by other factors, for instance, if he or she has the good fortune of cheap housing. These sharp income differences, of course, make for a wide diversity in standards of living. It is possible to find middle-class persons living in luxury apartments or in older but dignified *tugurios* (slum areas) in the older parts of the city, whereas others may live in new public housing units. Access to these new *viviendas públicas* or *multifamiliares* (public housing) can be a means for the working class to reach the threshold of the middle class.

Aspirations and Frustrations

The middle class is caught in a frantic attempt at maintaining minimum standards of decency. In order to obtain satisfactory housing and assure a modicum of privacy for family members, most middle-class families need multiple breadwinners in order to cover rent, food, and other necessities. Luxury taxes, currency with low purchasing power, and lack of assembly plants can combine to make the cost of a new Chevrolet or Volkswagen twice as high as in a neighboring country. The need to meet these consumer demands results in extensive moonlighting. A Brazilian survey found 78 percent of the families surveyed depend on five salaries, at least two for the household head, and usually more than one for other adult members.[44]

The newer middle class occasionally wish to enjoy the lifestyle displayed by images of the middle and upper classes in the mass media, especially television. At the same time, this new stratum must adhere to the cult of respectability associated with the older middle class, including proper attention to kinship and religious ceremonies. For example, a marriage in the middle class takes place in church in contrast to the consensual union characterizing the lower class. A maid is necessary for housework, opening the front gate, and carrying packages from the store in order to preserve, at least in appearance, the upper- and middle-class ceremonial avoidance of manual tasks. Still another feature of this refinement is attendance of the children at a private rather than a public school. Whether Buenos Aires or Bogotá, public elementary schools are disdained because of class symbolism and the danger of unsavory peer group associations the children might encounter. Private secondary schools are even more indispensable. Also, in industrialized nations the middle class assume a freer lifestyle even though the struggle to keep ahead remains acute. According to a Mexican sociologist, as the middle class became more affluent in the Alemán regime after World War II they aped U.S. behavior patterns, whether dating folkways or culinary habits, as inspired by movies and television. This euphoria for a *norteamericano* lifestyle became less evident by the 1970s as industrialization reached a more mature level and Mexicans found their own norms.[45]

As compared with the upper class, the middle class suffers more from inflation. For instance, in 1995 Venezuela had the highest rate of inflation (54%); over twenty-five years the share of the income spent on food rose from 28 to 72 percent; and the middle class has been reduced by a third.[46] Even if price stabilization exists for certain categories of older housing and for some basic foodstuffs in Latin America, the items most desired by the bourgeoisie are usually exempt from price controls. Further, persons who want to find a home in the new *viviendas* or *urbanizaciones*—they could seldom assume the cost of building their own—are faced with the high cost of such homes. Since interest rates in most countries run from 15 to 35 percent annually, the ubiquitous installment buying is a costly affair. As merchandizing is on a *norteamericano* basis, a large amount of middle-class consumer income finds its way into plastic and interest.

Variations in the Middle Class: Urban and Rural

The heterogeneity of the middle class can scarcely be overemphasized. Besides differences between the old and new, rural and urban middle classes, there are ethnic variations. In every major city immigrants assume managerial and commercial leadership roles that place them in the upper-middle and even among the new upper class. In southern Brazil, the middle class is largely composed of third- and fourth-generation Europeans who only gradually accepted traditional Brazilian values. Similarly, German migrants in southern Chile for more than one hundred years upheld a middle-class way of life. With some strain on validity, Argentines like to pride themselves as having a solid middle class with relatively open mobility, partly because they feel unhampered by ethnic strains.[47]

At various layers of the middle class, upward mobility occurs along differing avenues: A mechanic takes an extra course to become a foreman or acquires training linked to a new industrial process; or schoolteachers enroll in university courses in their off-hours in order to qualify for a better position. In a different style, the rural middle class is composed of independent farmers, artisans, and shopkeepers, who are self-employed, in contrast to the salaried employees of the city. This independence is often the very source of its instability.

The middle class in rural areas is proportionately smaller than in the city. In Brazil, class position, including the middle, is largely set by the number of hectares one owns.[48] Only one of rural Mexico's seven social classes can be considered as "middle," that is, the owners of medium-size farms (the classes include in order: older *latifundistas*, newer *latifundistas*, the "middles," *minifundistas, ejidatarios*, Indians, and laborers).[49] Also, the standard of living and pattern of social participation are more subdued in the rural community than in the city. Visible manifestations of status are of less concern. Furniture is simpler, but most houses have interior plumbing, running water, and a radio in addition to copious family portraits and religious mementos. Further, social life assumes a racial and class character in most rural communities. The Club Sociale in Minas Velhas in central Brazil caters only to the whites who play checkers, backgammon, and cards. The town's Afro-Brazilians witness the occasional dances from outside the windows. Similarly, in Itá on the Amazon River the festivals accompanying saints' days are not the same for the "uppers" and "lowers." On the day of Saint Benedict, the patron of the Negro, for example, a lower-class brotherhood is permitted to follow behind the saint's image in the *folia* (procession).

Festas (parties) are a major focus of social and organizational life, for most residents of Itá. Social life revolves mainly around friends and kinship; birthdays and other anniversaries become an occasion for celebration. These festivities seldom include lower-class persons. Even if the middle class incurs considerable financial debt from the celebrations, they do much to reduce the humdrum of the tropical town with its unvarying climate. The degree to which clubs impose class barriers depends on the size and traditionalism of the local social structure.

Community and Social Participation in the Urban Sector

In my investigation of four cities (San Salvador, San José, Bogotá and Santiago), I found greater social, community, and religious involvement among the middle class than among the lower. Also, the middle class has more exposure to mass media. In Santiago, for instance, almost twice as many of the middle as of the lower class read the newspaper daily (71.2% and 40.5%, respectively). Moreover, the paper chosen is the more literate *Mercurio* instead of the sensationalized afternoon papers. Movie attendance follows the same pattern. Weekly attendance of movies by the middle class runs two to four times as high, depending on the city and the economic gap between the two classes. Because of subtitles and more sophisticated themes, the middle class prefer North American and European movies, which represent their level of aspirations, whereas the lower class are more dedicated to Mexican and Argentine pictures, which pose no linguistic difficulty.

The middle-class lifestyle is revealed in friendship and kinship patterns, at least as revealed in questionnaire responses. When people in Santiago were asked "How many real (*íntimo*) friends do you have?," class differences came out sharply—an average of 3.1 friends in the middle class and only 1.3 in the lower class. The differences in the other cities were of a similar magnitude. In contrast, social relationships in San Salvador seem limited in both classes: Possibly in an overcrowded nation one problem is maintaining a sense of social distance! Or does living in a semifeudalistic culture lead to a sense of interpersonal isolation?

Although frequency of social interaction varies between national cultures, visiting with friends and relatives is consistently higher in the middle class. For example, in Bogotá half the middle-class sample but only one-eighth of the lower-class sample report a "social activity" as often as once a month. The expense of entertainment is probably the most important reason for infrequent social activity, along with distance and other complexities of city living. In keeping with Latin American tradition, ties with relatives have priority over those with friends (nearly three times as many middle- as lower-class residents of Santiago reported weekly meetings with relatives). Besides, members of the lower class are cut off from their relatives as they migrate to the city.

Values, Attitudes, and Orientation to Change

Middle-class persons emphasize stability and yet have a sense of mobility and the importance of education as a means of realizing their goals.

As compared to the upper class, they are more reactive than proactive. They have a vested interest in the status quo and yet are responsive to change, as we shall see later in this chapter. The middle class in Latin America, as elsewhere, conforms more to societal norms, especially when these are interpreted as a means of upward mobility. Church attendance and preference for the legal–religious ceremony over the consensual type of marital union are marked in countries where the middle class has only recently gained a foothold. According to a Brazilian study, the middle class is more liberal in theory than in practice, at least in the area of sexual conduct.[50]

In using items from a modernism scale with Bogotá and Santiago samples, I found clear-cut differences between lower and middle class. For example, in Santiago the middle class are more resistant to a principally familial or kinship orientation and less rigid in their belief systems. In other words, its members are universalist and rationalistic in assessing given judgments, stressing achievement over ascription. Middle-class subjects embrace an urban lifestyle, emphasize the efficacy of both personal and societal planning, and believe that the socioeconomic universe is capable of being controlled. These findings only bear out what common sense might assume and are associated with the educational advantages of the middle class, yet they underscore the difference between the middle and lower classes in the degree of orientation to change and potential for socioeconomic development—not without ambivalence. The more educated the individual the more likely he or she accepts social change, but only if certain privileges are not threatened. Members of the lower class perceive social injustices, but often feel helpless to effect changes in the status quo.

The middle class is regarded as the fulcrum of both change and stability; that is, its members favor neither revolution on one side nor stagnation on the other. They are occasionally driven to an acute awareness of the need for deep social change, as in Chile when the Pinochet economic program affected them almost as adversely as it did the lower class—half the social programs were curtailed between 1973 and 1980. As one objective, the middle sectors give a high priority to education. A second goal for the middle class is increased industrialization, an emphasis shifting from small plants producing consumer items to heavier industry such as automobile assembly and fabrication of steel and other metals.[51]

The Roman Catholic Church is a pivot for many in the middle class. For instance, in Popayán the middle class plays the conspicuous role in Holy Week processions.[52] A Chilean survey revealed the middle class to be more Catholic than the lower class, which leans toward Pentecostalism, although the upper class was even more exclusively Catholic.[53] In El Salvador, Protestants represent a lower economic position and vote more to the left than do Catholics.[54] However, in Brazil, Protestants may vote either left or right, depending on the flavor of the religion—mainline or evangelical—and their social class. Presumably, class position is a more potent force in attitude formation than is religious belongingness, as they are interrelated.

THE LOWER CLASS

At least two-thirds of Latin America's total population is lower class—for the rural population it is four-fifths in most countries. For instance, the rural is one-fifth of Chile's population but accounts for half of its poverty.[55] Despite economic growth, the level of poverty for much of this lowest four-fifths shows little change, particularly as birthrates remain above average. In economically advanced countries, the ratio of the impoverished is lower. Even so, a less than happy profile is to be found, as in Brazil, where in 1980 the poorest 50 percent of the population received somewhat less (14.2%) of the gross domestic product (GDP) than did the richest 1 percent (who had 16.9% of the GDP).[56] As a smaller country and one in which social welfare has been a priority, Costa Rica shows less harsh extremes, but in neighboring Guatemala 83 percent lived in poverty in 1987, and of these 65 percent were classified as being in deep poverty.[57]

Not all members of the lower class are necessarily impoverished. The composition of the lower class includes a continuum as wide as that of the middle class: rural versus urban along with lower-lower, middle-lower, and upper-lower. One has only to consider the semiskilled worker on the assembly line, the lottery huckster, and the beggar who works the city center and returns each night to the mushrooming shack towns. Or one might think of a member of the servant staff in an elegant villa of the new industrial elite, or of the servant of a professor, or of a low-level government functionary. In other words, a critical distinction is found between *working* class and *lower* class. Both are to be considered as different from the middle class. However, the boundary between working class and middle class is an arbitrary one. According to a Mexican study, of the upper 5 percent of income distribution, 9 percent were in manual work (*obreros*); of the next highest bracket in income level, 23 percent belonged to manual occupations.[58] A skilled laborer often has a higher standard of living than a lower white-collar functionary.

The employment hierarchy of the lower class is illustrated in Querétaro. Generally, unionized workers were in the upper-lower, or identified as the working class. In contrast, the lower-lower class included farm laborers, watchmen, street vendors, sweepers, porters, and servant girls, who received about half the remuneration of other manual workers.[59] Naturally, overlapping occurs between the less and more experienced, between urban and rural wages, and between levels of national economic development. At present, the minimum legal wage in several countries is barely more than four dollars a day, which means for a family of four, more than half of the income goes into a subsistence diet—one almost without protein and that is based on carbohydrates, often a variation of rice, corn, manioc, or beans, depending on the major products of the area. Between 1978 and 1991, the minimum wage in Mexico dropped an average of 12 percent annually in purchasing power.

Industrialization, growth of cities, and rising literacy have reduced somewhat the percentage of individuals in the lower class, but in raw numbers the lower class increases each year, particularly since 1980 when national indebtedness reduced the disposable income in many countries. These changes have served to widen markedly the occupational spectrum of the lower class. The growth of secondary and tertiary types of employment at the expense of the primary sector means new job classifications and different degrees of involvement for migrants from rural areas. Migrants often remain peripheral to industrial employment. Many in the lower class are found in this "no man's land" between the rural-transitional and the urban–service–industrial. The lower class consequently is diffused, unorganized, and fluid. Except for a socialist regime like Cuba, marginality, both economically and politically, best describes the situation of the lower class.

The Rural Proletariat

The portrait of agricultural labor presented in Chapter 4 leaves little doubt that most peasants live in destitution. Even so, differing levels of poverty exist. Many peasants have a larger, if somewhat more monotonous, food supply than do segments of the urban working class. Most sharecroppers are wage earners, and under the system of corporate agriculture a few social services have become intermittently available to them. Not least influential in bringing up wages, at least marginally, is a competing job market in the urban area. It does not follow that these changes occur in all countries or even in all areas or historical periods within the same country; the positive effects of aid programs, technological advances, and migration are undeniable. The character of the agrarian lower class has changed in a number of ways by corporate or industrialized agriculture. This process awakens a class feeling among the rural proletariat, as reflected in peasant movements.

Changes in communication and transportation have made for more differentiation in the rural lower class and middle class throughout Latin America. Also, in many communities the distinction between lower and middle class rests on the boundary of Indian and mestizo. In Huaylas, a town in the Huancayo area of the Peruvian Andes, the class structure is based on community rather than national criteria (10% upper class, 60% middle class, and 30% lower class). The lower class is characterized by manual labor, nonownership of land, an austere living standard with a limited variation in diet, preference for Quechua over Spanish, lack of leadership in the political processes, nonparticipation in formal organizations such as the *hermanidades* of the church, and limited contact with coastal cities.[60] In a number of towns, villages, and agricultural areas, the distinction between middle and lower class is nebulous, partly because of a common level of poverty. Other subtle distinctions can be found. In a rural community in central Mexico, the wage-earning "semi-proletarian" women felt slightly superior to the "campesinas," who lived on isolated *ejidos* and ranchos.[61]

Insecurity and Lifestyle

If anything, pressures on the urban working class are more severe than those on the campesinos, partly because this group is confronted by more affluent sectors of the middle and upper class. Nor is this situation new. In late nineteenth-century Brazil, as in most countries, conditions such as long working hours for women and children as well as men, with brutal treatment on the part of factory foremen and supervisors, were legion.[62] Similar events at the turn of the century are described for Buenos Aires, where much of the textile labor was supplied by children.[63] Today, for many families survival depends on whether the children can find "employment" in shoe shining, selling lottery tickets, or begging, or if the mother can rely on a succession of odd jobs such as laundress or seamstress. Prostitution is another possible occupation and is estimated to include at least 4 percent of the female population in many cities.

The level of living in most of Latin America appears favorable only when compared with that of Africa and Asia. In the poorer areas of Mexico and Colombia—certainly not the poorest countries in the hemisphere—unemployment rates are as high as 50 percent.[64] Life in *chozas* (huts) and one-room "apartments" in the *mesones* (single-room dwellings around a patio) I visited in San Salvador and Bogotá is little different from the shantytowns of Lima, Santiago, or Rio. The occupants routinely have a mat for a bed, perhaps a table and chair, usually no window, and only a door to the community patio, in which most families carry on their activities; for instance, meals are eaten here in order to escape the crowdedness and darkness of their quarters. The six to ten families who share a *mesón* among them have one "kitchen" facility and one or two toilets off the patio area.[65] Little warmth or optimism appears within the family, nor is there any feeling of camaraderie among the tenants inhabiting the *mesón*. Food can consume 70 percent of the budget, clothing is purchased second-hand, and recreation is confined to the blaring of radio "music" and TV serial dramas, profusely interspersed with commercials. Attendance once every few months at a movie or sports event offers a momentary escape. The "husband" may spend a sizeable portion of income in beer or *aguardiente*. Unemployment or underemployment of the male household head forces most women to find whatever work they can. In a sample of Rio slums, 73 percent of household heads were either unemployed or earning significantly less than the minimum wage.[66]

Poverty is characterized in various ways. Occasionally it is labeled as a deviant subculture—deviant because of social disorganization. In pointing to the "subculture of poverty," social scientists do not think of the term as altogether negative since individuals experiencing deprivation often develop traits of defiance, stoicism, innovation, and spontaneity.[67] Other observers see only misery for the lower class in the developing world. In any event, it is clear that those who reside in shack towns, whatever the national variations, live well below the level of, say, the skilled worker installed in public housing. For this lowest layer of the urban proletariat, the vicissitudes of life are related to illness and personality breakdown, inability to meet their expenses, and incapacity to engage in any kind of future orientation, including family planning. One hears much of poverty in the United States, but of the nearly three-fourths of Latin Americans constituting the lower class, most endure a different type of poverty than do the lowest one-sixth of its northern neighbors. And if poverty is a problem that has not been resolved for advanced nations, the solution is even more remote for those at a lower stage of economic development. According to the *official* figures for poverty in eleven countries in 1986, 37 percent were below the poverty line, varying from 13 percent in Argentina to 68 percent in Guatemala.[68] It is significant that in Guatemala in 1980 the upper 5 percent of the population received 59 percent of the income, and the lowest 50 percent received 7 percent.

The political climate can determine the fate of the lower class. For instance, in the democratic Chile of 1968 the poorest 40 percent of the population were allotted 13.4 percent of the GDP, but after a decade of the Pinochet regime they had only 6.4 percent. The lower-middle and lower classes suffered greatly, especially during the economic crisis of 1983, when abysmal nutrition and colder dwellings led to an increase in infectious diseases.[69] With the return to democracy and the Aylwin presidency in 1990, the free market economy continued. However, by increasing taxes the present government adopted social programs in housing, education, and stimuli to small businesses, in addition to reducing inflation and increasing the minimum wage. These reforms may explain why unemployment reportedly dropped after the fall of Pinochet from 25 to less than 15 percent and the poverty rate fell from 40 to 33 percent.[70]

Even more than political pressures, the economic debacle of the 1970s and 1980s lowered consumption levels in most countries, as the International Monetary Fund (IMF) forced governments to curtail imports and spending. The depression had a devastating effect on personal income;

for instance, between 1980 and 1992, the average real wage fell 53 percent in Venezuela and 60 percent in Peru,[71] with a severe repercussion on diet; between 1972 and 1979 the daily caloric intake of Peru's underclass fell from 1,900 to 1,500. For some areas, starvation is endemic. In Brazil's Northeast, children are 16 percent shorter and weigh 20 percent less than those of the same age in other parts of the country, where hunger also may exist.[72] The upper years are no less affected; for instance, in Bolivia 82 percent of the elderly have no pension coverage.[73]

Values and Roles in the Lower Class

It is not easy to characterize values for a population as widely divergent as the lower class, especially when we consider its regional and other subcultural variations. The values of both lower and middle classes have the peculiar stamp of Iberian culture transplanted to a frontier society and becoming fused with indigenous and African cultures. First, work is a central value in itself, and it also colors other values. The middle class rejects manual work, which the lower is forced to assume, if not always with enthusiasm. A statement so patronizing by a tourist guidebook, "the Chileans (or Salvadoreans, etc.) are hard workers," refers to a situation of necessity rather than volition. One national culture differs little in this respect from another, notwithstanding individual variations of personal initiative or habit systems. After all, competition for jobs leads many to consider work a value in itself. Second, although not explicitly admitted by Latin American males, women are a major value, especially for the lower class, since they are responsible for the survival and integrity of the family. With no dependable male support, at least in most consensual unions, the female household head must provide the economic, physical, and psychological support of the family. Third, land is a salient concern of campesinos. Land ownership may bring prestige to the upper class, but the value of land is much more than symbolic for those who are directly dependent on it for their survival.

Among the value clusters of the lower class are fatalism and resignation, and at the same time a need for escape. Many lower-class individuals accept the inevitability and differential rewards even though the number who protest the status quo is increasing. For example, in my Central American samples only one-fourth to one-half of the lower class felt any real antagonism toward the social class system. On this point, Marx spoke of "false consciousness" in reference to the inability of the actors to comprehend their class position or to enter into appropriate activity in combatting class inequality. Presumably, resentment in regard to the advantages of a higher class is a question of processing emotional reactions within a social network with highly variable cultural and individual variations.[74] Members of the lower class appear to accept the bleak world they inherit; fiestas, the pageant of the Church, and mass media are a means of making reality less harsh. The mass media provide variety, from *foletín* (short paperback novel) to *radionovela* to *telenovela*. Interestingly, a popular *telenovela* in Mexico was the tale of a demonic character who had a "will of iron"—a reaction to the sense of futility people felt after the financial crash of 1982 and the earthquake of 1985.[75]

Occupational roles are also revealing. Even if we take a single occupational category (e.g., the servant), an agrarian society evolving into an urban culture has varying role definitions and expectations coloring the individual's attitudes. I found that a servant was variously labeled a *sirviente* (servant) in El Salvador, a *muchacha* (girl) in Colombia, and an *empleada* (employee) in Chile. A servant may function in a set of ad hoc chores at the whim of each family member and become the scapegoat for frustrations with the employer's family, or on the other hand may operate according to an orderly assignment of specifically defined tasks. These differences correspond to the various segments of the lower class and its relation to the total status structure. La Paz, Bolivia, is probably not unique in eliciting the readjustment of servants because of the decline of the multiservant household and the socialization of wealth. Unquestionably, to this day, degradation of the servant continues.[76] However, forms of "disguised resistance" are practiced by servants, such as gossip, humor, and petty stealing.[77]

The rural hinterland provides the servant class, but political and economic processes affect the flow. In Chile, the land reform program of Allende tended to keep women in rural areas, but the harsher policies of Pinochet prompted their migration to the city.[78] In São Paulo, among other cities, unskilled female labor is increasingly more difficult to recruit for domestic service since factory and office positions are more attractive. This shift is symptomatic of a redefinition of goals and values taking place in the lower class.

PROBLEMS OF MOBILITY

As implied previously, there is no consensus about the degree of rigidity in the class structure in Latin America. Even Marx allowed for the existence of upward mobility—a "kind of exception that confirmed the rule of class closure."[79] Though upward mobility exists in all but the most agrarian societies, the state of flux in most of Latin America implies an open-ended question as to how far the individual in the lower and middle classes can climb. This situation of unsolidified classes arises as much from a changing social structure as from a society in which isolation and inadequate communication prevent an articulate definition of class identity.

The Social Setting

A situation of nonpermeability appears mainly in rural areas, where on the surface a two-class system is still evident. Yet the two classes tend to break down, as in Minas Velhas, Brazil, into other axes, such as urban–rural or white–black.

The middle-size city also limits social mobility. The implications of subcultural and institutional factors are made clear in Whiteford's study of two cities.[80] In both cities, people moved out of the lower class. In Popayán, this escape was based largely on education, which was readily available and for many almost free of charge since family income determined the amount of tuition. With Querétaro's more rapid economic growth, commercial and entrepreneurial activity became a primary medium of changing class. This channel was particularly favorable for movement from the lower-middle into the upper-middle and into the lower reaches of the upper class. In Popayán, entry into the lower-upper class was difficult because of the lingering mystique of *abolengo* (ancestry), and for both cities the upper-upper class remained a closed circle except in the rare event of a highly fortunate marriage. Kinship could often be used to one's advantage, as could the important *corbata* (a tie), which is based on political affiliations. In fact, party preferences cross class lines, and party affairs might find an upper-class Liberal rubbing elbows with worker groups.

Economic Growth, Education, and Redefinition of Social Class

The urban industrial climate of several countries, slow as it has been in developing, permits a degree of social mobility. In Argentina, this process began in the nineteenth century when the agrarian elite decided to modernize the country. The formation of foreign capital, construction of transportation arteries, industrialization and food processing, educational expansion, and sizeable immigration all abetted this mobility. A continuing process of migration from the countryside to the capital and other major cities permits movement upward in order to replace workers who have been upgraded. Immigration helps to foster this process, as the migrants readily adjust to the national culture and its upward mobile society. Beginning with the 1930s, the Argentine economy was growing at a lower rate; in the early 1990s, poverty and unemployment were keen political issues, with demands for redistribution of the wealth as the "trickle down" was no longer visible.[81]

In examining mobility in Brazil, José Pastore, along with other sociologists, distinguishes between *structural* mobility (the opening of channels within a given entity, particularly a growing economy) and *circulation* mobility (movement dependent on replacement and the candidate's abilities), both of which may be involved in intra- and intergenerational mobility. Compared to other Latin American countries, intergenerational mobility has characterized Brazil.[82] More than half (54%) in a national sample moved upward intra-generationally and 47 percent intergenerationally; downward migration was 4 and 11 percent, respectively. Secondary and especially tertiary sectors showed more growth than did the primary, and the industrial South was more vigorous than the North. In the Northeast, only one-third of the sample were better off than their fathers, whereas in São Paulo nearly two-thirds were. The ratio was still higher in Brasilia, with its explosion of tertiary jobs; yet large-scale poverty persists, and even the high mobility rates leave widespread inequality and dissatisfaction.[83]

Status needs would seem to be the most compelling drive for those about to enter the middle or upper class, and education is a principal means by which they hope to climb the social ladder. In a Santiago sample, the responses to the item, "What is your principal aspiration in life?" are of interest.[84] Whatever the limitations of this projective type of item, most respondents were deeply concerned with the prospects of their children's education. No less than two-thirds of the lower class and nine-tenths of the middle class *would like* to have their children pursue a university education, yet only one-fifth of the lower class and three-fourths of the middle-class sample *expected* to send their sons and daughters to the university—hardly a realistic estimate in view of the tight competition for university admission in Santiago.

The employment structure is still another variable. Upward mobility in urban centers is limited because of the high ratio of public and private office personnel to the total of the population employed. This tertiary sector can limit drastically upward mobility for the middle class. The building of a vast office bureaucracy, especially in Brazil, scarcely helps the expansion of industry. This development is inspired by foreign models of middle-class goals and values, which have come to be adopted by the lower-middle classes in a number of Latin American countries.

For most of Latin America, and notably for Brazil, one impetus to self-advancement originates in kinship structures, along with an intricate manipulation of associations within the social framework of the individual. The *cabide* (literally *cabide de emprego* or "employment hanger") refers to the upward mobile Brazilians' penchant for "personal connections not only through friendships, but ties of mutual obligation, and so on—a web of non-kin quite analogous to the web of kinship known from the standard ethnographic genealogy."[85] Various techniques are open to the upward mobile: first, the *tranbolim* (springboard) which serves as a launching pad; the use of the *pistalão*, the friend in the right place, who often is a relative; and the *futing* or "promenading with one's ears open."

Later on, one establishes a tactical coterie or *ingrejinha* (little church), which transmits cues, and might become a reciprocal in-group for getting jobs for each other. These techniques—variants of the *patrão* (patron) relationship—are not different from the mechanics of mobility in other parts of Latin America They are somewhat reminiscent of promotional networks in politics or even of business and professional activity in the United States. In Brazil, clientelism is perfected to an art form.

The entrepreneur may serve as one model of upward mobility. A late development in Latin America, the entrepreneur emerged as industrialists and a mercantile elite began to function as counterweights to the agrarian oligarchy. Entrepreneurs were often immigrants, especially in economies that might be labeled as "johnny-come-lately." Today, a new managerial elite has developed, often trained abroad, from the urban upper and upper-middle classes.

CLASS AND THE POLITICAL PROCESS

For most analysts of the class system, a major consideration is the relationship of social class to sociopolitical change. The debate hinges on the model one chooses—modernization, neo-Marxism, or some combination. Whatever one's theoretical leanings, a number of questions impinge on the relationship of class to political and economic events: How has class identity emerged? How does class belongingness affect political decision making? What is the relationship between economic and political elites? How is power shared with the middle class and working or lower class?

With increasing industrial employment, a working-class identity emerged in Latin America. This consciousness was a *fait accompli* in countries with well-defined unionization, such as Chile and Argentina. Attitudes became polarized later in Mexico, Brazil, and Venezuela. The distinction in Brazil between the political style of Vargas, who used the term *trabalhadores* (workers), and the more militant left, which prefers *operários* (craftsmen), indicates the ambiguity of the working class. Still, at least two political parties, the Workers Party and Communist Party of Brazil, were oriented to the needs of workers, who supported a kind of class politics dedicated to fundamental change but not for the overthrow of capitalism.[86] As hinted previously, the least class consciousness appears in those countries farthest from the process of modernization; instead, one encounters an undifferentiated mass of peasants and an urban Lumpenproletariat. Previously, the urban poor of Mexico City were inclined to support the political status quo.[87] However, frustration drove them to move to the left in recent elections.

A number of factors make change difficult for the working class and their unions: ineffective leadership, little bargaining power, lack of sustained organization, and inadequate channels for presenting their demands. Changes in the economy, such as the division between rural and urban, blue- and white-collar, and formal and informal labor, have a negative impact. All this is aggravated by the difficulty of international support, as represented by such structures as ORIT (Organización Regional Interamericana de Trabajadores).[88]

With national variations, the democratization process has evolved over the past half century or more. Even before 1900, Argentine elites made compromises with the middle and working classes. Moreover, worker unrest increases during periods of economic duress when industrialists unload their costs by higher prices and lower wages, with a strike wave resulting when conditions improve.[89] The evolution may depend on how classes view themselves. Possibly more than in other Latin American countries, a certain labor militancy evolved in Argentina. One reason is the solid front that developed during the Perón period. Also, a kind of consolidation developed from a trend toward wage equalization. In the 1935–1939 period, the differential between skilled and unskilled labor was 71 percent; by 1965 this gap was reduced to 13 percent.[90] In reality, the working class in many developing nations has assumed two psychological styles: (1) a "political class" for whom labor demands and political motivation are very acute, and (2) the "rank and file," who revolve about home, neighborhood, and clubs, labor demands being of secondary concern.[91]

In a very different milieu—Peru in the late 1920s—a labor movement demanded and landed—with support of APRA—a minimal wage and an eight-hour working day. But the struggle remained between the economic elites and the disenfranchised. The election of Fujimoro in 1990 represented the power of the *cholos*—the lower-income mestizo–Indian—against the *pitucos*—the white elites who had dominated Peruvian politics through the decades.[92] Peru has a history of interelite squabbles, which occasionally make their tenure insecure.[93] Even the *cholos* are not unified. A key factor is unionization, which can take the form of either radicalism or clientelism. That is, in the 1970s workers were increasingly enlisted in the pro-Communist Confederación de Trabajadores de Peru as opposed to the APRA-sponsored unions.[94] This problem relates to the rigidities imposed by a labor aristocracy. Social change is not too likely to emerge among those who are satisfied with the status quo.

Elites, Compromise, and Consensus

As we have seen, the frame of reference for elites has been a renunciation of their native roots for European and, more recently, North American products and lifestyle. The older aristocracy generally opposes social change because of its threat to their position. Among the exceptions was the late 1940s when the Peruvian rural oligarchy sponsored the Odría administration and its industrialization policy, without realizing it could sow the seeds of their destruction in the long run. All in all, the new upper class is more open to social change. But whether new or old, a struggle among political and economic elites can be a serious impediment to development or stability. Sometimes a crisis produces the unanimity of elites, as in Mexico following the assassination of President Obregón in 1929.[95] The older and newer upper classes will close ranks if their hegemony is seriously challenged from the left, a situation less likely to occur if the challenge comes from the military right.

In meeting the realities of workers' demands and political participation, national differences are found. For instance, the upper and middle classes in Argentina and Chile were more receptive to the franchise in the first half of the twentieth century than were these classes in Brazil. Because of regionalism and diversity of ideology, consensus among elites is rare, or at least difficult. For instance, in Chile the center-left government following Pinochet through a number of legislative maneuvers cautiously crafted an income tax that would meet social needs but not offend business interests.[96] In a different setting and time frame, the majority of Brazilian elites initially supported the military regime of 1964. Yet by 1973, because of a faltering economy, they knew that the military dictatorship had overstayed its welcome. It is worth mentioning that the great debates among Brazilian elites center on economic rather than moral issues. Questions of divorce, birth control, and abortion are of less saliency than they are in a number of other nations, both in Latin America and the world beyond.[97]

A central issue is whether elites make the basic decisions. Or do they share, whether voluntarily or involuntarily, with the middle and working classes? A significant response to this question is found in a study of the political process in Venezuela, where labor conflict increased after 1973 at the time of the fuel crisis. Partly because of the resources available, Venezuelan elites chose to balance capital accumulation and consumption needs. In part, the explanation lies in the decision of workers to forego present material gains in the hope that increased capital will bring future return. From the viewpoint of industrialists, reduction of conflict enhances productivity and profits. This "class-compromise" model evolved after the return of Venezuela to democracy in 1958.[98] That is, a capitalist regime in the democratic orbit must exhibit legitimacy as based on support from a given portion of the electorate. Mediation of a compromise becomes more difficult when class conflict intensifies or when private or especially public resources are low. Brazil, possibly more than other Latin American nations, wrestles with the maintenance of this equilibrium.[99]

A similar interpretation of change in decision making is the case of Mexico in its development since the 1910 Revolution. Viviane Brachet-Máquez sees four different perspectives as shaped by the political cli-

mate and style of national leadership: (1) clientelism—shaping of political power through informal exchange relationships; (2) pluralism—sharing of political power through competing groups, a process accelerated
after 1940; (3) authoritarian-corporatism—more often found in Brazil
and Argentina as a reaction to a crisis, but in Mexico specifically planned
to fulfill the aims of the Revolution; and (4) a "class perspective"—or a
power struggle among various divisions of the dominant class. More than
the other three, the class perspective considers political change as resulting from "global economic transformations." In other words, the state
acts an arbiter over class conflicts in the context of given economic forces.
As democratic aims are managed by "controlled participatory mechanisms" under state corporatism, this authoritarian-corporatist perspective seems to have been conspicuous; the other three have surfaced in
Latin American politics, especially Mexican.[100] These approaches to political power operate in the interplay of several factors: class, race, region,
and the personality of the leadership, as documented in a study of the
electoral process in Brazil.[101]

The Middle Class and Political Change

The emergence of the middle class has been no real threat to the oligarchy, except as it favors moderate change; for example, increased education, social security legislation, and agrarian reform. Nor do labor unions
pose any real danger to the upper stratum as they are too balkanized,
even in those countries where labor militancy is well established. Also,
leaders from the middle classes, whether in management, labor, the professions, or the civil service, often consider power more important than
reform. Consequently, they may sell out to the ruling upper class.

The middle class primarily shares support with other sectors of the
body politic. Not infrequently the middle sector turns to organized labor, which desires industrial expansion on one side and social welfare on
the other. A fluid situation exists between classes in certain historical settings. Opposition to the ruling elites, magnified by an economic breakdown in Chihuahua, Mexico, in 1910 brought unified action between the
middle classes, workers, and peasants.[102] In the shifting sands of Chilean
politics, Radicals and Christian Democrats have appealed to both sides
for strength in their alliance. Occasionally, both the top and bottom of
the social order revolt against the conservative elements of the traditional
upper and middle classes. In other words, as segments of all classes desire
social change, it is questionable whether class loyalties are the ultimate
determinant of voting patterns. Members of all classes may or may not
profit from political and economic reorganization. The particular historical juncture at which an individual moves upward or downward in
the pecking order may be more meaningful in explaining political attachments than is his or her overall class position.

Finally, the middle class insists on political moderation. The success of democratic middle-of-the-road governments of the late 1950s and early 1960s as well as the 1980s probably arose from the middle sectors, even though each nation had its own style and sequence of development. Especially when the middle sector is threatened by insurrection from the left, it may prefer the return of a quasi-military operation of the government. One may ask how much power rests with the middle class, since the oligarchy usually manipulates elections.

When a nation ignores the class equilibrium problem and simply administers a few palliatives to its lower sectors, democratic stability becomes doubtful. However, the paternalistic relationship between government and the masses in most nations would seem to forestall any kind of serious threat to power. Since unionization is a sort of substitute for the *patrón* relationship and a dispenser of various services in most countries, the Marxist formula of a working-class revolution is unlikely to take place in Latin America. The solution for the urban lower class may lie in mature industrialism, which might bring wages and consumer items closer together.

Conclusions: The Future of Class Influence

It is anticipated that the middle class in Latin American will increase from the present percentage of 30 to 35 percent, with wide variations in many cities, to perhaps a 40 percent level in the twenty-first century. The middle class will likely assume more decision making than it does at present. Before World War II, it had only a residual effect on the body politic.

A kind of revolution is taking place in the lower and middle classes, for which forces in Europe and the United States are indirectly responsible. On one side, these forces include the sale of toothpaste, fountain pens, and modern plumbing. They also undermine the stratified society characteristic of Latin America and much of the developing world. Dissent is spreading among members of the lower classes, who are now becoming exposed to the mass media. Also, the lower and working classes have lost much of their moorings with the discrediting of Marxism; reorientation and new directions must be found.[103]

Even though the older middle class may have more stable values than the recent *arrivistas*, insistence on moderation and progress in both sectors may be a realistic basis for Latin America's drive for economic growth and democratic institutions. Moreover, as the middle class brings in recruits from the upper-lower class, its political power should increase and not diminish. This depends on, among other things, industrialization, educational expansion, and a reshaping of political processes, namely the availability of structures for decision making to the mass of the electorate. These developments are moving slowly, however, and desirable changes in the political apparatus seem further off than ever in view of the ambivalence of national leadership in the early 1990s. The value system of the lower class, along with other layers of the social structure, will remain ambiguous until the direction of Latin America is defined more clearly.

Returning to the conceptual analysis early in the chapter, we recall that specific classes operate as subcultures by which we perceive and interpret our experiences. As we look at the high degree of stratification in Latin America, one may conclude that a conflict approach seems to be more useful than a functional one. Classical Marxism probably was most relevant to Latin America until the 1980s, at which time the return to nominally democratic regimes implies that a different social structure was developing. With the end of the Cold War, imperialist powers such as the United States are less likely to intervene on the side of either the economic elites or the middle class. Social movements dedicated to reducing inequality will possibly find a less hostile environment. The class struggle will assume the form of competing levels of competence and lifestyle, similar to the themes of other Western nations.[104] At the very least, countries such as Argentina, Brazil, Chile, and Mexico are moving toward a pluralistic social order in which stratification is based on criteria beyond ownership or one's niche in the bureaucracy. Each country displays a different profile, but the rigid, inherited pattern of wealth and social influence is being assailed by new professional elites. Clientelism still pervades; however, networks and their manipulations are more open to inquiry and criticism. These shifts are markedly slower in at least half the countries. Still, sociopolitical change in Paraguay, for instance, serves notice that social institutions, including the economic one, are in transition. A quasi-feudalism lingers in the rural area, but in the cities the class system shows less stability.

NOTES

1. Karl Marx, *Economy, Class and Social Revolution*, ed. Z. A. Jordan (New York: Scribner's, 1971), 143.

2. Alejandro Portes, "Latin American Class Structures: Their Composition and Change during the Last Decades," *Latin American Research Review* 20(3): 7–39 (1985).

3. Edward C. Hansen and Timothy C. Parrish, "Elites Versus the State: Toward an Anthropological Contribution to the Study of Hegemonic Power in Capitalist Society," in *Elites: Ethnographic Issues*, ed. George E. Marcus (Albuquerque: University of New Mexico Press, 1983), 257–277.

4. Ralf Dahrendorf, *Class and Class Conflict in Industrial Society* (Stanford, Calif.: Stanford University Press, 1959).

5. Ibid., 180f.

6. Hubert M. Blalock, Jr., *Understanding Social Inequality: Modeling Allocation Processes* (Newbury Park, Calif.: Sage Publications, 1991), 3.

7. Michael L. Conniff, "The National Elite," in *Elites and Masses in Historical Perspective*, ed. Michael L. Conniff and Frank D. McCann (Lincoln: University of Nebraska Press, 1989), 23–46.

8. Werner S. Landecker, *Class Crystallization* (New Brunswick, N.J.: Rutgers University Press, 1981).

9. Randall Collins, "Market Dynamics as the Engine of Historical Change," *Sociological Theory* 8: 111–135 (1990).

10. Philippe Van Parjis, "A Revolution in Class Theory," in *The Debate on Social Classes*, ed. Eric O. Wright (London: Verso, 1989), 213–241.

11. Alejandro Portes and John Walton, *Labor, Class, and the International System* (Orlando, Fla.: Academic Press, 1981), 123–135.

12. Hans Gerth and C. Wright Mills, *From Max Weber, Essays in Sociology* (New York: Oxford University Press, 1946).

13. Portes and Walton, *Labor, Class, and the International System*, 10.

14. Manuel Castells, *La Lucha de Clases en Chile* (Mexico, D.F.: Siglo Veinteuno Editores, 1971), 139.

15. Paul I. Singer, *Dominação e Disigualidade: Estructura de Classes e Repartição da Renda no Brasil* (Rio de Janeiro: Paz e Terra, 1981), 101.

16. Erik O. Wright et al., *The Debate on Classes* (London: Verso, 1989).

17. Eric O. Wright and Donmoon Cho, "The Relative Permeability of Class Boundaries to Cross-Class Friendships: A Comparative Study of the United States, Canada, Sweden, and Norway," *American Sociological Review* 57: 85–102 (1992).

18. Peter H. Smith, *Labyrinths of Power: Political Recruitment in Twentieth-Century Mexico* (Princeton, N.J.: Princeton University Press, 1979), 43.

19. Latin American Center, *Statistical Abstract of Latin America* (Los Angeles: University of California, 1995), 414.

20. John A. Booth and Thomas W. Walker, *Understanding Central America* (Boulder, Colo.: Westview Press, 1989), 97.

21. Jorge Papadopulos, "Pensamiento Social e Intervención Pública: Pobreza, Políticas Sociales y Democracia," *Revista Interamericana de Planificación* 28: 52–60 (1995).

22. Norman E. Whitten, Jr., *Class, Kinship, and Power in an Ecuadorian Town: The Negroes of San Lorenzo* (Stanford, Calif.: Stanford University Press, 1965), 109.

23. Robert C. Williamson, "Social Class and Orientation to Change: Some Relevant Factors in a Bogotá Sample," *Social Forces* 46: 317–328 (1968).

24. Andrew H. Whiteford, *Two Cities of Latin America* (Beloit, Wisc.: Beloit College, 1960).

25. W. Lloyd Warner, *The Status System of a Modern Community* (New Haven, Conn.: Yale University Press, 1942).

26. Singer, *Dominação e Disigualidade*, 41.

27. Juan P. Terra, *Distribución Social del Ingreso en Uruguay* (Montevideo: Centro Americano de Economía Humana, 1983), 113.

28. Alida C. Metcalf, *Family and Frontier in Colonial Brazil* (Berkeley: University of California Press, 1992), 66–68.

29. Angel Palerm Vich, "Factores Históricos de la Clase Media en México," in *Ensayos sobre las Clases Sociales en México* (Mexico, D.F.: Editorial Nuestro Tiempo, 1968), 71–88.

30. Ruben E. Reina, *Paraná: Social Boundaries in an Argentine City* (Austin: University of Texas Press, 1973), 198–199.

31. Charles Wagley, *An Introduction to Brazil*, rev. ed. (New York: Columbia University Press, 1971), 95.

32. Jorge P. Osterling, *Democracy in Colombia: Clientelist Politics and Guerilla Warfare* (New Brunswick, N.J.: Transaction Publishers, 1989), 34–35.

33. Arthur D. Murphy and Alex Stepick, *Social Inequality in Oaxaca: A History of Resistance and Change* (Philadelphia: Temple University Press, 1991), 112–113.

34. Peter McDonough, *Power and Ideology in Brazil* (Princeton, N.J.: Princeton University Press, 1981), 76–77.

35. Carlos M. Vilas, "Family Affairs: Class, Lineage and Politics in Contemporary Nicaragua," *Journal of Latin American Studies* 24: 309–341 (1992).

36. Frank Bonilla, *The Failure of Elites* (Cambridge, Mass.: MIT Press, 1970), 315f.

37. Bernardo Sorj, *Estado e Classes Sociais na Agricultura Brazileira* (Rio de Janeiro: Zahar Editores, 1980).

38. James R. Scobie, *Buenos Aires: Plaza to Suburb, 1870–1910* (New York: Oxford University Press, 1974), 215.

39. Nicholas Abercrombie and John Urry, *Capital, Labour and the Middle Classes* (London: George Allen & Unwin, 1983), 57–58.

40. Alan Gilbert, *The Latin American City* (London: Latin American Bureau, 1994), 54.

41. José Pastore, *Inequality and Social Mobility in Brazil* (Madison: University of Wisconsin Press, 1982), 160.

42. Scobie, *Buenos Aires*, 220.

43. Jonathan Kelley and M. D. R. Evans, "Class and Class Conflict in Six Western Nations," *American Sociological Review* 60: 157–178 (1995).

44. Tereza M. Frota Haguette, *O Mito das Estrategias de Sobrevivência* (Fortaleza: Edições UFC, 1982), 79.

45. Gabriel Careaga, *Mitos y Fantasías de la Clase Media en México* (Mexico, D.F.: Cal y Arena, 1980), 58–59.

46. Diana J. Schemo, "Whatever Happened to Venezuela's Middle Class?" *New York Times*, February 9, 1996, p. A3.

47. Julio Mafud, *Los Argentinos y el Status* (Buenos Aires: Editorial Américale, 1973), 53–54.

48. F. Cupertino, *Classes e Camadas Sociais no Brasil* (Rio de Janeiro: Editora Civilização Brasileira, 1978).

49. Francisco Gómez Jara, "La Estratificación Rural en Mexico," *Revista Mexicana de Sociologia* 32: 691–708 (1970).

50. Rose M. Murado, *Sexualidade da Mulher Brasileira* (Petropolis: Vozes, 1983), 321.

51. Gerardo L. Munck, "Authoritarianism, Modernization, and Democracy in Chile," *Latin American Research Review* 29(2): 188–211 (1994).

52. Andrew H. Whiteford, *An Andean City at Mid-Century* (East Lansing: Michigan StateUniversity Press, 1977), 197–199.

53. Carmen Galilea, *Valores en Chile de Hoy* (Santiago: Centro Bellarimino, 1982), 101.

54. Edwin Eloy Aguilar et al., "Protestantism in El Salvador: Conventional Wisdom versus Survey Evidence," *Latin American Research Review* 28(3): 119–140 (1993).

55. Susan George, *A Fate Worse than Debt* (New York: Grove Press, 1988), 132.

56. José de Arimateia da Cruz, "Democratic Consolidation and the Socio-Economic Crisis of Latin America," *Journal of Interamerican Studies and World Affairs* 35: 145–161 (1993).

57. Alejandro Portes, José Itzigsohn, and Carlos Dore-Cabral, "Urbanization in the Caribbean Basin: Social Change during the Years of the Crisis," *Latin American Research Review* 29(2): 3–38 (1994).

58. As cited in Gilbert W. Merkx, "Social Structure and Social Change in Twentieth-Century Latin America," in *Latin America: Its Problems and Its Promises,* ed. Jan Knippers Black (Boulder, Colo.: Westview Press, 1984), 148–161.

59. Whiteford, *Two Cities,* 82–93.

60. Paul L. Doughty, *Huaylas: An Andean District in Search of Progress* (Ithaca, N.Y.: Cornell University Press, 1968), 75–87.

61. Claudia B. Isaac, "Class Stratification and Cooperative Production among Rural Women in Central Mexico," *Latin American Research Review* 30(2): 123–150 (1995).

62. June E. Hahner, *Poverty and Politics: The Urban Poor in Brazil, 1870–1920* (Albuquerque: University of New Mexico Press, 1986), 193.

63. Diego Armus, *Mundo Urbano y Cultura Popular* (Buenos Aires: Editorial Sudamericano, 1990).

64. James D. Cockcroft, *Neighbors in Turmoil* (New York: Harper and Row, 1989), 392.

65. Robert C. Williamson, "Some Factors of Urbanism in a Quasi-Rural Setting: San Salvador and San Jose," *Sociology and Social Research* 47: 187–200 (1963).

66. Janice E. Perlman, *The Myth of Marginality: Urban Poverty and Politics in Rio de Janeiro* (Berkeley: University of California Press, 1976), 158–159.

67. Barbara Ehrenreich, *Fear of Falling: The Inner Life of the Middle Class* (New York: Pantheon Books, 1989), 49–53.

68. Comisión Económica para América Latina (CEPAL), *Statistical Yearbook for Latin America* (Santiago: United Nations, 1991), 45.

69. Pamela Constable and Arturo Valenzuela, *A Nation of Enemies: Chile under Pinochet* (New York: Morton, 1991), 233.

70. Nathaniel C. Nash, "Chile Advances in a War on Poverty," *New York Times,* April 4, 1993, p. 14.

71. *Statistical Abstract,* 426.

72. George, *A Fate Worse than Debt,* 136–138.

73. Margaret S. Sherraden, "Social Policy in Latin America: Questions of Growth, Equality, and Political Freedom," *Latin American Research Review* 30(1): 176–190 (1995).

74. J. M. Barbalet, "A Macro Sociology of Emotion: Class Resentment," *Sociological Theory* 10(2): 150–159 (1992).

75. William Rowe and Vivian Schelling, *Memory and Modernity: Popular Culture in Latin America* (New York: Verso, 1991), 110–112.

76. Leslie Gill, "Painted Faces: Conflict and Ambiguity in Domestic Servant–Employer Relations in La Paz, 1930–1988," *Latin American Research Review* 25(1): 119–136 (1990).

77. James C. Scott, *Domination and the Arts of Resistance* (New Haven, Conn.: Yale University Press, 1990), 198.

78. David E. Hojman, "Land Reform, Female Migration and the Market for Domestic Service in Chile," *Journal of Latin American Studies* 21: 105–132 (1989).

79. Dahrendorf, *Class and Class Conflict*, 59.

80. Whiteford, *Two Cities*.

81. Nancy R. Powers, "The Politics of Poverty in Argentina in the 1990s," *Journal of Interamerican Studies* 37(4): 89–138 (1995).

82. José Pastore, *Inequality and Social Mobility in Brazil* (Madison: University of Wisconsin Press, 1982), 99.

83. Ibid., 161.

84. Robert C. Williamson, "Social Class, Mobility, and Modernism: Chileans and Social Change," *Sociology and Social Research* 56: 149–163 (1972).

85. Anthony Leeds, "Brazilian Careers and Social Structure: A Case History and Model," in *Contemporary Cultures and Societies of Latin America*, 2d. ed., ed. Dwight B. Heath (New York: Random House, 1974), 285–306.

86. John D. French, *The Brazilian Workers' ABC: Class Conflict and Alliances in Modern São Paulo* (Chapel Hill: University of North Carolina Press, 1992), 283.

87. Susan Eckstein, *The Poverty of Revolution* (Princeton, N.J.: Princeton University Press, 1977), 138.

88. Hobart A. Spalding, "New Directions and Themes in Latin American Labor and Working-Class History," *Latin American Research Review* 28(1): 202–214 (1993).

89. Ronaldo Mack, "Cycles of Class Struggle and the Making of the Working Class in Argentina, 1890–1910," *Journal of Latin American Studies* 22: 26–39 (1990).

90. Ronaldo Munck, *Politics and Dependency in the Third World* (London: Zea Books, 1984), 165.

91. James F. Petras, *Class, State and Power in the Third World* (Totowa, N.J.: Rowman & Littlefield, 1981), 260–262.

92. Henry Dietz, "Elites in an Unconsolidated Democracy: Peru during the 1980s," in *Elites and Democratic Consolidation in Latin America and Southern Europe*, ed. John Higley and Richard Gunther (New York: Cambridge University Press, 1992), 237–256.

93. Philip Mauceri, "State Reform, Coalitions, and the Neoliberal *Autogolpe* in Peru," *Latin American Research Review* 30(1): 7–37 (1995).

94. Susan C. Stokes, "Politics and Latin America's Poor: Reflections from a Lima Shantytown," *Latin American Research Review* 26(2): 75–101 (1991).

95. Alan Knight, "Mexico's Elite Settlement: Conjuncture and Consequences," in *Elites and Democratic Consolidation in Latin America and Southern Europe*, ed. John Higley and Richard Gunther (New York: Cambridge University Press, 1992), 113–146.

96. Delia M. Boylan, "Taxation and Transition: The Politics of the 1990 Chilean Tax Reform," *Latin American Research Review* 31(1): 7–31 (1996).

97. Peter McDonough, *Power and Ideology in Brazil* (Princeton, N.J.: Princeton University Press, 1981), 233–236.

98. Kevin Neuhouser, "Democratic Stability in Venezuela: Elite Consensus or Class Compromise?" *American Sociological Review* 57: 117–135 (1992).

99. Kevin Neuhouser, "Foundations of Class Compromise: A Theoretical Basis for Understanding Diverse Patterns of Regime Outcomes," *Sociological Theory* 11: 97–116 (1993).

100. Viviane Brachet-Márquez, "Explaining Sociopolitical Change in Latin America: The Case of Mexico," *Latin American Research Review* 27(3): 91–122 (1992).

101. Glaucio A. Dillon Soares and Nelson de Valle Silva, "Urbanization, Race, and Class in Brazilian Politics," *Latin American Research Review* 22(2): 155–176 (1987).

102. Mark Wasserman, *Capitalists, Caciques, and Revolution* (Chapel Hill: University of North Carolina Press, 1984), 156–158.

103. Jorge Castañeda, *Utopia Unarmed: The Latin American Left after the Cold War* (New York: Knopf, 1994).

104. Hans Haferkamp, "Differentiation and Culture: Sociological Optimism under Scrutiny," in *Social Structure and Culture*, ed. Hans Haferkamp (Berlin: Walter de Gruyter, 1989), 101–123.

Chapter 7

The City: Basic Patterns

The twentieth century is the age of the city. For better or worse, cities continue to grow throughout the world, but most rapidly in sub-Sahara Africa and Latin America. Northwestern Europe and the United States have already reached the limits of city growth. Urbanization is occurring in developing areas, often without an adequate economic base. Migrants, who account for half the urban growth rate, have little reason to remain in their stagnant rural enclaves. Moreover, the gulf in lifestyle between these newly developing cities and their rural hinterland is much wider than what separates a Chicagoan from a resident of Prairie Center. The concept of a rural–urban continuum is more applicable to the highly integrated societies of Europe and North America than to Latin American cities. As elsewhere in the world, these cities usually represent the best and worst of their respective national cultures. Despite its squalor and frustrations, the city permits ascent to the top and participation in national decision making.

Latin Americanists often approach urbanism in a more global sense than do North American observers. They look at the total institutional structure, with special focus on the political and economic processes. In this chapter, we shall analyze urbanism's functional significance, especially in the economic and political life of the nation. Then we shall review the city in its historical and demographic perspective. Next, we shall consider the structure of the city from an ecological viewpoint. Chapter 8 will focus on migration patterns and the role of the slum dweller in both the older central barrios and the shantytowns encircling the city. This subject will lead to an examination of present and future problems, such as housing, as well as the scope of planning and its implementation.

THEORIES OF URBAN DEVELOPMENT

The approach to urban processes has moved through several cycles. Max Weber set the stage for a functional explanation in underlining the economic character of the city, which he defined as the "settlement the inhabitants of which live primarily off trade and commerce rather than agriculture."[1] He recognized the difference between producer and consumer and traced the history of the city in its changing economic and political functions. In a different vein, Louis Wirth analyzed the sociopsychological aspects of urban life—its heterogeneity, impersonality, and competitiveness.[2]

In the context of developing societies, a useful approach is the conflict and Marxian theories. This viewpoint was eloquently stated by David Harvey. He sees the demands of production causing certain inelasticities, as for instance the inability of market resources to be allocated equitably and the absence of adequate residence for the workers. Space and land are continuously restructured, but under capitalism they are subordinate to production rather than to social justice. As a "set of social relations," urbanism is more often "embedded in some broader structure (such as the social relations of production) rather than functioning as an autonomous structure."[3] Similarly, Manuel Castells views production as determining the organization of space.[4] The city embodies various spatial and symbolic forces, as skyscrapers are the cathedrals of an expanding corporate world. The modern city has moved through three periods: (1) internationalization of capital, (2) increasing challenges by organized labor and liberation movements, and (3) world conflict (at least until 1989) between capitalism and communism.[5] From another viewpoint, capitalist development requires an expanded labor force, with recruitment from the countryside, as exhibited in Latin America. However, as urbanization costs tend to rise, they must be met by labor or capital or both. Both land speculators and the state enter into the fray. Inevitably, workers are forced to struggle in order to maintain their equilibrium.[6]

In a slightly different context, theorists sought from the 1950s to the 1970s to relate urban processes in Latin America to various socioeconomic conceptualizations.[7] On one side, the city was viewed as a principal link in modernization, with a focus on how elites might provide leadership and innovation. On another side, neo-Marxists pointed to the subordinate function of cities in colonialism, both internal and external. Other neo-Marxists struck the dependency theme. Although it does not contradict either conflict or dependency theory, the more recent *world-*

system approach places urbanization in a broader context. In other words, one cannot understand macrolevel social change, including urbanization, without analyzing world-system processes.[8] This analysis takes us into a number of issues, such as hierarchy of urban systems, formal and informal sectors, and especially the role of labor. The model of core–periphery–semiperiphery, namely, the economic subordination of marginal to intermediate nations, stresses the notion of dependence on the dominant nations, with the status and bargaining power of labor reflecting this axis. The industrial–urban process has integrated—or co-opted—a given national economy into the capitalist system of the Western world. The cities of the core system have remained stable. However, cities in peripheral and semiperipheral nations have moved toward higher primacy; that is, a central city, usually the capital, dominates the economic life of the country. Historical processes produced this pattern. During the 1930s, the Depression reduced the scope of world trade. World War II, along with the rebuilding of Europe and Japan, further diminished the flow of manufactured goods from core to noncore, and Latin America was forced into import-substitution, which encouraged urban growth.[9] As an observer in Central America comments, "A traditional industry only becomes capitalist when it reaches the world market."[10] One aspect of this "economic circuitry of the world system" is the development of transfrontier industrial cities, as one finds along the Mexico–U.S. border. In these twin cities, such as El Paso–Ciudad Juárez, textile, electronics, and various assembly plants followed the formula of cheap labor with easy access to the United States and beyond.[11]

Even though the economic basis of the city may be paramount, the political power structure is hardly irrelevant. These structures remain elitist, more often the play of multiple elites. As cities grow in both size and scope, more open and competitive power structures emerge. Any redistribution of power rests on the relationships between the class structure and political processes.[12] The urban process becomes more complex as informational systems and international markets interlock with national elites. Moreover, possibly even more than in other parts of the Western world, the interrelation of public and private interests in Latin America is tinged with conflict.[13]

A Historical Note

Remains of Mesopotamian cities dating from approximately 2500 B.C. reveal that cities developed out of the Neolithic revolution. In Meso-America and in the Andean highlands, urban culture was evident well before the arrival of the Spanish. If the Aztecs, Mayans, and Incas did not have all the refinements of the ancient Mediterranean civilizations, their social organization achieved a complexity associated with urban culture.

The Spanish came to the New World as bona fide town dwellers, predominantly from the "agro-military towns of the central meseta," rather than from the trade and manufacturing centers of northern Spain.[14] This predilection for urban life can be attributed to the need to establish towns as protective settlements during the reconquest of Spain from the Moors as well as to retain their privileges of power. Consequently, colonizers of the newly conquered lands organized these towns along the lines of the *municipalidad*. Even though towns were frequently erected on the sites of indigenous urban agglomerations, as in Tenochtitlán, which became Mexico City, or in rare instances near the walls and monuments of pre-Colombian centers, such as the Inca empire of Cuzco, their fundamental design was a replica of what had been left behind on the Iberian peninsula. As an end result, urban centers controlled the trade; interregional contacts were discouraged, and ties with Spain were all-important.

A major feature of the Spanish city was the *plaza mayor*; its spaciousness and regularity stand in contrast to the narrow and tortuous character of the street pattern. This central plaza flanked by a church and public buildings remains the dominant landmark of most Latin American towns. The Portuguese were less addicted to the plaza concept, but along with the Spanish they took to the novel idea of a rectangular street arrangement when topography permitted. Mexico City, Bogotá, Lima, Santiago, and Rio de Janeiro still conform to this checkerboard design.

Except in Brazil, where a coastal position was preferred, the major cities were in the highlands. The *villa*, or secondary town, was established in order to facilitate transportation and trade; and a port complemented the inland town, as did Vera Cruz, for example, which became the "break-of-bulk" point to the Mexican capital. Towns in the interior often conformed to a major site of a pre-Colombian civilization. Perhaps the most picturesque urban developments were the boom towns of Guanajuato, Taxco, and Potosí nestled in the mining areas of the highlands. The process of urbanization involved a certain amount of trial and error: Towns were abandoned because of unfavorable climate or soil condition, and the decline of the Indian population led to the demise of some lowland towns. The development of cities in the *altiplano* was also unpredictable. La Paz, for instance, eventually outgrew Sucre and in time became the capital because of its more favorable location for trade.

The *municipalidad* was based on the principle of a municipal corporation composed of *vecinos*, or property-owning citizens, governed by a *cabildo* (town council) with the *alcalde* (mayor) as chief administrator. Tracts of adjacent farmland were assigned to the citizens. At the edge of the *villa* was the *ejido* or pasturage area, a kind of town common. Gradually the town demarcated barrios for nonwhite servants and laborers, who far outnumbered their white overlords.

Since census materials are untrustworthy, the size of towns is always in doubt, but it is safe to say that Mexico City was the largest city of the Spanish-speaking world almost continuously from the middle of the sixteenth century until the early nineteenth century. It grew from perhaps 30,000 after the fall of Tenochtitlán to 100,000 in 1800. Still, San Luís Potosí in Bolivia was in 1650 the largest city in the Hemisphere with a population of 160,000, far more than its present size. The wealth of towns varied as much as their population. Mexico City, drawing upon the rich mines in its hinterland, had families with incomes as high as 200,000 pesos, thirty times the income of a Lima aristocrat. However different their development, they were the most powerful cities of New Spain.

Urban culture in colonial Latin America was centered on the municipal center as the point of departure for settlement of the hinterland. This primordial city passed from the stage of port and fortress to one of bureaucracy—military, civil, and clerical.[15] The relation of the given city to the empire depended on its economic contribution to the crown. The lack of integration of the city with its hinterland was documented by the marginal position of the indigenous and even large segments of the mestizo population.[16] Urban settlements were often based on the premise that *encomiendas* were a means of assuring the Crown's rule as well as realizing the dreams of self-enrichment for the colonists. Three aspects stand out: achievement of socioeconomic needs for Spain and Portugal, distortion of the original purpose of the *encomienda*, and sacredness of the private ownership of land.[17]

The National Period

The nineteenth century gave a more cosmopolitan stamp to the city. The Spanish architectural style was still important, but European patterns became dominant. Mexico City assumed a French character, especially with the laying out of the tree-lined boulevards such as the Paseo de la Reforma and Chapultepec Park. Similarly, Lima had its Paseo Colón and other boulevards, Santiago constructed the Alameda, and Montevideo developed the Rambla waterfront. Buenos Aires, aspiring to be the Paris of the New World, created the Avenida de Mayo to link its historic civic center with the Congreso.

Conspicuous social, political, and economic changes occurred in the decades after independence, as Richard Morse documents for São Paulo: consolidation of political control, commercial and intellectual contact with foreign countries as opposed to colonial mercantilist rigidity, migration of the rural elite to the city for its political and economic advantages, strengthening of urban credit facilities, rise of humanistic doctrines toward serfdom, and emergence of the labor movement.[18] Most crucial of all was the beginning of the labor movement and European immigration. In 1883, more than 1,300 Europeans came to São Paulo, and the present-day elite of the city is dominated by their descendants. São Paulo's dramatic growth from the late nineteenth to the mid-twentieth century was also a result of the expansion of coffee production. More recently the concentration of industry has been in the south of Brazil, with São Paulo as the center of gravity between Minas Gerais and Rio Grande do Sul. The spark in this aggressive leadership was migration from abroad. By the late twentieth century, migration was overwhelmingly from Brazil itself. In 1980, 57 percent of greater São Paulo were in-migrants, of which over one-third came from other urban areas.[19]

As transportation improved, primate cities established closer relationships with other urban agglomerations. At the same time, North American influences began to supplant those of Europe. In Mexico, highway links with the United States brought an influx of tourists and commercialism, the spread of supermarkets in the 1960s being one tangible result. More important for the cities was the industrialization after World War I. Although the great spurt of growth in the cities occurred during and after World War II, the urban trend was visible as early as the 1930s. An exception is El Salvador, where the urban population actually decreased from 38.3 to 36.5 percent between 1930 and 1950.[20] This decrease can be explained by a negative correlation between urbanization and agricultural density.[21] At present, cities in all countries are growing more rapidly than the general population.

POPULATION TRENDS

Cities reached their greatest growth rate after 1960. In a sense, this rate of urbanization continued an already emerging trend in the growth of cities; that is, the dominance of the capital city. Urban growth reflects a number of factors, including the total growth of the country and the state of the economy, both rural and urban. For instance, in the 1960s and 1970s urban population was growing by 5.0 percent or more per year in Bolivia and Honduras, with the rural growth rate at 0.5 and 2.3, respectively; whereas Chile's urban growth was 2.1 and its rural only 0.1.[22] Industry and commerce, of course, stimulate growth. Cities in Africa and Asia, and to a lesser extent most of Latin America, grow independently of industrialization, with their growth resulting merely from hordes of immigrants who are searching for a better life. On the other hand, urbanization in Buenos Aires or in São Paulo (which in 1990 was seven times its 1940 size) is on a firmer foundation, as industrialization has grown roughly in proportion to the population increase.

Latin America is close to the world average in urbanization. Although it is less urbanized than North America or Europe, it is much more so than Asia or Africa. If we consider as urban those inhabitants living in towns of 2,500 or more, 71 percent of Latin Americans are urban. One striking aspect of Latin America's population is the clustering in cities of over one million inhabitants. In that respect, it leads the world with an average of 3.6 million people in no less than forty-one metropolises (as compared to Asia's average of 3.1 million, North America's 2.7 million, and Europe's 2.5 million).[23] Vast differences are found among the Latin American countries in the amount of urbanization. Uruguay, Argentina, Chile, Venezuela, and Brazil (in declining order) surpass the 1995 U.S. ratio of 75 percent urban population; whereas Mexico's ratio is 71 percent, Honduras's is 47, and Haiti's a mere 32 percent.[24] Even if we limit the calculation of urbanization to cities with 20,000 or more inhabitants (instead of the U.S. demarcation of 2,500), Argentina, Chile, and Uruguay are still more than two-thirds urban, a distinction held by only a dozen or so Westernized nations. It is startling to think that in the year 2000 one in three inhabitants in Mexico and South America will probably be living in cities of more than four million people; in 1970 the ratio was one in five.[25] On the whole, Latin America is more urbanized than Latin Europe, even though it is not as industrially developed. Finally, the rate of urbanization is decelerating. For instance, Mexico City was growing at 5.6 percent per year between 1940 and 1980, but by only 3.0 percent between 1980 and 1990.[26]

Primacy: Trends and Significance

As mentioned previously, Latin American cities show a strong, if uneven, tendency toward primacy (see Table 7.1) or the movement of a given city, usually the capital, to a position of demographic, industrial, and financial dominance, both in the national and world scene. The most extreme cases are Panama City and Montevideo, which account for nearly half of the population of their respective nations, as seen in Table 7.1. However, Brazil, Mexico, and Colombia divide their urban population between several major cities. The dynamic of primacy has intrigued urban sociologists. Historically, primate cities such as Buenos Aires and Montevideo were port cities, whereas Santiago and Caracas as inland cities grew during the nineteenth century at a slower rate than their respective countries.[27] Despite their inland location, Mexico City and Bogotá flourished because they were pre-Colombian centers of population and as capitals could direct the economy. Primacy is not only demographic but also economic. For instance, Santiago produces over half of Chile's GNP.[28] This megacephalic tendency has a long but jagged history. In the early nineteenth century, several factors led to a "primacy dip," such as a population loss of port cities to the hinterland, agricultural expansion, and the vulnerability of urban population to epidemics, among others.[29]

TABLE 7.1
Population of Largest Metropolitan Areas and Their Ranking

Country	Largest City	In Thousands 1950	1990	Percentage of Population in Largest City 1990
ARGENTINA	Buenos Aires	5,130	11,580	34.8
BOLIVIA	La Paz	300	1,320	18.1
BRAZIL	Rio/São Paulo	3,450	18,420	12.2
CHILE	Santiago	1,330	4,700	35.7
COLOMBIA	Bogotá	680	5,590	17.6
COSTA RICA	San José	180	1,040	34.8
CUBA	Havana	1,081	2,090	20.3
DOMINICAN REP.	Santo Domingo	220	2,200	30.7
ECUADOR	Guayaquil	259	1,738	16.0
EL SALVADOR	San Salvador	213	1,051	20.0
GUATEMALA	Guatemala City	337	2,183	23.7
HAITI	Port-au-Prince	130	460	7.1
HONDURAS	Tegucigalpa	140	520	10.1
MEXICO	Mexico City	2,880	19,370	21.9
NICARAGUA	Managua	109	1,148	27.7
PANAMA	Panama City	217	1,175	48.6
PARAGUAY	Asunción	200	1,270	29.7
PERU	Lima-Callao	1,010	6,500	29.1
URUGUAY	Montevideo	1,086	1,363	43.5
VENEZUELA	Caracas	680	3,960	20.1

Source: Latin American Center, *Statistical Abstract of Latin America* (Los Angeles: University of California, 1995), Tables 633 and 634.

Only in the last generation have secondary cities begun to assert their industrial and political importance.

Primacy has interesting historical and economic overtones. As one example, Argentina represents a struggle between the *porteños* (residents of Buenos Aires) and the pampas. Until the nineteenth century, the western towns were the principal urban agglomeration. With the railroad age and massive migration from Europe, Buenos Aires was growing early in the twentieth century at 5 percent per year. More recently, its growth rate fell to only 2 percent, far lower than most other Latin American cities. In view of its more acute regionalism, Brazil offers a different chronicle with at least a half dozen major cities, and Ecuador is described as the "tale of two cities," Guayaquil and Quito. By the 1970s, migrants

from the countryside were moving into cities such as São Paulo and
Mexico City at a rate comparable to African and Asian cities, and at the
end of the decade these two cities had three and four million squatters,
respectively.[30] The economic crisis of the 1980s, with rising unemployment and limited funds for investment, has decelerated city growth, especially in primate cities.[31]

Despite some acceleration of growth, secondary cities account for a
small part of the Latin American population as compared to other developing areas. Almost 40 percent of the urban inhabitants in 1980 were in
urban places with a population of less than 100,000, and 43 percent lived
in the primary city. Only in Bolivia, Colombia, and Mexico did secondary cities account for one-third or more of the urban population.[32] In the
significance of secondary cities, as with primary ones, economic factors
are central. For example, Quetzaltenango is secondary to Guatemala City,
but since 1973, it is growing twice as fast and represents a core administrative function for western Guatemala—with proportionately more commercial enterprises and professionals (notably lawyers) than the capital.[33]
An intriguing pattern emerging from economic trends is found in certain
countries of the Caribbean area. In Guatemala, with its economic recession and state-induced violence, primacy is on the decline. Countries with
a tourist boom outdistancing industry have shown a reverse of primacy,
as in the Dominican Republic. In Costa Rica, with growth in both tourism and export-oriented industry, a megacity is developing around the
capital of San José.[34]

The present status of primacy, as implied, is related to the world-system. As one aspect, urban primacy accelerated in the 1920s in Latin
American countries, whereas "mature" cities in core nations (London,
New York, and Paris) experienced little growth.[35] Primacy appeared in
Latin America, diffusing later to Asia, and most recently to Africa. Its
significance is found in the siphoning off of precious resources from the
countryside in order to meet the needs of the capital.[36] Primacy appears
to be fostered by various aspects of colonialism, notably export dependency and the consequence of import substitution. Another facet is rural
collapse. As one export crop succeeds another, workers are displaced and
move to the urban center.[37] Other explanations point to the concentration of wealth and the differential sophistication of labor in the city.[38]

Demographic Variables and the Future

Assessing the rate of future urban growth is difficult, since it depends
on migration combined with rates of natural increase, which in many
areas are only slightly below rural rates. Expanding industrialization will,
in all probability, be accompanied by further urban growth, even though
the rate of urban increase is already slower. It is significant that the rich-

est agricultural countries, Argentina and Uruguay, also have high rates of urban conglomeration.

Future growth rests on demographic variables. Gender is one variable: Urban sex ratios are generally lower, as noted in Chapter 3. Because cities offer more opportunities for employment of women than do rural areas (where a preference for male occupations predominates), women disproportionately migrate to the cities. However, as Latin America is broadening the nature of its tertiary employment, the sex ratio is becoming more equalized, but, as with most of the world, women are paid less than men for their labor. As in the rest of the world, the age structure in Latin American cities reveals a relatively old population, albeit with regional variations. Urban birthrates are low as compared with other areas of the developing world; they are also lower than in the rural. However, accurate statistics are difficult to obtain since data regarding woman/child ratios are seldom complete. As members of consensual unions are counted as single individuals, the "number" of married persons is indefinite.

Because of more adequate health services in the city, life expectancy is greater. Even though some cities report higher mortality and morbidity than the rest of the nation, more careful reporting may be the reason.[39] In view of the inability of agricultural productivity to keep pace with population growth, the city may suffer more than the country in the competition for what limited commodities exist. Wartime experience in Europe showed that persons farthest from the source of supply are the losers. Consequently, mortality may eventually increase for urban dwellers, notably the poor.

FUNCTIONAL SIGNIFICANCE OF THE CITY

In any culture, the city carries on a number of critical tasks: manufacturing, commerce, and transportation, along with institutional functions such as education, religion, and the arts and sciences. Cities appeared in human society when skill specialization and partial liberation from the primary requirements of the society were attained. At the apex of the occupational hierarchy, a clerical, military, and governmental bureaucracy emerged first in the classical Mediterranean world and later in the pre-Colombian civilization of the New World. The heritage of Greece and Rome persisted in the urban institutions of medieval Spain and Portugal, later to be transferred across the Atlantic. The elaboration of urban culture following the Industrial Revolution did not reach Latin America until nearly a century after it had changed the fabric of life in Western Europe and North America. The city must be considered as a geographic entity made up of economic or production space and of social space.[40]

Economic, political, and social processes are all vital to the city's function in the total society, or, as John Walton describes Guadalajara, a city can involve a civic culture, a modernity culture, a working-class culture, and a political culture.[41] In other words, what specific roles does the city play in the commercial and industrial growth of the society? To what degree can the city operate as a positive factor in the development of responsible government? How is the individual shaped by the urban environment?

Economic Forces

Because the rate of urbanization in Latin America is nearly twice the rate of industrial expansion, it appears that the region is overurbanized. In most of the developing world, urbanization outdistances industrialization. Per capita economic growth runs between 1 and 3 percent for most nations in the 1990s. Hence we must be cautious in expecting urbanization to produce industrialization. Nor does industrialization, or the secondary sector, necessarily depend on a city, since industries occasionally crop up in rural areas.

On the whole, the city offers the more promising environment for industrialization. A principal reason is the relatively high development of capital and skills in the urban as compared to the rural area. This dualism has a number of implications. For one, technical innovations are more likely to affect the urban than the rural worker. Even though lagging the norms of the Western world, urban workers in Latin America indirectly benefit from the feudalistic practices of the countryside. Discriminatory wage rates and large-scale migration to the city are part of this pattern. On that point, it is hypothesized that an increase in the wage difference between the formal and informal sectors in the city tends to decrease migration to the city, and as a result lower urban growth rates.[42] Parenthetically, whether in Brazil or Costa Rica, capital investment is concentrated in cities (often only primate cities), while rural areas fall ever farther behind. Increasingly, cities and even small towns are forced to consider their economic relationships to their hinterland, both industrialization and its ecological results, as reflected in a survey of Costa Rica.[43]

Probably São Paulo offers the most notable example of urban industrialization in Latin America. Its metropolitan area accounted for 40 percent of the manufacturing in Brazil in 1980. In addition to its industrial output, the city usually incorporates the financial, information processing, and research-development sectors. For instance, in Colombia at least six cities are significantly industrialized, yet Nicaragua's capital Managua is only beginning the transition to secondary development.

As implied, the hope of expanding economic growth in the cities was shattered in the 1970s and especially the 1980s. Several factors are relevant in this retrogression.[44] One is the huge indebtedness and the lack of funds for investment, all of which has a greater impact on the city than on the countryside. As cities depend on international capital, funds are not available for the infrastructure—water and sewer systems, surfacing of streets, and other facilities.[45] Another factor in financial underpinning is the political drift to the right of the major Western capitalist nations. Among the indirect results of this lack of international funding were a two-thirds decrease in the average income of manual workers in urban Peru from 1980 to 1990 and an increase in mortality rates for children in Chile between 1975 and 1983.[46]

Formal and Informal Labor

The city offers a wide variety of employment, both in quality and quantity. The postwar economy introduced more refinements in the capitalist system. Marketing has especially been affected by influences from abroad, notably North America. As one of many examples, the rise of *intermedias* (middlemen) became apparent in the marketing of Salvadorian coffee.[47] Informal labor becomes all the more critical in perhaps three-fourths of urban families; nearly everyone, irrespective of age or gender, is expected to contribute to the family income. Informalization has several socio-economic effects: a "decentralized model of economic organization," reduction of labor costs, and a more diversified form of work and social settings, among others.[48] Of course, the borderline between formal and informal is not a firm one.

The balance between the formal and informal economies varied during the industrialization period. For instance, the GNP for Latin America doubled between 1950 and 1980, with some decline in the informal economy during the first two decades, but the worsening economic climate of the 1970s and 1980s elicited a growth in the informal sectors, which was a result of more improvisation of economic products and, consequently, lower incomes.[49] In this connection, Castells denotes four variants of work in the urban economy: (1) salaried workers in the traditional or formal capitalist sector; (2) small merchants and handicraft persons; (3) purveyors of services—shoeshine boys, porters, guides, or others who do not fall into the conventional capitalistic norms of production; and (4) "sellers of their bodies"—prostitutes, beggars, and delinquents, who "exchange their survival against the possibility of potential destruction."[50] Only the first of these categories truly belongs to the formal economy. It is reckoned that two-thirds of the workers in Lima are in the underground economy, particularly in the garment industry.[51] Both formal and informal workers are found in the tertiary sector. Indeed, theorists disagree about the ultimate effects of "tertiarization."

Since no agrarian reform program can resolve the dilemma of a crowded rural landscape, cities must come to the rescue. With the overflow of migrants, there is always hope of expanding the industrial base. In reality, unemployment affects one-fourth to one-half of the workforce (depending on the particular country), leaving thousands in every city clamoring for any kind of employment, which usually means the informal area. Data from Bolivia reveal a floating population that moves back and forth between the rural and urban informal labor market.[52] The industrial climate is frequently the key. For instance, in Haiti, nearly all employment is in the informal sector.[53] In the case of Brazil, both Recife and Porto Alegre have a population of one million, but the latter has a onethird larger number of economically active population.[54] Even relatively advanced societies suffer from this desperate search for employment. In a survey of urban Uruguay, 35 percent of the working class were involved in informal work, of which nearly half (48 percent) were selfemployed. In the depression of the 1980s, many of the poverty-stricken population were struggling for economic survival, whatever the means.[55] One striking aspect of the informal economy is its enormous growth. A study of street vendors found a fourfold increase in Querétero, Mexico, between 1985 and 1993.[56] A major problem for informal commercial labor is where to find an opening in an overcrowded setting. Possibly most troubling is the degree to which informal labor falls on women and children. For instance, in 1988 in Guadalajara 35.5 percent of women were paid less than the minimum wage as compared to 16 percent of men. The UNESCO estimate of thirty million street children would seem to be excessive, but statistics on school dropouts indicate otherwise.[57] Finally, among the factors in the growth—and crisis—of informal labor are migration, shifts in industrialization, low wages in the formal sector, and the threshold of globalization.

Migration, Mobility, and the Economy

Economic variables also affect the growth of the city through migration. As an example, of the total population of São Paulo in 1973, more than two-thirds (68 percent) were migrants—one of the highest rates among developing nations.[58] The exodus to the city is determined not only by available opportunities but by the economic base of the hinterland and the socioeconomic characteristics of the migrants. One variant is the boom towns of the Amazon, which provide labor necessary for resource extraction, but after the initial labor demand fades away, migrants move on to other areas.[59]

Cities such as Buenos Aires, São Paulo, and Santiago, which have long been commercial and industrial centers with a relatively settled workforce, offer a contrast to Lima, Bogotá, or even Mexico City, where migration presumably occurs disproportionately among subsistence workers. The goal and site selection of a migrant are different for an industrialized country as compared to countries in which the economy is less developed. For instance, migrants to Santiago must present higher "credentials"; that is, they must have more education and be more skilled than migrants going to a Central American city. Also, the migrant to the city in developed countries is more likely to be from a provincial town than from a rural area.

Several factors affect migration. One is wage-rate differentials. At least in industrialized areas, migrants tend to move up the wage-rate gradient; they move from low-wage to high-wage areas.[60] Women suffer more than men in wages, ability to find housing, and lengthy commuting to work, not to mention the lack of day care centers.[61] An increasing gap between the formal and informal sectors inhibits urban migration. As wages rise, workers are displaced and wages fall in both sectors.[62] Family needs, fear of the unknown, and overcrowdedness of the city also discourage migration.

In view of the discussion of social mobility in Chapter 6, rigidity in the urban stratification system is indirectly related to economic growth. For example, the migrant goes to the city without skills but with a feeling of reliance on the *patrón* and the heritage of a complex relationship between subordination and superordination. Another limiting factor is the migrant's inability to take advantage of what training facilities and educational media exist within the city. Migration to the city has also been a factor in keeping wage rates low. Consequently, crises in the city will continue because of the lack of an industrial base that provides employment for the flow of migrants. One may question whether the tertiary sector can supply either sufficient capital or employment for meaningful economic growth.

Political Forces

Does the city environment facilitate the growth of democracy and stability of governmental institutions? For most observers, the answer is yes, but the unequal development of various countries might leave some doubt. The case of Argentina is an example. After the 1870s, it enjoyed a limited democracy, which gave way to mass democracy in 1916. The appearance of dictatorial elements after 1930 was preceded by a growing urban population. The Province of Buenos Aires grew from 37 percent in 1896 to 53 percent in 1914, and to 62 percent of the Argentine population in 1947. The processes of urbanization, education, foreign immigration, and economic growth threatened the previously unassailable position of the largely rural elite, which consequently opted for military rule in 1930. Juan Perón made a more drastic move away from democracy than even his immediate predecessors and did respond to the needs of the urban masses, from whom he received his major support. In 1966, again with tacit support of the urban working and middle classes, successive military dictatorships took power for nearly two decades. In conclusion, urbanization and its accompanying social changes do not necessarily assure either free participation by the mass of the electorate or government stability.

Democratic governments exist in countries with both high and low rates of urbanization, as do authoritarian regimes. Uruguay with high urbanization has a lengthy history of democracy, as does Costa Rica with low urbanization; dictatorships have flourished in Argentina with high urbanization and Paraguay with low. A complex relationship is found between voting patterns and the type of economic activity. In Chile, for instance, Communist voting in the postwar period was more evident in the copper, coal mining, and nitrate zones than in greater Santiago or in the Valparaiso–Viña del Mar area. However, as a result of the Pinochet regime, the political left is as conspicuous in the capital as in the mining areas.

Inevitably, the city affects political processes in certain respects. First, the urban milieu offers a variegated set of political postures, alliances, and coalitions. Symbiotic relationships develop between one party and another, usually crossing ethnic and class lines. In nearly all nations, the middle class has to compromise its interests and seek political bedfellows. Labor unions, among other groups, are forced to achieve a modus operandi with other power centers, very likely with some segment of the urban middle class. Whatever the alliances, class differences are more important than the degree of urbanization. In any case, the urban milieu includes a wide range of political options. Opposition parties in Mexico have little vitality outside the cities. It was the rural population that secured (possibly by fraud) the victory of Salinas in 1988, even though they had the least to gain by his modernization program.[63] In Venezuela, neither of the two leading parties has received overwhelming support in Caracas because of the city's multifarious electorate.

Second, migrants have no small political significance. For one thing, escape to the city reduces their frustration, at least until they become disenchanted with the urban status quo. More precisely, peasant leagues and militancy in the countryside would have greater support were it not for the safety-valve effect of cityward migration. The proliferating shantytowns are assumed to be cauldrons of revolutionary activity. Examination of the political attitudes of squatter settlements reveals, on the contrary, a varying attitude from the minimally politicized slum dwellers of Guatemala and the Dominican Republic to the involved residents in the shantytowns of Caracas and Santiago. For instance, according to a survey of Venezuelan *rancherios*, migrants have generally supported the distinctly minority parties rather than the "middle-of-the-road" Acción Demócrata or COPEI. In particular, Caracas *rancho* dwellers are articulate in their demands on the government for services, although they are by no means the political force represented by labor unions or other organized pressure groups. In comparison, squatters in Chile are militantly committed to the left.

Third, political and economic heterogeneity characterizes the city. Hence the urban environment is scarcely able to insure political integrity, either for the local community or the national society. Nonetheless, cities have successfully challenged the hacienda tradition and unquestionably hold the balance of power in highly urbanized countries. Moreover, in producing counterelites the city provides innovations in the political order. Rival interest groups appear as urbanization is accelerated in economic development. But the intervention of an agrarian elite, conflicting interests in the city, and lack of politicization among recent migrants can inhibit the exercise of power. Further, urbanization without adequate industrialization remains a problem. Consequently, the role of services is all important. On that point, the municipality is deficient in a number of services ranging from utilities to self-help projects—presumably more attributable to lack of finances than insufficient concern.[64]

Imagery, Identity, and the Rural–Urban Continuum

The meaning of urban identity has been explored by social psychologists and urban geographers over the last generation. Visual and related perceptions of our urban milieu are of increasing interest. One has only to compare the richly textured streets and monuments of Mexico City to the industrial profile of twentieth-century León or Aguas Caliente or the historic structures of Bogotá with the commercial port city of Barranquila. Studies show that city residents tend to identify primarily with the historic center rather than with the periphery.[65] Of course, imagery changes considerably with the type of city: the museum city, the bordertown, the commercial center.[66] Imagery may also grow out of historical processes. Medellín moved from the mining era (1650–1850) to the coffee era after 1875, followed by the industrial era beginning after 1910.[67] (A cynic might point to the drug era of the 1980s.) Some urban areas change more rapidly than do others, but residents depend on familiar spatial images. As implied, a predominant perceptual stimulus of many Latin American cities is the central plaza surrounded by the central church and public buildings. As with European cities, street nomenclature can provide a sense of national identity. For instance, Asunción, Paraguay, has no less than thirty streets named after historical events.[68]

The question of urban identity is not a new one. Early in this century, Georg Simmel was concerned with roles and social relationships.[69] More recent observers are preoccupied with the constraints of bureaucracy. As our sense of intimacy lessens, we are increasingly forced to rely on police and other social controls to achieve what social networks might accomplish in the village.[70] According to a study of selected barrios in Caracas, feelings of belonging to a given site grew out of a sense of identity based on length of tenure, preference for the physical setting, and interpersonal networks.[71]

The relative attractiveness of the urban environment is frequently said to be the result of certain opportunities it provides—individual freedom, anonymity, role segmentalization, and norm variability. In Chapter 6, we alluded to several dimensions in connection with social class. In other words, both urbanism and middle-class belonging are associated with Gesellschaft norms and attitudes, an association demonstrated by a comparison of an urban with a rural community in El Salvador. The El Salvador urban sample as compared to the rural sample revealed greater community and social involvement, larger exposure to mass media, and rationalistic rather than traditional beliefs.[72]

What are the effects of urbanization on migrants in developing areas of the world? As one answer, a study of the Guajiro Indians in Colombia points to shifts in role relationships and personality traits. The peasants become less able to control economic relationships as competitive wage labor is substituted for pastoralism. The conjugal union assumes more importance than extended kinship; socialization practices move toward a give-and-take relationship and away from the more severe norm restrictions in the tribal group. Secondary contacts vie with primary group controls throughout the person's life; not least in importance in this respect is the influence of formal education.[73]

The folk–urban hypothesis held that the values and ideology of a folk society have a more satisfying adjustment level than do those of the urban community. Robert Redfield conceived of the folk community as "small, isolated, nonliterate and homogeneous, with a strong sense of group solidarity."[74] The idealized representation of the rural milieu has led to an extended controversy. Personal and social disorganization supposedly occurs as the villager has to adjust to the employer–employee relationship and various fleeting involvements of the city. Louis Wirth[75] did not believe that any city could become a folk society, yet migrants to the city may bring their rural traditions with them. Neighborhood associations and even commercial institutions, whether shop or tavern, may improvise a kind of personal identity for a given setting. Whether La Boca in Buenos Aires or Candelario in Bogotá, a barrio has its own lifestyle. Residents of the city develop loyalties to their particular locality and see themselves as members of an "urban village."[76] The urban–rural axis is conditioned by subcultural and individual behavior patterns.[77] Also, one may ask whether Latin America is currently developing suburbia; if so, will it identify with the city, or will it develop a lifestyle of its own? Or, as in North America, will it show a specific pattern in indexes like anonymity, tolerance, community bonds, alienation, and deviant behavior that is somewhere between city and country?[78]

We shall examine more systematically the problem of the rural–urban continuum and, particularly, the role of the migrant in Chapter 8, but the supposed superiority of either the rural or urban environment is a matter of value judgment. Nor would social scientists agree as to what is archaic and traditional at one end of the continuum and what is modern at the other end.[79] The question of marginality in contemporary society is not resolved. Industrialization of the service sector, changes in communication and transportation, and varied lifestyles characterize urban life. However, the question of the ultimate quality of urban life—which varies remarkably for time and place—has yet to be determined.

ECOLOGICAL PATTERNS

Ecology refers to the organism's and society's utilization of space. Social systems involve people, organizations, and technology, all of which operate in a given milieu. Ecology also includes the way that individuals and groups bring meaning to their environment and how they organize territory and their spatial boundaries. Compared to cities in Europe and North America, the Latin American city has a somewhat different approach to spatial relationships since it is composed of highly diverse cultural types and is influenced by location and economic function. For one thing, cities vary in their degree of *nucleation*, or central dominance. The pre-Colombian cities were rigidly planned, with the elite in the central area and the lower classes in villages or agglomerations of huts on the periphery. The Spanish scheme for cities, in theory highly nucleated, had a plaza around which a central district was established; however, the development of barrios patterned according to ethnic status gave this type of city an unnucleated character. The city still lacks communality because of its separate enclaves. Jurisdictional boundaries, topographic barriers, and inadequate transportation facilities are all part of this nonnucleation. Instead of being nucleated, cities have tend to be *crescive*, that is, they develop in a relatively unplanned fashion.

Probably more than anything else, the highly stratified nature of a society determines its ecology. Although Santiago, for example, has a certain degree of unity imposed by the central business and administrative center, sharp sociocultural differences exist between the several *comunas* that make up the metropolitan area. Even a casual observer perceives the city to be divided into the middle- and upper-class "*barrio alto*" to the northeast and the vast lower-class area to the south, with less expansion of the city to the northwest. Size and quality of buildings, architectural styles, landscaping, and the extension of services (from the presence of sewers and street lighting to the availability and comfort of buses) all support this perception of two Santiagos instead of one. Nevertheless, the differences between the two often involve shades of gray rather than white and black.

In major cities, skyscraper apartments and luxury villas are physically not far from impoverished neighborhoods in all their variations, from the dreary, decaying *conventillos* (slums) adjoining the older part of town to the vast shantytowns on the city's edge and in interstitial areas. At the same time, to a passerby on the street, traditional upper-class homes with their blank walls are often indistinguishable from less affluent quarters. Since residences were formerly oriented to an interior patio, exhibiting opulence on the exterior was of little concern. In the postwar period, the upper class adopted the North American style of homes in the suburbs, but in smaller cities like Popayán upper-class residents still cling to the favored locations near the center, with the middle class in the next adjacent area. The lower class still prefers, or is forced, to live beyond the city boundary, where taxes—and facilities—are lower or nonexistent.

If one turns to the classical University of Chicago model of urban ecology—concentric zone, sector, and multiple nuclei—we would have difficulty in arriving at consistent generalizations regarding the ecological structure of the average city. Obviously, not all Latin American cities are the same. The *concentric* approach—that ecological zones, such as lower-class housing, commercial establishments, and other zones compose circular areas from the center outward—has been applied to the older, medium-size cities. However, the zones are in reverse of the American pattern of higher status as one travels from the central business district outward. Moreover, the unnucleated or crescive character of the Latin American city does not generally correspond to the concentric zone model.

The *sector* theory is based on the division of the city into quadrants which retain a degree of consistency from the center to the outer boundary. A study of three Mexican provincial cities suggests a need to revise the inverse concentric zone theory, since major arteries have a determining effect on the adjacent residential areas.[80] For most of this century in Guadalajara, the two eastern quadrants, Libertad and Reforma, have been the locus of the underclass; in Hidalgo and Juárez to the west reside the middle and upper classes. Land values are not greatly different between the two halves of the city, the eastern half simply has a significantly higher density. Also, the urban infrastructure (paving, lighting, water, and the like) favor the western half.[81] In other examples, if one travels northward on Bogotá's Avenida Séptima, one encounters a predominantly middle- and upper-class population, as on Providencia, a major boulevard in Santiago, or along the succession of beaches stretching southwest from the center of Rio de Janeiro. In time, the sector pattern may change or expand its course. Whereas nearly a century ago in Mexico City some four-fifths of the upper-middle and upper classes lived along or near the Reforma and Insurgentes, since World War II they occupy the plush Lomas de Chapultepec, Pedregal, and San Angel. As with Guadalajara, the lower class lives in the east and north, while the middle class lives more to the west and parts of the south.

Generally, most Latin American cities show a combination of sector and concentric zone development. Figure 7.1 presents such an arrangement with a "zone of maturity" encompassing the better housing and public services, "in situ accretion" as a transitional area with diverse housing, "disamenity" areas containing industries, utilities, warehouses, and waste areas, and a "commercial spine" providing commercial services on a sector basis.

FIGURE 7.1
A Model of Latin American Urban Structure

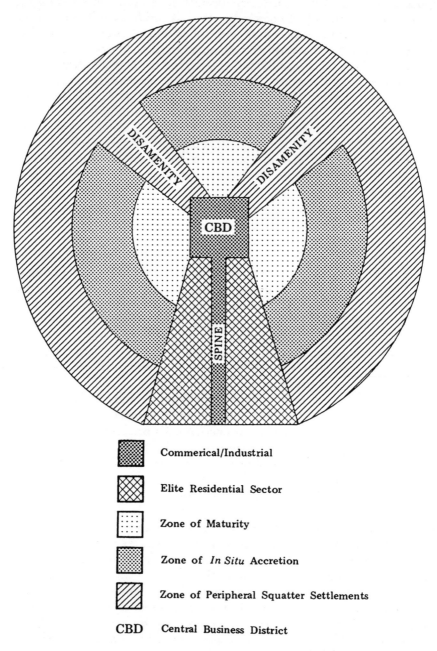

Commerical/Industrial

Elite Residential Sector

Zone of Maturity

Zone of *In Situ* Accretion

Zone of Peripheral Squatter Settlements

CBD   Central Business District

Source: Adapted by permission of the American Geographical Society, from Ernst C. Griffin and Larry R. Ford, "A Model of Latin American City Structure," *Geographical Review* 70: 397–422 (1980).

However, topographical features as well as historical development, economic forces, and migration make for *multiple nuclei*. As *favelas* have evolved into self-contained communities, often isolated by enormous topographic barriers, Rio de Janeiro has become a series of separate enclaves. Commercial districts are occasionally found in the outer rim as transportation difficulties render the "million class" cities unmanageable for commuters. This centrifugal tendency has a historic tradition dating back to 1681, when the Laws of the Indies stipulated that nonwhites should live in their own *cercados* (enclosures). Mérida, Yucatán, is a case in point. The central area was reserved for the elite, and barrios grew up to accommodate the Mayas. Each barrio had its own plaza, church, and business houses and was characterized by a distinct manner of speech, housing, dress, and occupation. By the end of the century, however, residential segregation was no longer enforced.

Probably no major city in the world can be considered a truly integrated community. In Latin America, transportation costs, adjacency of workers' quarters to industrial areas, traditional siesta hours, and the traditional confinement of women to the home discourage centralization of the city. Further, as the income of the highest one-tenth of the city population is greater than that of the lower half, one may find even greater isolation and segregation in cities in Latin America than in Europe or North America.

In other words, ecological theories modeled on other parts of the world can be applied to Latin America only with caution. The sector approach may not have the defects of the concentric zone theory, which is based on processes of invasion and succession that occurred in Chicago more than a half century ago, but it is not applicable to all cities. Since it is rooted in the economic diversification of the community, the concept of multiple nuclei also has its limitations, that is, retailing, wholesaling, and light and heavy manufacturing. These functions are less conspicuous in the Latin American city. Moreover, the shift of cities toward new economic spheres—computerization, telecommunications, professional services—further challenges traditional ecological models. Advances in communication and transportation imply that accessibility is not necessarily linked to physical nearness. With these developments comes greater variability and flexibility in the use of land. As the economy takes on regional and international dimensions, new forms of cities (for instance, strip and nucleated cities) appear.[82]

Stability and Change

In an area undergoing rampant urbanization and some degree of social change, ecological patterns are not static. Nevertheless, provincial cities have until recently held to their stabilized residential integrity. The ecology of most Latin American cities is undergoing change. Vibrant cities like São Paulo are caught in the same need as their North American counterparts to use space more efficiently. In Bogotá, a zone of transition or *zona negra* now surrounds most of the central business districts. In Santiago, many dwellings in the fashionable areas around the Parque O'Higgins and south of the Moneda became multiples or rooming houses. *Succession* has also taken place in the area below San Cristóbal, whereas the pre-war truck garden area to the northeast of the city became a fashionable suburban development. Rio de Janeiro residents no longer consider Cocacabana the most prestigious area but instead now favor Ipenema and Leblon. For various reasons the integrity of a given area is no longer secure. In the case of Santiago, economic duress is forcing some middle-class families into lower-class areas in order to find affordable housing.

Increasingly, the city is dominated by the automobile. Despite currency restrictions and luxury taxes, most members of the upper-middle and upper class own a car (most seeming to be at least ten years old). Consequently, they no longer feel compelled to live near the center of the city. Urban sprawl characterizes most major cities after nearly four centuries of comparative residential and commercial stability. In large cities, architectural integrity is further tarnished by the gaping holes in central areas as older buildings, occasionally historical ones, are torn down to make more parking lots. Traffic falls unevenly on the city; for instance, in Bogotá, only 13 percent of the population have a car, but 40 percent of them are in the middle- and upper-class Norte. Another bias is on the part of the buses, of which 95 percent enter or cross the city center, even though 60 percent of their passengers neither begin nor end their trip in that area.[83] (I recall more than once sitting with only five or six passengers on a bus in Bogotá in a gridlock with another dozen buses carrying a similar load.) Since many cities are crescive and nonnucleated, traffic flow is not necessarily concentrated in the early morning and late afternoon hours but is continuous throughout the day. Adherence to the siesta hour is a factor but is gradually disappearing from major cities.

The urban structure in Venezuela was reshaped as a natural outgrowth of government income, incipient industrialization, and relatively unrestricted importation of automobiles. In Caracas, high-rise steel and glass office buildings and a combination of government, residential, and shopping facilities stand side by side the superhighways that cross the city. Most of the urban area occupies the valley floor and represents the broad spectrum of the social classes, but the hills above the valley are consistently dotted with *ranchos* of the poor.

Topography, sometimes in conjunction with climatic factors, often influences the location of upper-class residential areas. After World War II, wealthy Salvadorians chose upland locations outside the city of San Salvador to escape the heat. In La Paz, Bolivia, plush homes occupy the Obrajes ravine because of its less severe climate, the effect of a small but significant difference of being 1,300 feet below the altiplano at 12,500 feet. The search for climatic comfort is by no means confined to the upper strata. Both indigent natives and migrants may establish their first dwelling in cold, bleak El Alto, but eventually struggle to rent or buy a home or even a room in the more central and temperate Cuenca.[84]

Although the Latin American urban scene has possibly more ecological stability than the fluid class society of its northern neighbors, the newer and more dynamic cities have initiated some novel experimentation. Occasionally, innovation is overly imaginative, as illustrated by the Helicoid in Caracas, a twelve-story spiral ramp built on a hillside. This daring attempt to provide a new version of the shopping center is of questionable service to the public in general, but particularly to its nearest would-be clients, the rancho dwellers. On the other hand, there are the successful *galerías* in the centers of Rio, São Paulo, Bogotá, and Santiago, which offer both shops and restaurants, an arrangement now in vogue in Europe and the United States. For decades, Buenos Aires and Rio de Janeiro have wisely decided to bar auto traffic from their finer shopping streets of the central area.

New cities have appeared—Ciudad Sahagun in Mexico to relieve pressure on the capital and Ciudad Guayana in Venezuela for the development of a petrochemical center. Most daring of all was the creation of Brasilia, embodying a whole new concept of urban planning, with its concrete, steel, and glass structures and a number of satellite communities. Its occupancy in 1960 created problems for the former capital. As fewer federal funds became available, the economy of Rio de Janeiro deteriorated, creating a larger Lumpenproletariat whose delinquent behavior became a scourge to tourism, a mainstay of the city's income. Other countries have flirted with the idea of new capital cities, especially when the old capital is no longer the geographic or economic center of the nation, or simply because they are too unwieldy to be truly functional. In 1987, the Argentine government proposed to move the capital to Viedma, but political and financial realities decreed otherwise. The Peruvian dream of moving the capital to Cuzco for the symbolic value of being close to the indigenous tradition has been similarly frustrated.

Increasingly, cities must deal with a broader ecological question of contaminated air and water, as Mexico City, Santiago, and other metropoli are experiencing. The use of space is ever more under scrutiny. The socioeconomic consequences of centralization can be considered both at the micro level (the community) as well as at the macro level (the nation). These problems cross national boundaries. Transfrontier cities along the Rio Grande present a number of problems, such as sharing of resources, transport loads, and legal bottlenecks.[85]

Housing Types

To some degree, ecological areas can be classified according to the type of housing they contain. Any major city runs the gamut from stately town houses and apartments to slum and shantytown. Within each extreme there is variation. For instance, in San Salvador, El Salvador, I recall the mansions of the "fourteen families" as an extreme in "conspicuous consumption," one being a replica of a European castle (the owner's desire for a moat was blocked by the public authorities because of sanitation problems), another a copy of the White House in Washington, D.C., and still another inspired by a movie (Tara, the antebellum plantation home from *Gone With the Wind*). Among these stand the more modest seven-room bungalows of the upper-middle class, all interlaced with small coffee *fincas* and squatters' huts. With its maldistribution of wealth, San Salvador represents an extreme in residential distinctions. In most countries, the upper class discretely hide their palaces behind walls or hedges, likely because of the need for security.

Middle-class urban housing assumes various forms, including walk-up flats and similar multiples, since convenience to the center is a primary consideration and urban density is somewhere between European norms and those of the eastern United States. The movement toward public housing especially favors the middle class. The *multifamiliares* several stories high are a new part of the urban landscape. Near the periphery of the city are the four-, five-, and six-room houses, somewhat like those of the North American middle class, although both the size of the lot and the rooms tend to be smaller. Housing is, of course, a tangible symbol of social status, as with entry into the middle class. For mobile members of the lower class who move into the multiroom dwelling associated with urbane living, the effect may be a kind of enculturation. Mexicans who migrate to the bureaucratic housing arrangements of the United States may have a similar experience.[86] The concept of privacy, space, or family belonging, whether nuclear or extended, is likely to be altered. On that point, slum dwellers are generally renters paying from one-third to one-half of their income as determined by location, facilities, size of the quarters, and the particular city.

The squatter settlements are even more varied, consisting of improvised huts of tar paper, packing boxes, tin cans, and other scraps of building materials, usually with only a dirt floor. The more substantial shelters are of wattle-and-daub construction. The older or established structures are more elaborate, often of three or four rooms, and have solid flooring. The scope and patterning of these settlements will be further explored in Chapter 8.

NOTES

1. Max Weber, *The City*, tr. Don Martindale and Gertrud Neuwirth (New York: Free Press, 1958), 66.

2. Louis Wirth, "Urbanism as a Way of Life," *American Journal of Sociology* 44: 3–24 (1938).

3. David Harvey, *Social Justice and the City* (Baltimore, Md.: Johns Hopkins University Press, 1973), 304.

4. Manuel Castells, *The Urban Question: A Marxist Approach* (Cambridge, Mass.: MIT Press, 1977), 130.

5. Manuel Castells, *The City and the Grassroots* (Berkeley: University of California Press, 1983).

6. Enzo Miglione, *Social Conflict* (New York: St. Martin's Press, 1981), 36–37.

7. John Walton, "Urban Hierarchies and Patterns of Dependence in Latin America: Theoretical Bases for a New Research Agenda," in *Current Perspectives in Latin American Urban Research*, ed. Alejandro Portes and Harley L. Browning (Austin: University of Texas Press, 1976), 43–69.

8. Michael Timberlake, "The World-Sytem Perspective and Urbanization," in *Urbanization in the World-Economy*, ed. Michael Timberlake (Orlando, Fla.: Academic Press, 1985), 3–52.

9. Brad Lyman, "Urban Primacy and World-System Position," *Urban Affairs Quarterly* 28(1): 22–37 (1992).

10. Carlos R. López, *Industrialización y Urbanización en El Salvador, 1969–1979* (San Salvador: Editores UCA, 1984), 138.

11. Lawrence A. Herzog, "Cross-National Urban Structure in the Era of Global Cities: The U.S.–Mexico Transfrontier Metropolis," *Urban Studies* 28: 519–533 (1991).

12. John Walton, "Structures of Power in Latin American Cities: Toward a Summary and Interpretation," in *Urban Latin America: The Political Condition from Above and Below*, ed. Alejandro Portes and John Walton (Austin: University of Texas Press, 1976), 136–168.

13. Jonas Figeroa Salas, "Urbanismo y Participación: La Construcción de la Otra Ciudad," *Revista Interamericana de Planificación* 26(103): 125–140 (1993).

14. Richard M. Morse, "Recent Research on Latin American Urbanization: A Selective Survey with Commentary," *Latin American Research Review* 1(fall): 35–74 (1965).

15. Angel Rama, *La Ciudad Letrada* (Hanover, N.H.: Ediciones del Norte, 1984).

16. Jean Casimir, "Definición y Funciones de la Ciudad en América Latina," *Revista Mexicana de Sociología* 32: 1497–1512 (1970).

17. Alejandro Portes and John Walton, *Urban Latin America: The Political Condition from Above and Below* (Austin: University of Texas Press, 1976), 16.

18. Richard M. Morse, *From Community to Metropolis* (Gainesville: University of Florida Press, 1958).

19. Vilmar Evangelista Faria, "São Paulo," in *The Metropolis Era, Mega-Cities*, vol. 2, ed. Mattei Dogan and John D. Kasarda (Newbury Park, Calif.: Sage Publications, 1988), 294–309.

20. Robert C. Williamson, "Population Dynamics in El Salvador," *Sociology and Social Research* 43: 421–426 (1959).

21. Kingsley Davis and Hilda H. Golden, "Urbanization and the Development of Pre-Industrial Areas," in *Cities and Society*, ed. Paul K. Hatt and Albert J. Reiss (New York: Free Press, 1957), 120–140.

22. Robert V. Kemper, "Urbanization in Latin American Development," in *Latin America: Perspectives on a Region*, ed. Jack W. Hopkins (New York: Holmes & Meier, 1987), 229–242.

23. Thomas Angotti, "The Unhappy Marriage of Dependent Urbanization and Metropolitan Planning in Latin America," paper presented at meeting of Latin American Studies Association, Los Angeles, September 25, 1992.

24. World Population Data Sheet (Washington, D.C.: Population Reference Bureau, 1996).

25. Graciela Schneider, "Latin America: A Tale of Cities," *International Social Science Journal* 42: 337–351 (1990).

26. Alan Gilbert, "Third World Cities: The Changing National Settlement System," *Urban Studies* 30: 721–740 (1993).

27. Richard M. Morse, "Trends and Issues in Latin American Urban Research, 1965–1970" (Part II), *Latin American Research Review* 6(summer): 19–76, (1971).

28. John T. Martin et al., *Book of World City Rankings* (New York: Free Press, 1986), 150.

29. Richard M. Morse, "Cities as People," in *Rethinking the Latin American City*, ed. Richard M. Morse and Jorge E. Hardoy (Baltimore: Johns Hopkins University Press, 1992), 3–19.

30. David T. Herbert and Colin J. Thomas, *Cities in Space: City as Place* (Savage, Md.: Barnes and Noble, 1990), 50.

31. Alejandro Portes, "Latin American Urbanization during the Years of the Crisis," *Latin American Research Review* 24(3): 7–44 (1989).

32. Dennis A. Rondinelli, *Secondary Cities in Developing Countries* (Newbury Park, Calif.: Sage Publications, 1983), 68.

33. Carol A. Smith, "Class Relationships and Urbanization in Guatemala: Toward an Alternative Theory of Urban Primacy," in *Urbanization in the World-Economy*, ed. Michael Timberlake (Orlando, Fla.: Academic Press, 1985), 121–167.

34. Alejandro Portes, José Itzigsohn, and Carlos Dore-Cabral, "Urbanization in the Caribbean Basin during the Years of the Crisis," *Latin American Research Review* 29(2): 3–38 (1994).

35. Christopher K. Chase-Dunn, "The System of World Cities, A.D. 800–1975," in *Urbanization in the World-Economy*, ed. Michael Timberlake (Orlando, Fla.: Academic Press, 1985), 269–292.

36. Lyman, "Urban Primacy."

37. Carol A. Smith, "Theories and Measures of Urban Primacy: A Critique," in *Urbanization in the World-Economy*, ed. Michael Timberlake (Orlando, Fla.: Academic Press, 1985), 87–117.

38. Portes, "Latin American Urbanization."

39. Peter M. Ward, *Mexico City: The Production and Reproduction of an Urban Environment* (Boston: G. K. Hall, 1990), 33.

40. Allen J. Scott, *Metropolis: From the Division of Labor to Urban Form* (Berkeley: University of California Press, 1988), 217.

41. John Walton, "Culture and Economy in the Shaping of Urban Life: General Issues and Latin American Examples," in *The City in a Cultural Context*, ed. John A. Agnew, John Mercer, and David E. Sopher (Boston: Allen and Unwin, 1984), 76–95.

42. Allen C. Kelley and Jeffrey G. Williamson, *What Drives Third World City Growth?* (Princeton: N.J.: Princeton University Press, 1984), 184.

43. Aire Romein, "The Production Structure of Smaller Towns in Rural Regions in Latin America: A Case from Northern Costa Rica," *Urban Studies* 32: 491–506 (1995).

44. Alan Gilbert, "Third World Cities: Housing, Infrastructure, and Servicing," *Urban Studies* 29: 435–460 (1992).

45. Thomas Angotti, *Metropolis 2000: Planning, Poverty and Politics* (London: Routledge, 1993).

46. Alan Gilbert, *The Latin American City* (London: Latin American Bureau, 1994), 74–77.

47. Carlos R. López, *Industrializión y Urbanización en El Salvador* (San Salvador: UCA Editores, 1984), 128.

48. Manuel Castells and Alejandro Portes, "World Underneath: The Origins, Dynamics, and Effects of the Informal Economy," in *The Informal Economy: Studies in Advanced and Less Developed Countries*, ed. Alejandro Portes, Manuel Castells, and Lauren A. Benton (Baltimore: Johns Hopkins University Press, 1989), 11–37.

49. Ibid.

50. Castells, *The City*, 183–184.

51. Thomas J. La Belle, *Nonformal Education in Latin America and the Caribbean: Stability, Reform or Revolution?* (New York: Praeger, 1986), 126.

52. H. C. F. Mansilla, "La Economía Informal y las Modificationes del Movimiento Sindical en Bolivia," *Revista Paraguaya de Sociología* 30(86): 113–126 (1993).

53. Portes, Itzigsohn, and Dore-Cabral, "Urbanization during the Years of Crisis," 27.

54. Speridão Faissol, "Brazil's Urban System in 1980: Basic Dimensions and Spatial Structure in Relation to Social and Economic Development," in *World Patterns of Modern Urban Change*, ed. Michael P. Conzen (Chicago: University of Chicago, Department of Geography Research Paper 217-218, 1986), 183–184.

55. Juan C. Fortuna and Suzana Prates, "Informal Sector versus Informalized Labor Relations," in *The Informal Economy: Studies in Advanced and Less Developed Countries*, ed. Alejandro Portes, Manuel Castells, and Lauren A. Benton (Baltimore: Johns Hopkins University Press, 1989), 78–94.

56. Donna J. Keren, "Rethinking Street Vending: The Other Side of 'Modernization,'" unpublished manuscript, 1994.

57. Gilbert, *The Latin American City*, 77.

58. Herbert and Thomas, *Cities in Space*, 50.

59. Brian J. Godfrey, "Boom Towns of the Amazon," *Geographical Review* 80: 103–115 (1990).

60. Christopher H. Exline, Gary L. Peters, and Robert P. Larkin, *The City: Patterns and Processes in the Urban Ecosystem* (Boulder, Colo.: Westview Press, 1982), 163.

61. Afsaneh Assadian and Jan Ondrich, "Residential Location, Housing Demand and Labour Supply Decisions of One- and Two-Earner Households: The Case of Bogotá, Colombia," *Urban Studies* 30: 73–86 (1993).

62. Kelley and Williamson, *Third World City Growth*, 185.

63. Gilbert, *The Latin American City*, 152.

64. Ward, *Mexico City*, 175–177; Bruce Herrick, *Urban Poverty and Economic Development* (New York: St. Martin's Press, 1981), 156–157.

65. Gerhard Schneider, "Psychological Identity of and Identification with Urban Neighborhoods," in *The Quality of Urban Life*, ed. Dieter Frank (Berlin: de Gruyter, 1986), 203–218.

66. Fernando Campara Paz et al., *Ciudades Intermedias* (La Paz: Instituto de Investigaciones Sociales, 1987).

67. David W. Dent, "Urban Development and Governmental Response: The Case of Medellin," in *Latin American Urban Research*, ed. Wayne A. Cornelius and Robert V. Kemper (Newbury Park, Calif.: Sage Publications, 1978), 127–153.

68. Homer Aschmann, "Calendar Dates as Street Names in Asuncion, Paraguay," *Names* 34(2): 146–153 (1986).

69. Georg Simmel, *The Sociology of Georg Simmel*, tr. Kurt Wolff (New York: Free Press, 1950).

70. M. P. Smith, *The City and Social Theory* (New York: St. Martin's Press, 1979), 109.

71. Rubén Monasaterios, *Comportamiento Territorial Humano en Habitat Urbano* (Caracas: Universidad Central de Venezuela, 1981).

72. Robert C. Williamson, "The Rural–Urban Continuum and Social Class: A Salvadorean Sample," in *Studium Sociale*, ed. Karl G. Specht et al. (Cologne: Westdeutscher Verlag, 1964), 691–704.

73. Lawrence C. Watson, *Guajiro Personality and Urbanization* (Los Angeles: Latin American Center, University of California, 1968).

74. Robert Redfield, "The Folk Society," *American Journal of Sociology* 52: 293–308 (1947).

75. Wirth, "Urbanism as a Way of Life," 21–24.

76. Nathan Glazer, "Note on the Sociological Images of the City," in *Cities of the Mind*, ed. Lloyd Rodwin and Robert M. Holister (New York: Plenum Press, 1984), 337–344.

77. Ulf Hannerz, *Exploring the City: Inquiries Toward an Urban Anthropology* (New York: Columbia University Press, 1980), 68–72.

78. Charles R. Tittle and Mark C. Stafford, "Urban Theory, Urbanism, and Suburban Residence," *Social Forces* 70: 725–744 (1992).

79. Martha de Alzate, "Hacia una 'Modernización' en Colombia: Análisis Crítico," in *Transición Social en Colombia*, ed. L. A. Costa Pinto (Bogotá: CID, Universidad Nacional, 1970), 63–84.

80. Fernando Peñalosa, "Ecological Organization of the Transitional City: Some Mexican Evidence," *Social Forces* 46: 221–229 (1967).

81. John Walton, "Guadalajara: Creating the Divided City," in *Latin American Urban Research*, vol. 6, ed. Wayne A. Cornelius and Robert V. Kemper (Thousand Oaks, Calif.: Sage Publications, 1978), 25–50.

82. W. Parker Frisbie and John D. Kasarda, "Spatial Processes," in *Handbook of Sociology*, ed. Neil J. Smelser (Newbury Park, Calif.: Sage Publications, 1988), 129–166.

83. Departmiento de Adminstración de Planificación Distrital, *El Futuro de Bogotá* (Bogotá: Banco Internacional de Reconstrucción, 1980), 12.

84. Paul Van Lindert, "Moving Up or Staying Down? Migrant-Native Residential Mobility in La Paz," *Urban Studies* 28: 433–463 (1991).

85. Herzog, "Cross-National Urban Structure," 523.

86. Ellen J. Pader, "Spatiality and Social Change: Domestic Space Use in Mexico and the United States," *American Ethnologist* 20: 114–137 (1993).

Chapter 8

The City: "New" Suburbs and "Old" Problems

Latin America has given rise to a new kind suburb: the squatter colonies which surround the urban core. As with other developing areas of the world, these mushrooming shantytowns cling to unused areas, infiltrate a ravine or hillside, or occasionally appear as enclaves in the central city. This process was underway largely after World War II, gaining momentum with accelerated urban growth. The new suburbs, along with the central slums, pose a number of implications for the economic, political, and social life of the city and the nation. Indeed, since a sizeable population of most cities are migrants from the provinces, the city serves as a microcosm of the entire country.

In addition to analyzing the profile of these migrant colonies, we shall examine the problems of the city, especially housing and the role of the planner in resolving them. As cities are changing at a more rapid rate than rural areas, we must ask whether these changes are controlled or uncontrolled. How may economic and political elites along with *técnicos* initiate change?

THE MIGRANT AND SQUATTER SETTLEMENTS

To many observers, the disturbing feature of the sprawling urban areas of the developing world is the agglomeration of shacks of all vintages, nearly all built by the present residents. Their growth is staggering. Alan Gilbert estimates that in Mexico City approximately 14 percent were in these squatter settlements in 1952, but by 1990 the ratio rose to 60 percent. Other cities have shown comparable growth.[1] In Latin America a rich vocabulary has emerged: *villa miseria* in Argentina, *cantegriles* in Uruguay, *favela* in Brazil, *callampa* in Chile, *barriada* in Peru, *rancho* in Venezuela, *invasión* or *barrio negro* in Colombia, *barrio proletario* in Mexico, and *poblaciones* in two or three other countries. Several terms appear in the same country—*colonia nueva, colonia perdida, barrio negro, barrio popular, barrio proletario, cordones de miseria,* among others. As these colonies and their labels have been popularized by the mass media, avid readers of the news can apply the correct term to the respective country, misled though they may be by sensational accounts of crime and disorder in these makeshift communities.

Portrait of the Shantytown

Because of their heterogeneity, these squatter towns do not easily lend themselves to generalizations. The *favelas* of Rio de Janeiro and other Brazilian cities form a continuum from the isolated squatters on vacant or partially vacant lots to settlements covering several acres and accommodating two thousand to four thousand people. The *callampas* of Santiago form a similar spectrum. Their location can be in suburbs, in interstitial areas along transportation arteries, on river banks, or in refuse dumps. They may be on private or public land, with or without legal or illegal public services and utilities. The shantytowns in any city can be old or new, legal or illegal way stations on the pilgrimage from the countryside to the city, or the abodes of second-generation, upward-mobile migrants. Some colonies are organized by Acción Comunal, while others have neither group support nor self-help. The *barriadas* have a long history in Lima and embody every style, from primitive huts sparsely set in a new colony among sandy wastelands to highly settled communities in more favored locations.

A widespread feeling holds that marginal *poblaciones*, presumably composed of unassimilable indigenous groups transferred to the city, are a source of personal and social disorganization, a breeding ground of communism, and an economic drain on the country's resources. These beliefs are perhaps as common among middle- and upper-class Latin Americans as among foreigners who have never seen a *favela* or a *barriada*. Although a grain of truth is to be found in most of the generalizations, the populations inhabiting these beehives are as diverse as the city at large. Any statement regarding social organization or political and economic behavior would have to be examined according to the specific situation. Many shantytown dwellers are on the fringe of the middle class, and the majority are either city-born or have spent at least five years in the city. In contrast is the misery of Port-au-Prince, Haiti, where squatters have invaded nearly all the city. By 1988, 72 percent of the population were without running water, and only 8 percent had anything resembing modern plumbing.[2]

Organization of Squatter Colonies

According to Alejandro Portes, three types of settlements are to be found: (1) spontaneous settlements, formed illegally on empty land by accretion; (2) invasions of a relatively large number of participants on private or public land, with plots generally allocated in advance; and (3) clandestine subdivisions arranged by landowners who work through "coyotes," as these agents are called in Meso-America.[3] Most settlements generally appear on an ad hoc basis. In some cases, a few settlers try a foothold on wasteland outside the city, only to be joined by others. Since the 1960s, Mexico has attempted to control the subdivisions, but illegal sales occur by *ejiditarios*.[4] The government is reluctant to aggravate the level of poverty by restricting migrants' access to a residential site. Giving up pasturage areas to expanding housing needs poses a dilemma. The PRI walks a tight rope between trying to keep both urbanites and campesinos happy by encouraging food production and at the same time permitting extension of the city to newcomers.[5]

In several countries, space may be rented out by a middleman acting for a wealthy landowner, who makes a profit charging the squatter rent for unused land, usually on the edge of the city. Such a case is Quiñonez, an area of a few hundred acres owned by one of El Salvador's wealthiest families and housing over two thousand people. The land was more attractive than the *mesones* (primitive one-room dwellings around a patio), which rented at two to three times the price of leasing the land. Materials for building the dwellings could be paid for in a few months, the work usually being done by the occupants themselves. The vast majority lived in primitive shacks and carried water as much as five hundred feet to their dwelling. The more ambitious built outhouses somewhere on the 4,000 square feet each plot was allotted.[6]

In most countries, an *invasión* involves illegal but coordinated activities of a group of migrants. In Venezuela, the leader generally has the support of a political party, which insures only minimal reprisals. In contrast to the Pérez Jiménez period prior to 1958, democratic regimes (Acción Demócrata or COPEI) make possible concessions in the form of services by the local government. As in nearly all areas of urban life, clientelism enters the search for living quarters.

In Peru, *barriadas* are generally set up in an organized manner, usually by an association of future residents of the project. This association eventually agitates for a legal title and for public utilities. In this respect, the *barriadas* are different from the *calletones*, which are entirely ad hoc migrant settlements. Marked differences in initiative and resources are found between individual *barriadas*. Some *invasiones* of squatters occur gradually and unnoticed, whereas establishment of other colonies may be precipitous and well publicized. For instance, 5,000 persons in 1954 set up a colony during a single night outside Lima. More often the settlement develops over a period of weeks or months. During the military period (1968–1980), government aid became available to the squatters in organizing their settlements.

The location and form of the barrios provides several clues as to their social and economic significance. As an example, in Venezuelan cities most *ranchos* are located in areas of questionable utility; that is, no profitable exploitation seems possible. Still, certain utilitarian aspects are evident: nearness to access routes to the city, industrial areas, and middle- and upper-class housing for the availability of domestic servants. Each settlement presents its own profile. Some interplay takes place between the physical aspects, spatial dimensions, and other characteristics of the locality and the needs of the individuals shaping the community. As residents undergo a variety of experiences, the settlement can hardly fail to change.

Settlements and Urban Housing

Subtle distinctions in settlements and housing appear in each city. In Bogotá, one distinguishes between (1) a *barrio clandestino*, an unofficial subdivision in which plots of unused land are sold without legal permit; (2) *invasiones*, or squatter colonies on public and private lands; and (3) *urbanizaciones*, or subdivisions which meet the city specifications and have public services.[7] Generally, in Bogotá invasions are rare. Of the city's some eight hundred barrios, only twenty-one settlements are considered as invasions.[8] Once they acquire the means, residents tend to move out of their *tugurios* (tenements) to the *barrio clandestino* (the *urbanización* is generally beyond their means) for fresher air, more space, or a feeling of ownership.[9] In Rio, Lima, and other cities, Anthony Leeds demarcates seven kinds of housing or settlements: (1) rooming house (*cabeza de porco* or *casas subdividas*); (2) a series of one- or two-room rental units known by a variety of names—*callejón, vecindad, mesón, corral* (perhaps a dozen units share a couple of toilets and wash basins); (3) "temporary" government housing, the labels varying with the country; (4) the *conjunto* as called in Rio, a complex of multiple dwellings designated for a given occupational group—military, labor union, and so on; (5) *vilas* or emergency subdivisions usually located outside the city designed for people who have likely been forced out of the *favela* (whether by natural disaster or government edict); (6) *suburbios*, privately owned homes on official streets but with no paving or other services; and (7) a miscellany of *tugurios*, or slums, including rooming houses, bordellos, pensions, and cheap hotels.[10]

Each city has its gestalt of tenant arrangements. Rentals account for one-fourth to more than one-half of the residents of many cities. However, according to a study of two Mexican cities, Guadalajara and Puebla, the average household pays 13 percent of their income in housing. In smaller towns, the average is lower, and in certain other countries (Bogotá and Cali in Colombia) rent reaches 18 percent. Landlords are small scale, especially in squatter areas. Significantly, in Puebla one-fourth of landlords live in the same building as their tenants and receive a meager return.[11] In Mexico City, a lack of rent controls and government funding severely limits the rental market. Consequently, many households subdivide in order to make room for kin.[12] In La Paz, where geographic location is important, the trend is from relatively long-term rental to "self-help owner occupancy," but residential mobility depends on job mobility.[13]

Background and Aspirations

Who are the migrants to these rapidly growing settlements? Migrants in the colony are more likely to belong to a relatively skilled occupation and have greater financial resources than are settlers in the central slum area. In other words, they are predominantly lower class but contain middle-class elements. Significantly, only 22 percent come from localities with populations of less than two thousand.

Integration in the shantytown and the larger community varies with the migrant's adaptability to the economic and social systems of the city. A survey of a squatter settlement on the edge of a provincial river town in Argentina points to a dichotomy between the reticence of those immigrants of lower educational level with a history of rural employment and the enterprising spirit of the residents whose background and drive lead them to find skilled manual jobs in the city.[14] Social networks can reflect either an urban or a rural orientation.

SLUM AND SHANTYTOWN: SUBSTANCE AND STYLE

The significance of the squatter settlements is perceived in various ways. For some observers, shantytowns and the *tugurio* are a kind of "shelter strategy" which permits the economically disenfranced to cope with poverty.[15] Others see them as a kind of "peasantization" of the city—undoubtedly more appropriate to Africa than to Latin America.[16] Most investigations of these communities reject the label of "culture of poverty."

Diversity of Setting

As implied, every degree of physical, social, and legal status is found in the settlement. Some colonies approach the status of a recognized suburb, although more of them have only a tenuous economic and legal existence. In a comparison of two *barrios populares* in Cali, Colombia, Nueva Floresta stands out in retrospect with its stores, bars, and a public school.[17] A barber shop also provides injections—the classic, omnipresent, multipurpose treatment throughout Latin America. In the newest annex of the *barrio*, however, utilities and commercial facilities are poorer and residents are not too concerned about the appearance of their dwellings. No public school is to be found, but a parochial complex is available for those families who are interested. In contrast, El Rodeo, a conglomeration of bamboo shacks adjoining La Floresta, represents a more precarious status. Unlike La Floresta, housing is completely improvised and has at best a rustic appearance; no water is available for sewage disposal and electricity is pirated. A number of *tiendas* serve drinks, chipped ice is distributed by bicycle, and oil for cooking is sold by itinerant trucks. Even though a kind of modus operandi evolved, the *barrio* has a temporary quality. Residents fear that a forced eviction may come at any time.

The function and distribution of squatter enclaves grow out of urban realities and the inevitability of mass migration in a developing economy. The spread of "squatments" results from several factors: relationship of the city to its hinterland, differential labor needs, housing opportunities, and the power systems of the society. A change in rural and urban wage levels or land values can be critical. Because of juxtaposition of these factors, variation among shantytowns is enormous. Settlements may be of low or high density or internal or external to the city. They may be loosely confederated or highly consolidated. Also, these squattertowns are generally newer than *tugurios* and have less social disorganization. In the center of the city an improvised shantytown may interlace the *tugurios*. Any absolute distinction between these two residential areas is misleading. Both become the locus of informal labor and with their cheap rent are a means of supporting the formal economy and transfer of capital to the ruling elites.[18]

The wide variation in *barriadas* is shown in a study of Lima. The National System of Support to Social Mobilization (SINAMOS) in the late 1970s recognized a population of more than one million in 191 "young towns" (*pueblos jóvenes*), of which nearly one-third (98) of the settlements were of less than 500 residents, almost one-quarter (74) between 500 and 1,000, with the largest number between 1,000 and 10,000, and only 19 pueblos of more than 10,000. In Modella Milagrosa, most residents varied from upper-lower to lower-middle class, with more than half the houses having at least four rooms, even though the vast majority of the inhabitants were *obreros* (workers). The remainder were *empleados* (white-collar workers), in whose homes a maid could be found, often brought in from the sierra.[19] All this stands in opposition to the more marginal *barriadas*.

In Mexico City, Susan Eckstein compared "La Colonia," a legalized squattertown, with "El Centro," a run-down central *tugurio* area, and "La Unidad," a lower- to middle-class housing development. After a 1954 invasion, *coyotes* (illicit brokers) sold plots to prospective owners (often the same parcel to more than one party). Struggles ensued both among the residents and with the authorities for title to the land. As dwellings were improved, the government acknowledged legality and began providing utilities—at excessive cost to many residents, who then migrated to another *colonia proletaria*. Gradually, the area became more middle than lower class, but most occupants were migrants to the capital. Although relatively new, La Colonia has less crime and other indexes of social disorganization than El Centro; however, it does not have El Centro's subculture of long-standing customs, rituals, and fiestas. Nor does La Colonia have the networks associated with rural life; both formal and informal associations are rare. One feature all three barrios shared is crowding. La Unidad, for instance, housed 80,000 persons in 10,000 units.[20]

Migrants, Economics, and the Shantytown

Rather divergent viewpoints surface about the economic, social, and political integration of squatter settlements into the larger local and national community. One factor is migration. In a study of two villages in central Peru, 39 percent were migrating primarily because they needed more income, and 25 percent wanted to join kin already working. The remaining responses reflected either the availability of work or the need to be near relatives. Those choosing Lima were particularly guided by work possibilities, whereas those who preferred to work in the mines and refineries in La Oroya reported other pressures, especially the need to care for aging parents or their desire to be near their land. As compared to the blue-collared (*obreros*) workers, the white-collared (*empleados*) workers were more inclined to stay in the urban setting, rather than return to their original habitat.[21] All individuals migrating must deal with a number of inputs—job expectations, intervening obstacles, and evaluation of gains and losses.

Perhaps the most salient feature of the settlements besides their heterogeneity is their endurance. Estimates of unemployment run from less than 10 to more than 30 percent. The problem is more one of underemployment than of unemployment. Even so, migrants are markedly more involved in the labor force than they were before they began their trek to the city. However bleak the profile of the settlements, they make at least four major contributions to the national economy: (1) investment in housing and land improvement, (2) enhancement of the employment structure, (3) development of small businesses from itinerant vendors and one-room *tiendas* to banks and movie houses, and (4) indirect capital gains from the involvement of the total community as well as government and international funding agencies.[22] An example of the economic contribution of squatters and shantytowns was the building of Brasilia. The settlements that once gave shelter to thousands of workers still remain on the fringes of that city and continue to nourish both the formal and informal economy of the capital.

Social Networks

An important element in the migrant's personal and social adjustment to the city is the security offered by kinship. The movement of one family member into the settlement is the prelude to the arrival of close and not so close relatives. For instance, migrants depend heavily on kinship for finding their moorings in Rio. The *favelados* provide the newcomers with financial assistance, temporary lodging, and employment, or even build or buy them a *favela* house. *Compadres* (godparents) can be as important as blood relatives. Observers point to the matricentric structure of many slum families in Latin America; yet over one-fourth of the families in a given Lima *barriada* housed at least one relative of the male household head, whereas kinsmen of the wife were found in only one-twelfth of the homes.[23]

The atmosphere of the particular shantytown determines to what degree neighbors constitute a major source of social assistance and particularly how they may function in a crisis. In Quiñonez, a San Salvador shacktown, I recall how severe illness and death brought forth a pattern of mutual aid. Borrowing of food and money came into play between certain families. Nevertheless, residents of Quiñonez missed the close ties they had with kin and neighbors in their former rural areas.

Within certain limits, *extensity*, or the presence of a large number of acquaintances, is concurrent with *intensity*, or the ability to establish close relationships. Each neighborhood has its own style of social network. For instance, Puerto Rican slums seldom have the solidarity that characterize the *invasiones* of Lima. A socialist regime seemingly offers various networks and organizations in which the residents can find social outlets, as a study of the barrios of Managua shows.[24]

Whatever the distress caused by the pressure of too many people, the squatter settlement offers considerable drama. Gossip is a major means of both communication and vicarious experience. Moreover, washing and drying clothes and other outdoor activities bring women together and an overexposure to other peoples' problems. Besides communicating by means of gossip, neighbors hurl *insultas* and *indirectas* at each other. These depend on "double meaning and ambiguous phrasing," and are sometimes "addressed to the person being insulted or are improvised into lyrics sung so that they will be overheard."[25] Although ostensibly fictitious, one has little doubt as to whom they refer. Gossip or slander in these various forms, although cause for annoyance, do exert a kind of social control, as found in a worker's barrio in Popayán.[26] As a result, the search for privacy is unrelenting.

Mass Media, Recreation, and Voluntary Associations

Exposure to mass media in the new urban slums is limited because of the inhabitants' poverty. In reality, the amount of newspaper reading and radio listening varies according to their availability. At least half the residents appear to read a newspaper. Since perhaps half the dwellings lack electricity, radio and television exposure is shared.

Sport and recreation loom high in the settlements; the *favelado* is a devotee of *fútbol* (soccer). The lower class find in this sport a passionate escape from their marginal status. As everywhere else, athletic competition bridges social classes; achievement occasionally rises above ascription. Another recreational outlet in the *favela* is *jogo do bicho*, an animal gambling game such as cock fighting. Men, women, or children play in the hope of winning a bet, their one chance for financial success in life. Likewise, sport enables the Peruvian male in the *barriada* to express his *machismo* and keep alive the intercommunity rivalry he acquired in the sierra.[27]

Urban social and organizational life moves in several directions. Drinking appears to be the most widespread diversion. Beyond the usual taverns are social clubs. As with other activities, club membership is a means of becoming a *criollo*, for it initiates the individual into new dress, speech, gestures, dances, food, and drink.[28] Social relationships are enriched through acceptance by a *hampa* (gang) or one of the *barriada* clubs. Dating and courtship—these practices are spreading from middle- to lower-class Latin America—are facilitated by these *criollo* connections. The club is an important integrative influence in most *barriadas*. Since clubs exist in nearly all coastal and sierra towns of Peru, these regional affiliations become for the migrant a medium of socialization in the capital city. The more active members include both workers and white-collar employees. Although clubs are usually male oriented, women may join. The clubs can serve athletic, social, and political purposes. When they function as unions or have political overtones, they are usually registered with the government. These kinds of voluntary association are not limited to Lima. Rio's *favelas* contain a similar elaborate system of associations, organizing public utilities, dance groups for carnivals, and land purchases, to name a few activities. Among the organizations in Catacumba (an extensive Rio *favela*), the Residents Association, with perhaps five hundred participants, promotes social activities as well as certain services, including a medical clinic.[29] Residents of the *ranchos* of Caracas tend to organize for political goals, both national and local, not least for the purpose of consolidating the struggle for property rights and legal titles. This social and political integration tends to reduce hostilities among neighbors. On the other hand, one can find squatter settlements in which voluntary associations hardly exist.

Throughout Latin America, squatters' recognition of common problems leads to the search for solutions through pressure groups. Women are often more mobilized to effect social action than are men, as in a water crisis in Monterrey, Mexico.[30] Newcomers to the city, however, may not always discover a voluntary association, political or otherwise. I found that as compared to more settled residents, few recent migrants to Bogotá and San Salvador were members of the Junta Comunal (town council) or recreational and political associations. This finding is dependent, however, on the type of *barrio* under study. If moving to a shantytown represents upward mobility, organizational membership and voting may be higher than in the more settled central area of the city.

Social Disorganization and Mental Health

Although necessary to the city's economic life, shantytowns are in many respects physically, socially, and politically isolated to what happens in the city itself. Personality characteristics of squatters may be somewhat different than those of other urban and rural populations. The personal factor, along with various institutional supports, including substitutes for the "fiesta system" and other networks, shape the migrant's adjustment to the urban setting.[31] Findings as to the level of adjustment, both personal and social, are not consistent. We are handicapped by not having sufficient comparisons between various parts of the city concerning rates of delinquency and mental breakdown. Despite exceptions, the nuclear family and kinship ties provide a means of personal and social control.

Inevitably, personal and social disorganization exists in the marginal settlements. A study of the *gamines* (homeless boys) of Bogotá found no greater number among the shantytowns than among the general slums of the city.[32] Most shantytowns have inadequate police protection and are more poorly lighted than older parts of the city. However, theft and violence are seldom appealing when one's neighbor is on a comparable level of poverty. Life is sufficiently busy in most settlements to make it difficult for a delinquency to take place without its being known to some observer or another. Delinquents may go elsewhere for their activity, whether drugs, theft, or prostitution. Whether one looks at the urban or the rural milieu, psychosomatic disorders are common to both populations. In a study of Lima *barriadas*, a serious problem was reported to be the lack of privacy both in the dwelling and the community.[33]

It is difficult to deal conclusively with questions of social pathology; to compare the effects of various urban subcultures on the incidence of neurotic and psychotic behavior is an even more elusive task. A San Juan

study assessing mental health indexes in a slum as opposed to public housing (*caserío*) revealed no difference in mental breakdown. The investigation did show a preference for the permissive if depressing atmosphere
of the slum over the bureaucratic controls of the housing project.[34] Still,
alienation, anomie, depression, and anxiety symptoms are almost inescapable for many urban migrants.

The *Favela* as a Test Case

Observers do not agree on the adjustment of the squatter. Consensus
can hardly be expected in view of the diversity among shantytowns and
their occupants. As the most chronicled of the settlements, the *favela* has
evoked a number of images and attitudes. Disenchantment with society
and government is evident. Yet as most respondents feel a sense of unity
with their fellow *favelados*, a complete sense of hopelessness is rare. A
somber portrait appeared in *favelada* Carolina Maria de Jesús's diary,
which became a best-seller in Brazil and abroad in the 1960s.[35] (Despite
the sale of some 300,000 copies in the United States, the author received
few royalties.[36]) *Favelados* rationalize their life in these enclaves, not least
because it expresses the urban values with which they are most familiar.
Moreover, notwithstanding the supposed rural character of the *favela*,
more than one-third of the population are city-born. As competition for
economic necessities and social status can be intense, the *favela* can be
highly dissociative. On the other hand, the *botequim* (bar) within the
favela is a means of reducing distance and tension since it permits a social
participation not possible in the workaday world.[37]

Whatever the limitations of squatter settlements, they offer the migrant a foothold in the urban environment. At a later stage, they provide
a permanent home. Most important, they are the primary answer to the
problem of low-cost housing in a rapidly growing city.

THE PRESENT AND FUTURE OF THE CITY

Latin America's population is to grow by 40 percent again by the year
2025, and well before that time over three-fourths of the population will
live in cities, as compared to approximately two-thirds today. The housing needs will continue to be gigantic. The factors surrounding urban
development are shown in Figure 8.1.

Services and Problems

Shantytowns share many problems with *tugurios* and even sectors of
middle-class urban areas. A myriad of problems are found in cities of
both the developed and underdeveloped world. For many observers,

FIGURE 8.1
Variables of Urban Development

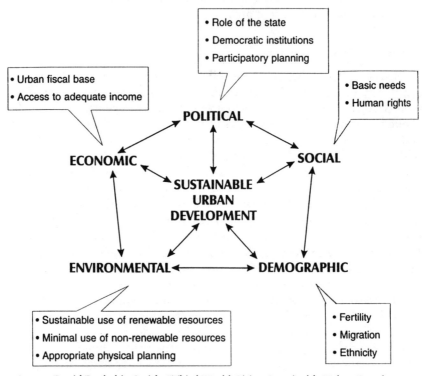

THIRD WORLD CITIES

• Role of the state
• Democratic institutions
• Participatory planning

• Urban fiscal base
• Access to adequate income

• Basic needs
• Human rights

POLITICAL

ECONOMIC   SOCIAL

SUSTAINABLE
URBAN
DEVELOPMENT

ENVIRONMENTAL   DEMOGRAPHIC

• Sustainable use of renewable resources
• Minimal use of non-renewable resources
• Appropriate physical planning

• Fertility
• Migration
• Ethnicity

Source: David Drakakis-Smith, "Third World Cities: Sustainable Urban Development, I," *Urban Studies* 32: 659–677 (1995), Carfax Publishing Company.

Mexico City with its nineteen million residents (no one knows how many) represents the maximum of urban crisis. Air pollution, especially from car emissions, compounded by dust storms during the dry season, is being combatted with restrictions on the use of cars, buses, and trucks. The servicing of utilities for a city growing by nearly half a million a year is a Herculean task. The provision of electricity has been better than of water; more homes were without water in 1980 than in 1970.[38] An inventory of the services for the poor areas of Oaxaca, Mexico, reveals that two-thirds of the residents have no water on their house site (several families spending nearly 20 percent of their income on water), and only one-fifth had sewer hookups.[39] These problems are generally worse for settlements and *suburbios* than for conventional barrios. Most services, including health care, are divided between the state and private enterprise. Puebla is probably typical of many cities in the parcelization of services in a host of private entities and government bureaus. Coordination improved during the 1980s, but hardly to the point of maintaining par with population growth.[40] In most countries, medical care, even in urban areas, falls short of the more advanced countries.

The Limits of Private and Public Housing

One can scarcely overstress the pressure of the housing need in both the urban and rural sector. In several countries, nearly half the dwellings have three persons per room. In Mexico, a country with an extensive public housing program, the average number of rooms per dwelling in 1980 was 2.1. Generally, urban residents fare better than rural ones; for instance, in Colombia in 1981 the difference was 2.3 versus 1.6 per room, respectively.

Unfortunately, neither private nor public capital is available to meet housing needs. Public housing is not as attractive to governments as is industrialization as a means of building the economy. Entrepreneurs are reluctant to commit sufficient capital for a variety of reasons: (1) political instability discourages long-term investments, (2) high risks are involved in loans to low-income or underemployed individuals, and (3) inflation invites only short-term loans. From the viewpoint of industrial planning, housing does have some advantages despite its slow financial return. That is, housing construction increases indirectly the probability of an adequate labor supply. In the meantime, lower-grade laborers are forced to rationalize slums and shantytowns.

My comparison of residents of public and private housing in Costa Rica and El Salvador does not support the negative responses found, for example, among San Juan and Caracas public housing residents. In San José and San Salvador, samples of both the lower and middle class had lived an average of approximately two years in various kinds of public housing. As compared to the residents in private housing, those in public facilities were more positive concerning upward mobility, membership in voluntary associations, voting participation, approval of birth control, and personal adjustment.[41] The psychological aspects of housing are always critical. That the applicants had a choice as to the type of housing was a factor in their favorable attitudes. Residents in most public housing may find a greater sense of future orientation and a stronger family orientation. At least as compared to those in conventional housing, interviewees in a *vivienda rural* in Venezuela showed more concern with savings and economic stability. However, construction of this rural housing project did not discourage migration to the *ranchos* of Ciudad Guayana as the authorities had hoped.[42]

Nearly all governments accept the concept of public housing—Argentina as early as in 1910. Yet almost everywhere, programs suffer from rigidities in building codes, lack of low-cost credit through savings and loan associations, unrealistic sites in terms of transport, shopping, and public facilities, and insufficient channeling of resources toward improvements in existing housing, including revitalization of shantytowns.

It is no surprise that richer countries make greater thrusts in public housing, often with mixed outcomes. In Venezuela, the *superbloques*, fifteen-story apartment houses for 450 families, were built during the regime of Pérez Jiménez (1952–1958), but without an orientation program of adjustment, communal living was difficult for rural migrants. Once Pérez was removed from office, many tenants returned to their *ranchos*. Moreover, public housing in Venezuela, as elsewhere, has been beyond the pocketbook of those who most need it. Rojas Pinilla (1953–1957) had a program of building *multifamiliares* for certain classes of Colombian workers. Similarly, over one-third of the *favela* residents relocated in housing projects outside Rio de Janeiro felt dissatisfied with conditions—mortgage payments, transportation, and sociopsychological isolation from the city—even though the project was an improvement over their former dwellings.[43]

The political climate, of course, surrounds decision making. For instance, in Chile under the Christian Democrats in the late 1960s, "Operación Sitio" (Operation Site) provided land parcels, cooperatives, and self-help along with urban renewal programs, but inflation and bureaucracy frustrated the implementation. When Allende's Unidad Popular entered the scene in 1970, a more penetrating approach included, among other items, (1) threat of legal action against speculators and builders who gave inadequate service, (2) rent control, and (3) more equitable mortgage repayments.[44] The advent of the Pinochet regime in 1973 set back the cause of low-cost housing. With help from the World Bank, new units were constructed, but mostly for the middle class.[45]

Self-help projects offer possibly the most promising plan. They depend on a minimum amount of financial outlay and may require the cooperative labor of thirty or more families with supervision from technicians. The projects break down, however, because of credit restrictions, lack of trained professionals to follow through in their coordination, and inability of services and utilities to keep pace with the need. Cooperative and sustained teamwork is not inherent in the Latin American cultural pattern. But housing experts regard this development as a viable means by which the low-income family may find its way out of improvised shacks and overpopulated slums. Indeed, self-help is precisely how squatter settlements are built. Aware of the failures of a number of mammoth, bureaucratized housing projects, governments now encourage self-help projects. Initiative and ego-involvement are usually more effective than superimposition from state functionaries.

Public housing remains a goal, but few specialists have illusions about the delay in its realization. It is one more case of the inability of market mechanisms to allocate resources equitably. Probably 40 percent of the population in most Latin America countries are in need of outside intervention in housing.[46] For betterment of urban services there should be reduction of clientelism and paternalism, emphasis on decision making at the local level concerning housing preferences, and improvement of technical assistance and relevant services. Despite financial barriers, this goal is realizable if political and bureaucratic obstacles can be removed.

Latin America is allocating proportionately less of its total national income to housing than are most areas of the world with a lower rate of population growth. Savings and loan associations must be funded in order for public programs to reach beyond the urban lower-middle class. Coordination of local, private, national, and international programs is necessary. Fortunately, some implementation of private and public resources in urban housing is occurring, often under the auspices of international aid agencies.

DIRECTIONS OF URBAN PLANNING

Latin American cities have an intermittent history of urban planning. The Law of the Indies in 1681 stipulated that space utilization should conform to the needs of the citizens: the model of the plaza, a grid street pattern, and self-contained *barrios*. For decades, most countries have given serious, if uneven, attention to the design of the city. In 1898, Aarão Reis planned Belo Horizonte, the capital of Minas Gerais, according to a design of radial streets and ring boulevards superimposed on a gridiron pattern. Early in the twentieth century, Buenos Aires adopted a master plan (*Plan de Urbanización*) for the purpose of establishing a greater integrity of the city's streets, buildings, and parks. Similarly, Chile established the National Department of Urbanism for consultation in Santiago and provincial cities. Mexico City has a lengthy history of creating monuments expressing both cosmopolitanism and nationalism, as in the 1910 centennial celebration.[47] A still different theme of urban planning was the development of historical monuments, such as in Taxco, Mexico, where no construction can take place without approval of the planning board.

An important adjunct to the efforts of planning boards, if somewhat limited and uncoordinated, is the innovativeness of their architects. For half a century, Brazil has profited from the work of a dozen eminent architects. Major figures were Lucio Costa and especially Oscar Niemeyer, who designed Brasilia, with government, commercial, and recreational centers located along one axis and housing along the other. Critics charge that the housing is more impressive as architectural design than as functional living quarters.[48] With its "petrodollars," Caracas led other capitals in experimentation with its superhighways and novel complexes of commercial and living quarters. However, the visitor to any city can hardly fail to see the shacktowns alongside the more dazzling architectural achievements.

No less than in the United States, urban planners in Latin America are able to grapple only with externals. Planning should involve a number of objectives: (1) arrangement and design of streets, transportation facilities, and public buildings; (2) control of zoning to segregate business, industrial, and residential uses; (3) provision for the cultural and physical needs of residents by means of parks, schools, libraries, as well as control of air and water pollution and disposal of other waste products; (4) slum clearance and construction of housing projects; and (5) integration of the city within the regional and national scheme. In most Latin American cities, urban planning boards can solve only a few of these problems, principally because of diffused decision-making power and severe financial limitations. Even more serious is the inability to focus on the essential polarization of urban society, the haves and have-nots. In Mexico, the PRI has not been able to resolve the aspirations of the city masses.[49] A Brazilian sociologist notes that no urban planning is effective without changing the economic structure, notably the wage structure.[50] Some of the variables in urban planning are suggested in Figure 8.1.

The Limits of Planning

It is a cliché to say that the dilemmas of the modern city are unsolvable. The problems associated with the movement, employment, and housing of ten to twenty million people in the megapolis, whether Mexico City, São Paulo, Los Angeles, Tokyo, or Cairo, are compounded by the conflict of different interest groups for space and power within the city. An additional problem is contamination of the physical environment. The parameters of planning are occasionally more hopeful when cities are new and evolving, with less accretion of old structures. Architects in Buenos Aires complain of the irony of new complexes and suburbs on one side and on the other the decay of older buildings.[51] Except for the largest cities, land values are generally more manageable in newer urban areas. However, real estate speculation is rampant, especially in Brazil, where latifundio just outside the city may give way to an urban minifundio as speculators lay out new *urbanizaciones*. With probably less suburban sprawl than in the United States, the territory surrounding the city is relatively accessible to the planner. Also, central areas of high density are interspersed with open spaces.

São Paulo remains a challenging example. With a population rise in less than fifty years from two to fourteen million, it is next to Mexico City the most rapidly growing of the ten largest cities of the world. As a result, the average speed of a vehicle in its city streets is claimed to be only six miles per hour, and travel time for many workers is four hours a day. To meet these and other needs, a Basic Urban Plan (PUB) was adopted after consultation with urban experts from Europe and the United States. Fortunately, a restructuring of taxation increased the city's budget to allow for increased spending in housing, transportation, and social services.

Centralism is an area of special concern for urban planners in Latin America. Mexico encouraged the location of business and industry in the Federal District, but by 1960 it recognized the danger of uncontrolled urbanization. As a result, an industrial satellite city, Ciudad Bernardino de Sahagún, was founded with the contribution of both public and private financing. For example, international firms Fiat and Toyota have responded to this venture in decentralization. Other planned cities were projected for various regions of the country, not only for industrial development but also as a means of absorbing the surplus agricultural labor. In one diversionary move, the Chilean government attempted to promote industry in remote parts of the country, only to find Santiago continuing its high rate of growth. Finally, the authorities promoted the relocation of the automotive industry to a smaller community in the central valley but in proximity to the capital. Santiago became the focus of a metropolitan region with a number of satellite cities within a radius of some sixty miles.

Other problems remain in Latin American urban planning. One is the difficulty of coordinating the work of planning agencies. Only fragmentary liaison is found between national economic planning and the specific roles a city has to assume in this process; nor are adequate financial resources given to municipalities by the national government. Most countries have only begun systematic data collecting in regard to market areas, flow of migrants, or potential tax revenue. Another problem is the confusion and vacillation in planning boards because of insecurity among office holders, conflict of local power groups, and, most critical, inadequate financing of the projects. Urban planners devise projects only to find themselves caught in a political impasse or overruled by one vested interest or another. The bureaucracy of federal and local agencies, along with meeting the demands of the private sector, frustrates the urban planner, as documented in Colombia.[52] Historically, the bases for local democracy in Latin America are deficient. Until political power is decentralized, most cities are relegated to marginal status in national decision making.[53]

As another point, state and private industrialization and commercial activity are seldom integrated with welfare and cultural functions; in fact, little coordination exists between social security, education, and housing. The *juntas progresistas* and other *barrio* councils rarely communicate with planning agencies for the total metropolitan area. Fundamental is the need for economic coordination in urban planning. Unrealistic goals are too often the norm.[54] A report from Chile points to the necessity of permitting the public to enter into the decision-making process in a variety of projects, from water distribution to the location and transport system of a new airport.[55]

Frustration at the lack of effective planning and its implementation, especially for programs aimed at the *clase popular*, have led to grassroots organizations, perhaps in Mexico more than in other countries. The evolution of these movements was also in reaction to what were perceived as cataclysmic events—the 1968 attack on university students, the 1985 earthquake, the 1988 fraudulent election—and the failure of PRI to resolve these crises. These "urban popular movements" often begin in neighborhoods, then coalesce into citywide, regional, and eventually national groupings. Probably foremost among the complaints is the inability of the government to provide housing, but hardly less salient are problems of wage levels, personal security, utilities, and other needs of exploding cities. Indirectly, authorities refined the planning mechanisms, but ideological conflicts and financial realities remain.[56]

Planning, Reform, and the Community

Problems of centralism, coordination, vacillation, and local conflict are typified in Brazil. The combination of speculation, bureaucracy, and public needs becomes self-defeating for the planner. The semantics of urban change is itself a reflection of this confusion. Usually the government stresses building wide avenues and skyscrapers. If there is any interest in humanitarian values, it is in slum or *favela* eradication, followed by the movement of the occupants to *multifamiliares* outside the city with the inevitable breaking of ties with the neighborhood. More progressive planners favor an integrated approach to planning through interdisciplinary consultation with geographers, economists, sociologists, and urbanists. These planners prefer to move toward a labor-oriented economy rather than a capital-consuming industry. They insist on reform in income levels, taxation, and zoning. Finally, as one looks at such factors as shelter, employment, and the infrastructure, a most important consideration is the emphasis on local needs, decision making, and input, rather than simply superimposing national criteria and needs.[57]

Despite these attempts to cope with the situation, Latin America's rampant urbanization inhibits the planner. In recent years, economic realities, especially the trend toward privatization, have led governments to be less concerned with planning and intervention.[58] Will the city grow without a meaningful structure or a resolution of the problems facing its citizens? Some compromise may be made, but priority will likely be placed on economic growth without sufficient attention to its impact on urban populations and their needs. In the meantime, *favelas* and *barriadas* will continue to exist side by side with the *autopista*, *galería*, and *superbloque*. These problems are found throughout Latin America. For instance, in Bogotá a host of agencies, government and NGOs, confront a number of challenges: controlling land speculation, developing public parks, revising urban legal codes, in addition to developing housing and transport.[59] Hardly surprising, in a 1990 survey of the world's ninety-eight largest metropolitan areas in respect to living standards (as based on food costs, number of persons per room, infant mortality rates, education, and other indexes), no Latin American city was in the highest one-third, and three (Mexico City, Lima, and Recife) were below the average for cities in the developing world.[60]

THE CITY AND NATIONAL DEVELOPMENT

In assessing the significance of the Latin American city, we return to the questions raised in Chapter 7. What is the meaning of the city in the economic and political sphere? As towns become cities and the city becomes a metropolis, if not a megapolis (São Paulo is predicted to reach twenty million by 2000, and Mexico City is likely there already), the question remains whether economic development can accommodate this increase. Although urbanization is correlated with industrialization, lack of capital and technical skills among new urban migrants is not reassuring. Planning must consider not only the state apparatus but also the informal and formal economy stretching from household and barrio to the corporate structures.[61] In several countries, Colombia among others, the municipal government has little autonomy; consequently, NGOs are committed to pressuring the national government to redress grievances ranging from waste removal to health services.[62]

Although urbanization (as defined as size of urban population) is moderately correlated with electoral participation, the relationship is less clear concerning correlation with the stability of constitutional government. For example, the level of welfare and related urban services may be more predictive than urbanization itself in determining government legitimacy. In Mexico City, politicians fear the entry of *técnicos* into the decision-making process. However, since 1982 opposition parties have forced more professional management on the PRI-appointed mayor.[63] These qualifications underline the tenuous nature of generalizations regarding urban processes.

Spatial integration, innovation, and modernization are central in urban planning. Future research may determine, for instance, the optimal rural–urban balance for given stages of development in national planning and development. Urban development strategy must involve several objectives: more equitable distribution of income, establishing the relationship between centralization and decentralization, ecological protection, urban development (restoring and expanding the infrastructure through housing and transport and regional or nonmetropolitan development), and encouraging location of industrial and related activities in appropriate "growth centers."[64] In less developed countries, revitalization strategies have to proceed on an integrated rural–urban development plan.[65] The long-range goal is the quality of life—a self-identity or a sense of familiarity and security as well as esthetic considerations.[66]

Cities in an International Perspective

Most cities in Latin America are in a transitional stage, with advanced technologies and consumption standards existing side by side with the marginal life styles of the slum and the shantytown. On that point it was once said that the problem of Latin American cities is not one of overurbanization but of underindustrialization. Today, that viewpoint would seem too simplistic.

Although the Latin American city is closer to the European city than are the cities of Asia and Africa, the mix of indigenous and Western traditions may mean a city different from its prototype imported from across the Atlantic. Whatever the course of development of Latin American cities in the world scene, sophisticated cities of the Northern Hemisphere hardly offer a model of urban development. Cities as diverse as Rome, Bogotá, and Philadelphia are in serious disarray, if not for the same reasons. The Anglo-American city increasingly resembles its Latin American counterpart in regard to economic disparities, homelessness, crime, and violence.

The primary function of cities may be economic, but other functions—governmental, educational, cultural, and recreational—play a differentiating role and are only marginally related to the economic one. Further, the city reflects not only the social statuses of its population but also variations in the life cycle. Cities function in a hierarchical arrangement domestically and internationally.[67] Consequently, any outline for future evolution of the city will have to be multilineal and subject to revision, especially as the Latin American city has come of age more recently than its European and North American counterparts.

NOTES

1. Alan Gilbert, *The Latin American City* (London: Latin American Bureau, 1994), 82.

2. Alejandro Portes, José Itzigsohn, and Carlos-Dobral, "Urbanization in the Caribbean Basin: Social Change during the Years of the Crisis," *Latin American Research Review* 29(2): 3–37 (1994).

3. Alejandro Portes, "The Economy and Ecology of Urban Poverty," in *Urban Latin America*, ed. Alejandro Portes and John Walton (Austin: University of Texas Press, 1976), 7–69.

4. Peter M. Ward, "Mexico City," in *Problems and Planning in Third World Cities*, ed. Michael Pacione (New York: St. Martin's Press, 1981), 28–64.

5. Nicolas López Tamayo, "La Urbanización de los Ejidos en la Ciudad de Puebla, México," *Revista Interamericana de Planificación* 27(107–108): 110–124 (1994).

6. Robert C. Williamson, "Some Factors in Urbanism in a Quasi-Rural Setting: San Salvador and San José," *Sociology and Social Research* 47: 187–200 (1963).

7. William L. Flinn, "The Process of Migration to a Shantytown in Bogotá, Colombia," *Inter-American Economic Affairs* 22(autumn): 77–88 (1968).

8. Alan Gilbert, "Bogotá," in *Problems and Planning in Third World Cities*, ed. Michael Pacione (New York: St. Martin's Press, 1981), 65–93.

9. William L. Flinn, "Rural and Intra-Urban Migration in Colombia: Two Case Studies in Bogotá," in *Latin American Urban Research*, vol. 1, ed. Francine F. Rabinovitz and Felicity M. Trueblood (Newbury Park, Calif.: Sage Publications, 1974), 83–93.

10. Anthony Leeds, "Housing-Settlement Types, Arrangements for Living, Proletarianization, and the Social Structure of the City," in *Latin American Urban Research*, vol. 4, ed. Wayne A. Cornelius and Felicity M. Trueblood (Newbury Park, Calif.: Sage Publications, 1974), 67–99.

11. Alan Gilbert and Ann Varley, "The Mexican Landlord: Rental Housing in Guadalajara and Puebla," *Urban Studies* 27(1): 23–44 (1990).

12. Peter M. Ward, *Mexico City: The Production and Reproduction of an Urban Environment* (Boston: G. K. Hall, 1990), 56.

13. Paul Van Lindert, "Moving Up or Staying Down? Migrant-Native Residential Mobility in La Paz," *Urban Studies* 28: 433–463 (1991).

14. Allison M. MacEwen, "Stability and Change in a Shanty Town: A Summary of Some Research Findings," *Sociology* 6(January): 41–57 (1972).

15. Terence McGee, "Conservation and Dissolution in the Third World City," in *Urbanism and Urbanization*, ed. Noel Iverson (Leiden, Holland: E. J. Brill, 1984), 107–126.

16. Michael P. Conzen, ed., *World Patterns of Modern Urban Change* (Chicago: University of Chicago, Department of Geography Research Paper 217-218, 1986), 107–126.

17. Lloyd H. Rogler, "Slum Neighborhoods in Latin America," *Journal of Inter-American Studies* 9: 507–528 (1967).

18. Bryan Roberts, "Transitional Cities," in *Rethinking the Latin American City*, ed. Richard M. Morse and Jorge E. Hardoy (Baltimore: Johns Hopkins University Press, 1992), 50–65.

19. Peter Lloyd, *The Young Towns of Lima: Aspects of Urbanization in Peru* (Cambridge: Cambridge University Press, 1980), 47–63.

20. Susan Eckstein, *The Poverty of Revolution* (Princeton, N.J.: Princeton University Press, 1977), 53–64.

21. Julian Laite, "The Migrant Response in Central Peru," in *The Urbanization of the Third World*, ed. Josef Gugler (New York: Oxford University Press, 1988), 61–73.

22. William Mangin, "Latin American Squatter Settlements: A Problem and a Solution," *Latin American Research Review* 2(summer): 65–98 (1967).

23. Ibid., 81.

24. Michael J. Higgins and Tanya Leigh Coen, *!Oigame, !Oigame: Struggle and Change in a Nicaraguan Urban Community* (Boulder, Colo.: Westview Press, 1992), 56.

25. Rogler, "Slum Neighborhoods," 525.

26. Michael B. Whiteford, *The Forgotten Ones: Colombian Countrymen in an Urban Setting* (Gainesville: University Presses of Florida, 1976), 70–71.

27. William P. Mangin, "The Role of Regional Associations in the Adaptation of Rural Migrants to Cities in Peru," in *Contemporary Cultures and Societies of Latin America*, ed. Dwight B. Heath and Richard N. Adams (New York: Random House, 1965), 311–323.

28. Ozzie G. Simmons, "The Criollo Outlook in the Mestizo Culture of Coastal Peru," in *Contemporary Cultures and Societies of Latin America*, ed. Dwight B. Heath and Richard N. Adams (New York: Random House, 1965), 518–530.

29. Janice E. Perlman, *The Myth of Marginality: Urban Poverty and Politics in Rio de Janeiro* (Berkeley: University of California Press, 1976), 29–30.

30. Vivienne Bennent, "Gender, Class, and Water: Women and the Politics of Water Service in Monterrey, Mexico," *Latin American Perspectives* 22(2): 76–99 (1995).

31. Bryan R. Roberts, "The Interrelationships of City and Provinces in Peru and Guatemala," in *Latin American Urban Research*, vol. 4, ed. Wayne A. Cornelius and Felicity M. Trueblood (Newbury Park, Calif.: Sage Publications, 1974), 207–235.

32. Cecilia Muñoz V. and Ximena Pachón C., "El Mundo Gamín: Un Fenómeno Urbano," in *Vida Urbana y Urbanismo*, ed. Carlos Castillo (Bogotá: Instituto Colombiano de Cultura, 1977), 47–56.

33. Oscar E. Gómez Peralta, *Las Poblaciones Marginales en el Peru* (Lima: Gómez y Hijos, 1990), 86–88.

34. August B. Hollingshead and Lloyd H. Rogler, "Attitudes toward Slums and Public Housing in Puerto Rico," in *The Urban Condition*, ed. Leonard J. Duhl (New York: Basic Books, 1968), 229–245.

35. Carolina Maria de Jesús, *Child of the Dark* (New York: E. P. Dutton and Co., 1962).

36. Robert M. Levine, "The Cautionary Tale of Carolina Maria de Jesús," *Latin American Research Review* 29(1): 55–84 (1994).

37. Luís A. Machado da Silva, "O Significado do Botequim," *America Latina* 12(July/September): 160–182 (1969).

38. Ward, *Mexico City*, 175–176.

39. Arthur D. Murphy and Alex Stepick, *Social Inequality in Oaxaca* (Philadelphia: Temple University Press, 1991), 56.

40. Jaime Castilo Palma, "Puebla: Agentes Dominantes en la Producción de Servicios," *Ciudades* 11: 42–47 (1991).

41. Robert C. Williamson, "Psychological Correlates of Housing in Central America," *Journal of Inter-American Studies* 6: 489–499 (1964).

42. John Stuart MacDonald and Beatrice D. MacDonald, "Jobs and Housing Alternative Developments in the Venezuela Guyana," *Journal of Inter-American Studies and World Affairs* 13(October): 342–366 (1971).

43. Lawrence F. Salmen, "A Perspective on the Resettlement of Squatters in Brazil," *America Latina* 12(January/March): 73–95 (1969).

44. Eduardo E. Lozano, "Housing the Urban Poor in Chile: Contrasting Experiences under 'Christian Democracy' and Unidad Popular," in *Latin American Urban Research*, vol. 4, ed. Wayne A. Cornelius and Felicity M. Trueblood (Newbury Park, Calif.: Sage Publications, 1975), 177–194.

45. Pamela Constable and Arturo Valenzuela, *A Nation of Enemies: Chile under Pinochet* (New York: Norton, 1991), 235.

46. Fernando Guardia-Butron, "La Situación de la Vivienda Popular en América Latina," *Revista Paraguaya de Sociología* 24: 7–21 (1991).

47. Mauricio Tenorio Trillo, "1910 Mexico City: Space and Nation in the City of the *Centenario*," *Journal of Latin American Studies* 28: 71–104 (1996).

48. Paul Rabinow, "A Modern Tour of Brazil," in *Modernity and Identity*, ed. Scott Lash and Jonathan Friedman (Cambridge, Mass.: Blackwell, 1992), 248–264.

49. Jorge Montano, *Los Pobres de la Ciudad en los Asentamientos Espontáneos: Poder y Político* (México, D. F.: Siglo Veintiuno Editores, 1976), 211.

50. Tersa M. Frota Haguete, *O Mito das Estrategías de Sobrevivência* (Fortaleza: Ediocões UFC, 1982), 111.

51. Rita Schlaen et al., *Buenos Aires: Una Estrategía Urbana Alternativa* (Buenos Aires: Ediciones Fundación, 1988), 117–123.

52. Julio Carrizosa et al., "La Dimención Ambiental en la Planificación del Desarrollo de la Sabana de Bogotá" (Buenos Aires: CEPAL-Instituto National de Desarrollo, 1988).

53. Jordi Borja, "Past, Present, and Future of Local Government in Latin America," in *Rethinking the Latin American City*, ed. Richard M. Morse and Jorge E. Hardoy (Baltimore: Johns Hopkins University Press, 1992), 131–143.

54. Antonio Daher, "Macro-economía de la Externalidad Urbana," *Revista Interamericana de Planificación* 23: 253–263 (1990).

55. Antonio Daher, "Liderazgo Municipal: Modernidad para el País," *Revista Internacional de Planificación* 27(105): 125–131 (1994).

56. Vivienne Bennett, "The Evolution of Urban Popular Movements in Mexico between 1968 and 1988," in *The Making of Social Movements in Latin America*, ed. Arturo Escobar and Sonia E. Alvarez (Boulder, Colo.: Westview Press, 1992), 240–259.

57. C. L. Choguill, "Crisis, Chaos, Crunch? Planning for Urban Growth in the Developing World," *Urban Studies* 31: 935–945 (1994).

58. Alan Gilbert, "Third World Cities: The Changing National Settlement System," *Urban Studies* 30: 721–740 (1993).

59. Pedro Santana Rodriguez, "Local Governments, Decentralization, and Democracy in Colombia," in *New Paths to Democratic Development in Latin America*, ed. Charles A. Reilly (Boulder, Colo.: Lynne Rienner, 1995), 165–178.

60. Abu J. M. Sufian, "A Multivariate Analysis of the Determinants of Urban Quality of Life in the World's Largest Metropolitan Areas," *Urban Studies* 30: 1319–1329 (1993).

61. John Friedman, *Life Space and Economic Space: Essays in Third World Planning* (New Brunswick, N.J.: Transaction Books, 1988), 125–134.

62. Rodriquez, "Local Governments, Decentralization, and Democracy in Colombia," 165–177.

63. Peter Ward, *Welfare Politics in Mexico: Papering over the Cracks* (London: Allen & Unwin, 1986), 98–100.

64. Brian J. L. Berry and John D. Kasarda, *Contemporary Urban Ecology* (New York: Macmillan, 1977), 405.

65. Philip M. Hauser et al., *Population and the Urban Future* (Albany: State University Press of New York, 1982), 160–163.

66. Harold M. Proshanksy and Abbe K. Fabian, "Psychological Aspects of the Quality of Urban Life," in *The Quality of Urban Life*, ed. Dieter Frank (Berlin: de Gruyter, 1986), 19–29.

67. Brian J. L. Berry, "Latent Structure of Urban Systems: Research Methods and Findings," in *Systems of Cities*, ed. L. S. Bourne and J. W. Simmons (New York: Oxford University Press, 1978), 220–232.

Chapter 9

Keys to Latin America's Future

The present volume analyzes a number of predominant social systems in Latin America in the context of institutions and processes. Often the focus has been on discontinuities more than achievements. As I stated early in the book, Latin America can be understood properly only by a native, and even though I have been critical, my years in Latin America have endeared a number of countries and places to me.

It is appropriate to compare the present situation in Latin America with that of the United States. In the 1950s and 1960s, the United States led the world, producing one-third of the planet's economy. Its monetary situation was unassailable. One could walk the streets of any metropolis and feel relatively safe. Except for several cities, the air was relatively pure; the nation's education system was still in high gear. Today, however, the United States does not stand so far from what is called the Third World. Indebtedness of four trillion dollars places it in a fiscal category not too different on a per capita basis from that of Argentina, Brazil, Chile, or Mexico. Equally scandalous is the report that the richest 1 percent of the population own nearly 40 percent of the wealth. In personal security, environmental contamination, educational achievement, and upward mobility, the *norteamericano* probably enjoys some advantage over the Latin American, but the gap is far narrower than it once was. Nonetheless, Latin America still lags behind most of the Western world, caught as it is in its "enervating debt trap, sharpening social inequities, deterioration of public institutions in several nations."[1]

This book is rooted in the idea of a "social equilibrium," or the "control of resources among actors." However, if the actors confer control of resources to others unilaterally, in the hope of arriving at an individual equilibrium, the results may be other than a satisfactory equilibrium.[2] In other words, variations of structural–functional and of conflict theory are apparent in Latin America and other parts of the world. Episodes of competitiveness, dominance, oppression, aggression, and co-option interplay with those of cooperation, concession, and consensus. For example, settlements among the elites have been very significant in Costa Rica, have a mixed record in Brazil, and are perhaps least impressive in Peru.[3] The conflict between the economically disenfranchised and the middle and upper classes remains.

Institutions and Processes

We have examined a number of social systems, both favorable and unfavorable. The Latin American economy, diverse though it is from one nation to the next, generally displays limited productivity and poor distribution, with well over half of the population receiving less than what they should. Despite the tragedy of the Lost Decade—the 1980s—Chile pioneered in neoliberalism with its emphasis on free trade and a reduction of state intervention and became the harbinger for other nations. With Carlos Salinas, Mexico also ventured into this reformed capitalist model—though marred by extensive corruption. Despite the setbacks of 1994, its economy grew ninefold from 1950 to 1988, and is already the tenth largest GNP of the world. Brazil has become another success story with its apparent control of inflation and a strong move toward privatization. As many of us think of President Cardoso as something of a twentieth-century Jeffersonian, Brazil should have a dynamic future. These scenarios do not make the economic perils such as the maldistribution of income in Brazil, Mexico, and their smaller and poorer neighbors insignificant. Still, the economic profile is less bleak than it was a decade ago.

Since few classically authoritarian states exist in 1996 in the Hemisphere, the political panorama is marked by a somewhat optimistic note. One hopeful aspect is the end of the Cold War, which has discouraged meddling by the United States, or more euphemistically, the advent of a more egalitarian relationship between North and South. As with the economic sphere, there appears to be more of a spirit of cooperation between the republics, the Peru–Ecuador border trouble notwithstanding. NAFTA and the General Agreement on Tariffs and Trade (GATT), for example, involve governments as well as agribusiness and industry. But as with the economic elites, political leaders still cling to their traditional position of privilege. In other words, it is time to move beyond the "politics of survival" to the "politics of development."[4] Even more than in the postindustrial nations, government and nongovernment agencies are faced with enormous challenges.[5]

Likewise, the demography of Latin America illustrates a more than partial success. Population growth is less frightening than in the 1960s, but it is still threatening as the rise in life expectancy almost equals the fall in fertility in several countries. The demographic profile is even more diverse than is the economic or political one when one compares Uruguay with Honduras. Of course, demographic processes cannot be separated from macroeconomic events and political decision making. Possibly the most disturbing aspect is the situation regarding public health, pensions, and other aspects of social welfare. Agricultural production and distribution are also related to population trends. The rural population is especially frustrated in its lack of services. No less important is the need for agrarian reform, to which so much lip service has been rendered but relatively little effective action given.

Ethnicity and class have moved somewhat away from a caste-like structure that characterized the first four centuries of Latin America. The twentieth century, especially since World War II, has witnessed a blurring of racial categories, most notably in Brazil, Colombia, and Mexico. Yet in these countries and probably all others, a remarkable correlation exists between whiteness of the skin and socioeconomic status. Certain countries have a relatively small number of ethnic minorities, the minorities are sufficiently integrated with the bulk of the population so that little discrimination results, or prejudice and segregation are less visible than in those countries with a large, salient indigenous population (Bolivia, Ecuador, Guatemala, and Peru). A glaring aspect of the class system in comparison with the Western world is the enormity of the lower class—two-thirds to three-fourths in most countries, of which more than half live in poverty. The middle class together with the upper working class composes more than half of the population in cities such as Buenos Aires, Montevideo, São Paulo, or Santiago. Consequently, it wields considerable political power. More to the point, the middle class in most countries is constantly struggling for a decent standard of living. For the lower class, the struggle simply for survival is a nonending one. For instance, in nearly half the countries in 1992, urban real minimum wages were less than two-thirds of what they were in 1980.[6] As Latin America moves toward the twenty-first century with its concern for a free market, one focus must be on those disinherited. Instead of a debate on growth versus equality, it should be "growth *and* equality."[7]

That I dedicated two chapters to the city points to the importance of this growing urban landscape. Cities are increasing more rapidly than is the general population. To many people, the city connotes decay, traffic, pollution, corruption, and violence. As in North America, policy makers must somehow cope with these problems, including the tide of migrants from the countryside. Despite the darker side of the urban environment, the Latin American city offers captivating recreational, cultural, educational, and artistic assets. (As a film buff, I found in Bogotá, to mention only one metropolis, an assortment of European films as rich as that in New York!)

Whither Latin America?

Various historical processes are rationalized implicitly or explicitly in various religious and political ideologies. In examining the evolution of Latin America from the colonial period to the 1970s, Alejandro Portes and John Walton outline a succession ranging from (1) patrimonialism—the Deity working through Crown and Church with the help of mercantilism to insure a hierarchical social order; (2) nineteenth-century positivism and its mix of revised natural law and evolutionism; (3) marginality with the emergence of working-class consciousness and the pressure of socialist doctrines in the 1930s and 1940s as elaborated into populism à la Vargas and Perón; and (4) developmentalism, with its various expressions from Christian Democrats to reform-minded militarists.[8] In the intervening years arose a new phase based on neoliberal economic policies oriented to a world-system with a trend toward democratic regimes, at least on the surface. One common thread running through these phases is the need to protect economic elites, even though the expanding urban working and middle classes seek a more comprehensive distribution of income. Other pressures of change include the revolution in mass media and communication and a growing social conscience among religious communities. The uneven effect of these forces on the twenty republics and their class, ethnic, and regional constituencies hardly needs to be restated.

After World War II, Latin America faced two general options of socioeconomic change, each with variations: first, modernization in a capitalistic system in (1) democratic pluralism, (2) the uniparty model of Mexico, or (3) military rule with Velasco Alvarado or quasi-military with Fujimori, both in Peru; second, the socialist route either by the Soviet plan based on the decay of capitalist structures (a scenario that lost credibility with the collapse of the Soviet system after 1989) or inspired by rural grassroots, as outlined by Castro, Che Guevara, or at worst, the Maoist-oriented Sendero Luminoso of contemporary Peru.[9]

Development and Modernization

The concept of modernization has suffered from its facile functionalism, yet in some respects it remains a viable option to Latin America as a developing area. Modernization can be approached in differing theoretical frameworks.[10] One is the evolutionary viewpoint voiced by European and North American theorists who see it as a phased, homogenizing, progressive, and irreversible process. Another is the functionalist outlook, which points to a systematic and transformative process, stressing the interrelationships between institutions involving the entire social order. Modernization can also be identified in a number of ways. Among other concepts, it means social differentiation of labor, development of a market economy, application of technology and automation, social and organizational innovations, and such sociopsychological attributes as individualism and acceptance of the scientific method.[11] Among the questions to be addressed are where, when, how, and under what conditions to modernize? What are the basic problems and techniques? Ideally, modernization might provide the end of oligarchical rule and a modification of the trappings of personalism and clientelism. In the past, industrialization was emphasized as a means of overhauling an agrarian and monocultural economy.

More relevant than the ambiguities surrounding modernism is the necessity to expand an employment market for an ever-growing labor force. As with much of the developing world, the Latin American economy is still skewed toward the primary and tertiary sectors, with too little development in the secondary or manufacturing area. The tertiary or service sector is overloaded with economically marginal occupations, such as lottery agents, domestic servants, and a mushrooming number of government employees. In reality, all three sectors have shown a continuous flow of informal more than formal labor. This expansion is a result of (1) population growth, (2) economic stagnation, including the lack of employment opportunities in both agricultural and urban areas and the discontinuity between formal and informal labor, and (3) internal migration from the rural hinterland to the urban shanytowns. One thrust must be to rehabilitate the agricultural economy through agrarian reform measures and community development projects, which means genuine changes in land ownership. Equally compelling is the need to broaden the urban economy, including expansion of industrialization as well as technical and professional services. Spurring local, regional, and national governments into action are the NGOs, which have found a new momentum since the 1970s.[12] External debt, monetary instability, lack of capital, an inadequately trained labor force, inability to find an export market, and gross disparity of income are among the barriers to facilitating leadership and an infrastructure necessary for industrialization and meaningful tertiary employment. In other words, the challenge remains. The United States could do much to further economic advances in Latin America by promoting higher stability in the world economy, expanding international financing, and encouraging access to its own markets, as currently planned by NAFTA. The protectionism of the 1980s was fatal to the developing world.[13] According to public opinion surveys in Mexico, the majority of the population overwhelmingly favor free trade.[14] Nonetheless, the effects of NAFTA and GATT are yet to be tested. Whatever the outcome, the thought of an expanding *maquiladora* and similar programs has frightened laborers, social workers, and environmentalists on both sides of the Rio Grande.

Another aspect of the problems surrounding modernization is the network of social and political factors underlying a backward economy. Both traditionalism and modernism are intermeshed with processes of population growth, rigidities of the class structure, and urbanization. Modernization also carries the burden of foreign intervention through investment capital and market access.

Most Western nations faced these problems as they emerged from an agrarian economy in the nineteenth century. Latin America has experienced a different cultural development in terms of its indigenous populations and traditions, unique pattern of government and religion, and basic value orientations. Moreover, it confronts a world marked by "rising expectations." Europe and North America had a century to make the transition to a modern industrial order, but Latin America is making the leap in a markedly shorter time span. Individuals need to adjust to novel occupational demands, to complex stimuli from the mass media, and to systems of government. Most nations are struggling with complications of the democratic process. In five thousand years of complex societies, democracy can be considered as a relatively new form of political behavior. The intricate responses underlying representative government have not been fully achieved even among the more advanced nations of the world.

Chile is among those instances of democracy giving way to militarism followed by a return to a representative, pluralistic society. New ideologies, policies, and articulation that are neither Marxist or neoliberal are being adopted.[15] In various respects, we are witnessing the twilight of an old system more than the emergence of a new one.[16] Whatever the difficulties in their transition to a pluralistic government, several Latin American nations have to recognize the ineffectiveness of old formulas. Political parties based on class, more often to the right than to the left, are not the only avenue of obtaining power or seeking social change. A newer means of effecting change is through "resource mobilization," or bringing to bear organizational skills, communication networks, human labor, and other commodities.[17] In this connection, the 1980s saw the rise of varied social movements, including women's movements in several countries, peasants' struggle for land, the candidacy of Cuauhtémoc Cárdenas in the 1988 Mexican election, and the sustained protest against Pinochet, all against the background of defiance, if not violence. As implied in Chapter 1, new political models are in order.

The term "developing nations" points to still other dimensions. How much of development—or modernization—is quantitative or qualitative? To what degree does economic growth become human development? Does development, like modernization, imply an internationalization of the economy? What are the allowable limits to growth? The answers or the options are limited. Notably for Central America and Haiti—both subject to U.S. intervention through much of this century—the outcomes are in a state of flux.

Most developing nations strive to move from the periphery to the semi-periphery. The gap between developing and advanced nations is not yet bridged, but it is more than occasionally arbitrary, especially in qualitative aspects. Development and growth have to be judged in the context of a satisfactory equilibrium. Most indexes of growth suggest that world trade, for example, is moving faster than the social system can adjust, as shown in inflation and unemployment indexes, particularly in the 1970s and 1980s.[18]

A recurring theme in this book refers to rigidities in the class structure and the significance of the middle class. The upward movement of white-collar employees and professionals has been a near-revolution in Latin America during the late twentieth century, even if the middle class, which numbers less than one-third of most nations, has a rather slippery tenure of power. The full implications of the middle class and those members who form a new elite are not known. A body of research has accumulated on the aspirations and attitudes associated with different social backgrounds through both survey and case-study methods. In another decade, hopefully, we may be better prepared to assess the ideology and roles actors can assume in the future development of their society.

One might argue that the middle sectors receive a disproportionate amount of attention. Unquestionably the lower sector needs to gain more education, income, and social power. Any wider share of the nation's income—which in the end spells power—the lower classes are to receive would have to come from the upper sector. The oligarchy—whether land-holders, military chieftains, or the newer entrepreneurs—are not disposed to accommodate this urban and rural proletariat. Up to the present moment, the lower sectors have few means of organizing themselves in order to achieve power. If for no other reason, the lack of effective labor unions would inhibit their seizure of power. However, revolutionary fervor combined with appropriate leadership could make possible this transfer of power. This tactic was attempted in Peru in 1968 and 1990 (in both cases with dubious outcomes), and it may occur in other countries as a new generation of military leaders is inspired by populist appeals. Seemingly, military adventurists are no longer fashionable.

Any discussion of the present and future of Latin America must come to grips with the formidable inadequacies of the government apparatus.

Several governments have shown an intellectual aspiration for democracy and at the same time have fallen short of their ideal. Certainly, easy categorizations are not helpful. For instance, Mexico as one of the more progressive countries offers a constitutional government interlaced with cronyism and corruption but as yet is not a constitutional democracy. Still, as compared to some of its southern neighbors, most of its people have reasonably extensive civil rights and a rising rate of employment with some upward movement in the social scale. In other words, we should be wary of conventional criteria for judging specifically what a democracy means. This does not belie the fact that in advanced nations, such as Argentina, societal strains arise whereby no democratic government from 1930 to 1980 lasted more than a few years. Few nations have incorporated the working class into decision making. Among the exceptions are Peron's Argentina and the quasi-Communist regimes of Guatemala, Chile, and Nicaragua—often experiments of short duration because of domestic or international pressures, notably from the United States. Mexico is a more enduring but limited example of workers' involvement in the government. It is too soon to predict the eventual outcome for beleaguered Cuba.

The Colossus of the North: An Uneasy Presence

Through most of the nineteenth century to at least the first half of this century, the United States dominated the political life of the Hemisphere, especially Central America and the Caribbean. The vision of the Eisenhower regime of the 1950s encompassed the lands to the south as part of a crusade to rid the world of Communism. In the Kennedy period, the vision became one of a progressive reform with the Alliance for Progress, but one that was ever less dynamic as other concerns grew more salient both in the north and south of the Hemisphere. For the Johnson (except for the Dominican episode) and Nixon administrations, a lower profile became the style. The Carter outlook was one of cautious interventionism with a stress on human rights, at least in the early period of his regime.

The 1980s in Latin America—the so-called Lost Decade—was dominated by a central theme of attempting to resolve the financial collapse with measures to reduce economic dependence, combined with rescheduling and restructuring the debt. The "diffusion of economic power" from the United States to Latin America was suspended. However, the "economic hegemony" of Washington and New York could still demand payment of the debt.[19] The other theme of the Reagan administration was direct intervention in Central America and a reversal of the human rights policy of Carter. With the end of the Cold War, the Bush administration held to a lower key, except for the attack on Panama in 1989. The Clinton administration has generally, if unevenly, striven for accommodation and cooperation.

One continuing theme is economic. Financial interests are perceived somewhat differently between North and South. For Latin America, private investments have meant, and mean today, that products leaving their respective countries are worth several times more than the payments and investments from abroad. The potential capital of the Latin American economy is diminishing while the profits of the invested capital grow and multiply at an enormous rate, more abroad than in the relevant country. If this characterization does not completely stand the test of economic validity, it is apparently what many Latin Americans think. Few North American entrepreneurs invest abroad for reasons other than profit making, which can be defined as a form of exploitation, even though in many instances they are making life more satisfying for a limited number of workers and consumers in Latin America. The U.S. public appears ambivalent if not hostile toward the welfare of their southern neighbors, as the controversy over NAFTA shows.

Probably the United States's most dramatic aid program, the Alliance for Progress was enacted in 1961 with high expectations but floundered in large part because of excessive congressional scrutiny and the inability or unwillingness of most Latin American governments to make realistic plans. (In the end the Alliance turned into military assistance programs for a variety of dictatorial regimes.) To a limited degree, success within the Hemisphere depends on the elimination of trade barriers between the two Americas and the eventual realization of a common market among the Latin American nations themselves. Usually, regional groupings offer more promise than grandiose structures such as the Organization of American States (OAS). An impressive example is the Contadora initiative in the 1980s as a plan to end the struggle in Nicaragua between Sandinistas and Contras.

Beyond the economic relations between the United States and its Latin American neighbors, the political picture is blurred by a lack of understanding. The faults of misunderstanding lie on both sides of the relationship and are attributable to the basic asymmetry of power, differing historical experiences, and divergence of goals and interests.[20] Frequently, the U.S. power elites are confused and divided as to which side should be given support. More often the decision lies with the financial elites, since they have the power to bequeath to North Americans what they most want, that is, profits and security for their investments—and in the past, hemispheric solidarity against Communism. U.S. policy stresses a market economy and lip service to democracy. Establishing democracy has usually meant a "quick-fix" approach with little awareness of the complexity of electoral behavior.[21] Labels such as "free elections" and "political reform" are more the focus than the basic nature of government processes.

After the advent of Castroism an awareness of sectors beyond the elites developed, but less priority was given to the economically depressed, who make up at least two-thirds of the population. Almost no lobby exists for this lower sector in Washington. Besides this inadequate perception of the needs of Latin Americans, the United States tends to alternate between the threat of military intervention or economic sanctions and the periodic doling out of financial or technical aid to those nations or groups within a nation that Congress perceives as meriting attention. The policy is self-defeating. Nor does decision making by larger structures such as the United States or the OAS prove to be much wiser, as the debates over Cuba and Haiti have shown.

Toward a New Century

The awareness that the North American hegemony has reached a twilight stage should lead the United States to find some fresh approaches. For instance, one might hope for success in associations like NAFTA and GATT (however problematic their effects), increased exchange programs, and more opportunities for interaction between persons on a cross-national basis. On the economic front, the United States could provide funds or other kinds of aid for Latin America with no necessary expectation of a return on the investment. Also, a change in the attitudes and behavior patterns is in order among American industrial, commercial, and diplomatic personnel living in the twenty republics—not to mention the status of Hispanics in the United States.

These solutions can be only painfully arrived at by a people who at the moment are inclined more toward greed and power than humility. Somehow North Americans will learn that if they cannot change their relationships with their neighbors, the hope even for moderate reform will be frustrated. As stated in Chapter 1, it is difficult to generalize about the twenty republics, and even more precarious to make future predictions. What is apparent at the present juncture is the striking change that has engulfed Latin America in the last third of the twentieth century. In the international scene it has displayed a move toward autonomy and self-reliance with a desire to enter a less peripheral role in the world market. The economic front is partly characterized by a struggle against indebtedness and a rise of neoliberalism. A most depressing aspect is the inability to move toward a redistribution of the income in order to provide a true consumers' market.

In the political landscape, an almost complete sweep of democratic regimes in the 1980s raises several intriguing questions. For one, the pressure toward democratization has seemingly come less from traditional political parties than from the rise of social movements. These are not new to Latin America but they have shown a wide range of strategies and ideologies—feminism, ecology, Christian Marxism, to mention but a few—and a sense of urgency for change.[22] The more important question is whether democracy can continue in view of the gulf between the "haves and have-nots" (or the class struggle, to use a Marxist term). Can cooperation and integration overcome marginality and dissolution? Otherwise put, will the mass of Latin Americans eventually turn to a militant or violent revolutionary solution for their problems? It would seem that the answer is no, but varied uncertainties in Cuba, Haiti, Peru, and elsewhere all present an uneasy scenario for the future, especially as the United States itself seems so uncertain of the meaning and goals of its socioeconomic and political order.

Guideposts for the Future

It is hazardous if not fatal for a social scientist to draw up a series of "dos and don'ts." Nonetheless, a few suggestions or caveats, both general and specific, can be tentatively offered beyond the observations in the preceding chapters and in this chapter:

1. Economic and political elites must somehow come to terms with the needs of the society. The leaders seem insensitive to the acute maldistribution of wealth. It is significant that President Salinas was able to force a somewhat larger portion of upper-income Mexicans to pay an income tax while at the same time rewarding his cronies. In this connection the reward structure should be directed toward symbolic and other forms of prestige. Other segments of society—science, education, the arts, and social service—deserve greater recognition.

2. The power structure must remain civilian. Happily, a downgrading of the military is already taking place. Yet for most countries the military still receives a larger amount of the federal budget than does education.

3. Increased focus on international agencies and cooperation would be welcome, whether in multinational corporations, agricultural quotas, or the drug trade. Strains of nationalism and parochialism still act as barriers to economic, political, and social progress.

4. Although Latin America is currently oriented to democratic procedures, a twilight of authoritarianism and excessive bureaucracy lingers on. Efficiency in organizations, both public and private, would gain by introducing more flexibility in the hierarchy.

If I am to deliver an ultimatum to my Latin American neighbors, I am even more inclined to look at the inadequacies of my own nation. Among possible directions for the United States are the following:

1. A particularly dangerous trend among North Americans is the recent drift into a quasi-isolationism. The ambivalence about our involvement in Somalia, Haiti, and Bosnia is symptomatic of this outlook. On a global scale, this kind of detachment between the two World Wars had serious consequences. Undoubtedly it will again.

2. The failure to recognize Castro's Cuba again demonstrates how political expediency overrules common sense. It is questionable whether the United States embargo had any validity during the Cold War. It certainly has none today. This intransigence only illustrates our isolation from the Western world—and means considerable suffering for the Cuban people.

3. The United States needs to continue its international nonmilitary aid programs—forsaken in 1995 by the Republican Congress. Again, this hiatus relates to a creeping isolationism.

4. The economic and political leaders of the United States must consider societal needs and not purely profit-and-loss statements. The implementation of NAFTA should not rest merely on trade advantages, but rather on the quality of life for citizens of all countries involved.

5. North Americans need to resolve their domestic problems. Dangerous trends such as the drive toward monolingualism or Proposition 187 in California and its implicit and explicit intolerance toward Hispanics do not augur well for future relations with Latin America.

It may be redundant to say that both Latin America and North America are at the crossroads, but in reality an ever accelerating rate of change characterizes both areas. At the time of writing these words, various transformations are occurring. The United States is assessing the direction of its social and economic system, and the outcome of the 1996 election will determine what the parameters of this process will be. The Mexican legislature is on the threshold of adopting new mechanisms to insure a multiparty political structure. Several other Latin American governments are in comparable phases of decision making. In other words, if one cannot assume an optimistic outcome for the future, it would be even more foolhardy to predict a pessimistic scenario.

NOTES

1. Abraham F. Lowenthal, *Partners in Conflict: The United States and Latin America in the 1990s*, rev. ed. (Baltimore: Johns Hopkins University Press, 1990), ix.

2. James S. Coleman, *Foundations of Social Theory* (Cambridge, Mass.: Harvard University Press, 1990), 42.

3. John Higley and Richard Gunther, eds., *Elites and Democratic Consolidation in Latin America and Southern Europe* (New York: Cambridge University Press, 1992).

4. John W. Sloan, *Public Policy in Latin America* (Pittsburgh: University of Pittsburgh Press, 1984), 250.

5. Charles A. Reilly, ed., *New Paths to Democratic Development in Latin America: The Rise of the NGO–Municipal Collaboration* (Boulder, Colo.: Lynne Rienner, 1995).

6. Latin American Center, *Statistical Abstract of Latin America* (Los Angeles: University of California, 1995), 424.

7. Margaret S. Sherraden, "Social Policy in Latin America: Questions of Growth, Equality, and Political Freedom," *Latin American Research Review* 30(1): 176–190 (1995).

8. Alejandro Portes and John Walton, *Labor, Class, and the International System* (Orlando, Fla.: Academic Press, 1981).

9. Lowenthal, *Partners in Conflict*, 20–25.

10. Alvin Y. So, *Social Change and Development* (Newbury Park, Calif.: Sage Publications, 1990), 33–36.

11. Gino Germani, *The Sociology of Modernization* (New Brunswick, N.J.: Transaction Books, 1981), 61.

12. Reilly, *New Paths to Democratic Development.*

13. John Sheahan, "Economic Forces and U.S. Policies," in *Expanding Democracy: The United States and Latin America,* ed. Abraham F. Lowenthal (Baltimore: Johns Hopkins University Press, 1991), 331–355.

14. Robert A. Pastor, *Whirlpool: U.S. Policy toward Latin America and the Caribbean* (Princeton, N.J.: Princeton University Press, 1992), 275.

15. Manuel A. Garretón and Malva Espinosa, "Reforma del Estado o Cambio en la Mártriz Socio-politica? El Caso Chileno," *Revista de Ciencias Sociales* 5(December): 7–20 (1992).

16. Alan Touraine, "From the Mobilizing State to Democratic Politics," in *Redefining the State in Latin America,* ed. Colin I. Bradford, Jr. (Paris: Organization for Economic Cooperation and Development, 1994), 45–65.

17. Susan Eckstein, *Power and Popular Protest: Latin American Social Movements* (Berkeley: University of California Press, 1989), 6–7.

18. Henry Teune, *Growth* (Newbury Park, Calif.: Sage Publications, 1988), 17.

19. Guy Poitras, *The Ordeal of Hegemony: The United States and Latin America* (Boulder, Colo.: Westview Press, 1990), 151–154.

20. James D. Cochraine, "The Troubled and Misunderstood Relationship: The United States and Latin America," *Latin American Research Review* 28(2): 232–245 (1993).

21. Harold Molineu, "The Inter-American System: Searching for a New Framework," *Latin American Research Review* 29(1): 215–226 (1994).

22. Arturo Escobar and Sonia E. Alvarez, eds., *The Making of Social Movements in Latin America* (Boulder, Colo.: Westview Press, 1992).

Selected Bibiography

Baer, Werner, Joseph Petry, and Murray Simpson (eds.). *Latin America: The Crisis of the Eighties and the Opportunities of the Nineties*. Champaign, Ill.: University of Illinois Press, 1991.

Baloyra, Enrique and James A. Morris. *Conflict and Change in Cuba*. Albuquerque: University of New Mexico Press, 1993.

Berryman, Philip. *Liberation Theology*. Philadelphia: Temple University Press, 1987.

Booth, John A. and Thomas W. Walker. *Understanding Central America*. Boulder, Colo.: Westview Press, 1989.

Brachet-Márquez, Viviane. *The Dynamics of Domination: State, Class, and Social Reform in Mexico, 1910–1990*. Pittsburgh: University of Pittsburgh Press, 1994.

Bradford, Colin I., Jr. (ed.). *Redefining the State in Latin America*. Paris: Organization for Economic Cooperation and Development, 1994.

Castañeda, Jorge. *Utopia Unarmed: The Latin American Left after the Cold War*. New York: Knopf, 1994.

Cubitt, Tessa. *Latin American Society*. London: Longman, 1988.

Dealy, Glen C. *The Latin Americans: Spirit and Ethos*. Boulder, Colo.: Westview Press, 1992.

Di Tella, Torcuato S. *Latin American Politics: A Theoretical Framework*. Austin: University of Texas, 1990.

Dorner, Peter. *Latin American Land Reforms in Theory and Practice*. Madison: University of Wisconsin Press, 1992.

Duncan, Cynthia M. *Rural Poverty in Latin America*. Westport, Conn.: Praeger, 1992.

Durand, Francisco. *Business and Politics in Peru*. Boulder, Colo.: Westview Press, 1994.

Early, John D. *The Demographic Structure and Evolution of a Peasant System: The Guatemalan Population*. Boca Raton: University Presses of Florida, 1982.

Eckstein, Susan (ed.). *Power and Popular Protest: Latin American Social Movements*. Berkeley: University of California Press, 1989.

George, Susan. *A Fate Worse Than Debt*. New York: Grove Press, 1988.

Gilbert, Alan. *The Latin American City*. London: Latin American Bureau, 1994.

Grindle, Merilee S. *State and Countryside: Development Policy and Agrarian Politics in Latin America*. Baltimore: Johns Hopkins University Press, 1986.

Hahner, June E. *Women in Latin American History*. Los Angeles: Latin American Center, University of California, 1980.

Hart, John M. *Revolutionary Mexico*. Berkeley: University of California Press, 1987.

Hawkins, John. *Inverse Images: The Meaning of Culture, Ethnicity and Family in Postcolonial Guatemala*. Albuquerque: University of New Mexico Press, 1984.

Higgins, Michael J. and Tanya Leigh Coen. *!Oigame, !Oigame: Struggle and Change in a Nicaraguan Community*. Boulder, Colo.: Westview Press, 1992.

Hopkins, Jack W. (ed.). *Latin America: Perspectives on a Region*. New York: Holmes & Meier, 1987.

Kirk, John M. and George W. Schuyler (eds.). *Central America: Democracy, Development and Change*. New York: Praeger, 1988.

LaBelle, Thomas J. *Nonformal Education in Latin America and the Caribbean: Stability, Reform or Revolution?* New York: Praeger, 1986.

Lancaster, Roger. *Life Is Hard: Machismo, Danger, and the Intimacy of Power in Nicaragua*. Berkeley: University of California Press, 1992.

Latin American Center. *Statistical Abstract of Latin America*. Los Angeles: University of California, 1995.

Levine, Daniel H. *Popular Voices in Latin American Catholicism*. Princeton, N.J.: Princeton University Press, 1992.

McDonough, Peter. *Power and Ideology in Brazil*. Princeton, N.J.: Princeton University Press, 1981.

Morales-Gómez, Daniel A. and Carlos A. Torres. *Education, Policy and Social Change: Experiences from Latin America*. Westport, Conn.: Praeger, 1992.

Moreira Alves, Maria. *State and Opposition in Military Brazil*. Austin: University of Texas Press, 1985.

Morse, Richard M. and Jorge E. Hardoy (eds.). *Rethinking the Latin American City*. Baltimore: Johns Hopkins University Press, 1992.

Murphy, Arthur D. and Alex Stepick. *Social Inequality in Oaxaca*. Philadelphia: Temple University Press, 1991.

Nash, June and Helen Safa (eds.). *Women and Change in Latin America*. South Hadley, Mass.: Bergin & Garvey, 1985.

Osterling, Jorge P. *Democracy in Colombia: Clientelist Politics and Guerrilla Warfare*. New Brunswick, N.J.: Transaction Publishers, 1989.

Pastor, Robert A. *Whirlpool: U.S. Foreign Policy toward Latin America and the Caribbean*. Princeton, N.J.: Princeton University Press, 1992.

Portes, Alejandro and Harley L. Browning (eds.). *Current Perspectives in Latin American Urban Research*. Austin: University of Texas Press, 1976.

Reichel-Dolmatoff, Gerardo and Alicia Reichel-Dolmatoff. *The People of Aritama: The Cultural Personality of a Colombian Mestizo Village*. Chicago: University of Chicago Press, 1961.

Rock, David. *Argentina 1516–1987: From Spanish Colonialism to Alfonsín*. Berkeley: University of California Press, 1987.

Roett, Riordan. *Brazil: Politics in a Patrimonial Society*, 3d ed. Westport, Conn.: Praeger, 1992.

Rowe, William and Vivian Schelling. *Memory and Modernity: Popular Culture in Latin America*. New York: Verso, 1991.

Sanderson, Steven E. *The Politics of Trade in Latin American Development*. Stanford, Calif.: Stanford University Press, 1992.

Singelmann, Peter. *Structures of Domination amd Peasant Movements in Latin America*. Columbia: University of Missouri Press, 1981.

Sloan, John W. *Public Policy in Latin America*. Pittsburgh: University of Pittsburgh Press, 1984.

Smith, Peter H. *Labyrinths of Power: Political Recruitment in Twentieth Century Mexico*. Princeton, N.J.: Princeton University Press, 1979.

Stoll, David. *Is Latin American Turning Protestant? The Politics of Evangelical Growth*. Berkeley: University of California Press, 1994.

Taussig, Michael T. *The Devil and Commodity Fetishism in South America*. Chapel Hill: University of North Carolina Press, 1980.

Torres, Carlos A. *The Politics of Nonformal Education in Latin America*. Westport, Conn.: Praeger, 1990.

Ward, Peter M. *Mexico City: The Production and Reproduction of an Urban Environment*. Boston: G. K. Hall, 1990.

Whiteford, Andrew H. *Two Cities of Latin America*. Beloit, Wisc.: Beloit College, 1960.

Whitten, Norman E., Jr. *Class, Kinship, and Power in an Ecuadorian Town: The Negroes of San Lorenzo*. Stanford, Calif.: Stanford University Press, 1965.

Wiarda, Howard and Harvey F. Kline (eds.). *Latin American Politics and Development*, 3d ed. Boulder, Colo.: Westview Press, 1990.

Williams, Robert G. *Export Agriculture and the Crisis in Latin America*. Chapel Hill: University of North Carolina Press, 1986.

Williamson, Edwin. *The Penguin History of Latin America*. London: Allen Lane, Penguin Press, 1992.

Winn, Peter. *Americas: The Changing Face of Latin America and the Caribbean*. New York: Pantheon Books, 1992.

Index

ABOUT THE AUTHOR

ROBERT C. WILLIAMSON is Adjunct Professor of Sociology at Lehigh University and was a Fulbright Professor in Chile, Colombia, and El Salvador. He is the author of *Marriage and Family Relations* (1972) and *Minority Languages and Bilingualism* (1991).

ISBN 0-275-95750-0

9 780275 957506

90000>

EAN

HARDCOVER BAR CODE